A GIRL CALLED GEORGINA

OVER THE SEX BORDER

A GIRL CALLED GEORGINA

by

GEORGINA SOMERSET

OVER THE SEX BORDER

by

Georgina Turtle

The Book Guild Ltd.
Sussex, England

Over the Sex Border first published 1963 by Victor Gollancz Ltd. London.

This edition 1992 by The Book Guild Ltd.

ISBN 0 86332 785 0

British Library Cataloguing in Publication data for this book is available from the British Library

Key Words:

Hermaphroditism
Intersexuality
Change of sex
Transsexualism
Trans-homo-sexuality
Gender dysphoria

Cover design by Georgina Somerset

Published by The Book Guild Ltd.
25 High Street, Lewes, East Sussex, United Kingdom
Set in Baskerville
Typesetting by Dataset
St Leonards-on-Sea, Sussex
Printed by Antony Rowe Ltd., Chippenham, Wiltshire, England

A GIRL CALLED GEORGINA

GEORGINA – June 1962.
An engagement photograph. Courtesy *Daily Express.*

A GIRL CALLED GEORGINA

by

GEORGINA SOMERSET

L.D.S. R.C.S. Eng.

With a Foreword
by
GRANT WILLIAMS

M.SC., M.S., F.R.C.S.

The Book Guild Ltd.
Sussex, England

CONTENTS

LIST OF ILLUSTRATIONS

11

COLOUR ILLUSTRATIONS

12

FOREWORD

Sᴇxᴜᴀʟ ᴀᴍʙɪɢᴜɪᴛʏ is a baffling problem in many cases. Life is not divided into black or white, male or female, good or bad. Some fall into that grey area between. When it comes to sexuality many are blessed by knowing exactly how they stand in femininity or masculinity and are horrified, shocked, dismayed or uncomprehending for anyone else who has no such certainty, especially if that 'anyone else' is a member of the family.

Homosexuality has been well recognised since the Biblical book of Genesis. Tolerance and acceptance of that state (if not its practices) have come much later. The loneliness, despair and drying up of creativity, when homosexuality was not tolerated, was bleakly expressed in Oscar Wilde's dying words to his peeling wallpaper "One of us has to go!"

There are though other problems of gender identity. The rarest are hermaphrodites (carrying male and female genital organs) or pseudohermaphrodites who are best described as having ambiguous sexuality. They tend to be the result of endocrine abnormalities. There are then chromosome abnormalities causing sexual ambiguity, of which the Turners and other eponymous conditions are now well recognised disorders.

Gender dysphoria is usually applied now to those people who are convinced that they are the opposite of their biological gender. The true trans-sexual usually develops these convictions when they are young children, and frequently take to cross-dressing as a first step.

It is sad though, that many feel they can only be fully satisfied when they have a 'sex change'. Sex cannot be changed.

Nevertheless more and more people are going through these ablative procedures, feeling that their problem will magically fade away. There may be a reduction in neurotic behaviour, but there is no evidence that the all too frequent petty criminality (which often accompanies transsexualism) in fact improves. Sadly the suicide rate does not improve.

There is though a further consideration, in that it frequently

15

has a catastrophic effect on often elderly parents when their grown-up son goes through a 'sex change' procedure and then, as sometimes happens, regrets the operation bitterly. Transsexualism is a twilight area which has been hijacked. Transsexual prostitution is a big business.

I have met some delightful young women walking around in a man's body, and I was pleased to help them, but I have to confess that they are a rarity and the vast majority of transsexuals are totally unsuitable for surgery.

If the Author's book helps people and their relatives to know the details of intersexuality and transsexuality then she will have achieved much.

GRANT WILLIAMS
M.Sc., M.S., F.R.C.S.

ACKNOWLEDGEMENTS

My grateful thanks are extended to Mr. Grant Williams for so kindly agreeing to contribute and to write a foreword to this additional book accompanying the reprinting of my original study. He is a consultant Wimpole Street surgeon who was at one time engaged in gender reassignment surgery at London's Charing Cross Hospital, and is therefore well qualified to speak with authority on the subject. His knowledge of the present-day state of the art makes his views pertinent and valuable, particularly when large numbers of trans-homo-sexuals are now seeking surgery. Not least he has seen some of the disturbing aspects of the problem, of the heartbreak of relatives of those caught up in the machinery of 'sex change' euphoria and of the results. For the dotting of the i's, the insertion of the commas in the right places and the expert editing of this new work I must give thanks to my beloved husband, Christopher. Without his understanding, encouragement, love and dedication to my interests this autobiographical summary and study update would not have been possible.

G.C.S

A GIRL CALLED GEORGINA

AN ILLUSTRATED AUTOBIOGRAPHY
with
STUDY UPDATE

It is a long time now since I first put pen to paper in 1960 to draft the chapters and framework of my book *Over the Sex Border*, reprinted here. It goes back even further, however, to my early childhood in the Twenties when the condition of intersexuality first occupied my mind. Born at Purley in the Croydon district, south of London, on March 3rd, 1923 I was the youngest of three children, with a brother four years older and a sister two years older. My sexual status, therefore, should not have been of any significance to my parents. For reasons embarrassedly evaded by them, however, the registration of my birth was delayed beyond the normal time limit allowed, so that March 23rd was the date which came to be wrongly entered on my birth certificate. In the event, I was brought up as a boy called George Edwin Turtle, although obviously of ambiguous sex both physically and psychologically, and I grew up with interests of both sexes and genders, feeling the sensitivities of both sexes within me.

I did nevertheless feel more like a girl than a boy and went through an early phase of regarding myself as a girl, wondering why I was not allowed to be one or to wear girls' clothes. I longed to wear a pretty pink dress and hated being expected to like getting into scraps, getting dirty and into mischief, which I did not. I hated being mocked, too, for always wanting to be good and for expressing my feelings and emotions which I was not always able to suppress. Sex did not come into it and I never thought of myself growing up, of being a woman or having breasts. It was just being a girl – a girl child – that mattered.

Yet, in fact, I grew up as neither boy nor girl, developing neither male nor female secondary sexual characteristics, going through no normal puberty, and remaining of the basic female form without facial, body or even axillary hair, and only very scant fine pubic hair of feminine distribution. As an asexual I grew up happily enough as a boy in conformity with the sex of

Aged 2. In the garden at home in Croydon. 1925.
Sexless and happy.

my rearing, although shunning the aggressiveness of boys around me. When they reached pubertal age, however, I felt completely lost and out of place amongst them, causing me to fade into the background and pretend to take no notice. This appeared to make me introverted but, in fact, my sexual infantility caused me to remain warm and genial to all those with whom I came into contact and, as through the eyes of a child, regarded the world as a lovely and wonderful, even if rather challenging, place.

Being the youngest I was the last to be allowed to say anything, if at all, and being docile I ended up doing everything I was told and cannot ever remember doing anything wrong. Before I was aware of life we had moved to a quiet tree-lined road near West Croydon railway station and, from the bottom of the garden, where there was a signal box, I used to watch for hours the trains going by and the steam engines shunting in the nearby yards. I liked toy trains and mechanical things but not guns or boys' games and pranks. I liked dolls and cuddly toys and the prettiness and gentleness of femininity but not particularly girls' games or their 'silliness'. I liked all animals and hated anyone killing or harming any. I also liked helping with the cooking and sewing, but mostly I enjoyed pastimes of a non-sexual nature such as music, playing the piano, drawing, painting, theatricals, making things, playing cards and collecting, etc. Mostly I was just happy being alone with my crayons, a comic and a bag of sweets.

In 1928, at the age of five, I was sent to the Croydon High School for Boys for my education, where I excelled in science and mathematics, no doubt taking after my maternal grandfather Lang who had been Professor of Mathematics at Dulwich College in the previous century. A tendency to dyslexia, however, meant that I found translation difficult, so that in spite of hard work languages defeated me. This was borne out also when I came to be taught the piano for, although I enjoyed playing I found that, with almost perfect pitch, I was better able to play by ear and by understanding the mathematics of scales and chords than by sight reading and converting the written notes into music. Academically, I was nearly always top of the class and won a prize every year at the annual Speech Days for the ten years I was at school. My efforts at games, however, were ill-rewarded, and although my slim size and speed at running caused me to be given the position of wing three-quarter at rugby I found myself suddenly and, inexplicably at the time, outpaced by the whole school once the boys I raced against reached puberty.

After 'matriculating' at the age of fifteen, the threat of World War II caused the family to move away from the likely bombing target of Croydon aerodrome, which was close to where we lived, to the sleepy typically English village of Lower Kingswood at the top of Reigate Hill in Surrey. From here I became a sixth form pupil at Reigate Grammar School for Boys to continue my higher education studies. Born of loving parents, our family was very close. My father, one of a large poor Victorian family, handsome and with a likeness to film star Ronald Colman, had struggled to become a dentist, a profession at which he was most able. He worked hard and long hours to keep us all and to pay for us, his children, to receive private education. My mother, on the other hand, was from an upper class family, was ultra-feminine and an accomplished pianist of modern and classical music, able to play with or without music, and who at one time had sung and danced on the London stage and played the piano for the silent films.

From earliest childhood my one ambition was to be a doctor and a surgeon, and at Reigate Grammar School I studied and successfully passed my pre-medical examinations in the summer of 1940. My brother had failed to follow my father into dentistry as was my father's wish, and so it was when I became a student at King's College Hospital, with the Battle of Britain at its height, my father prevailed upon me to study dentistry, after him, instead of medicine. The hope was that I might be able to study both, but this meant a longer period of study and, in wartime, with students in a reserved occupation, the minimum period of study only was allowed. The inducement was that I could always return after the war and take medicine. So it was I survived my late 'teens during the war, studying dentistry at King's College Hospital in London, wondering each day if it

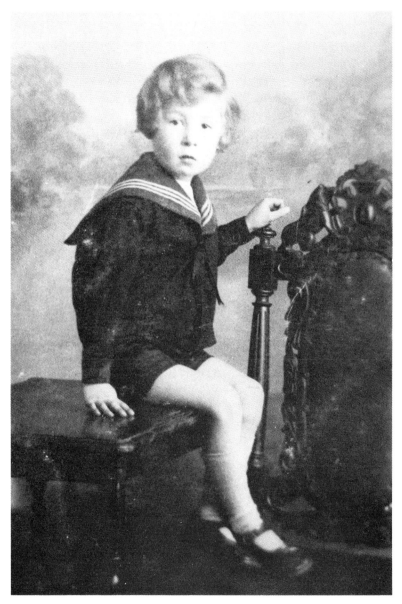

Aged 4. In sailor suit before having hair cut. 1927.

Aged 13. On holiday at Cliftonville, Margate.
1936. On 'rabbit'.

would still be there after each night's bombings and watching the night sky glow its angry red. Happily withdrawn into my medical books, I was glad of the excuse of the war to return to the familiarity and warmth of my home and escape from having to socialise.

As an observer of the war in the south east of England, however, I was able to watch and follow with some degree of excitement each day's happenings, sometimes right over my head, yet fearsome of the events, not really wanting to believe the reality of the terrible horror and drama that was being enacted around me and unfolding in the world. Being high up, from my bedroom window I had a wide panoramic view across the fields from right over Kent up to London. I was able, therefore, to follow the raiders from the moving band of converging searchlights and the red peppering of the anti-aircraft guns. Wave upon wave they came, night after night, their engines throbbing deeply under the weight of their deadly cargo, often dropping their bombs on the way. Far and near the night sky lit up momentarily with balls of light as the bombs exploded or persisted as a reddish glow as fires started. My heart sank to think that there were people somewhere out there right in the midst of it all.

Later there were the dreaded V1 'doodle bugs', coming in extra low over us because of our height above sea level, sometimes at the rate of two a minute, never ceasing day or night. Only the sight of the night sky filled with our own bombers forming up on another thousand-bomber raid gave heart. The Germans had started it all, tried to kill my beloved family and myself, bomb our home, flatten 'my' London and other cities, invade our country and had changed forever the face of the beautiful peaceful world I knew and loved. When they had been bombing Warsaw, Amsterdam, Coventry and London, and winning, they gloried in the destruction they were causing. Why should I not hate them now and be glad they knew what it was like to have some of their own medicine? The only two of my contemporaries who started at King's with me, Keith Turner and John Cox, two fine lads, became for a short time my friends until they decided to abandon their studies and go into the R.A.F. Keith wrote often to tell me of their progress and training and how they were at last ready to go out on missions. Then suddenly the letters stopped. Meanwhile I had watched the rows upon rows of little terraced houses in the streets around the hospital disappear into crater after crater, until only a waste land was left. To-day a fine 'new' Dental School stands on one of the sites, in Caldecot Road. Miraculously the hospital essentially survived. One can look back now knowing how it all ended but, at the time, no one ever knew what each to-morrow would bring and if they would survive it.

After qualifying in 1944, and a short appointment as resident house surgeon, I had to submit to an embarrassing preliminary medical examination for entry into the Armed Forces. Although it was a casual affair I had to step out of line into a private cubicle whilst another more senior doctor was called to examine me. Discussion ensued, but the consensus of opinion seemed to be that I could be passed at this stage as I would anyway later be undergoing a further more detailed medical examination prior to actual acceptance into one of the three services. In the event, when I subsequently volunteered for the Royal Navy, no further medical examination was carried out, for I had wanted to be accepted and attended my interview at Admiralty House immaculately dressed and with a neat 'short back and sides' haircut. The examiner, in the uniform of a naval surgeon, was more interested in why I wanted to go into the Navy and in my hobbies, and my answers seemed to go down well. I said I played the piano and a little golf, to which he replied laughingly, "You won't get much golf on board ship!" (Although the War in Europe was in its dying days the first atom bomb had not yet been dropped on Hiroshima and the War against Japan was still very much on, with *Kamikazi* attacks against the Allies' big ships.) Finally the examiner, seeming to suddenly realise that he had given me enough time, said, "There's no need to examine you medically is there? – You are alright, aren't you?" To which I, of course, replied, "Yes."

As a Surgeon Lieutenant (D), life in the Navy was to be a very happy time for me, although my parents felt uneasy about my being away from home. I found it a wonderful service and one

Surgeon Lieutenant (D) George Turtle LDS. RNVR.
Aged 22. London. 1945.

Surgeon Lieutenant (D) George Turtle LDS. RNVR. Aged 23.
Combined Services Hospital, Trincomalee, Ceylon. 1946.

Surgeon Lieutenant (D) George Turtle LDS. RNVR. (Right)
Aged 23. Aboard aircraft carrier *HMS Indomitable*. 1946.

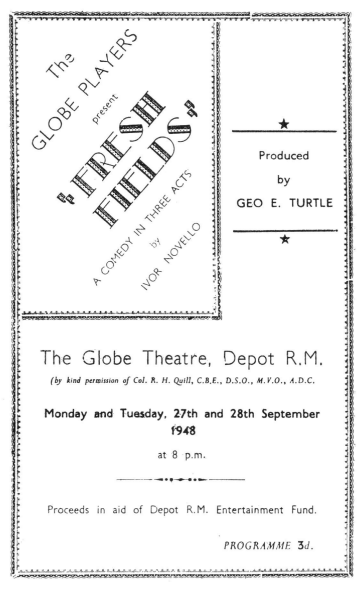

The Globe Players present

'FRESH FIELDS'

A COMEDY IN THREE ACTS by IVOR NOVELLO

★

Produced
by
GEO E. TURTLE

★

The Globe Theatre, Depot R.M.

(by kind permission of Col. R. H. Quill, C.B.E., D.S.O., M.V.O., A.D.C.)

**Monday and Tuesday, 27th and 28th September
1948**

at 8 p.m.

Proceeds in aid of Depot R.M. Entertainment Fund.

PROGRAMME **3**d.

Aged 25. Programme of play produced by me
at the R.M. Depot, Deal, Kent. 1948.

in which I remain to-day proud to have served, and I look back upon my years in it still with nostalgia. Those were the days when there was still a rum ration for the ratings and an allocation of duty free 'pussers' cigarettes or tobacco for all. I had companions of my own age, sharing the same mode of life and work. As an officer I was able to keep to myself and my asexuality made me the ideal person to be 'married' to the service. Although in no way homosexual or effeminate I was nevertheless perhaps more amiable, gentle and caring than most, and these qualities found me in favour with my superior officers who seemed even to 'father' me at times. I served variously at Portsmouth; Plymouth; the Combined Services Hospital, Trincomalee, Ceylon, and at the Royal Marine Depot, Deal. My outward journey to Ceylon was to Colombo aboard the aircraft carrier *Formidable*. My return was from Trincomalee on the aircraft carrier *Indomitable*. Both were fine ships. One of my 'flimsies', which are reports issued after each posting by the commanding officer and, in this case, was issued in 1946 after my service in Trincomalee, stated, 'he has conducted himself to my entire satisfaction. A capable and conscientious dental surgeon. He has a quiet disposition, popular with all and a willing help in all mess duties.'

At Deal I found myself 'drafted' into playing the ugly sister in pantomime, and after my performance was called out of line quite spontaneously by the producer on the final curtain to make a speech to the audience. Later I was elected to become chairman of the Depot Dramatic Society, going on to act in and produce a number of plays in their Globe Theatre. I hasten to add that the female parts were played by co-opted young women residents of Deal associated with the Depot.

It was upon my return to civilian life in November 1948, however, that my real troubles started and my intersexuality began to affect my life. The National Health Service had been going only a few months and, with all dental services free and patients queuing for treatment, building up a practice opposite the *Swan and Sugar Loaf*, South Croydon, in my father's name caused me to work excessively long hours in my surgery. I had no personal friends and no time for pleasures, so that my health

31

Programme

FRESH FIELDS

— CAST —

(In order of appearance)

MISS SWAINE	JEAN CLEMENTS
LUDLOW	TOM CHARD
LADY LILIAN BEDWORTHY	PAMELA SCOTT
LADY MARY CRABBE	JULIE DELLER
TIM CRABBE	GEOFF. NEWSTEAD
MRS. PIDGEON	MORA FORD
UNA PIDGEON	DINAH CHRISTOPHERSON
TOM LARCOMB	GEORGE TURTLE
LADY STRAWHOLM	BETTY BLAKE

Produced by GEORGE TURTLE.

Music will be provided by the Depot R.M. Orchestra, under the direction of Bandmaster H. S. L. Murray.

THE DEPOT R.M., DEAL, SOCIETY.

President	COLONEL R. H. QUILL, C.B.E., D.S.O., M.V.O., A.d.C.
Chairman	SURG.-LIEUT. (D.) G. E. TURTLE, R.N.V.R.
Secretary	INST.-LIEUT. F. J. CHINERY, R.N.

THERE WILL BE AN INTERVAL OF FIVE MINUTES BETWEEN ACTS.

SYNOPSIS OF SCENES

ACT I.

SCENE I. MORNING—ROOM OF A HOUSE IN BELGRAVIA—APRIL.

ACT II.

SCENE I. THE SAME—MAY.

SCENE II. THE SAME—TEN DAYS LATER.

ACT III.

SCENE I. THE SAME—LATE JUNE.

"Fresh Fields" was first produced at the Criterion Theatre, London, on January 5th, 1933, with Lilian Braithwaite in the lead as Lady Lilian Bedworthy.

Furniture and Effects kindly loaned by } MANOR HOUSE HOTEL, GLEN HOTEL, SHEPHERD'S CLUB

Telephones Supplied by G.P.O.

Stage Manager	PETER JONES
Assistant Stage Manager	ALAN BACON
Business Manager	GLYN WILLIAMS
Promoter	MICHAEL WILBERFORCE
Property Mistress	ELIZABETH CHINERY
Lighting By	SYDNEY WYATT and BERTRAM GREIG

The Producer wishes to convey his thanks to all those who have worked so well behind the scenes, so enabling this play to be presented to you.

Programme, R.M. Depot, Deal. 1948 — more details.
Chairman, producer and playing the lead.

deteriorated and I found it increasingly difficult to pretend to be the 'man' that my upbringing demanded of me. I could not understand why I should feel so feminine and could not broach my problem even to my family doctor. There were no textbooks for me to read about my problem, only lurid descriptions by one or two psychiatrists of various sexual perversions which not only sickened me but did not apply to me at all. Indeed, there was no other case known with whom I could compare myself or, for that matter, to encourage me falsely into a change of sex which I had come to realise was the only solution to my 'illness'. In 1945 my father, an eminent Freemason, had initiated my brother and I into the Craft. I had little choice other than to please him, the one I loved, especially as the cost of my studies, my books and upkeep to the age of 21 had not been inconsiderable and had been found by him. Rapid advancement in a small Lodge meant that I had to continue in office in order to avoid letting anyone down, and in 1953 became Worshipful Master. I resigned soon after, but my enforced indoctrination bore heavily upon my loyalty, strength and secret inner feelings. Adding to my troubles, in 1952 my mother, who had held the whole family together and who was the only one who knew silently of my plight, died suddenly and tragically at the age of 54 of peritonitis following a burst appendix. My private hell deepened.

News of the Christine Jorgensen case had not yet fully broken but when it did, instead of exciting me, it immensely distressed me as I felt no one would then believe that my own case had not been influenced by hers and that I might be different. I therefore struggled on, even taking a course of male hormones to try to overcome my sexual disorientation. They had little effect upon me, however, except to upset my normally placid nature and make me irritable, and in spite of them I found myself still gradually losing the fight to sustain the logic of my upbringing, becoming so desperate, in fact, that all I stood to lose, even life itself, became inconsequential. At last, seeking medical help in 1955, I had the good fortune to be introduced to Mr. Kenneth Walker, the eminent surgeon and philosopher, who had written extensively on social problems and was

Britain's, if not the world's, leading expert at the time. Meanwhile I had been asked to see a local psychiatrist, who was totally uninterested in my physical state, did not trouble to examine me, and instead spoke scornfully of a case of sex change about which he had read. He wrongly assumed that my problem was a psychological one, and promptly suggested that I enter the Warlingham Park mental hospital 'to be cured' and if necessary be given E.C.T. (electro-convulsive-therapy).

My father immediately objected, knowing that my problem was a biological one, and so it was I saw Professor Cawadias, London's leading sexologist. At last I had a full and thorough medical examination, and he told me afterwards that I was physically a hermaphrodite, that I had not developed as a male but had dominant female characteristics. I was unable to function as a male and he told me that I was biologically female, possessing female receptors in my body, and that I needed oestrogen "like a baby needs milk", which my own body could not produce. Male hormones, he continued, would have no effect upon my body, therefore, and affect me neither physically nor psychologically. Consequently, he said, speaking sympathetically but meaningfully, "hermaphrodites like you have to be looked upon as cripples in society". The very fact that I once had only one tiny testis, on the left, which was dysgenetic and earlier removed, suggested, he said, that the other gonad would almost certainly be an ovary, probably also dysgenetic and no doubt failed. (A laparotomy performed later for an appendectomy revealed the presence of a rudimentary uterus. Later still, a complex growth extending from the right inguinal region into the peritoneum had to be removed.) He therefore prescribed oestrogen therapy and, albeit cautiously, agreed the advisability of a change of sexual role.

My breasts responded quite dramatically and I knew he was right, but it was difficult to wipe away my whole male way of life and upbringing. Above all, how could I tell everyone in my family and expect them to understand? Kenneth Walker appealed to Sir Harold Gillies, the eminent plastic surgeon of the day, to help me, but when I saw him straight from my surgery in my black morning jacket and pin-striped trousers with 'short back and sides' haircut he dismissed me after only a few moments' consultation, without examining me, saying that he knew all about cases like mine and adding irritably, "I am already on the carpet with the General Medical Council for what I have done." The next day he wrote and said: 'Frankly, which may not appeal to you in the slightest, I have also a life to live, and my surgery is to a certain extent artistic and personal, and I do not really think you look or could be made to look like a woman.' (Four years later he wrote to say he was sorry about what he had said and to ask my help with getting one of his 'very deserving cases' a correction of their birth certificate. Regretfully I had to tell him that this was only possible if he was himself prepared to swear that the case was really **born** of the other sex. This he felt unable to do.)

In the event I had a small operation performed in the London Clinic in January 1957 by Mr. Patrick Clarkson, an eminent, kindly and dedicated Harley Street consultant plastic surgeon, which he termed a corrective procedure. It was not the so-called 'sex-change operation' of common knowledge to-day, and I even had to go out a week before and buy my very first outfit of female clothes in which to leave the Clinic. Indeed, I knew little of what a woman wore under her dress or skirt. With my hair still 'short back and sides' as expected of a professional gentleman of the day, I moved away from home to a rented bungalow near Bognor Regis in Sussex to let my hair grow and to establish myself in the female role. I had no friends, however, and life alone was not easy, not working and awaiting each post for news of my application for re-registration. My only companions were my Humber Hawk car, my radio and a cheap piano which I had bought and was a 'must'. Ironically, a week before approval was received for a correction of my birth certificate I was the victim of a most vicious and prolonged sex assault and rape late one freezing November night, being dragged into a field on the outskirts of the town. I desperately feared for my life and struggled home bleeding with my clothes torn off, soaking wet, traumatised and ill. Worse was that I could not go to the police or tell anyone, although I did of course write next day and tell my father. Needless to say, he was

Aged 34. A woman at Bognor. September 1957.
Eight months after coming out of the London Clinic.

terribly distressed and drove down from Croydon that weekend to see me. The effect on me, however, was that to proceed with my birth certificate correction was now a decision I could not make. I was in bed for weeks with pneumonia and a very high temperature, with only a kind neighbour coming in from time to time to see if I was alright. I felt so depressed and had such a sense of failure that suicide was much in my thoughts.

By the New Year my tenancy had run out and, with little money left and my upbringing winning the day, I cut off my long hair and went back to living as a man. I regretted it immediately, and whilst waiting for my hair to grow to be long enough to again resume my female role I did a locum dental job in Southampton for two months and then stayed in the Queen's Private Hotel in Regency Square in Brighton for another two months. One of the guests, a kindly elderly ex-actress, Mrs. Thomas, befriended me and I confided my secret to her. She used to tell me what the other guests talked about and said they were all wondering, "why doesn't that nice young man get his hair cut?" It was getting rather long by now for a man of that period and so I used to comb it well back behind my neck with haircream. Once on a trip into the Brighton shops I became the focus of attention of a group of rough looking men and, in a loud voice, one shouted out, "Well, look what we 'ave 'ere, Davy Crockett!" "Cor yes," said another, "Davy Crockett." "Hi yer Davy Crockett." It was a frightening moment, especially as I had a female anatomy, with developed breasts, under my male clothes.

The year was 1958 and looking back it seems funny to think that to-day, particularly in Brighton, anything now goes. Fortunately, with Mrs. Thomas's help, I found a nice little cottage to rent in Plumpton, a small village the other side of the Downs behind Brighton, and was relieved to move there and to be able to resume my proper female role once again. It was here that I became very friendly with Mr. and Mrs. Wilkes, the elderly owners of the cottage, the Manor house and sur-rounding grounds. Even so, a year passed without the trauma of the rape leaving me, and I remained in a state of total despair and stalemate. I was so desperate for help that I wrote to

Aged 35. Back as George after rape nightmare. January 1958.

Aged 35. Back as Georgina. Plumpton, Sussex. August 1958.

Professor Penrose, Emeritus Professor of Human Genetics at the University of London, to ask if he would undertake a chromosomal test to ascertain which sexual role was right for me. He replied most sympathetically but regretted that, in spite of claims, no test was at that time possible accurately to determine chromosomal sex, that my problem anyway would not be solved easily by knowing, and that other anatomical and biological factors had to be taken into consideration. (Indeed, it was not until later that year (1959) that Lejeune established the existence of the first human chromosomal abnormality.)

Then in the June (1959) my dear father died. Only a full autobiography could tell my whole unique story, of my ups and downs, of my crying myself to sleep on so many occasions, and give the details and full medical facts of my case, but these are not relevant here. Enough to say it was an act of love, duty and loyalty that caused me to have my shoulder length hair cut off yet again and to don a suit to enable me to appear at his funeral as the man everyone there thought me to be. This entailed asking my kind London psychiatrist, Dr. Maurice Partridge, to get me into hospital to have this done under sedation and a general anaesthetic, as I could not face up to it otherwise. I came round to a shocked nightmare with my head cold from the loss of my hair, my cared-for long nails cut down to the quicks, my male clothes by my bedside and the realisation that my beloved father was back at home – dead and alone. My distress was compounded by the fact that it was still a period when those who had short hair were regarded as male and those who had long hair were regarded as female, and, with my hair so short as to be bristly, I feared for my survival over the months that it would take for it to grow yet again.

So it was, in spite of my female anatomy, I lived outwardly again as a man for another nine months, carrying on my old practice in South Croydon and sorting out both my father's and my own affairs there before selling up. It was a very difficult and harrowing time and I hid away my female clothes, as it would have upset me too much to have even seen them. I became so desperate at one time, at the thought of the problems ahead, that to cheer myself up I rekindled my hopes of

Aged 36. Back as a 'man' (again!).
At father's funeral. July 1959.

41

becoming a doctor and approached King's College Hospital with a view to studying medicine. Alas, I was told that I could be the father of the students there and, as I already had a major professional qualification, it would be wrong for them to give up a place to me. The view was that I was too old at 36 and that someone qualifying much younger could serve the profession for a longer expected time. The fact that I could not have been a father to anyone was not the point. I understood the argument and retreated back into my state of loneliness and despair, and trying to sell the practice. Having finally succeeded, I moved to Hove in April 1960, having to change my outward sexual role 'on the way', leaving Croydon as a 'man' and arriving at my new home in Hove as a woman.

My birth certificate was eventually corrected on July 1st, 1960, but not until renewed medical reports had been submitted together with affidavits from Kenneth Walker, Professor Cawadias and my father, the latter having been signed some time before his death. Notwithstanding these, Mr. Clarkson, my surgeon, was also required to give a report as to my sexual anatomy at the time of surgery, whilst I had to give a written assurance that I had never been married or been capable of functioning as a male. The form of Statutory Declaration for the Correction of an error of fact or substance in a register of Births and Deaths, Pursuant to 1 and 2, Eliz. 2, Ch.20, S.29., commenced:

> 'In the matter of an error in the Register of the Birth of a girl registered as GEORGE EDWIN TURTLE which occurred on the 23rd day of March 1923, and was registered on the 30th April 1923 in the entry No. 283 in the register book for the Sub-District of South Croydon, in the County of Croydon C.B;
>
> I, . . . hereby declare that the above named child who at birth was thought to be of the male sex and whose birth was accordingly registered as George Edwin (a boy) was incorrectly registered, as the sex at the time of birth was indeterminate, and since the registration of birth the child has developed female

characteristics to such an extent that, in my opinion, the correct registration of birth was female, and the record of the birth should now be amended to show that the child is a girl named GEORGINA CAROL TURTLE.'

XB 013856

12100 R.57D

1 & 2 ELIZ. 2 CH. 20

CERTIFICATE

DIEU ET MON DROIT

OF BIRTH

Name and Surname........Georgina Carol Turtle.........................

Sex................Girl.........

Date of Birth................Twentythird March 1923....................

Place ⌠ Registration............Croydon
of ⎨ District
Birth ⎩ Sub-district ....South Croydon

Certified to have been compiled from records in the custody of the Registrar General. Given at the General Register Office, Somerset House, London, under the Seal of the said Office, the....4th day of........July........1960·

CAUTION :—*Any person who* (1) *falsifies any of the particulars on this certificate, or* (2) *uses a falsified certificate as true, knowing it to be false, is liable to prosecution.*

Aged 37. A Girl called Georgina.
A new birth certificate – July 1960.

So, **'A Girl called Georgina'** I was, and an indescribable feeling of serenity and joy and of belonging came over me.

The choice of names was mine. Georgina, the female

counterpart of George, was obvious but rather a mouthful, so for my second I decided to choose the short simple name of Carol, after Carol White, the name of the main character in a strip of the same name then running in the *Daily Mail*. (I did, in fact, use the simpler name of Carol for a few years before going back to Georgina – my friends now find it easier to just call me Gina.) By now the authorities had already come to refuse transsexuals, but my application was accepted on the basis that a Court ruling as to my dominant sex, both biologically and physically, as well as psychologically, would be that it was female. Indeed, I was so confident about this that when I was mentioned by name and compared with Jorgenson as being a transsexual, in a medical article in 1969, implying that I was homosexual, would have had breast implants, electrolysis and was probably not legally married, I had no choice but to instigate libel proceedings for, indeed, all these premises were totally false. I have never been homosexual, never needed nor had electrolysis, and my breast development is and always has been naturally produced, albeit stimulated by exogenous female hormones, and my 34 inch bust on a 30 inch chest frame remains the same to-day. I also married quite legally and in fact had to produce my birth certificate to obtain a special licence.

The preliminaries of the libel action dragged on for two years with 'further and better particulars' and every medical report I had ever had being submitted in evidence to the defendants. Blood tests and further medical examinations were called for and ordered by a Judge in Chambers, and although many believed that the ruling against April Ashley in 1970 would deter me I refused to give up, in spite of the heavy burden upon me financially. Blood tests revealed my chromosomal constitution for the first time, and that it was mosaic XO (Female Turners)/XY (male), regarded as representing true hermaphroditism, accounting for much of my physical development or lack of it (Polani P., *Errors of Sex Determination and Sex Chromosome Anomalies*, pp. 13, 25, 26. Ch.2 of *Gender Differences* by Ounsted and Taylor, Churchill Livingstone, 1972). Apart from the prolonged worry and many tearful nights, had I lost my action I would have faced bankruptcy, losing my home, my

Aged 37. Georgina at last, officially! July 1960.
At my piano. 'I enjoy being a girl'. Photo: Courtesy *Star.*

Aged 37. Georgina at last, officially. On the beach at Hove.
July 1960. Photo: Courtesy *Associated Newspapers.*

practice, and my sexual, social and marital status. In the event, two days before the case was due to be heard the defendants offered an apology, and in a statement read out in the High Court on November 23rd, 1972 by my counsel, Leon Brittan, later to become Home Secretary and now Sir Leon Brittan, said:

> "The plaintiff is a qualified dental practitioner. On April 30th 1923, her birth was registered as being that of a boy named 'George Edwin Turtle'. But on July 1st, 1960, the entry was corrected to read 'girl' on the production of medical evidence. In October 1962 she married Mr. Christopher Walter Henry Somerset. In the January 11th, 1969 issue of *Pulse International* there appeared an article which had been understood to impugn to imply that the birth certificate ought not to have been corrected and that she might not be legally married. Mrs. Somerset, who has for so long enjoyed a happy and stable marriage felt bound to bring these proceedings to remove any possible slur on her legal, sexual and marital status. The defendants have now seen the medical reports which were submitted to the Registrar in support of the application for the correction of the entry of the plaintiff's birth, and fully accept that the correction was properly made and, of course, Mrs Somerset's subsequent marriage was therefore perfectly lawful."

More than for myself perhaps I was relieved for my beloved husband who had stood by me throughout all the trauma and had stood to lose so much with me. I was also gratified that I had vindicated myself in the eyes of the authorities at Somerset House, the then Central Register Office, who had for so long, back in the late Fifties, had the difficult task of deliberating whether to allow my birth certificate correction.

Alone and in my innocence my story of sex change in 1960 made world headlines, and on the day the story broke my home was 'invaded' by press reporters and the telephone hardly stopped ringing. One such reporter, Charles Sandall from the *News of the World*, a sincere and likeable man, prevailed upon me to allow his paper to run an 'exclusive', for it seemed to me that I might have more influence over the content that way and perhaps be able to help the public and the medical profession to better understand the real meaning of sex change. Later I was to learn that I would be paid the sum of one hundred pounds. Yet many felt, quite wrongly, that I had not only sold my story for the money and the publicity, but also that I had received a princely sum for it. One local paper in relating my story stated that I intended to start up in practice in Hove and gave the name of my road. This, and the sensational approach of some national newspapers, led me into difficulties with the General Dental Council, since publicity or advertising of any kind was severely frowned upon in those days and against the regulations. Just when all was rosy with my world for the first time in my life my livelihood was under threat, and the only way I could stop the articles was by threatening to sue, something which I feel the media has never forgiven me for. One reporter became very excited when I told him and asked me to make sure that he was the first to be informed if I was 'struck off'! In the event I apologised to the General Dental Council and was given a reprimand, which I am sure was tinged with a certain amount of compassion for my circumstances, for which I was grateful.

In spite of the publicity the facts behind the headlines never came to light, and it was wrongly assumed that I was just a transsexual who had 'luckily' had my birth certificate corrected. Complex medical facts are not the forté of newspapers, and I was therefore inundated with letters from those we now know as transsexuals asking me to help them 'change sex as I had done'. The letters came from all over the world. I used to sit up half the night after a long surgery answering them, and then spent every evening and weekend receiving those into my home who had asked to come to see me to discuss their problems. Typical of the many hundreds of letters I received was the following, which shows dramatically the plight of the transsexual and the medical attitude to the problem at the time. It read:

'I am writing to you to ask you to help me. I am in a most awkward position and any help from you would be greatly appreciated. Since my very early child-hood, age two or three (which I can remember very well), I have felt like a girl and I have had all the habits, emotions, behaviour and thoughts which girls have. A year ago I consulted two psychiatrists whom I was told were the biggest leading experts on these sort of problems. They told me that mentally I was a complete woman but since I had the perfect body of a man it was not possible for me to achieve my sole ambition of becoming a woman. Then I saw two endocrinologists whom, I was told, were the biggest experts in Britain on this problem. They also told me I could not become a woman because I had the perfect body of a normal man. Then I wrote and explained the whole situation to Dr. Hamburger, the head of the Hormon Department of the Statens Seruminstitute in Denmark, who changed the sex of Christine Jorgensen. Dr. Hamburger told me that he could not help me because the treatment needed the permission of the Ministry of Justice and now they can give this permission only for a Danish subject. My last doctor, who was extremely sympathetic towards this and who has just retired, tried very hard to find out if there was a specialist in another country to help me, but she had no success. Please, Miss Turtle, help me, if you can! Please try not to break my heart!'

Later he wrote,

'Dear Miss Turtle, I received your very kind and wonderful letter two weeks ago. As soon as I read your letter, suddenly my life changed – since I have read your letter I feel so happy! I feel like dancing all the time! I simply do not know how to thank you for your benevolence and kindness.'

Later still he wrote to ask me, amongst other things, how he could get rid of all his heavy body and facial hair!

It was not long before I realised that, as far as I could make out, all were, within a reasonable scale of variation, really physically normal people and not like me at all. They ranged from the most hirsute, tall, heavily built masculine types to those who were small, immature and weakly. Some men came dressed as women and had obviously been transvestite for some time, but expressed a yearning for a full change of sexual status. Many were plainly passive homosexuals spurred on by their partners who came with them. Others were deeply psychologically disturbed individuals who just wanted to change without even knowing the anatomy or lifestyle of a woman. Of those who came cross-dressed to impress me or to enjoy the outing, a few were just passable, but others sadly looked more like Charley's Aunt. Several brought photographs of themselves dressed up, often in a sexual pose such as showing their suspenders. Many were married with children. Some brought their wives with them, and tragically I heard later that two of these wives had subsequently committed suicide. There were also female transsexualists who came dressed as men. It must, nevertheless, be said that most of all those I saw and heard from were basically sincere, nice people, who were so very happy for me and so very grateful that I was even prepared to listen to and understand their own troubles.

It surprised me that few if any knew just what was meant by a change of sex, of the surgery involved, of the limitations, of the legal implications, of the problems they would have to face, or of the really momentous nature of the goal they were seeking. Although not a transsexualist myself, I had experienced all the many social, medical and legal hurdles of changing my sexual status late in life in the pioneering days of the Fifties. These experiences had not only been subjective but objective also, through personal contact with various medical consultants and authorities so that, by now, I was well qualified. Indeed, most of the few London consultants dealing with the problem at that time referred their cases to me and I, likewise, referred mine back to them. One of these, Dr John Randell, consultant psychiatrist at the Charing Cross Hospital, was the most well known and I refer to him in my book. He was not an easy man to get on with and, although fascinated by the subject and inwardly sympathetic, he did not always convey this to his transsexual patients, sometimes reducing them to tears by bluntly refusing to believe anything which did not concur with his own dogmatic views. Sadly, he is no longer with us.

Mr Kenneth Walker, however, a consultant urologist, philosopher and writer, was, no doubt, the foremost pioneer of the subject, and describes in his 1955 book *Sex and Society* (Penguin Books), albeit briefly, a case of transsexualism he had then been seeing for over seven years! Although retired from active surgery when I first met him he used still to see and counsel patients in his Harley Street rooms, had a great personality and charm and listened most sympathetically to one's problems. From 1960 onwards, until his death a few years later, we freely exchanged referrals of our transsexual patients and it was he who agreed, most willingly, to write the foreword to my book. Others involved in the subject in those days included Dr. Peter Bishop of Guy's Hospital, Mr. Peter Fletcher, Dr. Joseph Adler, Dr. Clifford Allen and Mr. W. P. Greening, all from London, Dr. Sydney Brandon and Dr. Martin Roth from Newcastle, now both Professors, Dr. Charles Wolf of Switzerland and Dr. Walter Murmann of Milan, with most of whom I had correspondence about cases. Later there was Mr. Arthur Williams, consultant gynaecologist of Oxford, Mr. A. J. Evans of Harley Street and Mr. Peter Philip, consultant urologist of Charing Cross Hospital. Also eminent in the early days was Dr. Charles Armstrong, of Newcastle, a specialist on intersexuality and a staunch champion of the transsexual cause. Although it was not until later that I was to meet him, his name cannot be omitted from this list. Now, still alive and well at the marvellous age of 94, he remains actively dedicated to his work, a firm believer in the medical arguments that support the transsexuals' fight for full legal recognition.

It was a time when building up my new dental practice as a woman was a priority, and I was being pressed by several medical men to write my autobiography. I found I was repeating myself over and over again to those who were seeking my help, however, and seeing the distress on their faces and realising that doctors as well as the cases themselves were in the dark about the problem I decided to forego my autobiography, and instead write a comprehensive study of the subject which I thought would do the most good, and it is this study that is here reprinted.

There had not been a comparable book ever published, so that I had little to go on except all that I had picked up over the years and what few pickings I could find here and there in various medical works. Even Benjamin's book on the subject (*The Transsexual Phenomenon*), which was claimed to be the first, was not published in America until 1966, three years after mine. Started in 1960 with just fifty fully assessed cases to go on, my work was finished by the end of 1961 with two hundred cases then in my files. Some of these are now well known.

Christmas 1961 saw me struck down with pulmonary tuberculosis, however, and I had to spend seven months in King Edward VII Sanatorium, Midhurst in Sussex. By then I had met Christopher Somerset, my Prince Charming, and whilst there we became engaged and he lovingly cared for me whilst I regained my health. It had been love at first sight, and when we married at St. Margaret's, Westminster on October 13th, 1962 I was to become the first (and believed still the only) woman who had officially changed her sex ever to be married in a church under English law. I had asked my brother to give me away, then two uncles and then my family doctor. All declined. When I asked Mr Wilkes, whose cottage I had rented in 1958 and who had by now become a second father to me, he said he was "delighted to accept the honour". Amongst the hundred guests was my mother-in-law, Christopher's only surviving parent, and my sister. Needless to say, it was the happiest day of my life. After the reception at St. Ermins Hotel, we stayed overnight in the Cumberland Hotel before flying off to Paris for a five day honeymoon. News of our wedding, with different photographs, appeared on the front page in all editions of the London *Evening Standard* that Saturday night, and when my husband and I walked down Oxford Street that evening asking the

King Edward VII Sanatorium, Midhurst. 'Magically' engaged.
June 1962. On my room balcony. Aged 39.
Photo: Courtesy *Daily Express.*

Aged 39. Midhurst Sanatorium. Engaged. June 1962.
Allowed up briefly. Photo: Courtesy *Daily Express.*

1() *Daily Telegraph and Morning Post, Saturday, June 9, 1962*

COURT AND SOCIAL

Court Circular

BUCKINGHAM PALACE, June 8.
The Queen, accompanied by the

seas Airways Corporation) and Sir Basil Smallpeice (Managing Director, British Overseas Airways Corporation).
By command of Her Majesty, the

Forthcoming Marriages

Mr. C. W. H. Somerset and
Miss G. C. Turtle
The engagement is announced between Christopher Walter Henry, only son of the late Col. A. F. H. Somerset and of Mrs. B. M. Somerset, of Bournemouth, and Georgina Carol Turtle, L.D.S., R.C.S.Eng., of Hove, younger daughter of the late Mr. and Mrs. A. R. Turtle, of Croydon.

Our engagement is announced. *Daily Telegraph.* June 9th, 1962.

Miss Georgina Carol Turtle
and
Mr. Christopher Walter Henry Somerset
request the pleasure of the company of

on the occasion of their marriage
at St. Margaret's Church,
Westminster,
on Saturday, 13th October, 1962,
at 11-45 a.m.,
and afterwards to the Reception in the
St. Ermin's Hotel.

"Carisbrooke,"
6 Hayworth Road,
Hove 3, Sussex.

An early reply will be appreciated.

Our wedding invitation.

Married at St. Margaret's, Westminster – October 13th, 1962.
Now Mrs. Georgina Somerset. Photo: Courtesy *Mirrorpic*.

newsvendors for copies of their 'earlier' editions for our scrap book, looking straight at the paper with our photo staring out at them they asked, "What do you want it for?" The descriptive and warm account of our wedding by Vivien Batchelor, although inconsequentially minutely inaccurate in one or two places, is worth repeating here:

'It seemed like a normal fashionable wedding at St. Margaret's, Westminster to-day. The bridegroom was 30 minutes early in top hat and tails, the two bridesmaids in their pink organza dresses were on time, and the bride in her white nylon dress embroidered with silver lilies was 10 minutes late.

But this was a wedding with a difference, for the bride was Miss Georgina Turtle, 38, who began her career as a Surgeon Lieutenant in the Royal Navy and became a woman two years ago.

She met her bridegroom, engineer Christopher Somerset, 35, a distant kinsman of one of the premier Dukes of England, two years ago soon after she had officially changed her sex.

This is the first time that a woman, who has officially changed her sex, has ever married in a church under English law.

It was a busy morning for Gina – as she is known to her friends.

First there was a visit to a fashionable hairdresser. Her bridegroom fussed in the hotel lounge where the reception was being held, as time ticked by and she did not arrive back.

At last, just over an hour before she was due at the church, she arrived at the hotel in a taxi.

"It took a little longer than I thought," she said in a warm contralto voice as she patted her natural blonde waves and the upswept coif arranged by the hairdresser to hold the small pearl and diamond coronet from which her long veil flowed.

In the hotel bedroom her dress hung from the

curtains shielded by tissue paper.

She wore a pale pink foundation and coral lipstick. Her fingernails shone with colourless varnish. Apart from her coronet, her only jewellery was a gold cross.

The groom gave the bridesmaids, Miss Ann Dickins, 18, and Miss Shirley Goodhew, 14, a gold locket each, and left for the church while Georgina got ready.

She was given away by an old friend, a chemist, Mr. Herbert Wilkes.

Although she is tall, about 5ft 8in, she wore high heeled white satin shoes and her bridegroom husband towered above her.

At the reception, where the guests drank champagne, the couple cut a three-tiered white wedding cake. The menu cards bore the coat of arms of the bridegroom's family.

The bride's parents are dead and so is the bridegroom's father but his mother and her elder sister were there.

The bride's going-away dress was in fine beige check with a matching jacket and close-fitting silk hat. "I wanted some colour to brighten the dress," she said. She wore a gold "G".

When the couple return from their honeymoon in Paris, the bride has to go for a check-up on lung trouble which kept her in a Sussex sanatorium for seven months.'

The Sunday *People* carried the headline – 'Strangest fashionable wedding on record' and wrote:

'It was the strangest wedding any church has ever seen – let alone the debs' church where the greatest and most fashionable in the land are married.

A few years ago the bride was a pipe-smoking, beer-drinking naval officer. But yesterday as she left the church on the arm of her man, women shoppers

Aged 39. Wedding close-up with my 'Prince Charming'.
October 13th, 1962. Photo: Courtesy *News of the World.*

Another lovely wedding day picture, especially of my 'beloved'.
St. Margaret's, Westminster. October 13th, 1962.
Photo: Courtesy *Planet News.*

sighed: "Doesn't she look lovely."

They found it hard to realise that for the first 34 years of her life the bride had lived as a man. It was in 1960 that Somerset House issued a new birth certificate which officially changed the sex and Christian name of Surgeon Lieut. George Turtle R.N.

Now she is Mrs. Georgina Somerset, the bride who made history – for the marriage is believed to be the first in England of a man who changed into a woman.

St. Margaret's Westminster has never seen anything like it. For it wasn't a quiet wedding . . .

There were ushers wearing white carnations, a green and white awning over the church door, the wedding march and two bridesmaids in pink.

At the champagne reception childhood friends of the bride commented: "Most feminine." "She looks wonderful."

One male guest added: "A most delightful combination of surgery, science, art and charm." . . .'

All but one of the many British Sunday national newspapers at the time carried a report and most a photograph also, and when we arrived in Paris we found ourselves there also on the front page of *Le Journal du DIMANCHE*. We have a magical memory of our stay, visiting all the usual notable places – Montmartre, Le Sacré Coeur, Nôtre Dame and, of course, the Eiffel Tower, coming away with souvenirs which still grace our home.

It was not until the following year, July 1963, that my book, which I chose to call *Over the Sex Border*, was finally published. It was, in fact, turned down by several publishers before Gollancz championed the cause, for it was still a time when the subject was rather *risqué*. Consequently, it reached only a selective readership. The lack of any photographs also deterred the curious, but I did not want to sensationalise the subject and decided not to include any. Indeed, it was intended as an objective medical study and was not in any way autobiographical, much as many believed, quite wrongly, that part of its

Aged 39. My wedding day – facing the press and the crowds.
October 1962. Photo: Courtesy *Hawkins Press Photos.*

A wedding day toast to 'us'. October 13th, 1962.
London. Photo: Courtesy the *People*.

"Let me have one of you on your own". October 13th, 1962.
A wedding day picture of the bride. Photo: *Belgrave Press.*

Return from Paris honeymoon – Heathrow. October, 1962.
Photo: Courtesy *News of the World*.

contents at least were just this. In fact, my Chapter 3, on 'The Sufferer's Lonely World', was compiled entirely from letters I had received, some more than sixteen pages long, which are still in my possession in my confidential files.

During the 1960s articles and letters on the subject, both subjective and objective, kept my name in the public eye. As a pioneer, one of the first attempts to establish that sex was not something that could be readily and definitely determined, let alone before birth, was in a letter of mine published in the *Family Doctor* in June 1961. In it I said:

> 'I was particularly interested in the article by Dr. E. J. Trimmer on determining a baby's sex before it is born. Unfortunately, it would appear to the lay public that sex is a definite entity, capable of being determined with complete accuracy by what is known as the nuclear cell test.
>
> It is becoming more and more realised, however, that this test is not so conclusive as was at first thought. Also, to speak of nuclear sex is to differentiate only one aspect of sex. Indeed, an increasing number of cases are coming to light where the anatomical sex is different to the nuclear sex.
>
> This not only goes to show the unreliability of such methods of sex determination, but proves conversely that the whole make-up of sex is so complex that it can only be correctly assessed when all the factors of anatomical, nuclear, biological, psychological, and even social and environmental sex are taken into consideration.
>
> Not always are these conclusively in the one direction and, until some deeper explanation can be found for this, it would appear that we are a long way from the absolute truth and accuracy.'

Later, in a letter of mine published in the *British Medical Journal* (9 July 1966), I suggested that the medical profession could itself assist, 'by keeping an open mind and helping, not only by sympathising, but by understanding when the truth is offered them, instead of tossing it aside because of their own conditioning and sexual outlook upon life. 'It is interesting,' I went on, 'that most if not all medical studies (on transsexualism) have been made by men.' Attention drawn to this letter caused me to be invited to appear in a BBC *Horizon* programme on the subject of *Sex Change*. It was prompted by the retirement of Tamara Press and other female Russian athletes from the Olympic Games, causing their true sex to be called into question. It was the first time a sex-changeling had appeared on British television in a medical programme, and the first time the BBC had dared to allow a broadcast on such a then taboo subject. The media billed it as a 'shock' programme. I gave up a day in my surgery, cancelling a full appointment book, to go to Television Centre to give a forty minute filmed interview to Antony Isaacs. When I tuned in to see the programme on November 21st, 1966 I found only part had been devoted to the subject and the commentator, Christopher Chataway, opened and closed with the following sympathetic remarks:

"In our second item to-night we turn to one of those areas of human experience which many of us, doctors and scientists included, would rather ignore as being somewhat embarrassing, distasteful or so rare that it hardly merits serious attention. The subject is hermaphroditism or what is loosely or wrongly called Sexual Change. . . . To some, the idea of a change of sex has become a joke which makes sensational headlines every time a new case is reported but, for the individual concerned, it is far from a joke. It is a desperate situation which may well have built up over years of misery, uncertainty and misunderstanding. . . .

"Athletes provide only one example of the agonising dilemma facing those whose true sex is in doubt. Of all human predicaments this must surely be one of the most lonely, in a world where every detail of our social life is affected by whether we are men or women. To be uncertain of *this* must be to question one's very identity and, whatever doctors may do for these people, their mental suffering is surely something that the rest of us can never wholly understand."

Such words are warming to hear by those so afflicted but sadly the programme did not match up to my expectations, each contribution being separately edited and my own contribution edited to run for no more than a minute or so. No discussion took place. Subsequently I was told that I had said more than the BBC were prepared to screen, and a further appearance of mine scheduled for the *Late Night Line Up* programme was cancelled. Marsland Gander, reporting in the *Daily Telegraph*, put it this way:

'Last week, in the programme on BBC-2 on sex-changes, one participant in particular said far more than the BBC were prepared to broadcast and it was accordingly deleted by the producer. I mention this only as a corrective to the prevailing impression that in BBC circles almost anything goes.'

Over the decades my study of the subject has continued, and a re-reading of my work surprises me that so much of what I wrote still holds good to-day – some thirty years on – and I am pleased that, as a historic pioneering study, it is reprinted here to reach another generation of readers. As a work written for both doctor and patient it was difficult not to find one or the other either out of their depth or aggravated by medical simplicity. The hope was that each would accept the work for what it was intended to be and judge it upon its overall merit, rather than be critical of minor errors due largely to lack of established knowledge of the day. Indeed, my references to nuclear and chromosomal sex seem very elementary by to-day's standards, with even the experts of the day speculating and fumbling in the dark. In those early days I had only one work, *Symposium on Nuclear Sex* published in 1957, to help me.

Since then cytological studies have advanced by great strides, and we have come a long way from Barr's discovery of sex chromatin in 1949 and believing that a simple saliva test can tell the sex of an individual. A negative result, implying the absence of Barr bodies and the presence, therefore, of only one X chromosome, no longer means that the person is a male with XY constitution for it equally applies to a female with Turner's syndrome with XO constitution. Equally, a positive result, implying the presence of one or more Barr bodies and therefore of two (or more) X chromosomes, no longer implies that the person must be female of XX constitution, since this is also found in males with Klinefelter's syndrome of XXY constitution. Other variations of course occur, as do mosaics, and these can now be determined accurately by blood or skin analysis. Of the essence is that it is the Y chromosome which determines maleness, and it dominates over many other X chromosomes which may be present. The fact that those with Klinefelter's syndrome are almost certainly sterile and may present with some female physical characteristics does not, in itself, predispose to transsexualism. Much as one must sympathise with their predicament, those with such a constitution hoping that it gives some justification for their desire for a 'change' can only be disappointed, since this chromosomal aberration is not a mixed-sex, mosaic, aberration, occurs in about 1 in 700 males, and only very few of these are transsexuals – evidence enough that the aetiology of the problem is much more complex than genetic considerations alone.

Much as my chapter on nuclear sex is best viewed in relation to the year it was written, therefore, the main issues discussed remain accurate still to-day and none more so than the chapter on the legal aspects. Whether or not the findings in the April Ashley case in the High Court in 1970 or the findings in the European Court of Human Rights in the Mark Rees case in 1986 and the Caroline Cossey case in 1990 leave us saddened and dismayed at the apparent lack of compassion, it cannot be said that the arguments and warnings were not fully aired by me. Indeed, I sent a copy of my book to Mr. Justice Roger

Ormrod after the Corbett v. Corbett case concerning April Ashley and he kindly replied saying that it was not, in fact, amongst those referred to him during the case, but continued:

'I am particularly glad to see that you and I have arrived independently at the same conclusions as to the legal position and I must congratulate you on the way in which you dealt with the law on this subject. It is a confused area of law anyway and it is a great achievement for a layman to master it and to write so sympathetically about it as you have done. The rest of the book I found most interesting. Thank you again.'

In his summing up in this now famous case, he said:

"Operation cannot affect the true sex. The only cases where the term 'change of sex' is appropriate are those in which a mistake as to sex is made at birth and subsequently revealed by further medical investigation."

It is hard to fault this medically, although pressure has mounted in Britain ever since to upset this ruling. No doubt time, research and a better understanding of the aetiology of the syndrome may allow compassion to prevail over cold facts, especially in certain true cases of transsexualism where treatment has been sought early. Certainly, several countries of the world now accept what they permissively term the reality of the situation once surgery has been performed, even though most of these people have undergone no true change of their sex, cannot be said medically to have changed sex or to have *become* of the opposite sex. For *ALL* such cases to be given the same recognition regardless of their former social, marital and medical state is not only quite unjustified but morally wrong. What also of those – and there are a number – who regret it afterwards and wish to remain legally of their biological sex? The case of one such man is reported who regretted his 'sex-change operation' and, after 'reverting', legally married as a man again, the Registrar saying that he was quite satisfied that the groom was of the male sex in spite of his surgery (*Sunday Express* report, 'Sex change father weds girl of 18', London, 23 December, 1973, p.1). Indeed, one handicap to progress in England must be in trying to put *all* transsexuals similarly into one legal category, instead of aiming at the establishment of conditions whereby the more deserving transsexuals could be given full legal status *on individual merit*. Personal applications to a Court based on such individual merit prior to any surgery would also be helpful, especially if given strong medical support.

Transsexuals bewail the fact that they have no place in society and are left in a state of limbo after surgery. Yet it is they who land themselves in this state by ingesting vast quantities of opposite-sex hormones and beseeching to be castrated – circumstances which do not then give them the 'right' to upturn all the laws which previously applied to them. Whether or not they can help it does not alter *medically* what, often with misguided help, they have turned themselves into – at best sincere but demonstrably physically and sexually abnormal people and, at worst, psychotic, shameless, complicated curiosities. Following surgery male transsexuals certainly no longer possess male genitalia and can no longer be regarded as physically normal men. On the other hand, they cannot either be regarded as physically normal women and do not, in reality, become women. The problem is that not only does society expect people to be either male or female (enter either M or F in the box marked sex!) but that transsexuals themselves insist that as they are no longer men they *must* be women. In truth, transsexuals are neither and belong to a third gender, and a film about a fictitious male transsexual made in the United States of America some two decades ago recognised this fact, titling the film *The Third Sex*. In India to-day such a third gender is recognised, and men who wish to be women and have been totally castrated by having their penis and testes amputated are called eunuchs or *Hijras*. Whilst a few are said to be of ambiguous sex, the majority of the many thousands that exist in that country are little different to transsexuals around the world. Although *Hijras* accept the need to live in special communities, live mainly from prostitution and are regarded with a mixture of repulsion, fear, consent and disgust, India's culture accepts them as possessing certain religious powers. This is due to the fact that by accepting castration they are regarded as having renounced their sexuality, and that they themselves accept afterwards that they are neither male nor female. Nevertheless, similarities still exist with the recognised transsexual men of the Western world, in that their apparent (pre-surgery) homosexual love of other men only appears to be accepted and reciprocated by a certain type of male after the procedure of castration has been undertaken and the eunuch taken to living as a woman. Often strong relationships are then formed although, unlike transsexuals, who invariably insist that they have become women, acceptance by the eunuchs that they belong to a particular community and to a third gender is not disputed.

Medicine is the same the world over and the time has come for a universal agreement on the management of transsexuals, but the giving of a new birth certificate will always be a difficult issue since in all honesty the transsexual was correctly registered at the time of birth, often proving this beyond doubt by fathering children, whatever arguments may be put forward to the contrary. Indeed, to suggest that all post-surgical cases should be given new birth certificates and allowed to marry is untenable, because it would be morally and ethically wrong and dishonest for a father or a grandfather to be allowed to say he was born a girl and to remarry as a bride. The sad part is that, however permissive society becomes, these cases will always have to accept that biologically and organically they are really no more than feminised males or masculinised females, and will forever remain, regardless of their altered anatomy, of the male or female sex to which they were born. Their claim for legal recognition on the grounds that they were born of the other sex or have since changed their sex by operation can only be a fantasy, and to accept this and instead to argue their case on grou..ds of compassion would serve them better. Many male cases speaking independently confirm what I have long maintained, that they had never seriously dreamed of 'changing sex' until they started taking female hormones. The idea of helping transsexuals, often self-diagnosed, by freely giving or allowing them easily to obtain such hormones in the first instance is, therefore, completely misguided and of negative value *until* the full facts have been made clear to them and their case has been fully assessed by qualified specialists in the field. Writing recently in the *Journal of the Royal Society of Medicine* (Volume 82, August 1989) I said:

> 'The fantasy to "change sex" ONLY becomes a progressively irreversible determination AFTER the administration and influence of opposite-sex hormones. Even after surgery these physically normal men do not "become women" – the prostate is retained and they are "merely mutilated, by castration, into a simulacrum of the opposite sex" (Allen, C., "Change of Sex", *Nursing Mirror*, 9 August, 1963). Moreover they lack the formative years in their desired role and have a past from which there is no escape, even in dreams. As stated by Dr. Socarides (American Psychoanalytic Association, 31 January, 1969), "You don't change the body to conform to *anything* and, after the operation, the patient remains what he or she was born, and the psychic problems are the same or worse." . . . There are, of course, times when we must place a TRUE intersexual into their correct role, but if we do not accept facts we are living in the same fantasy world as our patients, and will end up as sick as those we are trying to help.'

Later, as a Fellow of the Royal Society of Medicine, in the same Journal (Volume 83, June 1990), in a further letter I wrote:

> 'Transsexualism is an affliction which appears inborn, remains throughout life and defies all "cure", and I have always maintained that there is a

proportion of applicants for gender change who are worthy of every assistance, having helped many on their way. These *true* transsexuals are rare, often asexual and, although popular, usually lonely, sensitive souls, and it is these who primarily deserve our pity and time-consuming help. However, large numbers of homosexuals, antisocials, exhibitionists and perverts have for some time been jumping onto the transsexual bandwagon, bringing the subject and the medical profession into disrepute. These are more aptly trans-homo-sexuals, often having their partners at their side when having surgery, many afterwards becoming prostitutes. It is among this majority that the phases of homosexuality, transvestism, soul-searching and guilt do exist – and form part of the maturing transsexual process, catalysed by the administration of opposite sex hormones. This could explain why, despite up to 100 cases a year receiving surgery at one London teaching hospital alone, waiting lists remain long . . . they **must** believe their change is not the illusion it is. The fantasy world in which these sufferers live both before and after "sex-change" surgery makes them **unreal people in an unreal world**. It is **this** predicament for which we have to have deep compassion.'

It is sad that so many transsexuals go into their 'sex change' without apparently knowing or being told the facts such as are enumerated here. The only real hope for transsexuals is that their condition should be diagnosed as early as possible so that they have less past behind them and more future to enjoy in their desired role. In 1960 my belief was that enlightenment would enable this to be so and that, with time and a more unisexual society, the condition would diminish and the critical age for action become lower. Yet, to-day, the average age still remains around 30 to 35 based on several thousand cases, and compares exactly with the graph shown in Chapter Two based on just fifty cases. Indeed, cases still go on marrying and having children before seeking help with their problem, thereby involving others in the tragedy of their lives. This is the unacceptable face of transsexualism since there is no need for it in these days of Gender Identity Clinics, when the subject is common knowledge and, sadly, provides easy material for cheap laughs on television. Indeed, why transsexuals who profess to have felt of the opposite sex since the age of two or three should reach thirty or more, and often have married with children, before suddenly becoming obsessed with the idea of 'changing sex' is something that needs much more in-depth psychiatric research.

The ideal is for a child to be brought up by his or her own loving parents, within the faith of their choosing, to marry and have their own children and to die with their children and grandchildren around them and to whom they can pass on the family heirlooms. The sterilising of transsexuals in furtherance of their quest is a desperate expedient, and the loss of God's greatest gift to be able to reproduce is a sadness that only old age will bring home to them. No doctor should legally be allowed to carry out such a procedure without exhaustive assessment of their patient and supportive approval. Yet, instead of fewer and fewer cases coming to light as one would expect over the years, the opposite is occurring, perhaps connected with the increasing permissiveness of society and the now commonplace coverage of the subject by the media. An added factor must be the commercial advertisements which increasingly appear in the tabloid press and elsewhere and which provide encouragement by offering advice and help for transvestites, transsexuals and homosexuals.

The fact is that surgery and sex hormone therapy is being given freely these days to all-comers, both under the National Health Service and privately, up to 500 cases a year receiving surgery in Britain alone. The result is that many reach the stage of being unable to 'go on' or 'go back' and end up committing suicide. When one realises that this is the outcome and the only way out for up to 30 per cent of cases, the real tragedy of the problem becomes apparent. For this the medical profession must be held fully responsible, since without their help in the form of opposite-sex hormone therapy and plastic-surgery procedures the illusion of a 'sex-change' as is known to-day would be quite impossible. All that results from giving hormones and telling the patient to go away and prove themselves in the new role is to land them in a deeper hole from which there is no escape, for, however unsuccessful they may be, functionally they will have rendered themselves irreversibly infertile and, psychologically, unable to face up to failure and having to turn back. Certainly medical and surgical help should not be given to patients unless both the surgeon and psychiatrist are prepared to continue to help them with their ensuing rehabilitation, for it is after surgery that the real problems begin. Indeed, if surgeons found themselves afterwards involved with prolonged correspondence, both official and otherwise, and with each of their patient's personal and family difficulties, they might reflect more seriously on the propriety of their actions and be less inclined to help other than the most deserving cases. Unfortunately, surgery can be obtained privately in many parts of the world just for the asking and the paying and the patient can disappear into the night as quickly as he came, leaving another country, perhaps, and its society to pick up the pieces.

The matter of the biological sex is one we hear more about these days and deserves clarification, as few appear to understand why it should be offered as such a powerful argument against transsexuals when they may present so acceptably in their new role. A man may have his penis and testes amputated and the penile and scrotal skin inverted to form an artificial vagina. He may have breast implants and tedious, often painful, electrolysis to remove his facial and body hair. He may be feminised bodily by the administration of large continuous doses of oestrogens. The result may well be a person who looks to all outward appearances to be a woman and acceptable as such in society. Plastic surgery is the art of deception and the plastic surgeon may be well satisfied with his efforts at pleasing his patient. What we have, however, is a person who has no female reproductive system whatever and now no male external genitalia, but with parts of his internal male reproductive system remaining. The prostate gland, one of those important in the male reproductive system, remains as does parts of the Vas. The ability to enjoy sex depends much upon the prostate, as old men who have had to have it removed will attest to. The ability to enjoy sex after a 'sex change' is due to the retention of this male gland and it is pressure upon it, either in a masturbatory process or by the penis of another pressing on it through the artificial vagina wall, that will stimulate orgasm. In some cases even massive doses of female hormones will not have caused it to atrophy, and some wet secretion of prostatic fluid may still occur. Consequently, therefore, discounting psychological delusion, neurologically, biologically and physiologically orgasm remains, and can only remain, male in type reaching a sudden climax.

The artificial vagina is just that – artificial. It is a blind pocket of skin formed from 'outside' skin often containing hair follicles, and is neither soft moist 'inner' skin nor contains the nerve endings which make up a normal vagina. (The use of a section of bowel to form a more natural 'vagina' is possible but not routinely undertaken, on account of the additional hazards and increased likelihood of post-operative complications of such surgery.) Where the penile skin has been inverted there will remain some erotic nerve endings but the brain, having been programmed, will interpret stimulation of these as still coming from the penis, in the same way that one might feel one's toes tingling after having a leg amputated. Being a blind pocket the artificial vagina needs keeping extra clean and, in most cases, the risk of contraction necessitates the wearing of a mould to keep it open or a dilator to enlarge it, which is not only likely to be inconvenient and uncomfortable but is a constant reminder of what the person is – an unreal woman. Quite often the 'vagina' is not deep enough or wide enough and intercourse, instead of being an enjoyable experience, can be painful and distressing, causing frustration and reluctance on the part of the transsexual to engage in such an activity. The person suffers none of the inconveniences of 'periods', of premenstrual tension or the fear of being rendered pregnant unwillingly as in a rape situation. The ingestion of prolonged high doses of oestrogen is also not without risk and over the years, and in different countries, there have been reports of several transsexuals dying from thrombosis or cancer of the breast as a result. Whilst high intake of the synthetic oestrogens such as ethinyloestradiol were mostly responsible for this and the more common prescribing these days of the natural oestrogens such as Premarin in normal dosage appears to carry less risk, transsexuals nevertheless become desperate enough to ingest *any* form of oestrogen that is available to them and have little regard for excessively exceeding the recommended dose. No operation is without some risk and the number who have died on the operating tables of the world having so-called 'sex-change surgery' is also not inconsequential. Indeed, the surgery involved is 'major' and complications are not uncommon. Anal and 'vaginal' fistulas, urethral constrictions and prostate problems can well be the legacy of such surgery and may present into old age if not sooner, to bring the patient face to face with the reality of the self-inflicted wound of having had their normal healthy bodies operated upon. Even the falseness of the silicone implants used to augment the breasts is ever-present, causing them to unnaturally stand up in the lying down position, and irritation from the silicone can produce serious problems at any time, the implants themselves not uncommonly leaking or shifting their position, causing not only deep concern but making further surgical intervention necessary.

A very important consideration also is the voice, for no amount of female hormones will alter it, raise its pitch or enable the transsexual man to get away with the illusion of the change without some further act of deception. Efforts to shorten the vocal chords by surgery have been tried and, in some cases, had a limited success, only for a relapse to occur later. For others, the results may be disastrous and leave the voice even deeper or mutilated. Such surgery, therefore, is too hazardous to be a serious consideration. The alternative is to have the voice trained. Much, it seems, is possible by voice therapy but patience and perseverence are necessary and, in the end, the result depends upon having to remember to speak in a particular way. Any lapse in concentration and the old deep voice will return.

The effect, therefore, is produced by having to 'act', which in most cases is what the transsexual is trying to get away from. Such a permanent pretence leaves the transsexual only too aware of what he is and can defeat the process of rehabilitation. The outcome is often a husky 'transsexual' voice, which can be tell-tale, particularly if there are other aspects of sexual doubt about the individual. Speaking on the telephone, where only the lower frequencies are mostly reproduced, can also cause embarrassment should the transsexual be called 'sir', which is quite possible however successful the feminine appearance. The male transsexual wants to be thought of and looked upon as a woman, not as some pantomime dame whose artificially pitched-up voice is 'just what it is' and part of the joke. The deep male voice is a secondary sexual characteristic and a result of male hormones at puberty causing the larynx to enlarge. Castration before puberty can save the transsexual much trouble, therefore, so that the earlier he makes up his mind about the 'change' the more successful his rehabilitation is likely to be. Even laryngeal surgery stands a better chance when the patient is young and the tissues softer, but, unfortunately, transsexuals rarely come to any decision until well after puberty when their sexual libido has built up and become channelled perversely into inflaming their long smouldering revulsion to their sexual organs and gender status.

In the case of female transsexualists a similar compilation of biological factors can be drawn up, although perhaps not so extreme. They have no male reproductive tract and not all of the female reproductive tract is necessarily removed. Removal of the breasts surgically can leave much scarring, especially if these are large and, although it is feasible to build up an artificial penis and insert a prosthesis simulating testes, a technique in which the Americans boast expertise, it presents a challenge with several operations being necessary and many cases live out their lives as men without undergoing any surgery of this kind. The administration of high regular doses of male sex hormones, usually by intramuscular injection, is also not without hazard, causing an upsurge in libido which cannot always be channelled to advantage. Further, these have not only androgenic but anabolic effects, so that the patient, apart from becoming more aggressive and more likely to suffer hair loss may, in the long term, face other, unanticipated, risks to health and a possible reduction in their expectancy of life. One advantage over the male transsexual is that the voice can be altered by opposite-sex hormones, making it deeper and thus helping the illusion in the desired role. The growing of the all-important beard also presents little problem once androgen therapy has been maintained for a year or two.

In both sexes, whenever the person goes into hospital they will be asked for a full medical history, and they would be unwise to tell other than the whole truth. The opprobrium of society and possible ostracism by their family have to be taken into consideration, and suicide is not uncommon as a result of this factor alone. Even applications for life or medical insurance will mean they have to expose their secret if the application is to be valid. This would apply whether or not they had been granted a new birth certificate or even if they are legally married, since it is not the legal issues which are relevant here but their past medical history, which has to be fully divulged.

They can go through a ceremony of marriage and let no one know their circumstances, but, if they are cheating, it will have no validity as soon as the legal issues of the marriage are called into question. Even a staunch partner may tire of the marriage due to its abnormal nature and seek a divorce, exposing the individual to undesirable publicity. Even in countries where marriage is allowed, the bond will depend upon something other than a natural relationship and having their own children, and the problem of finding a partner who is willing to accept that the person was once of their own gender narrows the field. Indeed, it is usually denied that many marriages, whether allowed or not, are to homosexuals, but studies indicate that most partnerships arise from meetings in homosexual bars and haunts (Feldman, P., *Sex and Sexuality*, Longmans, 1987). Probably the same is true with lesbians. What also cannot be ignored, however apparently inconsequential, is that scientific examination of the bones even long after death will still reveal the true sex and give the ultimate lie to any claim that the deceased changed sex during their lifetime. All these are things which the transsexual would wish unsaid, may deny, or can blank out of their mind. There is no intention to be cruel, but in a medical study all relevant factors have to be considered and examined. Certainly it is better for them to know the worst from the start, that they might be forewarned of the problems that lie ahead, rather than have to face up to the reality of their position later when they can do nothing about it.

The premise that transsexuals are perhaps born with a brain of the opposite sex due to abnormal prenatal influences is as yet only hypothetical, but is sometimes put forward as an argument by those wishing to find justification for the condition, although so far no real evidence has emerged to support such a theory. Such a theory is also not compatible with some significant aspects of the syndrome and, indeed, many continue to show, even after surgery, their masculine attitude and aggressiveness towards all aspects of life whether business, social or former leisure activities. Nevertheless, some psychological influence causes the 'unwanted' scourge, the conflict with the otherwise normally developed physical sexual state and the resulting tragedies to the lives of those afflicted and their families. Psychiatric studies suggest that parental and environmental influences play a large part, especially in the case of the Primary Transsexual (Stoller, R., Ch.5, 'The Gender Disorders', *Sexual Deviation*, Ed. Rosen, I., Oxford University Press, 1979) so that there is no simple answer covering the whole range of transsexual types. Research must therefore go on in the hope that a 'cure' other than surgery may be found.

Whilst transsexuals are always asking us to accept the reality of the situation, by definition they are, within generally accepted limits, born physically and organically normal, with normal chromosomal constitution and two normally functioning gonads. A deep-seated psycho-sexual problem therefore exists, whether it takes the form of a deviation or a perversion, and as the antagonism to the sexual role builds up and the critical age is reached the patient is likely to become very ill mentally and perhaps suicidal. This is well known and tends to discount the suggestion by some that transsexualism is not a mental sickness. Why else would they have to consult doctors and psychiatrists, desperately seeking castration and that their bodies be changed? Long after the abstract issues have been discussed and re-discussed, however, it is the practical issues that remain, and the belief that major ablative surgery is the answer *in such a large number of cases* is one that can have neither a serious place in medicine nor be morally sustainable. To be considered cruel by humanitarians for holding such a view is for them to ignore the overall picture of suffering caused by encouraging those with the vaguest transsexual feelings or weaker mentality into a deeper abyss of uncertainty and unreality. It cannot be denied that in the case of *true* transsexuals there seems no other 'cure' and that many are helped into more contented and useful lives, but considering the entire animal world is taken up with mating habits and reproduction of the species the question whether the efforts of humans in illusorily changing the sex of thousands of their fellow beings is wholly justified is one that needs deep application, especially when the result is Dead Sea fruit.

Less than a few percent of transsexuals are true or primary transsexuals. These are generally the lonely, sensitive, asexual types of transsexual whose desire for a change is gender motivated. Their essential wish is to have their offending genitalia removed so that they cannot then be regarded as of their sex of upbringing and have to conform to all that is expected of them in that sexual role. This also enables them to dress and have the appearance of the sex of their desire – the sexual act itself is either not important or secondary, so that a functional vagina is not of the essence, except to assist psychologically in their acceptance of themselves in their new role and their right in society to it. These generally are not particularly attracted to partners and marriage is not part of their plans. Being the least sexual of the transsexual groups, however, they have greater need to depend upon being immersed happily in their work, and it is only when they are frustrated in this direction that thoughts of failure and suicide may creep in. These cases can be the easiest to diagnose and assist, and yet in spite of their worthiness are often the ones needing the most moral support. This is because it is often these who, ashamed at finding themselves 'tarred' and associated with the sordid sexual world of others, try the hardest to conform to normality and, finding it impossible, are more likely to end up feeling guilty and uncertain of what is right for them.

By far the majority of so-called transsexuals to-day are pseudo-transsexuals, a term generally embracing those whose desire for a 'change of sex' is sexually motivated. These include those of bisexual and homosexual orientation who are more aptly described as trans-homo-sexuals. It is these who appear better able to ignore the opprobrium of society, generally having their ready-made circle of friends of similar orientation around them, and whose sex drive continues to make life sweet long after the novelty of the 'change' has worn off. Those in this group are more likely to seek sexual partners or become prostitutes. Many in this group, however, are enticed and encouraged into a 'sex change' by frequenting clubs which are run for sexual and commercial purposes, often without realising the full consequences of their actions until it is too late. Regret at the loss of their sex organs and of the 'pleasure' derived from them, and the realisation of what they have become, then accounts for many suicides within this group.

Commercialism is very much a part of so-called trans-sexualism to-day. Transsexualism has indeed been hijacked; the pure and magical world of the true transsexual, far removed from homosexual connections and clubbing together, has become overwhelmed. To-day we have all-comers calling themselves transsexuals. Groups form to claim their 'rights' and many engage in activities associated with homosexuality, even often using the jargon of the homosexual community. In this context, a clearer picture unfolds when we consider the words of Mr. Gabriel Rotello, editor of an American homosexual magazine, (*Daily Telegraph* report, p.1, 8 April, 1991) speaking of the current fashion to abandon the term 'gay' in favour of reverting to the original word 'queer'. He said, 'When you are trying to describe the community and you have to list gays, lesbians, bisexuals, trans-sexuals (post-operation and pre-operation), it gets unwieldy. *Queer says it all.*' This is *not* transsexualism as of old nor *true* transsexualism. At one time a person who had 'changed their sex' was regarded as a brave person who had crossed the divide into the world of the unknown. To-day the subject has been turned into a nightmare, with all manner of transsexuals making increasing demands upon both the medical profession and society. Often to the delight of the case concerned, the media also seems to revel in referring to them as having changed sex, having had a sex change operation and done this or that in a most bizarre fashion. There are no inverted commas around the terms 'sex change' or 'sex-change operation' to indicate that they are misnomers, and some of these cases are no more than 'in the process of changing sex' and 'awaiting surgery'. It is beyond belief that the public can still be susceptible to stories of this kind or that the press themselves should still be interested in publishing them.

My chapter on the surgical procedure to give the male perineum the appearance of a female is historic in its approach at the time, and as in Jorgensen's case this involved three operations. Yet it was not the operations themselves which were significant – these had been carried out before, albeit crudely, on such as Lily Elbe with only limited success – the break-through was in the synthesising of the sex hormones which were for the first time to enable the male body to take on the desired female form and vice versa. To-day, of course, prolonged administration of opposite-sex hormones generally precedes the surgery, whilst the gender reassignment surgery itself is much more sophisticated. Because even massive doses of female hormones do not necessarily enlarge the breasts of male transsexuals appreciably, breast augmentation by the insertion of silicone prostheses is often also regarded as a normal procedure and undertaken at one and the same time.

I also advocated in my book that a whole team of specialists be set up to help these cases, and to-day we have the Gender Identity Clinics. The intention was that the few deserving cases should be properly vetted and, once helped surgically, be given every social and legal assistance. Yet to-day's overwhelming numbers seem to work against this principle, and even the consultants working for the clinics do not always have the time to act as a team to see and assess every case. Indeed, in some London NHS clinics transsexuals report that they have as little as one and a half hours a *year* of a psychiatrist's time! The question of cost also causes dissent, when National Health resources and excessive money have to be poured into what many regard as quite unnecessary and immoral procedures, when other 'more deserving' surgical cases have to wait. Certainly the money expended on each case alone is quite considerable and the results do not always produce useful or acceptable members of society. Those who pay privately may appear to make no demands upon others, but even these still deplete medical resources and often such patients are given what they demand without proper counselling, evaluation or assessment. Misled by sensational stories they have read, they wrongly believe a sex change operation is possible. Consequently, they sometimes complain that if the surgeon was prepared to operate then he should have been prepared to ensure their full legal status afterwards, but unfortunately, because of their sympathy, surgeons and psychiatrists themselves sometimes get carried away into the fantasy world of their patients. Private surgery is big business and can command large fees, so that money rather than justification for a 'change' can sometimes fault the system. Nevertheless, the success of a 'change' largely depends upon the individual's previous capability for work and their future continuance in it, so that it might be said that if patients can afford to pay they must already be successful. On this basis, for others seeking free NHS surgery, it implies that there is a greater need to be selective. This does not mean obstructively denying help to these just because they cannot afford to pay, but if they are poor as a result of being unable to work and cope with life in one role surgery may be contra-indicated, since a change of role may well bring a whole lot of new problems and render them even less able to cope with life than before. In either case the ability to be convincing in the role of their desire is *essential* if they are to work and function effectively after the 'change'.

The trouble with a comprehensive study is that such a formula requires putting in all the ingredients and stirring well.

It would be wrong, therefore, to imagine that all that is said applies necessarily or equally to all cases. Even within each category every case is really different, much as the outside world, the media and even the medical profession are apt to tar every case with the same brush. The fact that those who really change their sex are not transsexual, and that transsexuals do not really change their sex, is totally unrecognised or ignored. Even in my own case, should I reluctantly have to tell anyone that I have changed sex – yes, officially – it makes no difference. They have heard such claims many times before and a momentary uneasy pause ensues whilst I am silently assessed as 'one of those' they have read about, a transsexual or perhaps a pervert, and labelled quite falsely as one out of the transsexual's handbook who had felt like 'a woman trapped in a man's body'. In Chapter Five I paid particular heed to this differentiation and put into groups the basic types of cases as I saw them. It surprises me that I have seen no follow-up to this in any of my reading on the subject, especially in the material coming out from the United States which is prolific.

Like everything it goes in for, America has gone into transsexualism in a big way, and gives the impression that it alone has pioneered the recognition and advancement of knowledge of the subject. A great deal of energy and enthusiasm is expended in perfecting surgery supposedly to change the sex of individuals, and in convincing society of their achievement, and this is admirable and shows deep compassion. The lengths they go to, for example, to construct an artificial phallus to enable a female transsexual to live successfully in the male role and urinate in the standing position is commendable, but their ingenuity in trying to make the phallus also simulate a sexual organ capable of being manually erected for sexual play highlights the somewhat grotesque nature of the mock trans-formation and the disturbing moral issue of whether surgical skills should be used for such a purpose. Indeed, to many laymen, some of the literature technically detailing these and other transsexual surgical procedures must read more like under-the-counter pornography. It is therefore sad that the objectivity of the excellent work being done in this field tends to be blurred by an apparent readiness to accept the syndrome, rather than to increasing efforts to get to the root of the trouble and help discourage its proliferation. Certainly it is becoming rarer these days to see any arguments against supporting cases, either on medical, social or moral grounds. This is in spite of the increasing degradation of true transsexualism at the hands of the homosexual fraternity.

Numerous organisations and groups exist to-day both in America and in this country to help transsexuals, and yet most of these appear to be mutual admiration societies run by transsexuals themselves, who appear to be anxious to attract newcomers to their ranks, telling them how to 'get started' etc., on the basis of 'come in, the water is lovely'. Many also seem to be more like clubs for transsexuals at all stages of their gender role change and, whilst giving comfort and companionship to a particular type of transsexual who revels in comparing notes and 'mixing' with their own kind, they fail to help the lonely transsexual who does not feel, or wish to feel, part of an abnormal group. These would be distressed by the sight of other types, perhaps pre-operative transsexuals or transvestites in various confused manner of dress, some possibly showing a blue jowl under heavy make-up, and wish only to disassociate themselves from them and to merge unnoticed into society as an apparently normal person. For the same reason, even the thought of having to attend a Gender Identity Clinic or sit in a private waiting room with other transsexuals is off-putting. The handbooks and literature of these societies are generally well written and well informed, and cases often contribute to the overall picture by revealing their own experiences. Somehow, however, to the objective outsider there seems to be, in a lot of the literature, a sickening continuing reference to 'sex change' as if it titillates every time it is mentioned. It would also be unrealistic to expect this literature to be other than partisan and stories of so-called sex change are enthusiastically quoted from the media in news letters.

This is not to say that these societies in general do not play a very useful role in relieving the medical profession of much of the tedious work of taking sufferers under their wing, although the object of help does seem to be directed more towards assisting in a change of sexual role rather than to advising whether the disoriented soul will be a 'suitable case for treatment'. Nevertheless, it must also be said that many such organisations are run by kind, dedicated and sincere people, and the more avenues of help that exist the better. Some organisations are registered charities, such as the Beaumont Trust which was established back in 1975 to assist all those with any form of gender dysphoria problem, and more recently a branch of theirs, Gentrust, also a charitable trust, has been formed to specifically help transsexuals and their families. Although post-operative cases of gender dysphoria appear to be involved in running these trusts, where their subjective experiences must sympathetically colour their views, both do excellent work, include professionals as trustees and officers and provide referrals to appropriate organisations and professional counsellors, and their compassion, understanding and efficiency deserve praise. Their literature stresses that they are non-sexual organisations, are about gender and support, and are not contact organisations for sexual purposes. Certainly no person who has been in serious conflict with their gender role of upbringing since birth, and who does not mind getting 'involved', should be afraid or need be afraid of writing to or telephoning any of the helplines given at the end of this section for a sympathetic understanding of their dilemma. This applies equally to wives and other relatives who need help in coping with the distress of a loved one's problem. Nevertheless, whilst members' names are held to be strictly confidential and there may be no physical contact with other members, involvement with others does occur, at least through the newsletters. For those, therefore, who wish to remain entirely in ignorance of others and do not wish their own dream world to be intruded upon, there are now several psychiatrists specialising in the subject who are prepared to see patients privately, sympathetically and confidentially. A letter of referral should be sought from the general medical practitioner, who can obtain the names from the main starred clinics listed at the end of this work. The Brook Advisory Centres, another charitable organisation, must also be mentioned for the commendable work they do in specifically advising and counselling young people over such matters as contraception, and who are also happy to see those who may be concerned about their sexual orientation. Any parent who suspects a child may have any problem in this direction will be saving themselves and the child much anguish later on by seeking advice at the earliest possible time. Puberty is a particularly difficult and critical time and no-one need any longer suffer in silence.

In so far as all cases are different, in type and degree, it follows that when it comes to making rules and regulations affecting transsexuals the same differentiation must apply, so that not all are subject to the same conditions. Whilst we must dismiss the claims of many, therefore, this should not prevent society from recognising that some worthy young never-married transsexual deserves better than to be disallowed the chance of building a useful life for themselves. Indeed, there seems little argument that a hermaphrodite or true physical intersex should have the right to decide which sexual role they prefer *at the time of puberty*. There likewise seems no logical argument against allowing certain transsexuals the same privilege, therefore, and post-operative cases, beyond puberty in these circumstances, *under* the age of, say, twenty-one, should also be compassionately considered for a modified birth certificate and the legal right to marry in their chosen sexual role, given that their partner knows their history. This would require personal application. A marginal note on the birth certificate could then state that the person is a transsexual, give the date of surgery and the new names, with Statutory Declarations following from the applicant's surgeon and psychiatrist to confirm the facts. The shortened birth certificate need then only state the amended sex or perhaps bear an asterisk to indicate that a special note applied. Indeed, if such males *are* born with a female brain and have longed to be a girl from the age of three, twenty-one years seems a long enough time for them to recognise their gender dysphoria *in these enlightened times* and to seek treatment for it. At least such recognition would represent progress for the transsexual cause and encourage pubertal transsexuals, who had from childhood wished to have been born of the other sex, to seriously consider their desire for a social gender change at the optimum time in their lives. In due course, the age limit for allowing such cases these rights could be reviewed. Others older, however, who have been capable of, and experienced, physical sex in their born sex, perhaps married and with children, cannot really have it both ways and expect society or the authorities to approve their claims that an 'inborn' need justifies legal assumption of the opposite sexual role. For them their happiness must lie in their ability to live in their desired role, and in being grateful for the help they have received to make it possible. Only unhappiness can come from fighting society and from blaming society for their misfortune.

The sad death of Christine Jorgensen in May 1989, at the age of 62, marked the end of an era. Speaking after the death of Dr. Harry Benjamin at the age of 101 in August 1986, she said, "I never went along with the word transsexual because I think it's transgender; gender is who you are, sexual is who you sleep with. That's important, but I never mentioned that while Harry was living." In my book I likewise tried to veer away from the term transsexual and came up with the term O-sexual, the reasons for which I fully describe in the text. Essentially I saw these cases trying to escape from the social role of their upbringing, against which they rebelled and in which they felt out of place, into the opposite gender role, the only other one available. Yet few knew or could possibly know what belonging to the opposite role really meant or entailed, and could only see a woman as a man sexually sees a woman and vice versa. I judged that what most wanted was just to be left alone by society and not to have to conform. Some felt they belonged to both sexes at once and yet to neither. They essentially felt complete in themselves – 'O' – and wished to be free from sexual entanglements, hence the desire for complete castration. Christine Jorgensen seemed to epitomise this by never marrying, although she tried once and was refused permission because her birth certificate showed her as male; more than likely her heart was not in it anyway, for she later confessed, "Men are wary of me – and I am wary of the ones who aren't." She was just happy living as and being regarded as a woman, and that was the secret of her success and fulfilment. Terms other than transsexualism and transsexuality have come to be devised, amongst them Gender Dysphoria Syndrome. Whatever the merits or otherwise of changing the term, however, it seems unlikely that the established simple term 'transsexual' will disappear from general use. (For a time in the early days many only used one 's' in the spelling and this was the case in the first edition of my book. This has now been changed to two s's in the reprint here, which is certainly the norm to-day and no doubt rightly so.)

There may be no reason why people should not live as they wish or in the gender of their desire, but upbringing and past play a vital role and society can only exist on accurate records; if it bends the rules to suit a minority the result can only be chaos by undermining the historical reliability of all other records held. Happiness can only come to these individuals when they embark upon their momentous journey early in life, have not married or had children, avoid publicity and do not afterwards get involved in arguing for rights which are not justly theirs. Short of being able to get a new birth certificate and being allowed to marry, the compromise for them is to have a statutory declaration sworn and signed by a Commissioner of Oaths on the back of a *copy* of their birth certificate to indicate their change of sexual status. Then when they have to present their birth certificate for any reason no further questions have to be asked. For companionship, there is nothing to stop a transsexual and their partner living as common law husband and wife, although the legal pitfalls of such a relationship should not be underestimated, there being no provision in law to recognise their mutual dependence. Provided the transsexual and their partner remain happy together, however, legal problems need not arise, and it will be their mutual love that will sustain them.

For myself I have been fortunate in finding a wonderful companion to share my life in which love is more important than sex. In 1987 we celebrated our Silver Wedding Anniversary with twenty-five years of very happy marriage. Such love I never thought was possible. Only with my husband's help was I able to write my book and give of my best to my dental patients. I owe him everything for my successful rehabilitation and am proud to have his name. Indeed, for twenty-five years, both within the National Health Service and then privately, I worked full time in my Hove practice before retiring in 1985. Although selling up meant moving we still live in Hove, in a lovely house and garden with panoramic views over the town to the sea, and life remains full. I still like model trains and cuddly furry animals, playing my piano and composing music, working out puzzles and solving crosswords, cooking and gardening, and am fascinated with photography, both ciné and video, and with computers.

By nature, I have never thrown anything away, and my home is filled with filing cabinets and suitcases crammed full with documents, records, reports and every letter that has ever been written to me. I have my school reports, school photographs, my prize books, my school cap and even my old Hornby O gauge electric engine with a light on the front for which I had saved hard and long to buy in the early 1930s. The original track I also have, affordable at only one rail at a time and so there was nothing left for coaches. I have many thousands of feet of 9.5 mm ciné film of myself and family dating from 1950 and of 8.0 mm ciné film of myself and my husband dating from 1960. I have my documents whilst at King's College Hospital, my pay slips of the first money I ever earned for just £4.00, the sum I received for each **month's** work as Resident House Surgeon, students' group photographs, letters from Keith Turner in the R.A.F. before he was killed, tickets for the Victory in Europe dance in the hospital refectory; all my naval documents, programmes and press cuttings of the plays I acted in and produced at Deal, numerous naval photographs and my original naval cap; all my masonic meeting summonses with the notes I made for my speeches; and all the letters ever written between my mother and I, and my father and I, whilst away from home, and even telegrams sent to me on board ship.

I have all the considerable correspondence between my

medical advisers, my solicitors and Somerset House and myself; an enormous 'bundle' of legal papers relating to my libel action; several typewritten copies of my book which I had typed and retyped myself in full, often late at night to my husband's dictation, to take account of the many alterations and corrections in the editing. Making up another large file and of particular historical medical interest must be the many letters written to me from various consultants and doctors asking my help with their transsexual cases back in the 1960s and early 1970s, and including a copy of my replies. I also have all the letters written to me from transsexuals themselves since 1960, which I regard of course as confidential. One of my largest files is about my own case and includes thousands of press cuttings, photographs and articles and many letters I have written and had published on the subject, and reviews of my book and television appearance, etc. My archive material contains large numbers of medical articles, papers and various cuttings from journals; numerous newspaper cuttings about cases themselves; and many books and autobiographies spanning over forty years. As I get older I cannot help feeling that my collection deserves a better fate than being put on the bonfire one of these days when I die. Perhaps some of it will find a way into history, but essentially it is the present that matters, and there is a case for conceding to fresh thinking on the subject by a new generation as a new century dawns.

To those who assume that I still need to take oestrogens and that, judging from my recent photographs, I must be still on hormone replacement therapy (HRT), I should state that I have taken no oestrogens at all now for some twenty years. Although I well tolerated ethinyloestradiol orally for many years, as initially prescribed, and found this gave me a great sense of well-being, I eventually succumbed to the side-effects of cramp and a predisposition to migraine attacks – to which I was already prone. Of medical interest is the fact that, since leaving my body to its own endocrine functions, my health has improved and is certainly the better for the absence of these side-effects. Although it is difficult to assess what benefits I may otherwise be missing by not taking HRT as the years take their toll, I see no reason to risk upsetting my now stabilised hormonal balance to find out.

For the record, I am a regular size 12, weigh in at 130 lbs, am five foot eight inches tall, asthenic with long slender fingers, have brown eyes, blonde fair hair and a very fair complexion. My own story here is a fantastic and unique one, and each incident could occupy a whole chapter in a more detailed autobiography. Whether at the age of 68 now I choose to reopen all my scars, however, is doubtful, which is why I felt this remarkable medical account of my story, at least, should be written. To sit in front of my word processor tapping away at the keys is not something that particularly appeals to me, or to my husband for that matter, with the sun going down on the autumn of our lives. I am sure I have said enough, and to lose myself in my garden with the birds and my husband by my side does have its attractions.

I have now lived 34 years as a man and 34 years as a woman and it would be surprising if, after so many years of studying the many aspects of intersexuality, I had not become intimately involved. Even the fictitious Dr. Jekyll was, as a doctor, dedicated to his good-intentioned work before it destroyed him. I offer no comparison but I have, with some diffidence, decided to include a photograph of a rather surprising nature in my collection here. I have written much about the illusion and deception of a change of sexual role and pondered the reason why all the films known to me about the 'sex change' of male transsexuals, both fictional and non-fictional, should have the parts played by naturally born biological women. The reason for this irritating 'fudge' would seem an attempt to show the convincingness of the emergent female by conveying not only the right appearance but also the correct voice and mannerisms. However, if transsexuals really are intersexual as classified questionably in some medical works, I asked myself, why should male transsexuals themselves not be found to properly play the dual role? The reason would clearly seem to be that, in spite of claims and appearances, transsexuals are not intersexual. Indeed, male transsexuals always say they never want to see their male clothes again as long as they live and do not want to have anything whatever to do with masculinity. They even say they would like to blot out their former years and to pretend that they had been female all their lives. These are *not* things that an intersexual would think or say, and to play both parts for a film would be an eagerly accepted challenge. Indeed, such a challenge was too much for me and I rather dared myself to see if I could play both roles still at my age. Could an 'old' woman of 62 be accepted by society as a young man? I use the word 'young' because of my slim build and my soft, rosy, never-shaven face. My husband and I had a 40ft motor cruiser berthed at Brighton Marina, and jeans and a royal blue, baseball type, naval cap had become part of my weekend attire. I therefore took the unusual and rather improper step of engaging in just one act of transvestism. Tucking my long blonde hair well under my *Ark Royal* cap, therefore, wrapping cling film over my breasts, putting a sock into a pair of Y-fronts, and sporting a boy's jumper and pair of sun-glasses I was ready for the experiment. The last of the World War II destroyers, *HMS Cavalier*, happened to be berthed at the Marina as a show piece, and I took the opportunity of going aboard and, for the record, having my photograph taken. The resulting picture is shown here (Page 113). I regarded the result a success and that it proved how easily the public can be misled and are willing to take one at their face value. That said, however, I must add that after receiving nine 'sir's, just when I was least expecting it someone called me 'madam' – admittedly I was standing in front of a shop counter at the time, visible only above the waist and having momentarily taken off my sun-glasses, but it shows that, leaving theatrical effort aside, you cannot fool all the people all of the time. To see that, behind this masquerade, I really have not changed, you have only to see the subsequent pictures taken of me the following day, on the occasion of my Silver Wedding Anniversary and of me on holiday, still in my (same) bikini, at Sidmouth recently at the age of 66!

The dust-cover 'blurb' of my book opened with the words 'Doctors are still largely in the dark about transvestism and transsexualism.' It is of regret to me that I have to say that this is still true to-day. It sadly applies to the media and to the general public also. There are the few specialists, of course, who sympathise, understand and are willing to help, but doctors generally still know very little about the subject. Indeed, one general medical practitioner recently admitted to me not only his ignorance on the subject but his wish to remain in ignorance! Considering the sickening exploitation of the sexual side of the subject these days this reaction is understandable. Whilst such attitudes remain, transsexuals will have to continue the fight for survival, but the outcome is largely in their own hands by striving to turn the subject from a sick soap-opera joke into a serious, respectable issue.

I hope those of you with gender identity problems reading this will no longer be misled about the facts through sensational stories which may have fascinated you in the media. Seek what is in your heart through your own efforts, but remember that whatever logic you toss aside now will become a reality as you get older. Your friends and loved ones are irreplaceable, and 'everlasting life' is the perpetuation of life through your own genes. Nobody has the right to deny others the chance of happiness, but a 'sex change' is never a 'cure' for one's problems and can bring misery and misgivings as well. Do not be influenced by others or by what others tell you. One reputable psychiatrist once said to me, "Few are willing to admit to themselves, let alone to others, that they have made a mistake and are unhappy after all the trauma they have been through." The opprobrium of society in particular should not be disregarded. Accept that you can only change your social gender role and not your sex, and then you will not end up disillusioned, unsettled and fighting for an impossible goal. Above all, do not be proud of your disability and expect sympathy, and tell *no one* other then those who need to know. At least there is now more medical understanding than when I walked down Harley Street in tears back in 1955, for then even physical justification was not enough. It would be unworthy of me not to accept that I did have a certain amount of luck but I did, however, also have tremendous conviction that what I wanted and was doing was right, not just for myself but morally. This gave the necessary courage to press on in the face of almost total opposition. I was fortunate, however, in that there *were* a few who believed in me and I count amongst these my dear father, who supported me immensely, particularly in my darkest days, in spite of what must have been his own inner burden of worry and pain. Nevertheless, I met nothing other than great kindness wherever I went and from whoever I came into contact with, whether socially, medically or officially. Above all I found that, if one is sincere and truthful, compassion – deep compassion – does exist. There are still some to-day known to me of that era who were repeatedly turned away, heartbroken and suicidal, and yet who have managed to struggle on trying to do 'the right thing' and maintain the respect of society. For them, the magical dream of being a young girl has gone forever – they never wanted to be old women! They banged at the door and it creaked a little, making it easier for the next, but they themselves never 'made it' through. It is these less fortunate unknowns, not just the well known cases, that transsexuals have to thank to-day for the recognition given to the syndrome, and for their ability to readily obtain sympathetic help and understanding of their problem.

Remember especially that, however much attitudes may change and compassion prevail, basic medical facts will remain. Everyone has their own problems, and very many escape into other fantasy worlds by regular drinking (alcohol), often solitary, or attempt to blot out reality by taking drugs such as diazepam (Valium). Your problem is your own and only you alone can solve it, but **whatever** you decide it is certain that your dream world will remain unreal as the fantasy it is and stay with you to the grave. Indeed, if your fantasy were to become reality, the loss of the dream that has filled so much of your life would leave little but emptiness. To seek a 'sex change' must be something much more than an obsession. There must be a further reason, a purpose behind it, to sustain you. It is said that young people see visions – old people dream dreams. When you have achieved your 'change of sex' and found only disillusion-ment at the end of the rainbow, because you have come face to face with the reality that you can never really be of the sex of

97

your desire, there must still be something left, an ambition to go to bed with, to dream about and to make you want to get up the next morning. This is not to say that happiness and peace of mind need be an impossible goal or not worth pursuing, but these are more likely to come when life has a fuller meaning than sex or gender and when one's country's social and religious codes of good conduct, decency and morality are also observed, respected and complied with. Hopefully, knowledge will not only help you find an answer to your own difficulties but enable society to see where it can also help and offer compassion, rather than turning something that can bring contentment, joy and fulfilment into a subject for ridicule and rejection. To all those so afflicted my deepest sympathy goes out to you.

Georgina Carol Somerset
June 1991

SOME USEFUL SOURCES OF HELP AND ADVICE

Patients seeking NHS treatment need a letter of referral from their general medical practitioner. If such is refused, it may be wiser to change to the list of a more sympathetic doctor. Patients approaching clinics directly may be regarded as private patients and be asked to pay a consultation fee for advice. Some consultants working within NHS Gender Identity Clinics also have private consulting rooms but private patients should note that they are still likely to be accepted only with the consent or knowledge of their general practitioner.

Unless otherwise stated, correspondence to these clinics should, in the first instance, be addressed to the Consultant Psychiatrist, at the Department of Psychiatry. It is regretted that the names of psychiatrists and surgeons connected with these clinics or the names and addresses of those otherwise prepared to advise and help transsexual patients privately must be withheld in order to abide by the normal ethics of the medical profession. These names and addresses, nevertheless, are known to the author and are available from several sources, such as the organisations listed below, upon personal application from members of the medical profession who need these for referral purposes.

NHS GENDER IDENTITY CLINICS
(Unless otherwise stated)

London

** Maudsley Hospital, Denmark Hill, LONDON, SE5.
   Telephone: 071-703-6333.

** Guy's Hospital, St. Thomas Street, LONDON, SE1 9RT.
   Telephone: 071-955-5000.

** London Institute, 10 Warwick Road, Earl's Court Square, LONDON, SW5 9UH.
   Telephone: 071-373-0901. (Not strictly NHS)

   Charing Cross Hospital, Fulham Palace Road, LONDON, W6.
   Telephone: 071-846-1234. Ext. 1516.

Provinces

Queen Elizabeth Centre, BIRMINGHAM.

Barrow Gurney Hospital, Bristol Royal Hospital, Barrow, Gurney, BRISTOL.
(Referrals accepted *only* in respect of residents in the Bristol area.)

** St. James' University Hospital, LEEDS, LS9 7TF.
   Telephone: 0532-433144. Ext. 5647.
   (Referrals are *only* accepted in respect of persons resident in the Yorkshire Regional Hospital Board area.) (West Yorkshire and Humberside)

99

The Consultant Clinical Psychologist,
** Windsor Day Hospital, 40 Upper Parliament Street, LIVERPOOL, L8 7LF.
Telephone: 051-709-9061.

Prestwich Hospital. Manchester and Hope Hospital, MANCHESTER,
Salford.

** Royal Victoria Infirmary, Queen Victoria Road, NEWCASTLE-upon-
TYNE, NE1 4LP.
Telephone: 091-222-6000. Ext. 7168.
(The Gender Dysphoria Panel *only* accepts referrals from General
Practitioners and for individuals living in the Northern region.)

Mapperly Hospital, NOTTINGHAM.

Scotland

Ninewells Hospital, DUNDEE.

Andrew Duncan Clinic, Royal Edinburgh Hospital, EDINBURGH,
EH10 5HG.

Wittingham Hospital, GLASGOW.

Bangour Hospital, WEST LOTHIAN.

The Consultant Clinical Psychologist,
** Craig Phadrig Hospital, INVERNESS.
(Has NO clinic but sympathetically prepared to refer cases.)

** Only hospitals so starred have replied to the author's request to confirm the
information in this list. Some hospitals appearing in other previous lists have
now asked for their names to be removed, as being no longer applicable.

REGISTERED CHARITIES and TRUSTS

** Beaumont Trust. BM Charity, LONDON, WC1N 3XX.
Telephone: 071-730-7453.
(Non-membership trust – advice and referral for all general Gender
Dysphoria problems.)

** BM Gentrust, LONDON, WC1N 3XX.
Telephone: 071-730-7453 (7.00 p.m. – 11.00 p.m., Thursday only)
(Membership Trust – specifically for Transsexuals and their families.)

** Brook Advisory Centres, 153a, East Street, LONDON, SE17 2SD.
Telephone: 071-708-1234 (in the first instance).
(Offers a contraceptive and counselling service for young people and is
happy to see those concerned about their sexual orientation.)

** TV/TS Support Group, 2 French Place, off Bateman's Row, LONDON,
E1 6JB.
Telephone: 071-729-1466.

GEORGINA SOMERSET

TELEPHONE NETWORK

** Transnet (Chesterfield). Telephone: 0246-551100 (24 hour helpline).
(Co-ordinates countrywide system of telephone helplines.)

SOCIETIES and GROUPS

** Gender Dysphoria Trust International. BM Box No. 7624, LONDON,
WC1N 3XX.
Telephone: 0323-641100.

** Derby TV/TS Group, c/o Derby Self Help Project, Temple House, Mill Hill
Lane, DERBY, DE3 6RY.
Telephone: 0773-828973.

** All these societies have replied to the author's request to confirm that the
information given is up to date. Some societies appearing on other earlier
lists appear to have been disbanded. The list is not intended to be necessarily
complete.

For a sympathetic ear to one's cross-gender needs, the following may also be
contacted by referring to the local telephone book.

The Marriage Guidance Council.
The Samaritans.
The Citizens' Advice Bureau.

* Whilst every effort has been made to ensure the accuracy of the
information in this section, the author and publisher regret that
they are unable to accept responsibility for any errors or
omissions.

Aged 33. Lucerne, Switzerland. August 1956.
Last holiday as a 'man'.

On honeymoon in Paris. October 1962. Up the Eiffel Tower.
Premier étage is high enough! Aged 39.

On holiday in the Lake District, England. Summer 1965.
In my bikini. Aged 42.

On holiday in the Lake District, England. 1965. Aged 42.
"Anyone for tennis?"

On holiday in Parknasilla, Ireland. 1967. Aged 44.
Dressed for dinner.

On holiday. St. Ives, Cornwall. 1968. Aged 45.
One of both of us – dressed for dinner.

On holiday in France. 1972. Aged 49.
In my favourite colours – red and white.

At Dieppe – awaiting the ferry home. 1972.
After another lovely holiday in France with my dear husband.
In my 'sailor' dress. Aged 49.

On holiday at Cannes, France. 1973.
In my shorts. Aged 50.

On holiday at Cannes, France 1973.
In my bikini on the *Carlton* Hotel beach. Aged 50.

The Brighton Marina experiment! June 1985.
Aboard *HMS Cavalier.* Aged 62.

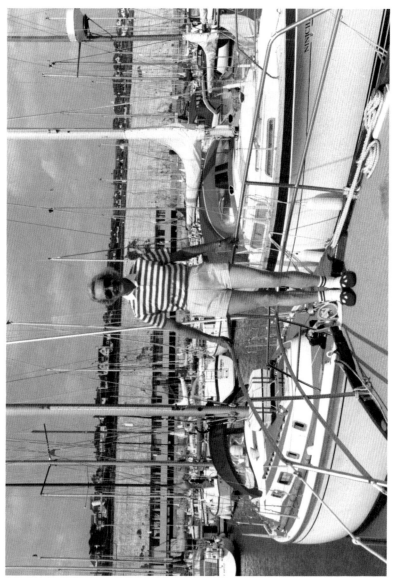

The Brighton Marina experiment – the day after. 1985.
Aboard our motor cruiser *Aranita.* Aged 62.

25th. Silver Wedding Anniversary, Hove. October 13th, 1987.
With my beloved husband, Christopher. Aged 64.

On holiday at Sidmouth, Devon. June 1989.
Still in my 'same' bikini! Aged 66.

Navy Days Portsmouth. August 1990. Aboard 'again' –
on aircraft carrier *HMS Ark Royal*. Aged 67.

On holiday in Devon. Summer 1990.
In the evening sunshine. Aged 67.

OVER THE SEX BORDER

OVER THE SEX BORDER

by

GEORGINA TURTLE

L.D.S. R.C.S. Eng.

With a Foreword
by

KENNETH WALKER

F.R.C.S.

The Book Guild Ltd.
Sussex, England

First to thine own self be true, and it must follow, as the night the day, thou cans't not then be false to any man.

Hamlet: Act I, Scene 3.

CONTENTS

127

Part III. The Adjustment

PREFACE to REPRINT

It may seem curious that this historical work should be reprinted here *following* my autobiography and study update, rather than preceding it as logical sequence would more correctly suggest. Thirty years is a long time in medicine, however, especially these days, and we have come a long way from the 1950s and early 1960s when few had heard the term transsexualism and fewer still knew what it meant. To-day there are few who do *not* know both the term and what it is all about. For this reason our starting point in history must be the present time, of which we already have a sense of knowledge and being, thereby enabling us to better appreciate what went before, the days of struggle, and to make comparisons.

Some comments about this work and how it came to be written have already been made in the preceding book, but some further comment seems desirable here concerning the text. When this work was written, transsexualism as a medical syndrome was very much in its infancy and the first few cases of 'sex change' made world headlines. The realisation that individuals could, in fact, be feminised by female hormones (or masculinised by male hormones), which were then becoming available, and then receive surgery, was like opening the flood gates to all those who had dreamed of 'changing their sex' since childhood and had been resigned that it was an impossibility. Now others had apparently done it – so it was not something impossible they were seeking after all!

Suddenly, everyone sought a ready supply of opposite-sex hormones and a surgeon to operate on them. Finding such a surgeon was rare; rarer still finding one who would agree to help. Sex hormones were also difficult to come by, and few would prescribe except in small quantities, fearing the consequences. This work is of that period, when transsexuals had to content themselves by dressing up as best they could in secret, and when the transvestite act was anything but easy, society expecting all men to have a neat 'short back and sides' haircut at all times and all women to have long flowing tresses suitably styled. To-day, when men can have their hair as long as they like, and wigs of all kinds are freely available, the problem does not arise and seems trivial, but in the days we describe wigs were only to be seen in the windows of the most elegant hairdressers, for their balding high-society female customers. The only other source was a theatrical costumier, if one was not too embarrassed to venture into such a place. The wig was hand-made from real hair and most expensive (about a month's gross average earnings) and questions would still be asked. The technique of electrolysis was also quite basic and electrolysists would certainly not treat men. It is little surprising that few looked the 'part' and found psychiatrists and surgeons difficult to convince. To-day, all manner of people calling themselves transsexuals start off with continuous high-level oestrogen therapy, long hair, sophisticated electrolysis to remove their facial and body hair, and are given cards to work in the role of their desire for two years pending consideration for gender reassignment surgery. The reader should remember these things when reading my account of the transsexual's behaviour in those days, and of the philosophy behind treating such cases.

What has not changed, however, is the syndrome itself, and for this reason the medical and legal arguments remain and time has not tarnished much of what is said here. The procedure for the correction of a birth certificate was drawn up originally for genuine cases of error, either by the midwife or for intersexes whose sex at puberty was found to be different to that of their rearing. It was not until about 1958 that the authorities came to realise the medical facts about transsexualism, from when, in spite of the required medical affidavits being presented, more mature individuals seeking such a 'correction' had their applications much more fully investigated. Realising that the Act allowing such changes to these documents was not intended to apply to transsexuals, whose birth details at the time were indeed correct, refusal resulted. To-day in England transsexuals are still not allowed such an amendment, remaining legally of their born sex and thus legally unable to marry in their changed role. With more and more cases of male transsexuals who have previously married and fathered children coming into the public eye, there seems even less reason for the authorities to change their views on the interpretation of the law as it stands.

Perhaps what should most be remembered is that it is *true* transsexualism that is the subject of this work and accounts for my occasional reference to the transsexual's 'O'. In my original version I constantly used such terms as O-sexualism, O-boy, O-girl, O-man and O-woman for ease of identification, and because it represented an inward quality rather than an expressive outward state. It was also easier to think of a person as being slightly 'O' if they had the vaguest transsexual feelings, showed some degree of gender perverseness or demonstrated aspects of intersexuality in their appearance or mannerisms. In to-day's world of transsexualism, however, it would be wrong not to bow to convention and in this reprint, therefore, only the recognised medical terms are used. Similarly, in referring to terms relating to transsexualism, two s's have been used in the spelling as opposed to the one 's' which appeared in the original copy. Since the term is derived from the word 'trans', meaning 'across', the spelling is correctly trans-sexualism or, with the more common usage of dropping the hyphen, transsexualism.

Georgina Somerset
June 1991

FOREWORD

IF ONE THING is certain it is that we medical men have a great deal to learn about Transvestism and Transsexualism. There is much confusion in medical circles about even the meaning of these two words. Transvestism was first described and named by Hirshfield about half a century ago. Transsexualism was only defined with any clarity in 1954. And both of these terms embrace many variations or different shades of themselves. The chief characteristic of transvestism is a strong urge to wear the clothing of the opposite sex. The desire may find expression in many different ways. It may be sufficient for the transvestite to wear under the outer clothing a garment, such as a vest, belonging to a member of the opposite sex. In other cases, much graver demands are made of the victim by the urge. It may even demand of a man that he appears in public completely arrayed in feminine attire, with all the usual feminine accessories in the way of handbag, hat and pointed shoes.

All this does not necessarily mean that a male transvestite of this kind is desirous of changing his sex and his mode of living for good. It is the transsexualist who harbours this ambition. The transsexualist will do everything within his or her power to be recognised and accepted as a member of the opposite sex. Nothing deflects a determined transsexualist from this aim. They are prepared to purchase what they want even at the cost of painful operations and of prolonged and expensive medical treatment. This does not mean that transsexualism is a natural sequel to transvestism. The two conditions are closely allied but they can, and often do, occur quite independently of one another. The transsexualist is, of course, the more difficult of the two to deal with, because the demands made on him or her are so much greater.

In every normal man there lurks a woman, and in every woman there lurks a man. Jung has given expression to this in his theory of the *animus* and *anima*, an idea which is closely related to the more ancient Chinese belief in the Ying and the

135

Yang principles. The two sexes, masculine and feminine, are not two clearly defined and separate entities, standing widely apart from one another. Rather we must look at them as two conditions which may approach one another and – to use Maranon's words – 'end by fusing in a phase of primitive ambiguity'.

Doubtfulness is indeed the main characteristic of the conditions known as transvestism and transsexualism. They provoke in the sexologist and the psychologist a host of unanswered questions. 'Is their cause a physical one or a psychological one?' 'Will such patients as these benefit more from endocrine or from psychological treatment?' The answer to the great majority of these questions is the word 'both'. As the causes of these problems are highly complex, so must our methods of dealing with them be very widely spread. That is a good reason for our welcoming Miss Georgina Turtle's very comprehensive and complete survey of a little understood subject. There was need for such a work as this and clearly she has given the problem much thought, based on her own experiences and those of the many people who have, as a result, come and conversed with her, confiding their troubles and seeking help.

KENNETH WALKER
F.R.C.S.

PREFACE

Bᴇᴀʀɪɴɢ ɪɴ ᴍɪɴᴅ the dangers associated with any book where the subject of sex-change is involved, it has not been without very careful consideration that I have decided there to be full justification for this work in its present form. First and foremost let me say that this is not a story about change of sex; neither does it represent my own case history, much as certain facts which may have emerged from it have found their place in the general pattern of knowledge that I have tried to accumulate here.

What I have aimed at in this work is enlightenment, not only for the individual but in the hope that the whole of humanity may come to a closer understanding of the many problems which are ever-present and all around us. Because of my own experiences, and my personal knowledge of the sufferings of many others, the problems of the men and women living on the centre of the sex line are those with which this book is concerned, but it is equally important that these problems are brought to the notice of, and understood by, every section of the public if the most good is to be done.

There are far more people than is generally supposed who are living tortured lives in their own private and lonely dream worlds of fantasy, rarely believing that others can possibly feel the same way or have suffered the same experiences. The conflict this causes can be largely attributed originally to the rigid and inflexible dividing line that society imposes between the sexes, requiring each to fit a set pattern. Considering the complexities of the factors which go to make up sex it must be realised that not one but many aspects are involved, and it is not surprising that there are those who find they do not conform to some particular aspect of this absolute pattern, due to some anatomical, psychological, biological or even environmental variation.

Without help and understanding of these circumstances the individuals can become reduced to a state of complete opposition to their way of life, unable to express their natural feelings and thus incapable of making their full and useful contribution to the world in which they live. It is hoped that my writing here will have something to offer them, for they too represent a part of the general public who, more often than not, only gain what information they do from the popular press. Large headlines are still given to the so-called freak who has re-established his or her sex status in the opposite denomination, and to such publicity rather than to any effective medical propaganda can be attributed the public's knowledge, or lack of it, on the subject. Many millions of ordinary people cannot be other than at a loss to understand, and it can only be left to their own particular nature to yield sympathy or cast scorn on the unfortunate victim.

I intentionally use the word 'unfortunate' for that indeed is what the victim is. It is only too tragic that such people should be adversely affected by sensationalism, and perhaps fit themselves into the pattern of seemingly similar cases, for no other reason than as an outlet to their emotions and pent-up feelings, seeking and accepting any explanation for their desperate state. The danger lies in the encouragement and satisfaction this gives developing into a kind of addiction, so that the sufferer gets less and less relief. This is apt to produce a vicious circle, since the build-up of tension increases as the craving develops, and each new effort to satisfy it brings forth its attendant obstacles and resultant frustration. Thus a limit may never appear to be reached, and it is often the realisation of this which shows the problem in all its magnitude, so that life itself loses its meaning and suicide may enter the mind as the only solution.

I cannot help feeling that the majority of non-medical literature on the subject to date has largely been of a sensational and misleading nature, and one major object of this work is to attempt to correct the misconceptions resulting from it. Every effort has therefore been made to keep strictly to the facts, all of which have been taken from true cases or authoritative sources. Only in this way, it is felt, can the knowledge which it contains possess the power to help those who need it. Although the many points covered are largely known throughout the medical profession as a whole, I am personally of the opinion that the subject tends to be scattered too much within their ranks, so that even the experts on the matter are often restricted to knowledge from their own individual cases and, instead of having a pool of knowledge to draw from, are quite often unaware of the opinions of their colleagues, which, even if they are known, are often contradictory. It is perhaps not surprising that this is so, in view of comparative inability to treat any one patient in a set manner, as the nature of the abnormality dictates that each case can only be dealt with on its own merit. I repeat, however, that it is most unfortunate that the medical profession are not more in unison to understand the problems involved, and thus offer to those so tormented and afflicted, not just one specialist, but a whole team of them working together in a common interest. Only in this way, I am sure, will the public be able to build up trust and knowledge of the body working jointly on their behalf.

Although it is true that much can still be learnt by these specialists the condition is not new, and literature has been published on the subject before and will continue no doubt to go on being written. I do not use the word 'new' in this sense, however, for as long as there has been man similar troubles must have existed, but, as with so many diseases, incurable in early times and now being treated by modern medicine and surgery, so the treatment of the troubles with which we are concerned here has brought more to notice the very existence of these conditions. It seems true to say – and facts, I understand, bear me out – that there is an upward rise in the number seeking treatment and in turn being assisted to live more balanced and happy lives. This, again, is not because the condition is on the increase, but rather that, with the widening realisation that they need no longer suffer in silence, the urge to seek assistance has grown. Even so, the present knowledge and experience of the medical profession is limited on this subject, so that, when the vital question asking the solution is put to them, a grave responsibility is incurred. In these circumstances it is only to be expected that they should hesitate to pass judgement, knowing as they do that their decision will have a profound effect on the individual's future happiness.

In establishing the pattern of this book, I have in the early chapters endeavoured to describe the sufferer's feelings and points of view. Later, the medical approach to the problem has been examined, whilst the closing chapters deal with the possibilities of adjustment and the legal aspects. As a result of attempting to render this work comprehensive the subject matter necessarily ranges from the most elementary facts of life and sex to the more advanced and controversial medical opinions. By the same token, it is hoped that the work will be read by both the lay public and members of the medical profession.

This is, then, an attempt to represent an entire picture of a problem which is not often seen comprehensively. Many of the everyday practical issues are discussed and related to one another, and various and different medical opinions quoted, to bring the whole matter into its true perspective. For the first time, transsexualists can wholly identify themselves with the secret thoughts, feelings and behaviour of those described and take comfort, not only that there are others like them, but that there is someone somewhere who understands. It is hoped, therefore, that it will be read from the beginning, since the subject is complex and, unless the condition is viewed in its logical and progressive sequence, there is a danger that the full implications of certain aspects of the problem may not be understood. Certainly there are a number of authoritative books which give mention to some of the conditions related here and which make interesting reading, but here my intention has been, for the first time, to bring together all the numerous factors involved into one book. If my work is new only in this respect, the hope is that my writing will create useful discussion and a better understanding on all sides. If in some measure it will assist to this end, so that even some of us may be more enlightened, then I feel this book may have something to offer humanity and I send it forth with that hope in mind.

It is with great feeling that I wish to express my profound gratitude to Mr. Kenneth Walker, F.R.C.S., for so kindly writing the Foreword; his outstanding contribution to the understanding of human problems is well known, and to him I owe my inspiration. My grateful thanks are also due to the authors of those works to which reference has been made and who have, in places, been quoted. Finally, with this book, I wish to couple the name of Mr. Christopher Somerset, whose constant encouragement and helpful discussion has made this work possible. For the considerable effort, time and interest he has given freely to this and to the editing, I shall ever remain indebted.

G.C.T.

PART I

THE PROBLEM

CHAPTER ONE

INTRODUCTION

Before we are able to gain an insight into the subject with which we are concerned, it seems essential that we first go into the meaning of the word 'Sex', and see how the biological processes, in the human, work to determine the differentiation of sex as far as is generally known. Sex, a word derived from the Latin *Seco*, meaning to cut, symbolises the division which exists by way of nature between the various characteristics of males and females, in their essential anatomical, psychological and social aspects. That these structural differences do exist between the sexes is unquestionably responsible for the sharp division which convention imposes upon them. Yet, much as 'sex' primarily denotes the individual's possession of male or female reproductive organs, it is also used to describe the physical attraction of one to another, the force causing the attraction, and the resultant behaviour. When this attraction takes place between persons of opposite sex the resultant behaviour falls within the bounds of normality, but when deviations occur it is then considered to fall into one of several abnormal categories.

At this point it will be helpful to enumerate, and to define, the medical terms which embrace these sexual conditions in their various forms:

(1) HETEROSEXUAL is applied to those who experience the normal physical attraction to the opposite sex.

(2) HOMOSEXUAL is applied to those whose attraction is to their own sex. When the condition occurs in the female, the term Lesbian is often applied.

(3) BISEXUAL is used to describe the state in which a person is capable of both heterosexual and homosexual feelings and behaviour in varying degrees.

(4) INTERSEXUAL describes the rare condition in which the individual appears to be of no distinct sex, having some

of the physical characteristics of both. In these cases the sex at birth may be considered indeterminate, and only become more well defined in later life. In still rarer cases, where organs of both sexes are present, the term hermaphroditism is used.

(5) TRANSVESTITE is the term applied to a person of either sex who obtains satisfaction from wearing the clothing of the opposite sex. The condition is often sexual in character, so that sexual pleasure and the masquerade become closely associated. The term Fetishism is then applied to these cases.

(6) FETISHISM implies the endowment of special significance to a certain object or objects, which form part of a ritual or ceremony essential to a particular activity. When this activity is sexual, in the male, these objects are often articles of female attire.

(7) TRANSSEXUALIST is the term applied to those who have developed physically normally in one sex but have the psychological characteristics of the other. There is therefore a desire to 'change sex' environmentally and, as far as possible, anatomically, although even after surgery the terms 'Transsexualist' and 'Transsexual' still apply.

As we shall be discussing the possibilities of abnormal conditions in this work, we must first devote some thought to the *normal* biological processes of reproduction and development. Let us therefore begin at the moment a human being is conceived within the mother. Here, conception is brought about by a single cell in the female (the ovum) being fertilised by a single cell from the male (spermatozoon). Each of these cells originates from the reproductive organs (gonads) of the respective individual, which comprise the testes in the male and the ovaries in the female. The ovum, the female-produced cell, is egg-shaped and, commencing its slow moving journey from the ovary, it passes into the fallopian tube, prior to reaching the womb (uterus). Whilst lying in the fallopian tube it occupies the favourable position to receive its counterpart, the male spermatozoon, which, in contrast, is a tadpole-shaped cell and rapid in its motion. During intercourse (coitus) the penis of the male enters the vagina of the female and ejects millions of spermatozoa into it. These then propel themselves, by way of the vagina and the fluid of the womb, into the fallopian tube, until one reaches, penetrates and fertilises the ovum already lying there as described. Once the male and female cells have fused conception has occurred, and a tough membrane develops around the ovum preventing the entry of further sperm cells. The fertilised ovum then continues its journey down the fallopian tube, dividing and multiplying as it goes, and about ten days later the little ball of already some thousands of cells reaches the womb, where it embeds itself in the prepared lining. At this stage, pregnancy has commenced.

Before discussing the development further, let us examine the make-up of the original cells forming the union. Each of these sex cells (sperm and ovum) contains a nucleus, and it is within this nucleus that chromosomes are found. In the normal human cell there are 46 chromosomes but in the *sex* cells there are only 23, so that, on fusion, a normal 46 chromosome cell results. Of the 23 chromosomes in the sex cells, one is a sex chromosome and the other 22, autosomes. All possess various characteristics, which determine the ultimate direction of development, although, whilst the autosomes appear to exert some influence on sexual determination, the sex chromosomes exert the greatest influence and are the deciding factor. These sex chromosomes are of two types, known as X and Y respectively and so called by virtue of their appearance, the X being the larger. As each sperm and ovum cell contains one sex chromosome, the fertilised cell, or zygote, thus contains two. The sex chromosome contained by the ovum is always X in character, but the sperm cells of the male contain either X or Y. Of all the sperm cells ejected, about one half bear the X chromosome and the other half the Y. Thus, depending upon whether an X or Y chromosome-containing sperm fertilises the ovum, an XX or XY combination results. Since, as we have seen, the mother can only produce the X chromosomes, it follows that an XX combination results in a female individual. Conversely, since only the father can contribute both X and Y chromosomes, the XY combination logically produces a male child.

Since development and growth take place by the zygote first dividing into two, and these cells again dividing into four and four into eight, etc, so the innumerable cells of the body are formed by this multiplication process. Each cell is therefore identical with the original zygote in its chromosomal combination. Later it will be seen how examination of the nucleus of the cells of the body at any time throughout life can give an indication of our nuclear or genetic sex, as it is called.

Further consideration of the make-up of the nucleus shows us that within the chromosomes are factors or units known as genes. These are responsible for the hereditary characteristics, occupy definite positions in the chromosomes, and, like them, exist in pairs, forming up when the single unit present in each of the sex cells (gametes) links up with its opposite number at fertilisation. The parents thus contribute their own characteristics and hereditary factors, such as colour of eyes, type of skin, and temperament, etc, the pairing up of their chromosomes and genes on fusion causing a balance to result, known as the genetic balance. The genes most concerned in the distinctive characters of the sexes are sited in the sex chromosomes, although, like them, it is considered that it is all the genes of all the chromosomes, pulling development in their respective directions, that sets the balance to determine the line of development and ultimate result.

The tissue from which the reproductive organs are formed is bisexual in character, so that this primitive gonadal organ (anlage), which is made up of a medulla and a cortex, is capable of developing into either a testis or an ovary. The direction of stimulation of the anlage depends upon the original chromosomal structure determined at the moment of conception and upon the resulting effects of genetic activators. These activators are closely allied to the male and female hormones of adult life. Thus, the potentials of either sex exist in the primordial tissues making up the anlage, so that when the activators in an XY zygote encourage the development of the medullary tissue and suppress the cortex, a testis develops. Conversely, in an XX individual the stimulation favours the cortical tissue and suppresses the medulla, so that an ovary develops. Rudimentary vestiges of the opposite sex still remain, however, characterised by the nipples in the male and the clitoris in the female. Although sex is thus determined at the moment of conception, it is not well defined until birth, when the zygote, having developed into the embryo, appears in the familiar form of an infant.

The stimulation that causes either a testis or ovary to develop is of comparatively short duration in embryonic life, but, once determined, the tissue will continue in its growth until functional maturity at puberty. During childhood no sex cells are produced by the gonads, but at puberty the glands of these organs increase their activity. The hormones or chemical substances produced by them are closely related, chemically, in both sexes, although the secondary sexual characteristics which will develop are dependent upon their exact nature. In the male, hormones which promote sexual development are known as androgens, and in the female, oestrogens, the particular hormones secreted by the interstitial cells of the testes being testosterone, while that secreted by the ovaries is oestrone. Not all androgens and oestrogens come from these sources, however, it being noteworthy that both appear in the blood stream of either sex and are excreted in the urine.

So it is that at puberty the hormonal factors proceed to differentiate more clearly, by way of the secondary sexual characteristics, the obvious physical states of male and female, with its resulting effects on behaviour and social life. For example, the female becomes aware of her reproductive role, brought about by the commencement of menstruation. This is a process whereby an unused ovum is discarded from the body, at the end of the reproductive cycle, which occurs approximately once every 28 days. This cycle consists of the production, by the ovaries, of an ovum, 14 days after commencement of the menstrual period. As we have seen, leading from the ovaries, situated in the abdominal cavity, are the fallopian tubes, and it is along one of these that the ovum passes on its way to the womb. If the ovum enters the womb in an unfertilised condition, instead of embedding itself it will remain until discarded at the next menstrual period. Discharge is then via the external opening of the vagina, together with the fluid of the womb and unused lining.

Having before us this picture of the reproductive processes in the human, we can now pass on to consider the various ways in which abnormalities may occur, attributable to both biological causes and those associated with the civilisation in which we live. An abnormality may be such that mere observation indicates its presence, or it may be that some specialised test is required to show the deviation from the normal. Further, other abnormalities may exist without a known means of detection. Beyond this determination of the actual existence of such deviations, whether they be in structure, appearance or character, from whole organs down to single cells or even specialised parts of cells, we must consider the reason or aetiology (cause) of such states. This, again, leads us from known causes to those which can only have theories advanced for them. There seems no better way then to go back to the original zygote cell and proceed through its development again, and see what forces may be brought to bear on it, genetically, biologically or environmentally, to bring about some degree of abnormality in the sense we know to-day.

The word 'environmental' is not used casually, for the study of sex, as related to flowers and many primitive animal forms, shows us that at the start the gametes are not specifically sexed, as are the ovum and spermatozoon in the human, but possess the potentialities of either sex, with the environmental factors controlling the direction of expression. By this method, however, there is no regulating balance to ensure an equal distribution of the sexes, and to improve upon this state of affairs it would appear that nature later evolved a more complex mechanism, whereby sex determination could be brought about by inherent characteristics of the gametes, relying less upon environmental influences. Thus, in the higher plants and lower animals we find the forms more predominantly one sex or the other, and more specialised still among the higher animals, although even here the potential still remains within the germ cell for an off-spring of either sex to develop given the appropriate stimulus. Although the gamete cells in the human have become highly specialised sex cells of specific denomination, we still find that every ovum contains bisexual potentialities so that, technically at least, a process does exist whereby the laid down genetic messages to cause sexual development in one particular direction could be reversed. Also, much as environmental forces no longer appear to play any part, if it can be argued that these may not have been completely suppressed it could offer an explanation why some intersexual elements might be introduced into the growing foetus. These are only rare or hypothetical considerations, however, the constitutional genetic activators invariably determining the direction of sexual development.

Nevertheless, whatever the sex chromosomal constitution may be, be it XX or XY, the formative tissues of the reproductive organs may still develop into either an ovary or a testis should the genetic balance at fertilisation be sufficiently disturbed, and very rare cases of apparent males with XX constitution and apparent females with XY constitution have come to light, although it is logical that they would be sterile. How this comes about is obscure, although the possibility of abnormal stimulation of either the medulla or cortex of the anlage, and corresponding suppression of the other at a critical time in development, could account for this. Causative factors could be genetic, endocrinal or even exogenous in character. In other rare instances there can be a failure of either the medulla or cortex to be stimulated properly or at all, resulting in gonadal dysgenesis where the gonads fail to develop normally or agenesis where no gonads develop, the individuals in such cases remaining physically feminine and without developing normal secondary sexual characteristics.

The final result therefore depends upon the degree of stimulation and suppression of each of these generations of cells, although, once the sexual direction has been established and testicular or ovarian tissue formed, this tissue itself maintains the development towards masculinity or femininity. It is as early as the seventh week of embryonic life that the anlage or foetus has established itself to form a testis or ovary, but whereas the development of the body continues in a basic direction virtually unaffected by a developing ovary, if a testis has formed the androgens secreted by it will bring about a deviation from the basic type, and the characteristics of normal male differentiation. It is interesting to note that it is the gonads which stimulate development of the ducts associated with the reproductive processes, so that any abnormality occurring after the gonads have formed may result not only in underdevelopment but in the failure of the ducts of the opposite sex to be fully suppressed. On the other hand, it is not impossible for both the medullary and cortical cells to be so stimulated as to cause an individual to have a mixture of both male and female gonadal tissue, each exerting their influence on development, so that a natural physical intersex may result. This influence lasts for but a brief period in early embryonic life, and although the primordial tissue soon becomes 'fixed' in its development, to form an ovary or a testis, it is perhaps difficult to assess what effect such abnormal intersexual factors may have on the individual in later years, not only physically but psychologically. Certainly, the possibility cannot be ruled out that many apparently intersexual individuals that exist to-day may still be unconsciously fighting the influence of this earlier brief stimulation, which may have occurred with no-one's knowledge. Yet that some intersexual factors do exert their influence on every individual, to form or mould the balance of their make-up, can be demonstrated by the presence of both male and female hormones in all of us to some degree.

Should, in fact, an actual mixture of sex reproductive organs be produced in one individual, be it a complete testis and a complete ovary or just elements of each, a condition known as hermaphroditism arises. Such cases of true hermaphroditism are extremely rare, medical help generally having to be given to assist development in its most pronounced form, but this is also often necessary in cases of false or 'pseudo' hermaphroditism, when usually endocrine factors cause under-development of the true sex characteristics and a failure of certain features of the opposite sex to be normally suppressed.

It is interesting to note that not even specialised sex genes and chromosomes are pure in their character. This is demonstrable by certain hereditary characteristics produced by some genes, which are carried on the sex chromosomes and are known as sex-linked genes. Typical examples in man are those producing colour blindness and haemophilia (deficiency in blood clotting factor), and, because of the association of these genes with the X chromosome only the male XY, bearing the abnormality in its only X, does not have a compensating *normal* X as does the female (XX). Consequently, the male exhibits the abnormality, whereas the female does not, although she is capable of transmitting the abnormal gene to her offspring. Certain characteristics may thus be directly linked to the genetic sex of the individual; harmful and abnormal conditions can therefore be closely associated with sex, and their inter-relationship may have more significance than is known to-day. Recent work in this field is already bringing to light much new and valuable evidence, especially in connection with nuclear sex, and the investigations of Professor W. M. Davidson and other eminent authorities lends much to the increasing sphere of knowledge on the subject, as will be discussed later. Other work seems to suggest that certain abnormalities, such as Mongolism (Down's syndrome with associated mental retardation), may be the result of an abnormal number of chromosomes, although the reason for this is not, at present, clear.

For the first few months of intra-uterine life no visible signs would indicate if the embryo is, in fact, male or female. Indeed, whatever the sex, the growing individual would appear to be female, because in the human the female is the basic negative type. Accordingly, at this stage, whether a boy or a girl baby is to result at birth, three openings would be similarly present in the genital region between the legs. In the girl these remain, to form the urinal opening from the bladder anteriorly, the vaginal opening behind, and the rectal opening posteriorly for the excretion of waste products. In a boy baby, however, six months before birth the two anterior openings join into one, to form the penis growing forward. Some simulation of the penis is, however, also found in the female, in the form of a tiny lump which is called the clitoris, and represents what would have developed into a penis given the appropriate androgenic stimulation.

When the infant is born the genital differences are usually sufficiently marked to assess accurately the anatomical sex, and a brief observation is generally enough to place the new-born baby into its proper category. It is reasonable enough to expect, however, that with the many hundreds of thousands of births annually circumstances may occur that give rise to some errors being made. These may be merely human errors of observation, or of recording, but they may also be due in some instances to under-development of the penis or over-development of the clitoris, so that no clearly defined direction of sexual development makes itself apparent, and only tests or later growth will establish the predominant sex. Generally, human errors soon come to light and are remedied, but cases of under-development of the penis or hypospadias may be brought up as girls, for two or three years, before the true sex is recognised. Should a distinct abnormality occur, however, it may only be at puberty or even later that an actual error in the sex determination comes to notice, when the secondary sexual characteristics become apparent. Cases have been known when an individual, brought up as a boy, has started to menstruate at puberty, and an individual reared as a girl has developed facial hair with a 'breaking' of the voice, and been found to possess 'internal' testes. As in the cases of true hermaphrodites, such occurrences are fortunately extremely rare.

Perhaps the one distinctive fact that emerges from all these errors, whether they be from human, developmental, or abnormal causes, is that there is never an actual *change* of sex, from the genetic or reproductive aspects. This is not to say that other aspects of sex may not change under the influence of internal or external forces, possibly glandular, hormonal, or environmental in nature, but that once tissue is developing or has developed to a major extent, even when it has been bipotential originally, the process becomes irreversible. Once the primordial tissue has been 'used' to develop, say a testis, whether surgical or natural reasons cause loss or suppression of

154

the organ's development there is no means left whereby an opposite organ, such as an ovary, may take its place. This is relative to each side of the body, of course, there being two testes or two ovaries normally present in each person.

Glandular Influences

The glands in the human body are vast in number, and form complex systems which perform specific functions to maintain life. They produce and secrete substances; substances which may have a local action only, such as saliva from the salivary glands or sweat from the sweat glands. The ductless or endocrine glands, however, are glands which secrete their products directly into the blood stream, and so have a general effect upon the body. Mainly, they comprise the pituitary at the base of the brain, the thyroid in the neck, the pancreas in the abdomen, and the two adrenals situated over the kidneys, as well as the ovaries or testes. The substances they secrete are called hormones and, due to their general effect, any disturbance in the amount or type of secretion can cause certain body changes to occur. These glands of the endocrine system are closely related and since their hormones act through the blood stream they also balance each other's effect, influencing each other. Indeed, it is the final result of their interaction which determines what is commonly termed the individual's glandular make-up. Should the hormone level from one gland be abnormally high or low, another gland is prompted to increase or decrease its secretions so that these will in turn cause the 'offending' gland to become suppressed or stimulated in its activity. In this way, nature helps to ensure that a balance is maintained.

Often, one gland produces many hormones from its different parts. The pituitary is such a gland, and indeed has so great a governing influence upon the other endocrine glands that it is generally regarded as playing the major role in the system. Hormone from the pituitary, therefore, by its action upon the testes or ovaries, governs sexual development. Furthermore, in the female, it is certain hormones from the anterior lobe of this gland which regulate the cyclic production of the ovum.

Complex hormones are also produced by the cortex of the adrenal glands, some of which are known to be androgenic, and these too may be stimulated or depressed by hormone from the pituitary. Once the glandular balance is established, then development will take place in accordance with these influencing factors and generally any fluctuation from the normal will be resisted.

How may abnormalities occur, then? First, the original make-up may have been so balanced as to cause over- or under-development in a certain direction, as, for example, we may find one man with very little body hair, and another considerably covered. A similar state of affairs can exist whereby the development which causes the physical differences between boys and girls may be disturbed by some ill-balancing of the 'androgenic' or 'oestrogenic' activators in the years up to puberty, so that the normal path of digression may be less marked. Although, of course, the essential differences appear more pronounced after puberty, in the years up to maturity the development of the boy and girl is still on opposing lines in body and bone structure, preparing the individual for the reproductive role nature intended. Not only does this over-or under-development, towards or away from the recognised genetic sex of the individual, produce visible physical effects, but these effects themselves often influence the person's mental outlook, to a degree which presents an even deeper subject for thought.

Secondly, the normal balance may be upset by pathological conditions or disease. Tumours or growths are perhaps the commonest, for these may cause the glandular tissue to increase or decrease in size. When a growth increases the size of the gland an excessive secretion of hormone occurs, beyond the normal adjusting mechanism of the system, so that the excessive influence of the hormone is allowed to affect the body without control. In this way, a tumour of the cortex of the adrenal gland, one of the functions of which is to secrete male hormone, may produce pronounced masculinisation in a woman and the development of male secondary sexual characteristics. On the other hand, disease may waste away a gland and limit or stop its work entirely, so that the normal supply of hormone is lost. The result depends upon the gland affected, the degree of the influence, and often the age of the individual.

Hormonal Influences

Having discussed how glandular disturbances may upset the hormonal balance of the body, we are led directly to consider the effects that such a deficiency of sex hormone may have on the individual, physically and psychologically, etc. Obviously, the earlier these disturbances occur the greater is the effect on the sexual development. This is particularly so before puberty and is typified by the eunuchoid boy, who has been castrated or has suffered testicular insufficiency due to other causes. The penis and testes will remain small; he will lack muscular development, fat deposits will be more feminine in type and distribution, the voice remains high-pitched, and the normal growth of masculine facial and body hair will not take place. At puberty, there is not the usual arousal of sex desire (excitement, erections, or the wish to masturbate), and the eunuch remains impotent and often psychologically inhibited, not only sexually because of the realisation of his body state but socially because of his awareness of his inadequacy. There seems little doubt that the male hormone, testosterone, plays a major part in the desire for normal sexual activity in man, and that, without the activating influence of this hormone, the psychological outlook on sex by the individual is subject to deviations. This should not be assumed, however, as a reason for abnormal sexual behaviour, as statistics do not bear this out and cases showing deficiency are relatively few.

Lack of oestrogen production in a young girl may equally result in sexual under-development, so that the normal commencement of menstruation may be delayed or fail to occur at all. Since the pattern of sexual feelings is different and not so acutely marked as in the male, however, the abnormality is not so apparent, and this is so too in the earlier years, as the development is not so away from basic type as in the male. In a later chapter the implications of hormonal changes after puberty, whether the result of external (exogenous) or internal (endogenous) factors, will be discussed.

Environmental Influences

Although all the internal factors determining sex may be normal, and the growing child genetically and physically a normal boy or girl, the influence of external factors or environment may have a profound effect, in a complex manner, on the sexual outlook and psychological approach to life of the individual. It is said that many psychological neuroses and subconscious states of mind dominating one's actions may be traced back to childhood, and that incidents occurring in these early formative years may have undue importance attached to them.

Searching back into the past in order to put the particular events into their proper perspective often relieves the conflict and is the accepted method adopted by psychiatrists to-day when, by a process of 'psycho-analysis', the mind is explored into to recapture the dim memories of childhood. The up-bringing of the child does, indeed, powerfully dominate the whole thought processes of later life, and the actions resulting through them. Particular qualities of the parents, apart from being transmitted in the genes, are largely passed on to the offspring, the behaviour, words and actions of the parents being observed and copied. By the time the child has learned to think for itself and form its own opinions the shadow of the earlier years has been cast on its mind, and the attempted reversal of a previously accepted fact or idea meets with great mental blocking. As it is easier to maintain the original idea or opinion, than to go through the emotional upheaval of changing it and the conflict of the loving parents being wrong, the compromise is to push the thought into the subconscious mind. Life goes on then without the conflict apparent, but it remains to mould the personality and become active whenever circumstances disturb the easy flow of life. The number of ways in which different incidents may occur and give rise to complex thoughts and behaviour, sexual and otherwise, is inestimable, many examples of which should be apparent from our everyday experiences.

Because of the prevalence of homosexuality, compared with other forms of sexual deviation, it seems natural that more attention and thought has been given to this subject. In so far as writings in search of the cause of this behaviour deal also with the possible internal and external influences, it is interesting to note that whilst some writers favour the theory of inversion, in which the condition may be due to some inborn constitutional factor or abnormal balance of the sex glands, producing a sort of feminised male, these seem to be in the minority, and analyses of cases give more credence to the majority view. In his book, *Homosexuality*, Dr. D. J. West writes:

> 'The theory of "true inversion" finds favour with some homosexuals because it releases them from all sense of responsibility. If the explanation of their condition lies in the way the glands work, then no one can expect them to be able to change. In the opinion of the present writer, however, the glandular theory of inversion has little to commend it.'

If, indeed, the support Dr. West goes on to give for his view is merited, as seems well justified, it shows even more clearly the tremendous effect that environmental factors bring to bear upon the individual, and how much importance must be given to them when assessing the reasons for any of the less common abnormal sexual states. Whatever the physical nature may be, the effective force of one's environment playing on the mind throughout life cannot be over-estimated, and the study of cases of intersexuality, brought up in the opposite sex to their predominating internal sex gland development, shows that the individuals accept and favour their sex of upbringing rather than that of their reproductive organs. As we shall see later on, this is a major consideration when any change of environmental sex comes under review for any purpose.

Psychological Influences

Many aspects of the problem with which we are concerned are closely related to the psychological attitude to life in general, and to sex in particular. In childhood and early adolescence, a homosexual phase is considered a normal and natural part of growing up, as a means of healthy self-expression. This may be seen in the hero-worship a boy exhibits for the captain of his school or to a whole team of players of a sport in which he is particularly interested. Likewise, a girl may look to her elders at school, being attracted by the admiration she holds for them. Generally, this attitude has no sexual significance and exists quite unconsciously, passing off with the approach of sexual and mental maturity to give way to normal adult sex feelings and attraction to the opposite sex. Puberty, the time when the body ceases to be that of a child and takes on adult form, with maturity of the sex reproductive organs, occurs at about the age of 12 in girls and 14 in boys. In the female it is the time when menstruation commences, with a rapid consciousness of widening of the hips, enlargement of the breasts and the appearance of pubic hair. In the male, consciousness of the enlargement of the penis and its increased activity and sensitivity, with the growth of pubic hair around it, is followed by the deepening of the voice and the appearance of hair on the face and body.

Apart from these changes, the psychological awareness of sex becomes apparent, often bringing with it mixed feelings of satisfaction and anxiety or shame, and if the individual is not helped to understand the normality of these events he may find himself even more deeply disturbed mentally, and complications may later arise due to this enforced repression.

The penis is capable of stiffening into 'erection' by blood being deflected into the many spaces in the spongy tissue of the organ, and sexual thoughts or continued handling may stimulate this enlargement. When the sexual excitement reaches its climax, seminal fluid, made up of sperm cells and fluid from the sex glands such as the prostate, emits in spurts from the penile opening by a series of spasmodic muscular contractions, and such a process is known as orgasm. Stimulation of the clitoris in the female can similarly produce orgasm, although there is nothing for her body to expel in the act and the effort required is usually greater. Full satisfaction is still possible, however, but may not sometimes come for some years after puberty. Stimulation of the sexually sensitive parts, known as the erotic areas, can thus produce orgasm in either sex, although whereas in the male the stage up to the climax and that back to normality is rapid, in the female, in contrast, both these stages are much slower, so that the climax takes longer to build up and the satisfaction of the act diminishes less markedly.

Much as the direction of sexual attraction in early adolescence is unconsciously homosexual, the first orgasms usually occur unconsciously also, for the sexual excitement that can be produced by touch and handling of the erotic areas leads to the realisation that the pleasure of orgasm can be induced in this way. This often encourages the deliberate handling of the sexual parts, and the self-production of orgasm in this way is called masturbation. Often the act is performed with a great sense of guilt, but it is generally accepted that most youngsters go through a phase of masturbation. Whereas this causes no bodily harm, it often produces anxiety and many conflicts of mind. The main danger is that the act may become compulsive and continued masturbation may carry on into adult life, using up much unnecessary energy by the individual that could be more usefully directed elsewhere. If, in fact, the practice is continued, the desire for normal sexual relationship may not mature, and this 'making love' to oneself can give rise to various sexual abnormalities and deviations. Often this may result from the guilt feelings the youngster has developed, through parents who feel that sex matters should not be discussed and should be looked upon with abhorrence.

Yet normal sexual relationship between the sexes, when justified, means the merging of the minds and interests so completely that the sexual enjoyment of each other's bodies, far from being a 'naughty but nice' experience, is an act of true affection, so in unison with the pattern of their mutual personalities that it leads to an even greater admiration and respect being built up between them. On the path to this maturity are all the conflicts and difficulties of one's own sexual approach, masturbation complexes, parental influences, education and social opportunity to grow up. Unless the individual faces up to all these things and is able to gain this greater insight into life, its purpose and its beauty, seeing sex in its right perspective as a part of the whole and not as a separate entity, then he or she will tend to remain alone in the immaturity of their own confined world. Many sexual problems are in fact caused by a failure to 'grow up', the individual remaining 'outside' and tending to dissociate himself from the conforming environment of society of which he is himself a member, needing their services as well as they need his.

'Libido' is a word that crops up a lot in relation to sex, and was regarded by Freud as the chief driving force in human life. As sexuality is inter-related so closely and complexly with life itself, both emotionally and physically, it is not surprising that all manner of conflicting theories and postulations have come from those authorities engaged in looking into the psychological processes in man. As behaviour and every human action is prompted by some underlying influence or force, the possible reason for anomalies may best be considered by studying these motivating factors. Because of this, we should have firmly fixed in our minds just what libido means. On the basis that the 'sex urge' is the most important of the impulses of our will to live, Freud, although terming libido as the fundamental source of emotional energy, seemed to intend the meaning generally to have more sexual significance.

Kenneth Walker and Peter Fletcher (*Sex and Society*, Penguin Books, 1955) expressed Freud's view in the following way:

> 'Freud believed that the "libido", the source of all behaviour, is a more or less fixed quantity of primitive emotional energy. It could be directed into many different channels of activity, but it was essentially sexual; that is to say, everything it constrained us to do was consciously or unconsciously designed to gratify a craving to love and be loved; a craving which would find its most direct and natural expression in sexual intercourse. He therefore believed that all sexual anomalies and perversions, indeed all emotional conflicts and neurotic disorders, were the result of the interruption or the faulty canalisation of the flow of energy.'

The limitations of this view, however, have given rise to much discussion and argument, on the basis that the 'sex urge' is but one of the primary motivating impulses which produce the vital energy and drive. The widely accepted theories of to-day attribute libido to three main urges: the Sex Urge; the Self Urge, implying the will to self-preservation; and the Social Urge, whence our love and desire of association with our fellow beings originates. All are closely related and we need not discuss their relative merits here, but the essence of a force setting up a reaction within us, prompting the manner of our thoughts, desires and behaviour in order to relieve us of the pressure of these forces, shows clearly how the influences of environment are a direct source of emotional stress and conflict. This comes to light in the outward expression of our personalities and behaviour, either in our conforming to normality or in our adopting abnormal practices.

The dictionary gives libido as coming from the Latin for 'lust', and one definition as 'The emotional craving which is said by psycho-analysts to lie behind all human impulse, the repression of which may give rise to pathological conditions.' Another dictionary defines it as 'The dynamic expression of sexual impulses.' In whichever sense the word is used, however, and whatever the interpretation given to it, it represents some inborn driving force to which the body reacts and expresses itself; it may be sexual in character, with the desire to love and be loved, or may be, in the wider meaning, a craving to satisfy a hunger or to live a fuller life in the company of the society which makes up our environment.

We can assume that libido embraces all these forces, and that 'loss of libido' implies the reduction in strength of one or more of them. Thus, whilst certain circumstances in life may reduce the sexual desire of the individual, bringing about this loss of libido, it may not follow that other means of pursuing life with interest are affected. On the other hand, circumstances may cause the *complete* loss of the will-to-live, should the force be particularly important to the person or the forces, working together, affect one another, and when this occurs a suicide state can be reached. Depression is probably known to all of us to some degree, and the associated loss of interest in everything, and lack of appetite or desire to eat, are typical signs of this loss of libido, usually occasioned by a build-up of emotional conflict and an inability to direct the force into a channel of expression and release. Such is common when mourning the loss of a loved one, and when crying acts as a 'safety valve' and assists a more speedy return to normal.

Deviations

As there is no set point about which we can ascertain the normal, there can be little measure as to what constitutes a deviation, or what degree of it is necessary before we can class it as such. In discussing these anomalies, therefore, we are more accurately describing the expression of the individual's thoughts, feelings and whole state, according to a particular pattern or classification. It is realised that people do not necessarily conform to set types and groups, but the salient aspects, once classed as typical, can then be considered as a common point for the basis of discussion and investigation.

When something we read or see in picture form arouses sexual excitement, it is said to be pornographic. Because the state and mind of individuals varies, however, what is pornographic to one may not be to another. First we must consider what may cause sexual excitement, and then the nature of the resulting behaviour it may cause. Briefly, then, we are concerned with the cause and effect of erotic deviations or expressive states. Apart from pornography, the cause of stimulation may be a part of the body, or it may be a particular object, such as an item of clothing, or it may be a mental image, thought, or a certain act. In the latter instance the act may be active or passive; actively it may take the form of sadism, in which there is a desire to be cruel and to inflict pain on others to promote the sexual satisfaction. It may be exhibitionist, in which the pleasure is derived by exposing the body, or perhaps only the sexual organs, for others to see. Amongst the passive forms is the condition known as masochism, as when pleasure is obtained, sexually, from being dominated or cruelly treated. The masochist enjoys suffering or being unwell and unhappy, and

164

therefore makes no effort to improve matters, having been conditioned to this attitude by environmental influences.

Sadism and masochism may be complimentary to each other, with a desire to both inflict and receive pain, and the term sado-masochism is then applied. All variations of these conditions occur in repressed personalities, where the sexual feelings are so dulled or desensitised that some greater sexual stimuli are required to produce the necessary excitement. The desire to inflict and receive pain is often satisfied by the individual inflicting the pain on himself, when the sex organs may well be the target for abuse.

Homosexuality is a subject in itself, and involves many millions in our civilisation to-day. It may exist in an active or passive form, and the attraction of a person to a member of the same sex may be an unconscious expression, as we have seen in early adolescence, or it may involve active sexual relationship, when the penis is inserted in the anus, or rectal opening, of another male (sodomy). Homosexuality is usually thought of in relation to the male sex but it is to be found also in the female, when methods of devising mutual sexual pleasure are practised. The condition is then called lesbianism. The partners do not always play both roles; more often one habitually takes the active part and the other the passive. Much has been written on the many aspects of homosexuality, probably because of its wide incidence and its effect on the society as a whole. True homosexuality is not our concern here, but the possibility of latent homosexuality occuring in other abnormal forms of sexual expression will require consideration when we come to discuss these later.

Transvestism, as with so many other conditions, is in danger of being applied, often too freely, as a means of pigeon-holing for ease of classification, and although on paper it can be described in typical form, by no means every case of supposed transvestism fits the recognised pattern, because the causative influences and resultant behaviour are not necessarily the same. To be a transvestite does not mean that, by deriving pleasure from wearing the garments of the opposite sex, there is necessarily any wish to 'change sex', anatomically or in role.

This, indeed, is the wish of the transsexualist. Both terms are, however, comparatively new; transvestism was first given its name by Hirschfield in 1910, and transsexualism popularised by Benjamin only as recently as 1954. Both are of immediate concern to us. In transvestism, the desire to wear the clothing of the opposite sex can manifest itself in many ways. The act may only take place behind closed doors, because of a guilt complex, fear of being found out, or through lack of other opportunity. It may take the form of wearing selected garments under the everyday clothes, or of dressing completely as the opposite sex in public, as a means of exhibitionism. Sometimes, the act is satisfaction in itself; generally, however, it has a sexual purpose and stimulates arousal. Though most of the gross abnormal sexual conditions are mainly associated with men, women are not unaffected by such practices and transvestism is to be found in both sexes. Transvestites are often found to be fetishistic in their behaviour, when there are particular items of clothing or other objects that become essential for the act to be performed. Such items or objects have for some reason developed a special sexual significance during the individual's life, and, when they are garments, the ritual is usually enacted by wearing them. Seeing themselves in a mirror often enhances stimulation of the transvestite's sexual feelings, leading to orgasm either by pure emotional arousal, handling of the erotic areas, or sado-masochism.

Transsexualism is not necessarily a natural follow-on to transvestism, much as they are often inter-related, for both conditions can, albeit rarely, occur independently. It is possible that a true transsexualist may have all the desires of belonging to the opposite sex, of wanting his anatomy changed, and of living in the opposite role, may perhaps even have some physical justification yet resist any act of transvestism. This may be due to a natural repression of the transvestist forces, a revulsion at the thought of a masquerade, or the desire to be true to themselves, their family, and to society. Nevertheless, the vast majority of transsexualists start cross-dressing from early childhood and this transvestism progresses, until eventually the act becomes permanent in preparation for what they hope will be surgery and their ultimate acceptance in the new role. By now, however, and in spite of them still possessing the genitalia of their birth, they cease to regard such behaviour as transvestism, their mental state convincing them that they are dressing naturally and are entitled so to do. Whatever the reason for the transsexual urge, however, even if it is closely connected with transvestism or homosexuality, the feelings of the individual are directed to the goal of a change of anatomical and environmental sex and the satisfaction it is assumed to bring.

Barely a few years ago the only word to be used medically in reference to anyone who cross-dressed, for *whatever reason*, was transvestite. The recent introduction of the term transsexualism to the vocabulary therefore was welcomed, admitting as it did that the term transvestism embraced too wide a field of cases and often classified them not too aptly or correctly. In the same way the writer, although accepting the descriptive value of the term transsexualism, feels that as transsexuals do not change their sex it is not strictly accurate. It also gives no indication of the supposed sex of the individual or of the direction of desire, without even more elaborately speaking of a male transsexualist or a female transsexualist. It does not tell us the sex at birth, whether the individual has received surgery or not or their present role. Further, it tends to label cases to an easy formula, as if to suggest a definite type of person and a stereotype condition of known cause, with set pattern of behaviour and an acknowledged method of treatment. This is, of course, not so.

Consideration of the facts that this work places before the reader will surely make it clear that the term transsexualism can, in itself, only be used as generalisation as it leaves no measure for closer examination. However, as the writer believes the degrees of the condition to be numerous, some differentiation is in fact essential between the extremes. Careful thought has been given to the suggestion of a term which may embrace **all** the transsexual *qualities* and yet equally remain simple, a term not intended to replace the term transsexualism but rather to be complementary to it, expressing more the qualities, emotions and personality inseparable from the condition

167

irrespective of the degree to which the individual wishes to change physically and regardless of body anatomy.

It is the writer's opinion that, in cases of true transsexualism, beneath the desire to 'change sex' lies a fundamental state of intersexuality, of completeness in oneself, and that the sexual feelings and thoughts are in conflict with the ability to express the emotions adequately because of the strong dividing line imposed by society between the sexes, impelling rigid conformity to an accepted pattern. The inability so to conform activates the opposite principle even more profoundly, and, although the completeness remains, the belief grows that to conform in the opposite role would be more natural and enable the ventilation of feelings which have had to be suppressed since birth.

As a symbol of this completeness or self-containment the writer has chosen the alphabetical letter 'O', which already appears in the terms heterO-sexuality and homO-sexuality, the term 'O-sexuality' suggesting a position somewhere between the two but opposite to the positive state of Bi-sexuality. Additionally, whilst O-sexuality symbolises the desire for castration and the acceptance of being rendered sterile the positive sexual qualities of both sexes remain, in contrast to the negative state of A-sexuality. To speak of an O-boy, an O-girl, an O-man or an O-woman therefore suggests a simple recognition of certain qualities in an individual and not only informs us whether they are of a pre- or post-pubertal age but also qualifies their born sex.

Perhaps the greatest single point that the writer can make in favour of the use of the term O-sexuality is that the desire to change the anatomical sex (transsexualism) can be modified, perhaps by experience, education or treatment, so that the desire no longer exists or has to be abandoned. Yet the reasons for the condition, which have given rise to certain qualities, cannot ever be altered, and in the same way the writer believes that these qualities will remain in the individual throughout life. It is said that a transsexualist never wants to be cured, but from the above it is more likely that he or she fears to lose the 'O' factor and accept basic heterosexuality, rather than not wanting to be guided to peace of mind and happiness. Even cases who have changed their environmental sex role still cling tenaciously to their 'O', and this is often the reason why the individual remains unsettled, their biological sex and upbringing always overshadowing their ability to wholly accept what they have become, and regrets creep in.

Although transsexualism is a syndrome applied to physically normal individuals whose only known sexual abnormality lies in the psychological plane and is the main concern of this work, as the title indicates the subject matter is change of sex and this can properly apply to cases of true physical intersexuality, pseudo-hermaphroditism or true hermaphroditism, where subsequent development has to be taken into account in later life to place them more correctly in the opposite sexual role to that of their rearing. In many cases the unfortunate individuals choose to remain in their 'wrong' sex to avoid all the upheaval that a change involves, but when this is not so, frequently before the full medical facts have been established, such individuals are often thought of and assumed to be transsexualists. The very expression of a desire to change sex in these cases makes them at least 'apparent' transsexuals. More likely it is their possession of the qualities of O-sexuality which the writer attributes to true transsexuals that causes this, rather than any real association with transsexualism.

The intention of this introduction, therefore, has been to put the whole subject into perspective, to show how physical abnormalities can occur, and to indicate not only the likely problems resulting from them but enable us to decide to what extent, if any, they may be relevant to transsexualism. More-over, the aim has been to present as generalised a picture as possible of life, sex and the forces that influence development, behaviour and the whole attitude of mind of the individual. It is hoped that by it, the subject now to be discussed in greater detail may be followed more easily, enabling the reader at the same time to formulate a better understanding of some of the problems that exist in the world in which we live.

CHAPTER TWO

INCIDENCE

IN ANY DISCUSSION concerning transsexualism it is inevitable that certain associations with transvestism and homosexuality will occur, and it will thus be necessary to look into these other sexual abnormalities and examine their relationship to the subject under investigation. There seems little doubt that homosexuality is the most widespread form of perversion, whilst of the other two conditions it seems safe to say that transvestism comes next and transsexualism last. If this were not so, the medical profession up and down the country would be pestered, and possibly overwhelmed, by patients expressing their wish to 'change' sex. On the other hand, transvestism is more openly recognised as being practised and can be assumed to be more widespread than is likely to be estimable, because, like homosexuality, of the secrecy with which the act is carried out.

It surely cannot be said that essentially normal heterosexual people, who may casually remark in passing that they wish they had been born of the opposite sex, come under the category of being transsexualists. As with every such condition, we find the same scale or range of variation, from the most extreme case to the one affected in but the smallest degree. At what stage, then, can we call a transsexualist a transsexualist? Without knowing this we are unlikely to be able, even with close research, to come to any near assessment of the incidence of the condition. If we are to include the example above, of the average normal heterosexual who may see some advantage in the opposite role, we should probably find that transsexualism had quite a considerable incidence, even more than the most pessimistic would suggest. As it is, we can happily rest back knowing that such thoughts in people's minds are but cursory, and that the logic of life, the normality of their sexual outlook and environmental forces more than offset the importance of this envy of the opposite sex.

The many authorities who have studied the incidence of homosexuality have equally found it necessary to think in terms of complete homosexuality and partial homosexuality for this very reason, for none of these states is absolute, and in fitting the many into a pattern we can only place them according to a man-made definition or generalisation. Such is so also with transsexualism. There is perhaps one marked difference, however, for much as the extreme homosexual or transvestite may go through life undetected and omitted from the statistics, extreme cases of transsexualism cannot fail to come to notice. The reason for this is that these cases require help in accomplishment of their goal, and, if their need is extreme and overpowering, before very long medical advice and assistance is sought. Also, there is the need for an employment card in the appropriate sex, so that figures of such changes by official bodies can help give some indication of the position. Admittedly this does not cover all the cases, but it does cover all those actively seeking treatment, and gives some basis for assessment which is not possible with homosexuality or transvestism.

Because of the great extent to which homosexuality affects our civilisation to-day it is natural that much work has been done on the subject, and Dr. A. C. Kinsey, investigating the sexual behaviour of some 4,000 American men, reported the figure of about 4 per cent as complete homosexuals and as high as 33 per cent for partial homosexuals. Other investigators have in the past put forward their own suggestions, and further estimates will no doubt continue to be made and be the subject of discussion and possible contradiction, because of the absence of the fixed point from which to work. If such is the case where much study and investigation has taken place, there seems little hope that any accurate assessment can be made as regards transvestism, much as it is now believed that the incidence is far higher than was originally thought.

Returning to transsexualism, we have dealt with those on the extreme end of the scale and have seen how a fairly accurate estimate of numbers seems possible. On the other hand, we have dismissed a group as not meriting inclusion. What now of those in between? The people in this group suffer silently with their troubles; some in ignorance of the reasons for their feelings, or too young to understand, others knowledgeable about their feelings and desires, releasing their emotions in the best way that they can. Of these, some may refuse to seek help, perhaps because of family or marriage ties, religious views, or other important considerations. Some may genuinely try to master their feelings, by essentially realising the illogicality of their state, whilst many may desire to seek treatment but are too shy or embarrassed to enquire how to go about it.

This is a subject which, without question, gets little sympathy from the general public, for it is an age-old adage that 'what we don't understand we don't agree with'. Whilst transsexualists are fully aware of this attitude, the greater problem seems the inability to gain any faith in the medical profession, because it is believed that they, too, do not and will not understand their feelings, let alone offer any advice that they may feel able to accept or otherwise help them in the direction of their goal. The main body of transsexualists therefore remain reluctant to seek medical help, not only because the whole manner of the trouble causes embarrassment, but because of the fear of not being understood. So the cases drift on in their own lonely worlds, going from one depression to another as the phases of tension and strain take on an almost cyclic pattern of build-up and easement. The covering up done by these transsexualists thus keeps us well in the dark as to the numbers involved in any particular country or community.

It seems certain that much of the behaviour of homosexuals and transvestites is likely to be confused with what is basically attributed also to transsexualists. A delight to make love to members of their own sex, and of dressing the part and masquerading in that role, by no means implies the wish to change the anatomical sex as in transsexualism. Of course, these conditions may all be present to some degree in one individual, but the essential qualities of transsexualists indicate a revulsion to sex in the form they know it, and equal revulsion to any form of masquerade. Much as transvestism may be present also, it is often the attendant guilt of 'dressing up' that enhances the desire to change the anatomical sex and role completely, so that

172

the expression of their dressing up can be continued without ridicule or the conflict that it causes in their own minds.

Investigations of certain native races in Africa, North America and New Guinea have shown how the male homosexual has been accepted in their social life and how an elaborate ceremony, to change the sex status of those men who do not fit the pattern of recognised masculinity, would often be enacted to enable the misfit to dress and live as a woman and take a 'husband'. Indeed, homosexuality has been found to have its place in every tribe, race and country, and in whichever era is studied. There is no reason to suppose otherwise, as we would expect to find traits and behaviours carried down through the ages on a matter so primitively basic in itself as sex. No doubt there have been phases in the culture of countries, brought on by wars or progress, whereby the incidence of such sexual abnormalities has increased or waned, but we see a society to-day, with all its modern thinking and knowledge, affected to quite a considerable degree with this perversion. Whether the condition is on the increase or decrease to-day we may never know, any more than whether we can attribute such a fluctuation to our modern civilisation and way of life. What is certain is that as all the possible causative factors are so wrapped up with life and all its environmental forces, then such states amongst the population of the world must be general in their distribution.

By examining this more widespread form of abnormality first we can see that transvestism and transsexualism, which may have originally developed from it, are likely to have a similar pattern of distribution, although of lesser incidence. The writer is of the opinion, however, that the incidence of transvestism is appreciably higher than is generally supposed to-day, and although the term is not supposed to apply to those who wear the clothes of the opposite sex for theatrical purposes or fancy dress it cannot be discounted that much of this behaviour produces a great sense of sexual excitement and pleasure, and is often used as an excuse and cover for it, in itself representing a form of latent or deliberate transvestism.

Whilst homosexuality and transvestism need consideration

173

because of their close affinity to transsexualism, it does not naturally follow that transsexualism is solely a development of these other states, although they are generally stages through which the transsexual passes. This is not always clearly seen as such, so that the individual states can appear confused. This is due to the transsexuals mentally identifying themselves with the opposite sex, leading to attraction to the sex of which they are anatomically the same (homosexuality), and to the ready expression of their feelings by dressing up in the clothes of the opposite sex (transvestism).

If we are to regard transsexualism purely as a wish to change the anatomical sex, and therefore the whole environmental and social role, irrevocably and permanently, it is the force that exerts itself in this direction which determines whether the condition will come to light, unless counteracted by the forces against a 'change' such as logic and opportunity. If, in fact, the desire remains under control, the individuals can continue in their normal role and live useful and happy lives, with the transsexual element suppressed. There must be a considerable number of people throughout the world to-day who are in just such a position, and if, as seems fair, we leave this group out of our estimation, the writer believes that, at present, the figures for true transsexualists would not be excessive in comparison with population. When we consider the possible incidence of homosexuality at 2 to 4 per cent in a country with a population of fifty million, this implies the existence of one to two million homosexuals. If there were this number of transsexualists, we should indeed know something about it! On the contrary, the average medical practitioner has up to now seen little if anything of the condition, and even specialists on the subject have relatively few cases from which to gain experience.

A comparatively recent article (26 December 1959) in the *British Medical Journal* by Dr. John B. Randell dealt with fifty cases of transvestism and transsexualism, discussing various aspects of these cases and the subjects in general. The importance of such an article lies perhaps in the fact that few have the opportunity of mustering fifty cases for investigation, and, even so, only thirty of these were transsexualists. If we are

174

to take this as an indication of the incidence of the condition we can see how low this is, bearing in mind that there are probably less than a handful of such specialists in the country with a similar number of cases as patients. To put the figure at 200 in this country for those who were actively seeking advice and help in 1959 would therefore seem reasonable. Perhaps that figure is nearer 300 to-day. Yet these cases only represent about 2 per cent to 10 per cent of those still secretly nursing their transsexual desires so that we can estimate, at the lowest level, a figure of 3,000, and at the highest a figure of some 15,000. These figures, of course, include both sexes. Even a close survey and investigation leaves many doubts, but granted that no actual basis for these figures can be given or the correctness or falseness of them ascertained, the writer's knowledge of the subject, the number who have sought her help and the evidence collected, does suggest a figure somewhere between those given.

We have as yet, however, only taken into consideration the indications of the subject collectively coming under the term transsexualism. What the writer believes to be much more widespread is O-sexuality, a condition described in the last chapter and which is essentially intersexuality in its psychological form. Whereas true intersexuality is intended to imply a physical state and suggests that the individual is between the sexes and belongs to neither, the O-sexual individual can be said to possess the qualities of both sexes *at one and the same time* and, because they cancel themselves out, an apparent form of intersexuality results.

Mention of this has been necessary only in order to differentiate the conditions and to show that transsexualism is in itself a development of the O-sexual qualities. Although transsexualism appears to be still comparatively uncommon amongst our civilisation, O-sexuality is on the contrary extensively present in far more of us than we would be prepared to admit, for in the completeness of our 'O' lies our selfishness, independence and individuality, which by virtue of our needs are factors which none of us are ever quite prepared to lose. None of us is either all masculine or all feminine in our ways, thoughts or interests, and just as there are men who take an interest around the house or in such activities as cooking or knitting, so there are women who are keen on sport, or follow pursuits usually attributed to men. There is no reason why this should not be so, as we are all brought up in a world of equal wonder and fascination to both sexes.

Many of us have qualities of both sexes, then, but the search for a partner in life is prompted by a need to make up those qualities we lack, in order to form a complete union. The feminine part of the husband enables him to take an interest in his wife's activities, and the masculine part of the wife will similarly enable her to take an interest in her husband's work and pleasure, without either losing their own respective qualities.

Quite often, however, these sexual qualities may be evenly matched in one individual, so that he or she becomes complete in themselves. This O-factor may be the reason why some men do not marry, or some women take to a career instead of settling down and rearing a family. The writer believes that this is largely so, and that the incidence of O-sexuals amongst us is quite high. Indeed, it is when we do not gain a true perspective of life that our completeness closes around us into a world of loneliness, immaturity and introspective thinking, and deviations occur.

We cannot look closely into the question of incidence on any subject without realising that the position is never stationary. What may be a latent quality in one individual one year may become quite active the following, and, equally, one who is normal may become abnormal. Can we rightly say that, as some die and pass off one end of the scale, others take their place from the other end? Much as this may be true when other subjects are considered, the writer believes that transsexualism can be a very variable condition. In a civilised community, where opinions can be freely expressed and newspapers enter into the daily life of everyone, much can be done to stimulate or suppress the everyday facts and actions that form the pattern of our lives, whether they are associated with our home town or places many thousands of miles away. In the past, when 'sex-change' had never been heard of and no medical knowledge was available, there was little that a troubled individual could do but face up to his problem, as indeed a man had to face up to a surgical operation without an anaesthetic. Those who found themselves compelled to live in the opposite role, for whatever reasons induced them to, did so in relative secrecy. To-day we hear of more and more cases of supposed 'sex-change', and, as the news is sped around the world, a fresh wave of trans-sexualist activity occurs. You have only to be slightly fascinated or transsexually minded and 'what others have done, I can do' manifests itself. Those who would normally be happy to go on as they are feel stimulated, as if at last they have found an answer to their conflicts and sexual emotions. Much as the condition has existed through the ages, then, circumstances and publicity, associated with the knowledge of medical and surgical help, has to-day made the deviation an established fact, and required the bringing into use of the new term transsexualism. There seems little doubt that the need for expression of one's sexual feelings and qualities has taken on new importance with the idolising of cases in the newspapers, and because of this the incidence of cases has unquestionably increased markedly in recent years.

From the records of cases which have come to light so far it would appear that the proportion of male transsexualists to female transsexualists is about three to one. This may be due to the fact that female transsexualists are able to assume the male role more easily without the essential need of surgery, so masking any real measure of the numbers involved. On the other hand, the driving force behind male sexuality can be powerful and be expressed in many devious forms, and if in addition the desire to be castrated is sado-masochisticly moti-vated to satisfy some latent childhood transsexual dream of belonging to the other sex, the transsexual drive can be much greater than that exerting itself on the female.

Fashion trends throughout the ages have fluctuated between bringing the sexes more together and then exaggerating the differences to the other extreme. At the present day, when the trend is towards the popularity of slacks for women and a wider variety of colour for the men, we find the dress of the sexes at the convergent stage. One often hears the remark that they cannot tell if a person is a man or a woman from the back. The shorter hair styles for women and the group of men going in for long and 'styled' hair accentuates this. Thus the predominant appearance is masculine. As a result, women are able to wear characteristically male garments, so that their transvestist act can better go unnoticed, and therefore any progression to transsexualism may, although latent, not manifest itself to the same extent as in the transsexual man. On the contrary, the male has to dress up in secret, and this, instead of relieving his feelings makes him become increasingly guilty about his feelings and deeds, thus heightening his wish to 'change' permanently in order to relieve him of these conflicts.

The average transsexualist is sufficiently aware of his state to do his best to cover up any abnormality within himself, and, except in the extreme later stages, his appearance is unlikely to give him away. Often he even tries to conform more to convention, which, although producing greater conflict of feeling, tends to make him smart in his dress and assume an aggressive manner, as a cover to his real self and shyness. Where evidence of femininity in a male transsexual or masculinity in a female transsexual is exhibited, however, it is often unconscious and unnatural. Generally, therefore, the appearance of anyone we may pass in the street gives little indication of this condition, except perhaps when some little thing giving satisfaction to the individual may be passed off as eccentricity. Such may be the mere buttoning of the coat on the 'wrong' side or the wearing of a blouse or shirt of the opposite sex. It must be said, however, that when the breaking point comes for these cases all logic and convention is lost, resulting in a 'couldn't care less' attitude, and all manner of exhibitionist ways may become marked in the appearance. At this stage, however, medical treatment, generally psychiatric, is usually needed or being obtained.

In order to study the relationship between severity of the condition and age, fifty fully assessed cases known to the writer have been taken for survey and assumed to represent a typical cross-section of all such cases. Since we can assume that an approximately equal number of transsexualists are born in each year, we can also say that at any one time the severity will be the greatest at the age at which the greatest number seek treatment. Also, as all cases included in the survey are those who have found their problem pressing enough to seek advice or treatment, it follows that an analysis of the numbers in each particular age group will indicate the relative incidence of severe cases at any given age. By taking the actual ages at which these cases first sought treatment, and plotting them against the number in each age group, the curve shown in Figure 1 is obtained.

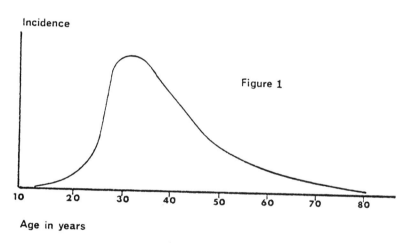

Figure 1

Incidence

Age in years

The curve is perhaps significant at once, because of its similarity to any curve showing the rise and fall of sexual activity throughout life. An interesting difference, however, is that the curve shows an immediate sharp rise commencing at about the age of 22, and not at about the age of puberty around 14. Although basically of the same pattern, therefore, there seems a delay of some eight years throughout, which we can interpret as the build-up period *after* puberty during which the problem is suppressed and fought off, before finally becoming too much to bear. Our curve shows the dangerous age to be between 22 and

28, during which time the problem becomes acute, and it is important to see that the best chance of assisting cases with their problem is therefore before this time. From about 28 to 32 the condition is at its peak of severity, and thereafter declines slowly into middle age, eventually tapering off as old age is approached. This does not mean that we may not find a case of 18, another of 30 and another of 70, all of equal severity, but rather that whilst assuming, for instance, that a hundred cases of each of these ages exist, only one case of 18 and one of 70 may be desperate enough to seek help, compared with possibly ten cases aged 30. Of the fifty cases under review there were actually one of 18, twenty-one between 25 and 34, and one of 77, amongst others. The total age of all the cases was 1,806 years, representing an average age of 36.12 years. As stated, the curve shows the best possible chance of adjustment to be before the age of 22, when the problem starts to get out of hand. Conversely, once the obsession has been fully built up, approaching the age of 30, the individual is likely to be well beyond the reach of help.

Full details of only forty male cases were available to enable an accurate examination and summary to be made of other aspects of the condition, the three tables given being compiled from the known information on these cases.

In Table I the civil status of these cases is summarised, the interesting feature being that as many as one-third are married. The records show that nearly all these latter cases married early in life, mostly in a supreme effort to overcome their problem. Amongst the single cases are those who have experienced no attraction to the opposite sex, and no desire for marriage, or who have been so aware of their condition and wrapped up in their 'O' as to remain content in their own lonely but uninvolved world.

TABLE I: CIVIL STATUS

	Married	Single	
No Issue . . .	9	27	
Issue	4	—	
Total . . .	13	27	= 40

In Table II the occupations have been classified on the basis shown. The figures show that the greatest incidence appears among the semi-skilled and skilled classes, accounting for twenty-three of the forty cases, but in considering this we must bear in mind that there are several times more people in this group in any country than there are in the highly skilled and

TABLE II: OCCUPATIONS

	Non-industrial	Industrial	
Unskilled . . .	4	−	4
Semi-skilled . . .	11	1	12
Skilled . . .	5	6	11
Highly skilled . .	4	3	7
Professional . . .	5	1	6
Total . . .	29	11	= 40

professional classes. The figure of thirteen cases found in the highly skilled and professional classes therefore is relatively high, and indicates that it is in this latter group that the highest percentage of cases are likely to be found.

TABLE III: POSITION IN FAMILY

	Younger brothers	Younger sisters	Elder brothers	Elder sisters		
Only children						14
First children	−	Yes			1	
	Yes	−			2	7
	Yes	Yes			4	
Last children			−	Yes	5	
			Yes	−	3	14
			Yes	Yes	6	
Intermediate children	−	Yes	Yes	−	2	
	Yes	−	Yes	−	2	5
	Yes	Yes	Yes	Yes	1	
					Total	40

A rather more complicated analysis has been attempted in Table III, to obtain some idea of the incidence of the condition in relation to position in family. Fourteen cases were 'only' children, and twenty-six had brothers and/or sisters. If we consider the possibility that the condition may be due in some measure to a parent wishing the child had been of the other sex, we can include the fourteen cases who were 'only' children, the seven who were first children, three who only had elder brothers, and four of the intermediate children who only had elder brothers when they were born. This makes a total of twenty-eight out of the forty, leaving only twelve cases with elder sisters. Although these figures rather indicate some causative factor associated with the parent's attitude to their child, it does leave nearly one-third of the cases unaccounted for. On the other hand, in looking for another factor in these remaining cases we see that five had *only* elder sisters, and wonder if upbringing in a predominantly female household may have encouraged the onset and maintenance of the condition. Of the seven cases now remaining we find that six of these were last children, with at least one brother and one sister, and if we wish to establish a possible parental reason for the condition in these cases we need only consider that, as the youngest, the child may have been pampered and been a mother's darling. How much of all this is conjecture and how much is fact is another matter; certainly, however much we generalise and try to see some simple and logical explanation for the condition, we must not fail to realise the possible existence of very real constitutional factors at work and understand that the condition is essentially personal and individual to each case, and that it is too serious a matter to be regarded other than in the light of all available facts and evidence.

CHAPTER THREE

THE SUFFERER'S LONELY WORLD

We ARE NOW ABOUT to step into the mind and world of a group of individuals who, through some of the influences we have been discussing, find themselves troubled and confused by their sexual feelings, state and behaviour, and quite often at a loss to explain them or to know the best way to approach their problem. Because of this they are certainly sufferers, and their inability to believe that anyone can understand leads them into a very lonely existence, feeling that if they cannot understand themselves, how can anyone else, human nature being what it is?

When we are born we know nothing of the world, and everything has to be taught to us by education or experience. Much as our first year or two of life is unconscious, certain influences are exerting themselves on our developing bodies and minds, just as much as the various factors we have discussed play their part from the moment of conception, when the sex gametes fuse into the zygote. To most of us, even going back to recall memories of when we were three years old is difficult enough, if indeed possible at all, and to assume that with all the wonders around us we should come to learn or know anything about sex, let alone the facts of life and such matters is, at such an early age, quite impossible.

Yet it is at about the age of three that we consciously come to realise what sex we are. Can we say it is because our inborn influences are showing signs of exerting themselves upon us, or is it that the word 'Boy' and 'Girl' come into our vocabulary, and we are told repeatedly that we are a good boy, or bad boy, or, otherwise, a good girl, or bad girl? Certainly our association with others, of about our own age, tells us that they are either boys or girls, and that we likewise belong to one of the two types. Apart from hearing the words constantly, we get the association of ideas that boys are dressed one way and girls another, so that we can easily tell what we are because of how we are dressed, or we may just come to learn that girls have long hair and boys do not. How much of all this, then, determines our first conscious awareness of our sex? In families where brothers and sisters are bathed together, the fact that boys have a penis and girls have not is obviously a factor we take early notice of, without knowing the reason for the differences or understanding their purpose.

The sufferers' first essential description of their feelings will be that, as long as they can remember, they have felt as if their sex has been wrong; they have always felt like a member of the opposite sex and thought a mistake must have been made, or, if not, wished that it had. One transsexual man said that when first told he was a boy he cried heartily, because he felt so much like a girl and wanted to be one. He was bitterly disappointed, and dearly wished he could change and be treated as a girl, and be able to wear their pretty frilly clothes. This is much the history of all these cases, the transsexual women saying that they had always wished they were a boy from their earliest recollections, and longed to be one. As the onset of these feelings is almost certainly back in early childhood (usually between 3 and 6) how can we account for them purely on a psychological basis, as they are feelings over which we have no control so early in life, when sex and environmental factors have had little time to exert their influence? Surely, they say, it is because there are some internal factors, perhaps of glandular or genetic origin, that have caused my state; nature must have intended me to be of the sex I feel, but for some reason my body has developed incorrectly. To the transsexuals searching for the cause of their trouble such an explanation seems the only answer, and comes to be accepted as such, for explanations and reasons are vital and necessary if an outlet for the confusion is to be found, and in order that some peace of mind may result.

Occasionally, definite external factors seem to precipitate the onset of the condition; for example, the tendencies of parental sexual perversion may become transferred into the child. The disappointment of a parent having a boy, but wanting a girl, and vice versa, may often manifest itself in abnormal upbringing and teachings, and there may be an attempt to feminise a boy in his ways, interests and outlook. Likewise a girl may be brought up assuming the role of a son, and expected to follow a family tradition in a masculine direction. Instances can be related where a mother, deserted by the father, has brought up a boy as a girl for the first few years of his life, because she wanted a girl, and therefore kept the child's hair long and dressed him in girls' clothes, so that neighbours always believed she had a daughter until circumstances later brought the matter out into the open. Such cases are rare, to this extreme, but varying degrees of such behaviour do exist, with untold harmful effect upon the child during its formative years.

Sometimes the parent may wish to humiliate the young boy, as a means of punishment and to satisfy their own perverted state; two such cases have personally related their stories to the writer. In the first, the boy was dressed in girls' clothes as a punishment for some little wrong deed, with the threat that this would happen again if he was naughty. The boy said, however, that once he had been so dressed he longed to be a girl, loved the girls' clothes, and dreaded the time when he would have to change back. The desire grew so much that he would deliberately be mischievous in the hope that the threats of being repeatedly dressed as a girl would materialise. In the second case, the unfortunate boy would, when quite young, be made to dress as a girl for a week at a time, as a punishment for some misdeed, and, being an only child, the clothes were bought specially for him. He used to be terrified of having to dress in this humiliating way, because all his friends jeered and made fun of him. The female clothes would even be washed and put on the line, in readiness for the next 'episode', and the boy would have them pointed out to him by his friends and be laughed at. The extreme mental anguish caused by living in such terror has never left the individual, although he is now a man of 44, and the effect has been to reverse the process so that some unconscious desire for, and love of, female clothes has resulted, manifesting itself in transvestist behaviour and a suppressed longing to be a woman. In both cases, some original revulsion probably existed to being made to appear as a 'cissy' and, as no power was present in them to prevent such parental cruelty, the only way out was to wish desperately that they were a girl as the humiliating practice would then have no significance.

Although such instances are mentioned, it should not be thought that they generalise in any way, for differing factors and influences, causing different circumstances, occur in each case, and by no means do we find that all sufferers are the only child, or the first-born, in spite of the ready-made answer from psychiatrists that the parents must have wanted a child of the opposite sex denomination. It must be remembered, too, because of the vast number of ways in which transsexualism may arise, that although some facts may appear to point very firmly to the reason in some cases, in others even deep investigation or analysis may prove fruitless, as so many internal factors may remain unknown. The child's attraction to certain toys seems to leave a distinct mental picture, and cases will say quite readily, when going into their past, that as a boy they remember liking girls' toys best, and craving after dolls and cuddly things, or likewise that as a girl they always wanted train sets and cricket bats, etc. Quite often these desires appear to be fulfilled, but when they are not, in the case of a boy, any household article may become the object of love, in place of a doll, and may take on such significance that he cannot perhaps go to sleep without it. In the case of a girl, frustration at not having the boyish toys she craves for may stimulate the masculine side in her even more, and some aspect of her father's interests or hobbies may provide her with suitable playthings.

Next we find the growing child at school, and the story of these unhappy souls continues. The boy, already aware of his feelings and state, may either retract into his shell (his 'O') through shyness and embarrassment, because of his conscious femininity and his assumption of inferiority for the tasks required of him in his masculine setting, or he may take the opposite approach and go to great lengths to prove how normal or even superior he is to the other boys, as a front and cover to his inner emotions and love of everything graceful, dainty and feminine. If he keeps to himself, feeling out of place and not fitted for the rough-and-tumble of a boy's life, most of his energy may be devoted to study rather than to sport. Sport at all times proves distasteful, for the sufferer feels inadequate, and the mere thought that as a result of his feeble efforts he may be called a 'cissy' causes great emotional upheaval, for it hits home at the very root of what the boy believes to be correct but is afraid to accept, and to have the truth laid bare is in his eyes the worst thing that could happen to him. That is why some may not remain subdued, but on the contrary develop a harder surface and over-act the aggressive role as a defensive mechanism. Nothing seems more pathetic to him than to be poor at a sport in which he is letting the side down, knowing that he is trying his hardest and still failing miserably. He complains that at school he is made to join in and is then criticised for a miserable and often effeminate display, as if it were his fault he is playing at all. Indeed, the sufferer would be much happier if he could come up to his expected sexual role, rather than be made to feel so humiliated, or if he could be released from his commitment of being forced to play. If only he could go and play with the girls, he thinks, and be one of them, his torment at the thought of games would disappear and he would be as happy as any around him, in his 'natural' surroundings.

Sometimes a younger brother may have added conflicts, by being expected to follow his elder brother who may exhibit all the accepted brilliance at boyish pursuits. Then, it seems, the weaker efforts of the transsexual boy are even more scorned, and, the more he tries to live up to what is expected of him, the more he finds life difficult or impossible. He may join the school cadet force because of this, only to find his state and qualities are entirely opposed to any successes in this field, and whilst others join long after him and take superior ranks he remains as he will always be, more and more shown up as the misfit that he is. This picture is very different to those who have not the ability, but who are able to conform and accept themselves because of their normality, and for whom all school activities represent the useful training they are meant to be, in preparation for facing the world. The sufferers do not therefore see any fault in the school system as it is but only in themselves, and are resentful at being given a role in life they feel they do not fit.

Even from early schooldays, there always seems the desire to remedy the 'mistake', and any opportunity to dress as a girl, at home in private, is seized upon. This early transvestist behaviour seems common in the majority of cases, and it is significant that there seems no ability to account to themselves for these feelings, or why such acts should produce the pleasure that they do. Certainly, there is no conscious eroticism or sexual pleasure, as may develop later, to enhance or encourage the act of dressing up, and it is done with the pure motive of achieving the mental peace of mind it gives. Amateur theatricals often provide an outlet for these expressions, and when picked for a female part in a school play, although the transsexual boy inwardly revels, outwardly he has to cover himself by pretending that he dislikes it, and force himself to be a little masculine even in the role, lest it is thought he may fit the part too well and be teased over it. Yet in spite of the front he puts up, it is surprising how often his feelings come to be recognised by those around him, and how often he is cast for the female part.

During all this time the individual is growing up, and in his own particular way (quite often unbeknown to himself) he is absorbing all the facts of things which interest him and are very much feminine in character. Even at this stage the outside world does not have the attraction it should, and the individual finds he is generally happier when he is not in company with his fellow beings, for not only can he be free from the possibility of criticism or of doing things unconsciously that may attract attention to his state, but, once alone, he can then indulge in the things that give him pleasure. Often because of this he may work harder scholastically to take his mind off his troubles, but against this is the emotional conflict, so that the resultant hard work may not always produce the expected result. Some male transsexualists are quite well established even before puberty, although sex as such still means little to them. They feel that if only they could go to sleep one night and wake up to find they no longer had a penis but were in fact a little girl nothing could make them happier, and many times they go to bed in tears, hoping this may happen.

Much of the conflict and emotional distress that transsexual men describe as a general pattern of their schooldays applies equally well to transsexual women. On the other hand, the girl who feels out of place is rather better able to tolerate her difficulties, for the qualities of dominance, leadership and physical prowess which she possesses, as part of her more masculine traits, are if anything an advantage to her, and, far from being criticised, she may well be praised for her 'stronger' characteristics. This not only partly compensates for her mental opposition to her surroundings, but provides her with an outlet to express herself more freely.

With the onset of puberty, even normal individuals are beset with all manner of problems, both physically and emotionally, in adapting themselves to their new circumstances and increasing awareness of their sexual sensitivity and outlook. Even more so does this prove a testing and disturbing time for transsexualists, for they now find their masculinity or femininity developing more and in opposition to everything they desire. The transsexual boy now finds he has new worries, for his hitherto girlish voice begins to 'break'; apart from his enlarging penis his testes add to his antagonism, and, to his horror, facial hair starts to grow. Each aspect of masculinity is in itself equally revolting, increasing his mental torture as he sees his ability to assume the female role become more and more difficult, and his goal less possible to attain. 'I hate this, and I hate that,' he says, mentioning everything he can think of relating to masculinity. In the transsexual girl, the commencement of menstruation and the development of the breasts equally give rise to frustration and conflict. In both sexes the arousal of sexual feelings, especially in the male, brings matters very much to a head, since the phase of masturbation, a source of conflict in itself, becomes symbolised into an expression the exact nature of which is not understood at the time.

This 'making love' to oneself develops little by little, the process taking on more and more complex deviations as the craving for satisfaction in a new and varied form increases. Usually, the mirror plays an important role, and the ability to see a 'partner' in the now transvestist sex act enables a greater meaning to be placed on this behaviour, the individual looking upon himself as playing both roles. From this feeling of being both sexes, the mind may now blot out the role to which the transsexualist is in such opposition, so that identification with the opposite sex becomes marked. In this way, the individual's feelings of belonging to the opposite sex, which have for so long been suppressed, are forced more to the surface, and the whole normal approach to sexual activity can be reversed until the behaviour and the feelings are matched in this mental image of the role in which the transsexualists see themselves, because of their need to force the pattern of their feelings to dominate any changing exigencies that life produces. At puberty, then, instead of a balancing effect occurring to encourage the opposing sexual forces to decline, as the physical reproductive role develops the inversion on the contrary becomes stimulated, and the mental antagonism to body function and to the anatomy becomes more highly aggravated, the desire to 'change sex' taking on new significance and importance.

Because of lack of knowledge or reason for the feelings, however, together with the assumption that they must be mad to feel as they do, and in the belief that no one would understand them anyway, the sufferers rarely take any active measures to seek advice or treatment but compensate for their increased burden by retreating more into their own world and inhibiting all normal forms of activity, so that less effort is necessary to maintain their 'front'. The result is that the individual fails to 'grow up' and remains 'immature', so that the feelings themselves remain bottled up. As the feelings increase in the years after puberty, then so do the inhibitions, the need to express the emotions of the sex opposite to that of their upbringing becoming more pressing and the sufferer going from one crisis to another. Denied the ability to express themselves the sufferers are forced into a dream world of fantasy, and the world of their desire is subconsciously built up as a refuge from reality. In it, the transsexual man sees himself as a beautiful young girl, in a pretty floral frock, long hair and high heeled shoes, etc, wanting to be pampered, looked after and loved. The transsexual woman sees herself as a dominating figure, striding about with hands in her trouser pockets and with the world to be conquered, etc.

Yet in reality they have to conform to accepted normality and they repel it vigorously, so that the conflict of the real and the unreal damps the energy, as the motive force is divided in its objective. The sufferers become unsettled and less able to cope with life and its challenges, and the escape to the lonely dream world becomes more and more compelling, so that the whole personality becomes obsessed with all manner of ideas, both normal and exaggerated, in an effort to make up for what they feel denied by life in reality. They feel as though their whole life has been and is an act, as being given a wrong part to take in a play. Nature has made a mistake, they will say, and really meant them to be of the other sex. They feel and think as one, but their body makes them the other. Everything about their body revolts them, and when their anatomy falls short of their desired picture they imagine changes about themselves as if they were a fact. This form of auto-suggestion often causes the transsexual man to believe he is developing breasts, or that his genital organs are diminishing in size.

Whatever the medical or sexual reason for the existence of such a condition, the feelings or emotions and their need for expression seem to be the prime motivating force, the build-up of tension due to 'bottling-up' driving the sufferer deeper and deeper into his problem and able to understand himself or accept logic less and less. Thus, although the feelings started off by unconsciously influencing the thoughts and behaviour, the tables are gradually turned so that the conscious thoughts and behaviour influence the feelings. The sufferer's lonely world therefore comes to take on weird and fantastic proportions, the feelings become exaggerated, and every conceivable notion of femininity or masculinity is visualised.

The vitally important thing to remember with these cases is that the feelings, the explanations, and the desires, all seem to fit a very steady pattern, *in spite of the fact* that one case may appear to have some constitutional reason for them whereas another may have no justification whatever and be physically

191

ultra-normal in every ascertainable respect.

We cannot better gain an insight into the dream world of fantasy than by letting the sufferer personally tell his own story. It is a story of hopes and fears; of longing and desire; of conflict and frustration; of endeavours to account logically for feelings which are themselves illogical; of efforts to blend fantasy with reality; and of the realisation that in the end the problem will remain in all its magnitude because, although the facts may be clear, to accept them is against instinct, nature and make-up. With no one to turn to the sufferer often finds release by writing of his troubles, even in the knowledge that they may never be read. He feels it is a way of expressing himself, and may enable him to reflect at a later date on his own problem and reasoning. In this way he hopes to sort out why he should feel as he does; whether he should condemn or accept his feelings; if condemning them, how he can return to normality and avoid a guilt complex, or, if accepting them, how he can convince others of his justification and need for help, and above all really convince himself that a change of role is wholly the answer to his search for satisfaction and happiness.

The writer has chosen the following case who has recently sought her help, and who has not only come to see her but written voluminously to her of his feelings – feelings which amply express those common to all male transsexualists. By following his writing here we can almost hear his mind tick. Although some editing has been necessary the words as written remain accurate and genuine, and are typical of what any psychiatrist or doctor may hear provided the sufferer can bring himself to tell his seemingly unbelievable story, at the risk of being misunderstood, rebuked, or told simply to pull himself together. But, Mr. X, you can speak freely here, without interruption, and will be given a sympathetic hearing, so let us hear your story.

"I am almost 26, and I feel I can no longer go on as I am. I feel I am a woman imprisoned in the body of a man, and I ask any woman what she would feel if, one day, she were told that tomorrow she would physically become a male, and, because society demanded it, have to behave like a man although she retained her feminine outlook on life. To any woman it would be hell, yet I feel my position is worse; I have had to endure what she would feel *all* my life. There is only one way out for me; to express myself properly as a woman, as I have yearned indescribably to do ever since I can remember.

"When quite small I somehow knew I was not like a normal little boy. At first I discovered I could escape from my unhappy world into a dream world where I was wonderfully contented. I found by improvising with my mother's things I was able to make believe I was grown up, and like my mother. I used to like to imagine I was a princess who would one day be rescued by a prince, and through him be able to do all the wonderful things a little girl could do. Then again, I liked to dream that one day I would find someone who would understand me and help me to change into a little girl. But all I did never had any reality about it. No one knew of my yearnings, and I could never wear or do openly the things my heart most desired. As a child I was a very pretty baby, and until I was about 4 I had lovely, almost shoulder length, golden curls. In fact, people have often refused to believe it was a little boy they were looking at in photographs – not that my parents dressed me as a girl. When finally I was taken to have my hair cut, I remember hating every snip of the scissors and crying most bitterly. I always hated boys' clothes and would much rather have worn pretty dresses, and it seemed quite natural to want to do the things little girls could do, play their games and play with their toys.

"I recall vividly being in a shop with my mother, when a young girl of about my own age picked up a pretty slip, and her face lit up as she said with feeling, "Isn't it beautiful?" Suddenly it was as if I were there

too, feeling the silky softness of the garment against
my skin, and equally suddenly I felt utterly alone and
just wanted to get away from that shop. It came home
to me poignantly that reality denied me such lovely
things. By the time I was 10 or 11 I was tall enough to
wear the clothes of a woman properly, and every
conceivable chance I got in private I would dress
myself from top to toe as a young woman. I would
arrange my hair (which I always kept rather long)
becomingly, and use cosmetics, and for a while I was
completely happy. Until I was about 18 I thought my
feelings and yearnings were signs of insanity, and that
is why I kept them to myself as well as I was able,
though perhaps people nearest to me guessed how I
felt. I even fought my feelings as I thought them
morally wrong, and strove to be more mannish by
throwing myself into male activities, however repugnant I found them to be. I heard about other
people who were like me; whom it was said nature
had intended to be a girl or boy as the case may be,
but somehow at birth something had gone radically
wrong. I was able to appreciate my position a little
better, although none of the heartache and frustration were removed, and I still felt, as I feel to-day,
that the ordinary layman would ridicule people like
me or believe they were insane.

"People have often told me I should have been a
girl. A boy at school once told me, 'You have hair just
like a girl.' A woman said, 'You have small hands, just
like a girl.' Another told me, 'You should have been a
girl with your nice legs and slim ankles.' My proudest
moment came, however, when a girl I knew told me I
would make a nice girl, as my expression and features
were most feminine. She was trying to persuade me to
dress in her clothes and enter a fancy-dress competi-
tion. I find I am constantly envying other girls their
chances to wear pretty clothes. I can't explain why I
like dresses or want to wear my hair long; it's not only

194

because I want to express my femininity but partly because I find them so glamorous and exciting. I love make-up, too; lipstick does so much to pep me up, and pretty, colourful beads have always attracted me. High heels and nylons do so much for my morale; I feel so well dressed and sleek, and my deportment improves wonderfully when I wear them. I love the variety, colour, and softness of women's clothes and the sparkle of jewellery, and the more pretty and feminine an object the more I am attracted to it and wish to wear it. When I am on my own at home I can put on a skirt or dress, and when so dressed in women's clothes I find I just don't want to take them off, although invariably there are all sorts of other calls upon my time. I believe I could be quite happy and contented wearing a dress or skirt for the rest of my life. In fact, if I could become a woman physically, I don't think I would ever want to wear slacks or jeans, however fashionable they may be.

"Generally speaking, there are certain things that girls don't do, simply because they aren't interested in them, and there are other things that they cannot do, because they are constitutionally or mentally so arranged. I am quite happy at home doing house-work, and love darning, cooking and shopping, and yet I am hopeless at practical or mechanical things, in which I show no interest at all. I am decidedly uncomfortable in the company of men, but with girls I am completely at ease and can talk naturally. I have never shown much interest in sports, except athletics, and sports that are the prerogative of men, like boxing, horse-racing and motor-car racing, I show complete indifference to. I like taking an interest in people and I love reading women's magazines. I ask awfully embarrassing questions about the mechanical side of my car (things which the average man would know), and as long as the thing goes I am quite happy. I am more concerned about its colour, style and comfort.

"In these different ways I am like a woman. I have always had a deep-rooted, all-powerful feeling that I wanted to be a girl, and was more like a girl, even when I was quite small. There is surely no earthly reason for me wanting this or feeling this way at such an early age unless something had gone wrong and I was meant to be born a baby girl. I have had this feeling all my life; it has never left me once; if I have not actually been thinking about it, it has always been at the back of my mind. With all my being I want to be able to express myself as a woman. There seems to be such a fountain of feeling, love and affection, gentleness and beauty inside me that is always compelling me to give expression to it in some way. I love children and anything small and helpless. I could never kill an insect. I feel quite sick if I see a poor little bird or a cat run over and lying in the gutter way. To me, the gentle, loving and pure things of life are best. I abhor war and bloodshed, I love sentimental tales with plenty of romance, and cannot help crying over deeply emotional films.

"My problem, then, is not so much that I want to live and express myself as a woman – that is pressing enough – but that deep down inside me, if I am truthful with myself, *I am a woman*. Everything that touches me in life touches me as a woman. My senses are those of a woman and my whole being is a woman; I just cannot get away from what I am. I don't want to change my sex just for the sake of doing it. Inside me I have a deep-rooted and sincere feeling that I am much more like a woman than a man, even if I am a man physically, and as far as my emotions are concerned I am very feminine. My difficulties are not confined to the way I feel things, but my outlook and expressions are also feminine. I know I cannot say that because a person likes doing a certain thing he or she belongs to a particular sex, but there will always be exceptions to the rule. In my case, practically *all* my interests – those that matter – are feminine. I used to be terribly embarrassed about this, and fought hard to develop masculine traits, but this was impossible because it was against my nature, though I must say I have been able to lead a reasonably successful life as a man, because I was able to hide my true feelings so well.

"I dare say, as I look and feel so feminine, I could leave my home town and begin a life as a young woman elsewhere. But I don't want to do that; it would be cheating. What I want is to know that I really **am** a girl, to be accepted **legally** as a girl, be accepted **socially** as a girl, and be able to do openly all the wonderful things a girl can do, without feeling as I do now, because I am a man, a pang of guilt or even acute embarrassment at times. I want to be accepted by the world as a girl. I want men to look upon me as a member of the opposite sex and treat me as a girl and I want other girls to acccept me as one of them. I have always envied girls' privileges, position and opportunities. I have never wanted the male prerogative in life; however many advantages it can bring, they hold no interest for me. I have never been proud of anything manly, or interested in a manly physique or large muscles. Ever since puberty I have been intensely envious of any girl with a good figure.

"I believe it would be impossible for me to live as a woman without any physical change, because I would feel insecure and that I was masquerading. Apart from the feeling that I was still physically male, I have strong feelings about the morality of dressing up as a woman and exhibiting myself in public under those circumstances. I do believe, however, that I could be very happy with hormone treatment to make my appearance more feminine, and with an operation for castration and plastic surgery for the creation of female characteristics in the external genitalia. Even

197

with this help I know that I might still have the mental conflict that underneath it all I was just a mutilated male, but at the moment I feel that I am a mutilated female. My foolish heart leaps at the thought of living as a woman, but I would have to know within my own mind that I was as nearly a girl as medical science could make me. It is true up to a point that I look like a young woman; my two main drawbacks are persistent facial and body hair and a broken bone in my nose; but I know I would definitely require medical aid before I could leave one life for another.

"Possibly my greatest regret, other than never being able, as a woman, to bear children, is that I shall never be able to recapture the wonderful experiences and joys of girlhood. If I had been given the choice at birth, I would have wished to have been born a girl. If only, I now think to myself, I could visit a beauty parlour and have the complete and invigorating and uplifting beauty treatment at the hands of an expert; if only I could go to a hair specialist and have my hair set in the latest style; if only I could gaze into a shop window at pretty hats or shoes without feeling conscious of my embarrassment; if only I could go into a powder-room and chat with the girls about fashions and beauty; if only I could go into a shop and hear the sales-girl say, 'Can I help you, Madam?'; if only I could get on a crowded bus and find a man give up his seat to me; if only I could be whirled around a dance floor in a pretty frock; oh! oh! if only, if only, if only, a thousand times over!

"A woman's greatest quality is her attribute of love – I mean here love in its purest form, love for her children, husband, and for the world in general, for by transmitting her love and care to her children she can help to make the world a better place to live in. However much one may argue the merits and demerits of male superiority over woman, I sincerely believe that no one is better at their own type of job, that actually she has the most important job to do in the world. To be able to run a home, have children and bring them up properly is the most worthwhile work anyone can do, and has something of a divine quality about it. I have always found I have a greater appreciation of the aesthetic things of life; of good music, nature and the arts. To me, the physical beauty of hill, dale, moorland and stream is more satisfying and invigorating than any mental or physical supremacy over another. The writings of the naturalist Hudson are particularly dear to me, and he seems to express something of what I feel about life and beauty. He writes: 'The blue sky, the brown soil beneath, the grass, the trees, the animals, the wind, the rain and stars are never strange to me; for I am in, and of, and one with them, and my flesh and the soil are one, and the heat in my blood and in the sunshine are one, and the winds and the tempests and my passions are one.' Elsewhere he writes: 'The sense of the beautiful is God's best gift to the human soul.' How I echo his sentiments exactly!

"While as I am anything to do with the male sex is abhorrent and out of the question, if I were able to change my physical sex my feelings towards men would change too, perhaps, and I would like to think they were attracted to me as a woman. I know I would like to marry, run a home of my own, and, as I would be unable to have children, adopt some perhaps. But I must say that I am really scared stiff about a change of sex, for I think to myself; 'Would I ever be able to accept not being able to bear a child or being a *real* woman? Would I ever be able to marry? Even if I could face my parents and friends after a change, would they accept me and would it be practical to live in the same place? Would I ever regret my step and, similarly, would I really be happy? Would I feel the many things I could do as a girl were still worthwhile and wonderful? How could I break off my present marriage to my wife, for whom I have a great deal of affection and regard?' So I hesitate at the cross-roads; I have a wife, parents and job to consider and, however much I want to be a woman, my feelings for all three are very deep. Could I ever feel justified in changing and living as I believe is right for me, knowing how hard and difficult it may be for others? Because of this, would I ever live in peace and contentment in the role that would otherwise give me such untold happiness? I firmly believe that my feelings and emotions are innate, but I recognise that I could be wrong and that I could be just all mixed up inside, having got my sexual values topsy-turvy. Oh! Where do you get with all this soul-searching?

"Facing up to reality, I suppose an attempt should be made to make an adjustment back along the masculine road, but I cannot help feeling I shall always be out of place in a masculine world. I dare say I would still feel my limitations as a female if I attempted treatment the other way, and that is why I have begun to reason that if I could somehow live as a woman, perhaps for a little while, I could gauge my true feelings much better than I do now. After all, I think, I have lived as a male all my life, without ever having the courage to find out how feminine I really am. To me womanhood and femininity are beautiful things to dream about and conjure with, and although I would not call myself effeminate I have always intensely disliked and been entirely unsuited for the challenge of masculinity. Men seem to be compelled to conquer things and show their strength. You might just say my feelings were for some reason wrong, and that nature did not intend me to be born a girl, but that certain things happened in my early life to make me yearn to be a woman and express myself as one. How I hate just to think about such a theory! I suppose anyone who is brought up in one sex while actually belonging to the other finds certain things in that sex attractive and other things easy to do, merely because of having to do them all their life. Therefore, while I believe my desire to change sex is genuine and sincere, I cannot help feeling that I might be deluding myself about my feelings, thoughts and emotions. I try to be as objective as I can about myself, yet there is this feeling of insecurity. However that may be, I cannot help remembering that, under certain circumstances, I react like a girl, and that in numerous things I have the outlook and appreciation of life that a woman has.

"Whatever treatment I have, if, as I truly believe myself to be, I am basically female, then, whatever anybody can do, they cannot remove these basic and innate feelings. I won't say that everything I do is entirely feminine, or everything I think, either; that, I would say, is impossible when one is brought up as a male, taught to be a boy, and forced to live in a man's world. Going to a boys' school or doing National Service come to mind, for at both you have the masculine drummed into you to the exclusion of the feminine, and woe betide you if you show undesirable traits of femininity. You quickly learn to subdue your true feelings, although, however much you try to submerge them, they still come out in some other way, sometimes disastrously. But however much I have had to toe the line as a man, my feelings and interests refuse to be banished. They may be dormant through necessity, but nevertheless they are there and very real. I have discovered this to be even more so in the past two years, which is why I don't want to go on with my present existence. The years seem to be slipping by and I am getting no nearer to expressing myself as nature intended, and I am heaping on my head untold misery at the same time. *I would give anything in the world, were it my own to give, if I could become a woman*. I feel so feminine in my outlook and mind that I believe only as a woman

201

can I find happiness and fulfilment in life, and I am certain that nature equipped me far better to adopt the role of female in this world than male. I have led a lonely, shy life because of my difficulties, and to go on with the folly of my present life will mean further frustration, regret and misery. I know I shall need all my courage in my efforts to become a member of what I rightfully believe is my true sex. *I am determined that I shall achieve my goal in the end.*"

This person who has just put his problem before us is still living with his conflict, and the solution to his troubles seems just as far off. Who can venture, after reading his story carefully, to presume that there is any ready-made answer? Whilst one cannot fail to have deep sympathy for the person behind the story, however, an objective analysis must be that we are dealing with someone who has a deep-seated psychological disturbance in more than the sexual plane. He has not only divided every aspect of masculinity and femininity into unrealistic definite compartments but his mind overflows with his thoughts to the point of repetition and verbosity. He speaks of being able to live as a woman as he is and yet in reality he is a physically normal man, with all the normal male secondary sexual characteristics and even tells us he is married. The world he lives in is one of fantasy and self-delusion and any psychiatrist would find much to delve into. That said, the overall transsexual feelings come through, the desires, the love of all fine things, the guilt, the conflict, the soul-searching; the only reason he can come up with is that nature must have made a mistake when he was born. We may scorn this but the question must still be answered. Why should he feel as he does and was there some intra-uterine influence acting on his developing brain after all? What he cannot fight, however, is what he physically and biologically is to-day, and whatever he decides, sadly, it is almost certain that his conflicts will remain. Later in this work, the feelings he so vividly expresses will be examined and commented upon. Whilst he would profess to be able to go on and on in similar vein, it more than illustrates the nature of the problem. It is the factual account of one case only but, although others may state that the *behaviour* pattern varies from their own, the majority will agree that the *feelings* are identical, and in that respect the words could be their own. Variations on the theme will be considered more fully when we come to establish a classification of the basic types.

What now of the world of the female transsexualist? Can we assume that the pattern is the same in the reverse direction? The writer believes that this is not generally so. Indeed, female transsexualism is so different that it might be said that true transsexualism as such only occurs in the male. The torment and frustration are there from early childhood, but there is more opportunity for the release of tension, which only tends to become overpowering when the urge dominates all thoughts and actions and brings the sufferer to a mental standstill. The outlet in the manner of clothes has already been discussed, as has the more ready acceptance of a woman taking an interest in the more masculine pursuits. The sexual aspect also does not appear to be so demanding, and the pairing up with another girl for companionship and to confide in, which is a common feature of these cases, helps to lessen the loneliness that the condition would otherwise create. These facts seem to be borne out by the lesser incidence of female transsexualists over male cases.

Since the need for expression throughout life has not been so thwarted the need to convince others as well as themselves has not been so overwhelming, as many practical issues have not intervened and less rigid conformity to femininity is expected of them. For obvious anatomical reasons, even the law is more lenient in its attitude to women dressing as men in public. There appears to be no resort to writing, as with the transsexual male having to argue his case, and the transsexual female often knows her goal without hesitation, her attitude appearing to be based more on the future than the past. In this way, the accounts they give of their difficulties are less elaborate, and although this does not mean that the sufferings and conflicts are any the less severe throughout life, there does seem a greater ability to cope positively with the problem.

The cases that have come to the writer's notice therefore appeared much more concerned with immediate issues and the problems involving their ability to assume the male role than with searching for reasons and reciting their past difficulties. Some feelings are, of course, typically the inverse of the male transsexualist, but the questions the male transsexualist asks himself, "Will I be accepted as a girl? Do I look passable as a woman? Will my family accept me? Are my physical features as feminine as I think? Will it affect my job?" etc., are types of questions missing in the female transsexualist. There are often practical reasons for this, for it is quite possible that the female transsexualist may, as a man, increase her status and earning ability, whereas the male transsexualist may, as a woman, have to accept a more humble position and reduced income.

If the female transsexualist *were* to speak of her feelings we may expect to hear something like this:

> "As long as I can remember I have been aware of these 'strange feelings' that somehow I was a boy, and hated to think that I was a girl. I disliked being called by a girl's name and always wanted a boy's name instead. My interests were masculine, and I always preferred boys' toys and playing with boys. I enjoyed all their games and activities, and felt fully at ease in any rough-and-tumble and used to be called a tomboy.
>
> "When I was at school I felt terribly out of place with the girls and their interests bored me, and I envied boys going into a neighbouring school and wished I could go with them. Being aware of my feelings I tried to subdue them at times, but my efforts to do so caused me constant torture and conflict. With puberty and the commencement of menstruation I became even more antagonistic to my role in life. I still wanted to be with the boys, not because I was attracted to them but because I felt one of them and so much more at ease in their company. I have always hated my body, and longed to wear male

clothes without the telling presence of my breasts.

"Much as I have had to go on as a woman my inner forces have always made me strive after manhood, and I know that to live as a man is the only way I can find peace and contentment in life. Having to wear dresses and feminine clothes always distressed me, whilst I found that wearing slacks and a shirt eased my tension a great deal, so that I began wearing them more and more and now wear them all the time. I also feel unnatural with long hair and keep it as short as possible. But, however much I am able to express myself in this way, I know I shall never be really happy until I can actually be the man that I feel within me. Having 'periods' causes me untold misery, any part of me that indicates femininity revolts me. I know other cases have been helped, and although I have so far been unsuccessful my feelings insist that I keep trying. I know in my heart of hearts that I shall only be able to live a full and happy life and enjoy what others are blessed with at birth – the naturalness and normality of their sex – when I can be freed from my life of acting and be enabled to assume my rightful role as a man."

This account is based on one particular case who at last it seems may be on the way to getting some help with her trouble. Indeed, whatever medical label a case may be given, no one has the right to approve or condemn another's efforts to seek happiness, and *if* the reward of help is true happiness humanity will not be the loser.

CHAPTER FOUR

GENERAL BEHAVIOUR

As the condition of transsexualism varies in degree within its own definable limits, and no sexual state is in itself static, we find that not only can one individual be assumed to lie on a point either left or right of the supposed normal defining any particular condition, but that the point itself may fluctuate on the scale according to factors of time and circumstance, Since it is the urges in life that prompt action, by causing our bodies to react to resolve the urge, so the transsexualists, by way of their disturbed urges, impulses, and associated feelings, have the need to express themselves accordingly. The general behaviour that results is therefore largely and directly due to these forces and feelings, imposed, by the condition, on the sufferer.

Although the feelings are often very similar in all cases, the practical aspects of life, upbringing, environment, and opportunity vary in each, and the behaviour pattern is not therefore necessarily the same. It may be that one person has a high regard for the moral code, and, much as the thought of dressing up and appearing in public may be of great appeal, the actual act may be suppressed. In discussing the general behaviour here, then, we must not consider it fully applicable to every case, or that the stronger the feelings the necessarily more devious the behaviour. Some with quite powerful desires and instincts manage to 'soldier on' in life, refraining from certain practices because their upbringing tells them it is wrong, because it goes against their own sense of what appears right, or out of regard for others such as their loved ones. Others may feel less guilty of their actions, give way easily to their impulses and feelings, have no loved ones to consider, and have ample opportunity to indulge in behaviour which provides an outlet for their sexual tension and conflict. It is thus the resultant of many complex factors and forces which gives rise to the final picture.

The activity would appear to follow very closely the curve

given in Chapter Two. Whatever the manner of the behaviour in early childhood, puberty acts as a marked stimulus, and in the years after, up to about 30, all manner of behaviour that is ever likely to be indulged in manifests itself with increasing need and forcefulness. Beyond this point there is a slow decline, as the limit of satisfaction is reached, the sexual drive lessens, and the individual learns to live with or find a way out of his problem. This is not to say that hope for an adjustment to the opposite role is ever lost throughout life, from the psychological point of view, but that, since the behaviour is directly associated with the sex urge, both lessen together. The only exception is to be found in those whose mental outlook has been so affected during the peak period as to continually drive them towards their goal, irrespective of all external factors, logical or practical.

From early childhood to puberty we find the main desire is to wear the clothes of the opposite sex, and the wish, in the male, to be rid of the penis. Whatever may have prompted these desires, the desire itself (to belong to the opposite sex) no doubt unconsciously prompts the behaviour, since it is significant that, as knowledge is so limited in these earlier years, the transsexual boy believes that the only things preventing him being the girl he so longs to be are his clothes and the presence of his penis. Up to puberty, then, the transsexual boy will dress up as a girl as often as he can, using perhaps his mother's or his sister's clothes. At first he may do this openly, being unaware that he must conform to his supposed sex, but even if this is not criticised by his parents at first, being passed off as a childish prank, in the end he is bound to discover his parents' displeasure and will continue his dressing up in secrecy. Often, only one frilly item of girls' clothing may be tucked away, and suffice to enable the youngster to see himself as a girl when wearing it. The penis, which to him represents his masculinity, has no place in his dream world and, finding it mars the pleasure of his dressing up, he may next conjure up some way of simulating its absence, by bandaging it around himself or wearing some tight garment of underclothing. Up to this time he knows little reason for his behaviour, and often sees little harm in it, beyond knowing that it gives some incomprehensible satisfaction.

The transsexual girl may equally derive great pleasure from dressing as a boy, or wearing any boyish article of clothing she can, and usually her 'tomboy' activities enable her to carry this off without too much comment, so that although the desire for a 'change' is as powerful as that of the transsexual boy, by virtue of having some form of outlet it may not build up to such dynamic proportions.

With puberty, the transsexual boy finds that dressing up, either in part or in whole, stimulates even greater excitement and pleasure, for, being sexual in character, the act encourages erotic play which usually terminates in masturbation and orgasm. Since the dressing up has usually by now become part of the individual's life, and is more demanding with the approach of puberty, the very first orgasm to be experienced may come quite unexpectedly during just such an episode of dressing up, and the ability to obtain pleasure in this way encourages a repetition of the procedure at intervals. Soon this becomes established as a routine, and should it be associated with a definite object or item of clothing fetishism results, the performance of the ritual necessitating the fetish object to be present, seen, or worn. Alternatively, the pleasure and relief of masturbation may provide the sole motive. For a time this behaviour may provide ample sexual gratification, but sooner or later the satisfaction wanes and loses its effect and new methods are conjured up to restore the loss. It is as if there has been a numbing of the erotic areas, and a greater stimulation is required to produce the same effect. When this occurs, sado-masochism may result, in which the individual resorts to all manner of violence upon his sexual organs. Such practices may already have been resorted to, to a lesser degree, up to puberty, when the boy plays with his penis, ties it up, or uses rubber bands on it. Later sado-masochism may take many forms, and may be directed at causing orgasm only, with maximum effect, or at prolonging the sexual pleasure and build-up before the climax is reached, thereby delaying the anticlimax of sexual apathy and indifference which normally follows orgasm.

All manner of devious behaviour may ensue from abnormal channelling of the sex urge. The strange behaviour of placing both feet into one trouser leg or dressing back to front often provides erotic stimulation. Another example is the forced retention of water, which not only promotes sexual excitement by bringing pressure to bear on the prostate, but also enables the bladder fullness to be mentally regarded as pregnancy, the ultimate feminine attribute. Because of the association of desire for a 'change' with the sado-masochistic urge, however, the satisfaction at inflicting severe violence on the male organs is enhanced by the wish to be rid of them, and the individual may feel like cutting them off, or beating them into non-existence, or inflicting such injury as he hopes may necessitate their removal. Such an emasculation complex comes to nearly all transsexualists at some time or another, when the condition becomes extreme and satisfaction can no longer be obtained other than as assumed in the role of the opposite sex. The desire of the sado-masochist to inflict injury and pain upon himself, and to be humbled, may prompt all manner of devious behaviour. Such may involve the application of a powerful tourniquet to the penis and testes; the application of irritating agents to the bulb and erotic areas; crushing of the organs, or suspension of them just out of reach of body support; severe tying of them back between the legs to assume their absence and sitting down to bring the weight of the body to bear upon them. Such actions are often enhanced by tying the hands and feet at the same time, to incapacitate themselves and so enhance the suffering. Yet it is often hard to conceive just where sexual stimulation and pleasure merges into actual pain and torture, since the sexual act itself is a sort of painful pleasure, some anaesthetisation effect occurring as the climax is approached, so that the mind and body lose themselves completely and exclude time, responsibility, and awareness, in order that nothing may interfere with the sexual act going through to its natural conclusion.

Often, however, the desire to dress up and the practice of sado-masochism does not form the entire picture, and some may also seek and find pleasure in a heterosexual relationship.

In these cases, the conflict between the two opposing forms of behaviour may lead the individual into practical as well as emotional difficulties, for the earlier feelings and influences still remain and, much as efforts are made to push the abnormal practices into the background on the realisation that conformity to normality is expected, generally the reason for the deviation, the surroundings, and mode of life have become so established as to prevent any alteration in the general pattern of the desire. Mostly, however, the transsexualist keeps to himself, feeling that it would be a fate worse than death to be found out, and the secret feelings which have for so long come to be accepted by the sufferer as something that must be put up with find their outlet in secret behaviour. This impelling need for secrecy, which moulds the whole life of the individual, serves to build up the tension more and more, and with it the wish to be rid of the pretence and come out into the open grows and grows. As a result the behaviour takes on more devious forms, each new episode to produce satisfaction reaching its peak of emotional expression and pleasure, only to wane after a time and for further new outlets to be envisaged and engaged in.

From dressing up in part as a woman behind locked doors of the bedroom or bathroom the male may next assume a complete change of clothes, either using garments of female members of the household or garments specially purchased for the purpose. At first the feel of the clothes may be sufficient to produce the necessary pleasure, but anything that the individual may later see of himself showing up his masculinity causes revulsion, so that not only the craving for creams, powders, and lipstick develop but the ability to mask the facial hair by make-up is an added attraction in assistance of the disguise. Circumstances may not permit a hair style longer than the conventional 'short back and sides', and at this stage the need for everything to be just right may not be present. Just a head scarf, or a large hat pulled well down, may suffice to enable the individual to picture his own transformation, or simply parting the hair on the supposed girls' side (on the right) may be enough. In some cases, the short hair itself may be arranged to the delight of the transsexual man, whilst in others, as the

210

condition progresses, a wig becomes more essential to the masquerade. Since the transsexual man is generally shy and easily embarrassed procuring a wig may present quite a problem, and he may well pass a hairdresser's exhibiting them in the window many times before he can find the courage to go in and ask to purchase one displayed. Although hairdressers may have doubts as to the use for which it is required, even if they believe it is for theatrical purposes the purchaser often gives little opportunity for a fitting as the hairdresser may wish, for he will feel his hot blushes and embarrassment, and cannot get out of the shop fast enough. Often, however great the desire may be for a wig, the courage needed to procure one defeats the transsexualist, coupled with the fear of his secret being exposed. Generally, however, wig-makers are co-operative and only too happy to sell their creations. Indeed, one often sees advertisements in popular newspapers offering to supply wigs to measurement, although again the need to give a name and address may act as a deterrent. The transsexualist may go through the phase of desiring a wig only while going through a phase of transvestist behaviour, but a pure transsexualist generally finds such a need is not present until perhaps every avenue of satisfaction and help has been explored and the condition reaches breaking-point. By then, however, all conscious awareness has often been lost and, instead of a wig, the natural hair is usually allowed to grow.

This dressing up in secret, often with sexual motive, may for a number of years form the entire pattern of the individual's sex life, but the tension of the secrecy, the fear of being found out, the logical self-reasoning that points to insanity, and the knowledge that, whatever the effort to 'be better', the build-up will surely come again, all add up to an even greater conflict because of the guilt complex that results. However the transsexualist may be able to account logically for his feelings and behaviour it is never enough to compensate for this guilt complex, which begins to enter the mind at work and at play. The inability to escape from all these worries hangs as a heavy cloud, sapping the energy and leaving the sufferer less capable of pushing ahead in life or of serving humanity to the full.

Sometimes, a way of escaping is to become more occupied and engrossed in work, and for a time this may ease the condition and the closer application to work may equally have its rewards. Work and no outside interests, however, have their disadvantages; before long the mental and physical states fatigue, and without the energy to suppress the abnormal behaviour the condition becomes more acute and even less controllable than before. This is a particularly typical state of affairs, for the efforts to suppress the feelings and behaviour are greatest when the individual is well, refreshed, and on top of things. Conversely, as the individual becomes tired so ability to cope with the problem decreases; he retreats into his fantasy world, gives in more easily, and his desire to express himself emotionally and femininely becomes more desperate. It is then that the wish to 'change sex' builds up to powerful proportions, and appears the only logical solution to resolve the conflict and torment.

Yet, by the very nature of the trouble, the transsexualist has few outside interests or friends, and in his loneliness becomes highly introverted with his problems. His whole state of wellbeing is therefore constantly threatened, so that the factors encouraging physical and mental fatigue are rife. Much of this follows, not only from the abnormal sex life, but from the suppression of the normal social life, for since his whole outlook on life is feminine his masculine role is, by normal male standards, inferior, so that a deep-rooted inferiority complex exists and may show itself in many ways. Often, this feeling of inferiority may be covered up by forced aggressiveness. The need to conform and to prove masculinity when in company finds the individual going out of his way to appear normal, and he may resort to drinking pints of beer and smoking a pipe when he would much rather be sipping a gin and smoking a cigarette. The knowledge of often saying things out of place in company may cause a happy-go-lucky and joking manner to develop, so that any *faux pas* may be passed off as a joke. The mental torture caused by these efforts to conform and to hide the true feelings produces untold suffering, so that the choice has to be made between sapping all the energy by maintaining

212

this front or withdrawing completely from all social life. Either way, the transsexual man finds even the compensating influence of friends denied him, for in the competitive field of sport and love in a masculine world he is unplaced, and cannot form a normal friendship with a man by unreservedly sharing in his interests. Equally he has no girl friends, since the ability to say, do, and behave as expected to the opposite sex is not in him. So the vicious circle turns again, and any efforts at normality only force the individual to withdraw even more into his own completeness and his lonely world. On the sexual plane efforts at normal heterosexuality usually prove equally frustrating, and so the inward battle continues to rage, especially as the moral issues at this stage generally prevent any acceptance of abnormal or devious ways of living.

With the sex and social life as well as the work of the individual now affected, escapism is freely resorted to in an endeavour to escape from the hard world of reality and its problems. Many find this possible by going frequently to films, for here they can be alone and project themselves into the chosen character. Some indeed may choose to 'live' in the part of the starred actress, as an outlet to their emotions. They may see themselves in the same clothes, or 'making love' in the same way. Generally, anything to stir the emotional side and bring a tear gives relief from the tension caused by the hard reality of the outside world beyond the cinema. In the same way, novels, plays, and hobbies may provide the means of escape, whilst in others the craving for drink or drugs may form the means of transporting the individual into a rosier, less real world, so that he may even become an alcoholic or drug addict. Once in the world of romanticism, all the thoughts and desires can be moulded to fit the picture the transsexualists see of themselves. Age, anatomy, clothes and convention can be made to show no similarity to the truth, and a perfect example of the person they would wish to be, living in the most gratifying circumstances of being loved, cared for, or humbled, can for a time dissipate all the inhibitions and give freedom and peace of mind. Such may not only apply to the sexual plane, but can embrace any form or aspect of life. The daydream may then be of being someone different, of having another job, perhaps, or of doing something exceptional, so that they may be different but admired for some particular uncommon quality, in contrast to being scorned for being different as they are.

When every avenue has been explored to solve the problem, satisfaction is still unachieved in the behaviour and escapism is found to be disappointing, a last bid is often made to induce normality by resorting to marriage. 'Perhaps,' they say, 'this will at last make me normal, and it is, after all, what is expected of me.' The danger is, however, that this may be nothing but a desperate form of escapism, which far from solving any problems may, on the contrary, only inflict greater suffering upon the individual, by proving his abnormality even more surely and burdening him with greater responsibility and worry in the involvement of someone else. There is also an unfortunate twist to such a final effort at normality, for the very thing from which the transsexual man is trying to escape confronts him at every turn – a ready wardrobe of clothes belonging to his wife, clothes which include everything to satisfy his desires. The opportunity to indulge in devious behaviour is thus presented to him whenever his wife may be out or away, and such a golden chance is usually too good to miss. Once he realises the possibilities, any opportunity of being alone may be seized upon to relieve his emotions, so that before long his abnormal practices may become a regular habit. If he is found out by his wife, either through his carelessness or by accident, this will be an even more tragic development since, with the need for secrecy gone, he may feel able to dress up at any time whether his wife is at home or not. Should she try to be understanding, hoping to help her husband with his problem, he may take advantage even more and lose all sense of guilt or shame, without realising the mental torture he is inflicting on her. It is hard to imagine the feelings of any young wife who has to face up to such a situation, and there can be no doubt that any compulsion to marriage as a solution to the male transsexualist's problem is usually completely misguided.

As the condition progresses the transvestist fantasies manifest themselves more and more, and the mind becomes increasingly occupied with thoughts and pictures of how he would wish himself to be in reality. Such daydreams may enter into every moment of the sufferer's life, so that other forms of escapism may now become unnecessary, and as the transsexualist curls up in his shell, disowns the outside world and retreats into his lonely world of fantasy, his day-long conscious thoughts become reproduced in his unconscious moments of sleep, in his dreams. Such dreams may take all manner of forms, and in them the transsexual man may alternate between being dressed as a man and then as a woman. If his moral sense is powerful, and he dreams he is dressed as a woman in public, the guilt complex may disturb him. He may be concerned about his acceptance and whether he looks the part; he may be conscious of his anatomy under his masquerade, even though he may be aware that he is, in fact, dreaming. Every aspect of his problem, his thoughts, feelings, past life, present behaviour, and his desires for the future, may become intermixed, and pleasure, disappointment, heartache and conflict will merge. Waking only produces bewilderment or a violent reaction to the return to reality, frustration and tiredness leaving him less energy to cope with the day ahead and the ever-mounting problems.

Somehow, the faith remains that things might improve, and at moments of less sexual need the tension seems a little easier, so that closer application to work or a hobby may temporarily make life happier, and the will to try and 'be better' may give new hope of adjustment to normality. By now, the hope is a little half-hearted, however, for the transsexual man has learned from experience that similar past efforts have only failed, and that his desires and behaviour will surely build up again. Unconsciously then, the conflict is ever-present under the surface, waiting like some volcano to erupt into activity. These phases of activity and quiescence are common with a large number of cases, and they take on an almost cyclic pattern. Quite often, these cycles have a monthly frequency, which leads the sufferer to think they may be associated with 'moon madness', or perhaps be connected with some suppressed physiological function of the female cycle.

An important fact to note is that, in the earlier stages of

transsexualism, it is during the time immediately preceding the sexual climax, when the demand for a relief from the sex urge is most pressing, that the devious behaviour and desire to 'change sex' is at its height, and that once relief is obtained the desire is temporarily dissipated. Immediately before orgasm the individual decides he must and will 'change sex' at all costs, and cannot see that anything could possibly make him think differently. Yet, almost dramatically, immediately after orgasm the desire goes completely, and the individual wonders what made him have such feelings. He cannot get out of his female attire and back to his recognised role quickly enough, and he is left with an immense feeling of shame. So repulsed is he by his whole behaviour that, to try and dismiss it from his mind and make sure it will not happen again, he often at this stage burns his clothes or any photographs he may have of himself dressed up. Later on, as the tension builds up again, he dearly regrets this action and starts all over again. The continued shame and guilt make him only more certain that, if he could 'change sex', he would be rid of all these conflicts and his abnormal sexual behaviour, and be able to live at ease as he wants without ridicule, secrecy, or loneliness. The wish for treatment and the knowledge of other cases being helped now combine, and the possibility of actually taking action becomes more real. Quite often, however, the reluctance to expose his secret results in treatment not being sought.

As the transsexual man sees himself more and more as a woman logicalities go to the wind, and he will begin to believe anything he wants to. His mannerisms will change to fit his desired role and he will mentally castrate himself, believing that he really is a woman and that nature made some terrible mistake at birth. To be attracted to a man now seems quite natural and in no way homosexual, yet he may in fact now choose quite unconsciously the road to recognised homosexuality, justified by his feelings, in order to gain an outlet for his emotions without undue upheaval in his life and affairs. If he does not take this road, however, homosexuality, latent or otherwise cannot be applied, for the attraction to his own sex is but a symptom of his condition, and unconsciously he will be

216

on the main road to transsexuality. During his weaker moments he may take to wearing female garments under his own male clothes, finding he can now do this without too much conflict, and gradually he may also find that he can dress up without the immediate need for sexual relief. Masturbation therefore comes to play a lesser role; the act of dressing up is not attended with such guilt feelings, and before long the periods of attempted normality become shorter with a longer period of satisfaction and more permanent wish to play the female role. There is an associated growing revulsion to male clothes, and any new garments that have to be bought are chosen for their softness and possible similarity to female ones.

The condition is now drawing near its climax, for efforts at suppressing the tension within himself rapidly become ineffective and impossible. He has tried all he can; he is worn out with pretending and acting and trying to conform. He can do nothing more but give in and accept what he feels to be his true self. The climax itself may often be precipitated by some emotional upheaval not connected with his problem, but it is likely in any case to be marked by a nervous breakdown, as the breaking-point is reached and the giving in to failure at attempted normality has to be accepted. Such a breakdown may show symptoms of pain in any part of the body (possibly the stomach or back), lack of energy, depression, shortness of breath, rapid fatigue, sleeplessness, lack of mental concentration, shaking, crying, loss of appetite, general lack of interest etc. The individual may be slow recovering from these symptoms, and they may indeed persist until help is given, but in any case all sense of shame has gone, all inhibitions are lost, and the condition is looked upon with an almost casual and callous regard. The true climax of transsexualism has now been reached, at an age generally between 25 and 30. From now on a very definite picture builds up, but it is not one of more happiness and less conflict. Instead, it is really the beginning of the heartache, the torment, the frustration and desperation. It is a road beset with obstacles and constant barriers and brick walls. It is a state in which whatever is bad can get worse, and whatever is worse can become impossible; whatever is impossible will be unsurmountable, yet whatever is unsurmountable must still be borne.

So far, the act of dressing up has not had to be complete to give the desired satisfaction, but from now on every effort is directed towards achieving as complete a change of role as possible, both in dress and anatomy. Whatever few female garments the transsexual man may have do not now prove enough, and systematically a whole wardrobe is gradually built up. This may be difficult if the individual is living at home, so that if circumstances permit he may get a flat or small place of his own. The problem of buying female clothes is often overcome by telling the shop assistant they are for his wife or girlfriend, whilst others more easily embarrassed may undertake such purchases through the post, a means which presents ample opportunity. In the privacy of his own little place the transsexual man can dress up as often and for as long as his leisure time permits, and this may be all day on his day off from work or all over a weekend, provided he is sure of no interruptions. The sexual act itself is usually by now almost disconnected with the act of dressing up, and no longer is there a return to normality and a sense of shame after orgasm. Instead, the dressing up can be done without any need for masturbation, and should the urge develop any orgasm is but a passing phase to be well rid of, so that the individual can settle down at peace within himself to enjoy his assumed role of femininity.

In order to play his off-duty part to the full the hair is now allowed to grow, and if this is impossible through circumstances of his work or thinning hair, etc., it is now that the procuring of a wig becomes an absolute necessity. His state may also induce an almost fanatical need for personal cleanliness, so that a daily bath may replace a weekly one, and the hair may come in for regular twice-weekly washing. In some cases the dressing up becomes routine every evening once work has finished, and a bath may then become a necessity as if to wash off the taint of the daytime masculinity and to prevent soiling his 'femininity'. The hands are a major concern of the transsexualist and he abhors getting them dirty or scratching them, and even during the week as a man he will treat them with excessive care and use hand-cream to try and make them, and keep them, soft. The nails will also be cared for in the same way, allowed to grow long and kept immaculate and polished, and any breakage will greatly distress him out of all proportion to the damage caused. As with so many little things, they become a symbol of his femininity, and he will become hardened to criticism or comment about them, so much do they mean to him. Often the need to prove his own femininity to himself is great, so that every aspect of femininity is closely studied. What the normal woman has long ago left behind in her 'teens' and through gradual experience the transsexual man, in unleashing his outlet of expression for the first time, overplays the part. Everything must be just right. A perfectionist state develops. He plucks his eyebrows, shaves his legs, and may also spend hours of his time every so often plucking his facial hair, irrespective of the pain it may cause and regardless of the effect being but short-lived. He will study the mannerisms of women with whom he may come into contact and copy them, and he will disassociate himself from all forms of masculine behaviour, even denying himself the pleasures that such behaviour may, by virtue of his upbringing and interests, normally give him. He will attempt to avoid all vulgarity, considering it unfeminine, and pay more attention to what he considers the finer and nicer things in life.

Perfume and jewellery will have great attraction for him, and he may tend to overdress himself with rings, bracelets, ear-rings, and brooches. He will love to paint his fingernails a bright red, and to use cosmetics to the maximum, in his delight to feel and, as he believes, look feminine. He will study his 'vital statistics' carefully, assessing that he has really quite a small waist and that his measurements are in keeping with his 'true sex'. Any arguments that may deny the truth of this are rejected by him as totally unacceptable, for so convinced is he of his feminine state that he has almost hypnotised himself into the role. Indeed, whatever his appearance may be when fully dressed up, any imperfections will be masked by the peace of mind it gives him. It is not long before he ventures out of an evening, to satisfy himself that he is passable in the role, taking advantage of the dusk or darkness to help him in the test. The danger of being arrested does not seem very real to him, for to him his masquerade has no sexual motive, but in spite of his sincerity the possibility of an unexpected incident demanding a reason for his pose cannot be ruled out. Once he is confident, the masquerade may be undertaken in daylight also, and an even greater satisfaction result from this type of exhibitionism and fooling the public, as well as from the ability to express himself freely as his nature demands. Any female hormones he may have managed to obtain and take are, in such a short space of time, unlikely to help him better look the part, but mentally they will be a boost to his ego and help him to feel 'right' in his role.

Back in the privacy of his home, whilst playing the female role, the transsexual man will take great pride and pleasure in doing all the normal feminine chores. He will enjoy making his place neat and tidy, doing housework and cooking, etc., as well as being happy doing his washing or sewing. He will say he is never happier than when living like this, and would give anything to be able to live as a woman permanently, looking upon the world as a cruel place when it eventually becomes necessary to resume wearing male clothes. The adoption of such a dual role becomes a very specialised art in some cases, although many others find such behaviour against their moral principles and confine their dressing up to the privacy of their own rooms. This means, however, that they cannot go out unless they redress as a man, and so, although they feel 'caged' and fed up with staying in, they invariably still choose to give up going out rather than take off their female clothes. Wearing female night attire has already become a well-established part of the picture, and to curl up within a frilly nightdress produces sheer delight, so much so that sleep would be denied them in any other way.

With the figure in mind a dread of putting on weight can develop, causing the individual to deny himself food which he would otherwise enjoy, and he may condition himself not to feel hungry in order to obey his obsession. Every aspect of the outside world distresses him, as wherever he goes and whatever he sees or does emphasises the sharp dividing line between the two sexes. If he walks down the street he will pass dress shop after dress shop, and, as a man, feel barred from even looking in the windows, let alone having the supreme satisfaction of going in, selecting, purchasing, and being able to wear such 'enrapturing creations'. At these thoughts he may become so emotionally distressed as to shed a tear, and his heart will ache for the 'change of sex' that means so much to him. If he picks up a newspaper he may see pictures of happy brides, or have his attention drawn by a special page for women. If he goes to a film, it will possibly be about love and marriage, and there may be children in it, and the impact that the wonderful natural feminine things in life will always be denied him, even if he is able to change his role, brings fresh depression to the conflict. There is no escape now from his condition; the obsession is complete. He must surely get help to assist him in a 'change' or life will just cease within him. 'If only I could get some female hormones,' he thinks, that would be a start, for surely he read somewhere how they had been given in other cases. He need not look further than all the cuttings he has carefully put away about other cases who have 'changed sex'. He doesn't know what effect they might have on him personally but is determined to go to any lengths to obtain some, and, if he has already confided in a medical adviser, he will press desperately for a prescription. If this is not the case, and he finds he is turned down by the chemist, an advertisement for hormone pellets for implanting into cockerels may catch his eye, and at great risk to his health he may obtain and take as many of these pellets by mouth as he dare, even though they make him violently ill. In spite of possible harm, he will refuse to believe they are doing him other than good, and may even envisage changes in himself. If he is wise, however, he will realise that his correct and only course is to seek proper medical treatment. Indeed, since the obsession is complete and he is set on a 'change' regardless of all factors, logical or otherwise, he **must** seek treatment in order to achieve his desire. Thus, his round of medical practitioners, psychiatrists, and surgeons commences.

In spite of earlier hesitations about discussing his problem with his own doctor, when he does get round to it now it is not so much to ask his advice as to tell him of his desire, and how determined he is to pursue the only course he has convinced himself is open to him. The sufferer never really believes his doctor can understand or know much about the subject, assuming that the chances of his having encountered even one other case is remote. Also, he feels his doctor, like so many, will only sex him on his genital organs, regardless of any other factors, and will doubtless tell him to pull himself together and conform to the role in which his organs place him. The challenge has become too great, however, for the male trans-sexualist to be deterred by anything the doctor may say; all he really wants is a prescription for female hormones and an introductory letter to a specialist on the subject. Just what help he gets depends largely on the doctor, and on his own circumstances and need. Some doctors may, in fact, prescribe female hormones in small doses for a short time, as a sedative measure or just to defer having to take any more immediate and definite action. Other doctors may be in close touch with a teaching hospital, and feel the case warrants being referred to it for more expert advice and treatment.

Should the transsexual man find his doctor entirely unco-operative he may change to another, but in any event, when the need is pressing enough, the patient will first be referred to a psychiatrist. At last he may open his heart of all his conflicts, feelings, behaviour, and desires, but although he now has someone in whom he can confide, and will make visit after visit to try and prove his justification for help with a 'change of sex', he will often feel no more relieved, since anything that is said against him reaching his goal only frustrates him more. He is likely to go from one psychiatrist to another, usually at his own expense, in the hope that eventually he may find someone who will believe in him and be willing to put him in touch with a surgeon who may consider giving him the operations he feels will make the difference between his being a man or a woman. By this time the antagonism to the male organs is acute, and the sufferer develops such an emasculation complex that he may even threaten to operate on himself, if no help is forthcoming. Although the extreme risk of such a procedure is pointed out to him he can see nothing else that matters, since anything that stands in the way of his objective must be crushed. So strong is the determination at this stage that the male transsexualist is prepared to walk over every obstacle and everybody, irrespective of what is practical, possible, or legal. He looks ahead in blinkers, seeing only his goal, so driven by his obsession that his mental state, if not already affected, falls prey to his condition. The urge is there and it must be satisfied, as surely as a violent itch builds up a frantic need to be resolved by scratching, regardless of the knowledge that such scratching may infect or injure the itching area and be a self-inflicted and detrimental action.

The sufferer insists that he will bear full responsibility for operations, and that whatever may have been the result in other cases (if there have been any regrets with them) he is altogether different. If only he can have the operations to remove his penis and testes, he says, this will make him the happiest person alive and transport him from a life of misery into a world of ecstasy and joy. He maintains he is only asking to be allowed to live as nature intended, and has a right to such an existence from humanity as surely as any individual. His only other major problem seems to be his facial hair, and his thoughts turn to a way of being rid of it. Treatment by electrolysis becomes a very serious consideration, and a real effort to obtain a home electrolysis outfit may be made. Disappointment is likely to be the outcome, however, in view of the skill required for self-treatment, the tough and usually numerous hair follicles, and the possibility of scarring. The more reliable and professional approach to the problem, by diathermy, finds the sufferer searching for a clinic that will be sympathetic and prepared to help, but even then the considerable patience required, as well as the cost, are deterrent factors, not to mention the time required for the vast number of visits. In the meantime the demand for surgery and the search for a surgeon to perform the operations continues. Nothing will deter the now confirmed transsexualist, for each refusal only makes him more determined than ever, and when he has exhausted the possible avenues of help in his own country he will probably spend his savings going abroad, searching one country after another for a surgeon to help him, only to be disappointed again and again. On his return he will renew his contacts, and proceed on his rounds of the teaching hospitals, for however much his hope is dampened it is never extinguished, and, though years may pass in the process, his determination to be successful in the end is never lost.

During all this time the pleasures of living have been passing him by, and he is so wrapped up in his conflict and problem that his introverted state envelops him. His energy is gone; he is not only desperate, but frantic for help. Every aspect of his torment is upon him, and life loses its purpose. From having renewed strength and hope for pressing his case he will sink to the lowest ebb of depression and despair, with attendant tiredness, loss of interest, and easy flow of tears. These states will fluctuate, each fresh hope only rising to be thwarted again and precipitate an even deeper and longer depression. Suicide comes constantly into the thoughts as the only way out, and the sufferer can amass any number of reasons for justifying ending everything. When things are at their blackest some do, in fact, plan suicide and may make an attempt at it. Occasionally one is unfortunately successful in his attempt, but the majority live to fight another day. And with each day the fight for life and existence continues.

Although the foregoing pattern of general behaviour is relevant to the condition of transsexualism in its overall form, it should be emphatically stressed that the picture is a composite one and does not necessarily apply to any one individual or case. The *manner* of the build-up is thus a constant and common feature, but, whereas the behaviour as outlined may fit one case accurately throughout, quite a large range of variation occurs in each individual, although this still remains within the framework given. We must remember, too, that the behaviour depends very much upon opportunity and circumstances, as well as class, upbringing, and the moral approach to life, and because of this the transvestist behaviour may be limited in its extent or even be entirely absent. In some, the extreme obsession may reach its climax rapidly, although much depends upon the individual seeking the right help at the right time or being fortunate in getting medical assistance, either with a 'change' or to a more logical approach to life. Some may have a greater degree of justification for readjustment to their desired role, and so possibly seek and obtain help as soon as the first breaking-point comes, before any undue devious behaviour has taken command. These may be on one extreme end of the scale and have no need to consider problems of facial and body hair, be completely neutral in their attitude to sex, possess no wardrobe of female clothes, and live and conform entirely to their supposed sex whilst their problem is medically sorted out. Others, on the other end of the scale, may progress through all the stages and phases of the behaviour, and embrace all the aspects of the problem in the manner described.

Much of what has been written about the various behaviour of the transsexualist should therefore be taken only as a guide, and by no means be attributed to every case as a hard and fast label. Such behaviour is in any case only a symptom of the condition, and, although it cannot be condoned, it should also not be unduly condemned by the supposedly normal and right-thinking people who are blessed with other but more acceptable forms of outlet for their sexual satisfaction and emotions. There can be no burying of the head in the sand, or pretending that such things do not exist because they are too 'nasty' to think about. Few things in a hard world of reality and suffering humanity are very nice, but to be willing to learn of problems, to try and understand them, and then be happy to share in overcoming them is the mark of both humility and greatness.

CHAPTER FIVE

BASIC TYPES OF CASES

WE HAVE ALREADY seen that no state or condition of sexuality is necessarily rigid in its specific application to any one group of individuals, and that, by virtue of large variations within the defined limits, even the conditions themselves can merge one into the other. In this sense to call a person a transsexualist can only be a generalisation, for the differing and complex causative factors which account for the resulting feelings and behaviour vary in each case, both in degree and type. Where factors and circumstances are similar, however, grouping of cases is possible to some extent. The writer has therefore formulated a classification of the basic types, to permit closer study of the subject and also to branch away from the necessity of generalisation, which, although useful, does not always apply equally and accurately in every case.

To establish a fixed point on which to base the different types the state of immaturity has been chosen, since it is the common feature of all cases. It can be likened to the point of intersection on an 'X', the two lower legs representing the range of variation in the causative factors, the intersection the common point of immaturity, and the two upper legs the divergent effects that may result. We can therefore base our classification and sub-division of cases on the reasons for this immaturity, and the manner in which they affect the individual. We must, however, fix firmly in our minds what we mean by immaturity, and it will help if we first consider the meaning of *maturity*.

Maturity can be defined as a state of being fully grown. It implies ripeness and having reached perfection. Although we are only concerned with the human aspect here it can apply to any number of processes, and represents a stage that is reached when the whole purpose of the development attains its desired and intended result to the full. Maturity or immaturity can only be accurate in meaning, therefore, when the process to which it refers is aptly qualified also. Often it is only considered in terms of physical development, but when applied to psychological or mental development its implications can be vast. As an example on the physical side, we may rightly assume that the production of the spermatozoa in the male, and of the ova in the female, at puberty, represents sexual maturity, since it is the function of the reproductive organs to produce these cells in order that another individual may be conceived and born. Yet we may be confused that a normal male, for instance, who is capable of intercourse and fathering a child, can be said to be immature. The reason is, of course, that the term can apply not only to body development but to the mental development as well, and, indeed, immaturity is a word to be found extensively in psychiatrists' reports. Strictly speaking, if we consider it to be a state appertaining to a person as a whole being, all the factors and processes involved must come under review. Thus the body processes cannot be separated from the mental development, or the urges from the resultant feelings and behaviour. In this sense, maturity may be said to be when all parts of the personality work together, sex being but one aspect of the ability to share in the mind and interests of the opposite partner, or of the world at large, in the fulfilment of pleasure and in bringing to perfection the whole state of well-being of the individual.

It is not difficult to see, then, why so many of us remain immature, and why being totally introverted or self-satisfyingly individual does not lend itself to an acceptable bond being formed between us and the rest of society, upon whom we rely for so much of our pleasure and satisfaction. Every one of us is constantly striving throughout life to find more happiness and satisfaction, and in this respect full perfection and maturity come to few if any of us. It is often a question, however, of what society considers normal and mature, or otherwise abnormal and immature, and by these standards we are judged. Since the majority of cases with whom we are about to deal have little or no apparent or known justification for their feelings, and are to all accepted standards anatomically normal, immaturity is applied in the psychological sense. Whatever the cause, they have failed to come to terms with life, unable to express

227

themselves as they would wish; their mental conflicts have jeopardised their normal development, and prevented them from reaping the satisfaction of usefulness in life.

Similarly, the sexual state has become stifled and deviated into abnormal ways, with continued masturbation a significant feature. Often, adverse factors of upbringing and environment, not strong enough to sway the 'growth' of the normal individual, may readily affect the transsexualist already in conflict with himself and ill at ease in his role. He may already have been told that it is wrong to do this and wrong to do that, and that sex is something not to be mentioned, so his guilt complex is easily engendered. In the male, hatred of his genital organs and of his sex may be increasingly stimulated in this way, leading to an emasculation complex and a furtherance of his feminine feelings, on the assumption that if he were a female he would only have to concern himself with the 'nicer' things in life, and not have to bother with sex. The latter is viewed on the basis that he need not play his sex part as the 'chaser', as expected of him as a man, but that his role of being 'chased' would exonerate him from all guilt and responsibility concerning the 'evil' act. Since immaturity is such a part of this condition it rarely resolves itself even with a change of role, since the factors which caused it are difficult to shut out.

We can now proceed to examine seven basic types of cases. Each example refers to an actual individual, although for obvious reasons precise details have been omitted where necessary in order to ensure that identification is in no way possible.

The Immature type

Although all cases are to some extent immature, some show this to a marked degree, the whole upbringing, attitude to life, knowledge of the outside world and sex, and inability to accept responsibility being features which are characteristic to the extreme of individuals in this category. The picture of just such a case presents itself in this way:

Mr. A, aged 25 and in the catering trade, has been subject all his life to over-doting parents, having to conform very much to home life and the parents' interests. As a result, he has been made to believe that whatever his parents say is right, is right, and whatever they say is wrong, is wrong, and he has not been allowed to think for himself. Everything has been done for him, as considered to be best for him, and any association with others of his own age has been resisted on the grounds that he may get into trouble or into bad habits. He has been sheltered from the outside world and has come to know little about it, and he finds it difficult to cope with everyday things. With few outside activities, and only occasional visits to the cinema with friends of the family much older than himself, he has had to fall back on the love of his parents. They have therefore come to mean very much to him, so that his own feelings and need for expression have been forced into the background under their dominating influence.

The result has been to cause a great deal of conflict in his mind, and recurrent bouts of depression have become a common feature, life at times seeming impossible. He is subject to moodiness, feeling he is tied to his parents and must do nothing to hurt them, whilst in his heart he craves to be free and live a life of his own. Yet he knows it would hurt him as much as his parents if he left home, and, not being brought up to face the world alone, he feels frightened at the thought of it, for even a long journey gives him the fear of being lost. The great problems of his transsexual feelings therefore build up on him, and, without the ability or desire to mix with others of his own age and share in their interests, his conflict and thoughts are churned over and over back in his own private dream world at home. Sexually, he has never been attracted to girls, because of the need to plough his affection back into his family. In the same way, normal masculine mental development has been retarded, and, instead of attaining confidence in himself and ability to accept responsibility, he has remained weak and only feels happy when protected and loved. His mannerisms have automatically and unconsciously taken the same pattern, pseudo-feminine in type. This has often encouraged the attention of those with homosexual tendencies, much to his displeasure, though naïvely knowing little of the reason for the attraction.

He has, if anything, striven to keep his feelings to himself, and confined his sexual relief to masturbation, having to play at 'secret service', as he puts it, in his own home. Any opportunity to practise transvestism does not therefore present itself, and being an only child he has little ability and too much embarrassment to procure female garments, although the thought of them thrills him very much. Putting on make-up proved an easier form of satisfaction, with less degree of risk, and, since puberty, the thought of possibly being able to 'change sex' and fit more easily into life has always been a longing wish. His circumstances, as well as his great sense of moral duty, mean that any thought of a 'sex change' has to be based on help, with his parents' consent. The knowledge that his parents do not understand, and that far from giving their blessing would if anything fight him over it, causes him to live in a permanent state of nervous tension. He is therefore easily upset, emotionally unstable, and has strong guilt feelings. By nature he is a very sensitive, kind and loving individual, and because of this his need to refrain from hurting his parents forces him to inhibit his desire for a change, much as it has come to mean the only thing in his lonely world. Unable to express himself, he mentally lives the lives of others he has read about who have supposedly changed sex, and a well-guarded scrap-book containing all the newspaper cuttings of such cases exists, to further the belief that what others have done he may still be able to do one day. Even to write about his problems overwhelms him emotionally and makes him unable to express himself adequately. He dislikes being called 'Mister', and feels so ashamed of his body that he declines to go swimming because of feeling embarrassed in a bathing costume.

A significant feature is his reluctance to seek medical advice and treatment. This is largely due to a fear of having to tell his secret, although his lack of drive and way of going about finding a specialist is also against him, because of his immature state. Once, when he did manage to tell a doctor of some of his difficulties, in the hope of getting hormones, he received a strong rebuke, and although he had relied upon the doctor's discretion and the confidence that any patient over 21 deserves and expects, his family were informed. This only increased his suffering, for, by inhibiting his desire to get proper medical help, because of his parents' even tighter hold on him, he was, in his own words, 'sentenced to a life of hell'. 'I just don't know how I am going to go on!' he said.

It is obvious that the parents are sincere in their intentions but in years he is a grown man, and still to have to give an account of his every movement, and just where he is going at any time and why, can only restrict Mr. A's own mental development and maintain his immaturity, which has all along been behind his desire to 'change sex'. There is little likelihood of an adjustment to normality while this state of affairs exists; this sort of thing cannot be hidden under the carpet – it can be suppressed for a time and then it will even more forcefully erupt. The facts must be faced by the parents. The facts must be logically explained to the individual. New interests and friends are essential. Above all, proper medical advice should be sought, and the individual must be taught how to stand on his own feet and to cope with life. At the moment his world seems empty and pointless, and there is little depth to his life, yet his gifts of love, kindness and sincerity can give so much happiness to himself and to the world, for they are gifts too fine to be denied humanity. They are the gifts of a child, but they can also be the gifts of an adult if only he can be helped along the road to maturity.

The Aesthetic type

These cases are typified by their sensitivity of feeling; their desire of everything that is fine and clean; their love of music and the arts; their affection for everything that is small, helpless, or needs looking after; their great powers of thought, and the possession of an obsessive personality. Their disassociation of all fine things from masculinity appears to be the key to the development of their transsexualist desire, since they feel they cannot express these finer emotions and still remain manly. Their conception of what applies to the male sex and what applies to the female sex is very rigid. They establish views

231

to the effect that with masculinity must be associated anything that is dirty, rough, coarse and vulgar, an inability to feel and sense beautiful things or to appreciate them, and above all an incapability to express deep love, either in a partnership or towards humanity generally. They consider a man's life is shallow and superficial, beset with challenges and impulsive activity to meet them, as a means to an end. On the other hand, they look upon femininity as a symbol of purity, cleanliness, finesse, charm and gracefulness, gentleness and beauty etc., representing the capability of real love and devotion, a deeper awareness of life, and an affinity with everything that is aesthetic, lovely and wonderful. Feeling they possess these latter qualities, these cases therefore shun their masculinity and stimulate their desire to be a woman.

Cases in this group are essentially intelligent and useful citizens of good class and education. They exhibit all the usual early feelings and behaviour of the transsexualist, but master their difficulties more capably. This is shown by the definite effort they make to act the male, and the success they make of it. They are more likely, therefore, to conform to heterosexuality, although the pressure in the opposite direction may tend from time to time to be too much for them, giving rise to some degree of bisexuality. Their immaturity is therefore dependent upon the fluctuating forces within them. Particularly significant is their capability of great drive once they have made up their mind about anything, and it is this drive which builds up the obsession to 'change sex'. Yet the obsession in turn increases the drive, so that a vicious circle results and, in this way, the matter can either go completely out of control or can be reversed to such an extent as to cause a return to normality, provided the illogicality of associating aesthetic characteristics with the female sex can be forcefully brought home to them.

The following example is of an individual who not long ago was plunging headlong into the unknown, through his extreme obsession. Circumstances presented themselves, however, whereby he has been able to discover the true facts, and by virtue of his own logical reasoning he has now made a swift return to normality as a male, and is left bewildered that he

232

could ever have had such fancies and ideas. Whether this is but another transient phase, however, only time will tell.

Mr. B, aged 34 and an engineer by profession is an only child. His father exerted considerable influence over him, expecting him to conform rigidly to his masculine role. Anything that was in the least feminine by thought, nature, or deed was denied him, and his love of the more aesthetic and beautiful things in life had to be suppressed under a hard and superficial front. He longed to express himself freely, but his love for his parents and his reasoning persuaded him that he must do what was 'right' and expected of him. He was a delicate and sensitive child and brought up to believe that sex should never be mentioned, and at puberty was told it was wrong for him to 'play' with his erotic areas. Even at the age of 18 he was discouraged from having anything to do with girls, on the grounds that there were more important things in life with which he should occupy his mind. This early suppression of his normal and natural sex feelings led him to find his sexual outlet in perversion, and female underclothes became, to him, the symbol of his desire to be a woman. To procure and wear such clothes gave him the sexual excitement that he was otherwise denied, and once he had started the occasional behaviour of wearing such items he found the softness and prettiness of them appealed to the aesthetic side of his nature. Gradually the aesthetic pleasure of dressing up became more important than the sexual aspect, and, by a process of rationalisation, he reasoned that if only he were a girl he could always dress as he wanted to, without secrecy or guilt, and at the same time give expression to all his finer feelings. Thus sex no longer mattered, and the possession of the male organs became not only a nuisance but completely abhorrent, standing between him and the life he so desired.

This produced an ever-increasing conflict, between the world as he was made to see it and the entirely opposite world of his dreams. The pattern of his behaviour was dominated by this conflict, and he would swing from masculinity to femininity and back again. During his masculine phase he would revert to excessive masculinity as his upbringing taught him, be completely heterosexual, dominant, energetic, and at home in a fight.

During his feminine phase he became shy and reticent, would over wash and bathe, be very particular about keeping his hands and nails clean, avoid dirty jobs, and want to be admired and made love to. His whole attitude of mind and personality would alter according to the clothes he was wearing, and, as a woman, he felt nicer, more natural, and experienced wonderful peace of mind. These feelings were missing when dressed as a man, and he strove more and more for an explanation of this, which led him to become introverted and to write of his troubles. These self-writings became a part of his efforts to try to find some logical explanation for his state and problem, and at the same time to convince himself that any desire for a 'change of sex' was justified and not just a superficial fancy. Once, during a masculine phase, he re-read some of his writings and was so swayed by them that it immediately produced a feminine phase.

Eventually, nothing short of a physical change of sex would make life worth living one day longer. Having decided this was the course, all the resources of his strong will, his education and his drive were mobilised in an attempt to achieve his object. In his obsession he would spend more than he could afford on female clothes, and, being a 'perfectionist', would pay great attention to small detail, not being content until he supplied his measurements for clothes to be made for him, for everything had to be just right and the best. In physique, Mr. B is tall and thin, athletic and with sensitive features, and although with rather less facial and body hair than one would expect to find in the average man any feminine characteristics he possesses appear to be well masked by his male clothes. Yet he had reached this stage whereby he had mentally come to look upon himself as a woman. 'It does not matter how ugly I might be,' he wrote, 'lack of physical attractiveness as a woman would be compensated by my charm, sincerity, and selflessness. It is having to pretend that makes life so intolerable. My body is the thing that causes me such mental distress, and it is surely easier to alter a body than a mind, for the mind is one's very soul and personality.' So obsessed was he by this time that he even rejected lifetime pleasures, because they appeared masculine and not in keeping with acceptance of his femininity. He would have still loved to have got under his car or looked into shop windows at model toys etc., but his obsession refused him permission to do it.

His capability, so typical of this group, enabled his determination to be employed to the full. His craving for female hormones did not go unrewarded, and for six months he took large daily doses, but they produced little effect beyond arresting his sexual activity and easing his tensions. It was to be but a first step to seeking help with a physical 'change of sex' by operation, for, to him, he either had to be all man or all woman. He readily accepted that there would be limitations to a 'change', however, but without one he felt he would either spiritually or physically die. Also, since he would rather be physically than spiritually dead, he said, he was left with little choice. He concluded his writings by saying: 'My plans are to obtain hormone treatment as a palliative, and to seek with all my strength for help with a physical change of sex. I am ashamed at such ignoble and unworthy aims, yet it is impossible that I will be any use to the world unless and until this is achieved. For I have one other ambition, and that is to serve my Creator, whoever or whatever He may be, and I seek only to loose the bonds that prevent me from doing it.'

As stated earlier, this case has now reverted completely to his normal male outlook on life, for his powers of logic and understanding have enabled him to see the flaws in his arguments. He has seen that nothing will alter him biologically and he realises that his second state might be worse than the first. Yet his finer feelings remain and neither will they ever alter. For why should they? If the world had more people with his judgement and depth of emotion, warmth of heart and love of God's gifts of life, it would be a long way towards offering mankind the peace and brotherhood that is so sadly lacking.

The Oedipus type

The Oedipus situation is one that is generally accepted to-day as being produced by the child's emotional disturbances and conflicts in the adjustment to its family influences and environment. When the development of transsexualism can be traced

235

to such a situation the Oedipus type of case emerges, and the general pattern and possible course of development arising out of these early conflicts forms the basis of our study of cases under this heading.

The Oedipus situation is one we are all supposed to experience to some degree during our upbringing, although in normal practice we gradually suppress it, and so important is it in influencing our minds that one can hardly envisage a book on psychological medicine without mention of it. It takes its name from the legend of Oedipus, a foundling, who on growing up and returning to his homeland unknowingly killed his father and married his own mother. When he found out what he had done he was so overcome with remorse that he gouged out his own eyes. In the male, the condition arises through the child developing a mother fixation. The earliest associations are with the mother, in the warmth of her breasts and in her love, long before the awareness of sex, but as the boy grows and learns to appreciate his sex he realises he is meant to grow up like his father. He therefore becomes jealous of his father's love for his mother, and so hates taking second place that his father becomes his rival, and he conjures up all manner of mental fantasy to oust his father's position. He knows he must repress these feelings, however, and this in itself is hurtful enough, but to realise it is wrong to have such feelings anyway produces immense conflict and guilt within him, and fear of punishment by mutilation or castration builds up. If these fears become exaggerated they may continue throughout life as a complex, instead of being left behind as part of the growing-up phase. When this occurs, the feeling that punishment should be meted out persists, and the thought that the guilt can only be removed by submitting to such punishment may lead the individual to wish and long for a castration, and gain peace of mind by being rid of sex completely.

We find cases in this group, then, typically antagonistic to their father and drawn to their mother; sex has been pushed into the background and they have developed a barrier to reality and are unable to accept logic, but put on a hard front to life. They are quite normal physically, and show no desire to exhibit female tendencies. Their transvestist behaviour is on a small scale only, and they have never had or sought after female hormones. Often in childhood they have been made to dress as a girl as punishment, and hated the ridicule so that the torment has never left them. They have lost their faith in humanity; they may take to drugs or to drink as a means of dulling their senses and conflict. Essentially they are confused about exactly what they want, and often show suicidal tendencies. Generally, then, these cases are forced into medical care, although their belief that a 'sex change' is the answer may not emerge because of lack of courage and the thought of ridicule – ridicule which has for so long been their dread and done so much to foster their problem.

Mr. C is just such a case. He is now 44, and has held high positions in the chemical processing industry. He is essentially masculine in appearance and physique, and makes no effort to appear otherwise. Having had one son, his parents wanted a girl when he was born, and there seems little doubt that his upbringing was affected by this (see also pages 184 and 185). His early life follows the pattern we have just been discussing, and the parents' desire for a girl may have prompted their action in dressing him as such as a pretext to punishment. This caused considerable mental torment, and life became so unbearable that at the age of 14 he ran away from home, making up his mind that no one would ever laugh at him or ridicule him again. He has never seemed to recapture his faith in humanity, and has acquired a hard, aggressive attitude to life, to the suppression of all his softer emotions. He never feels settled or appears to have any real objective in life, and although he has tried logically to understand himself the failure to find an explanation only increases his guilt feelings.

Although a part of him cries out to dress at times in women's clothes, the fear of ridicule should such behaviour be discovered opposes this. Often, however, he feels impelled to buy some female garments and hurries back to put them on in private, but almost immediately afterwards his sense of guilt makes him burn or otherwise destroy his newly acquired clothes. He has always suppressed anything to do with sex, and lived as if holding the lid down on a boiling kettle, involving constant effort, vigil and strain. From time to time the tension becomes too great, and he will leave his job and try to run away from the world and from himself. Because of this, he has no friends and feels a lonely outcast of society. In an effort to drown his troubles he has taken to drinking heavily. This, he says, often weakens his suppressions, so that it makes him more desperate to express his femininity. At other times, he says, it makes him feel that nothing is of use any more. His inability to cope with life has brought him into contact with psychiatrists, but only recently has he managed to tell something of his inner wish for femininity. This took so much out of him that he cried bitterly whilst telling his story.

Both his parents are dead, his brother has drifted away from him, and without friends he feels completely alone in the world, life going from one crisis to another. He admits that any attempted change of role would only make things more difficult for him, and even understands that it is, in his case, quite impractical and impossible, yet in spite of knowing this he is not altogether able to accept it. The denial of self-expression is interpreted by him as a denial of the feminine part of his make-up, yet his rigid refusal to be other than hard and completely masculine, in order to spare his guilt feelings, splits his personality and enables him to make use of one half of it only. The real craving, then, is not so much for femininity, much as it is rationalised into this, but the craving to be a whole person. Consequently, he does not really know what he does want, except to be released from some overpowering burden.

There seems little doubt that he has put up a strong barrier between himself and the outside world, and that this is very deep-rooted in its origin, back in childhood. Until the inner force demanding expression is free and this barrier can be eliminated by normal conscious reasoning, Mr. C's life is not likely to alter. Whilst the barrier is maintained words and logic are of no avail, and there is always the danger that things will go from bad to worse. The solution lies within himself, by appreciating his surroundings and by learning more of the outside world and what he can offer humanity. He is a person

238

of kind disposition and with a genuine character, but he often pities himself and reflects on his failings. He should count his blessings and remember that every new day is a challenge to us all, and that it is only through hope for the future that we can live to-day.

The Homosexual type

This type has been so called because of the possible origin of the condition and certain features of the behaviour pattern, but it does not follow that cases in this group are necessarily homosexuals in the accepted sense. Homosexuality can only be applied accurately once we have established, beyond a shadow of doubt, the true sex of the individual, taking into account all the known (as well as admitting to the unknown) complex factors that go to make up sex. If, for any reason, attraction to the assumed same sex presents itself, therefore, we must be careful to examine every aspect of this before we apply the term homosexuality. We do not look upon a girl's attraction to a man as homosexuality, because we accept and agree that the girl is a girl. Unquestionably, these cases, as with the others, are anatomically male, but the important thing to realise is that they are attracted to men because, mentally, they look upon themselves as female. Their attraction and therefore their homosexual leanings, then, are generally a symptom of this outlook. In true homosexuals, the desired relationship is only with another homosexual. The cases in this group, however, want what they see as a 'normal' heterosexual relationship and dismiss angrily any suggestion that they or their partners may be of homosexual orientation. They do not want the sex act that takes place between two men but the sex act as they see it between a man and a woman. Hence the provision of an artificial vagina is very necessary for those in this group, sex being an active ingredient of the 'change'. In this respect they are different from the generally accepted passive homosexual, who, although being sexually excited by taking the woman's passive role, would rebel at operation or losing his sexual ability because he would immediately lose the satisfaction of the masquerade, and be denied the sexual pleasure that is so much a part of his life.

From early childhood cases of this type may, because of their feminine outlook upon life, show their affection for other boys. Being more sexually minded than those in the other groups, their feelings extend into a form of love relationship, so that when with a boy playmate they may regard the association on the basis of a boy-and-girl sweetheart affair. These typical early homosexual leanings develop more as the individual grows up, and may be openly displayed in the professed enjoyment of playing female roles in amateur theatricals or at fancy-dress parties. In this respect they differ from the previous types mentioned, who fight shy of showing their feelings and become embarrassed should any indication of their secret world be exposed.

Again they differ, in that they usually have a large number of friends, many of whom know of the individual's feminine feelings and transsexual desires. Transvestism is practised openly, being rationalised as a process of rehabilitation to the role he one day will adopt, and as an expression of his 'true-self' and sex. The guilt complex is not evident, and a large wardrobe of female clothes and accompanying accessories relevant to a woman's life is generally amassed. It is the clothes, the thrill of the masquerade, and the feeling of being 'natural' which produces the satisfaction, and they think how wonderful it would be if only they could be like it all the time, able to go about the world freely in the female role, and will resentfully only be a man for the purposes of their work, adopting the female role at all other times and not hesitating to go out dressed as a woman, to a friend, to post a letter, or to buy feminine attire for themselves.

When the climax of this behaviour is reached, the hatred of having to change back and be a man again for work becomes so intense that every effort is made to be rid of the conflict of the dual role. They then press for an implant of female hormones and for operations to free them of their genital stereotyping, so that their dream world may come true and the full time life of a woman be theirs. Sometimes they will be forced to take the step of living permanently as an environ-

240

mental woman even without medical help but the desire for operation is always there, for, although they may mentally be able to assume the non-existence of their male organs, the wish to be a 'normal' woman sexually is everpresent, feeling that their attractiveness to a man depends upon it.

Although cases in this group have homosexual leanings, then, and exhibit marked transvestist behaviour, the state is still strictly one of transsexualism in spite of the more devious methods of expression and different approach to the goal. There is always a marked tendency to exhibitionism; to this group almost invariably belong those cases who find their way into the entertainment world as female impersonators and who, as a result, learn the art of how to make-up, to dress and to feminise themselves, often before the secondary sexual characteristics and the adult masculine way of life have become dominantly established. Any 'change' then often comes earlier than with other cases in this group, and is therefore likely to be more successful, both physically and psychologically. Unfortunately, publicity, however depraved, is generally revelled in, and full co-operation given to the Press to sensationalise their 'change', both to satisfy their exhibitionist trait and as a means of making easy money. At the same time, there is usually the further hope of glorying in their 'fantastic' achievement and of demanding a large salary in show business as a unique and public figure. It is, indeed, a great pity that the public are kept in the dark as to the true facts, just because this pays better commercially.

Mr. D is a case who comes under the general classification of this group. He is 42, of good education and social standing, and has two elder brothers. He has served several years in the Forces by choice, and is by profession an engineer. As a child he says he was often mistaken for a girl, because of the way he was dressed. He always felt like a girl, but at school hated the possibility of being thought a 'cissy', and counteracted this by deliberately assuming masculinity, playing rugby and cricket and even being good at them. He was happiest when called upon to play the female parts in plays, however, which relieved his inner feelings and made him feel natural; he would 'live' the part, and feel an attraction to the boy he played opposite. Since school, any opportunity to dress up in public has been seized upon, such as at amateur concerts, etc., and to see others dress up as the opposite sex has always produced a great thrill. Unfortunately, youngsters would often be encouraged in this behaviour.

He seems to have been well able to cope with life as a man, in spite of his conflicts, although he appears to have been to one doctor after another either because of his physical or mental state. Although he is attracted to men he emphatically rejects homosexuality, but having come to disregard himself as a man he justifies the attraction since he feels it is in no way sexual. Indeed, he professes that the loss of sex function by operation would not distress him but that, on the contrary, the gratification of being less masculine by such an operation, and therefore more feminine, would be immense. Mr. D, having seen so much of life, appears to be free of the mental barrier put up by so many other cases, although he similarly is unable to accept thngs he does not want to. His conversation is easy and flowing, and outwardly he gives the impression of knowing well which way he is going, as if he has the situation well under control. Inwardly, however, the conflict and tension are still there, leading so commonly to depression.

Mr. D has now been more and more accepting his femininity and living as a woman. To do this he has a small flat away from all possible disturbance and, with his parents dead, lives the life of his own choosing. Essentially, his work necessitates his being a man, but when he has finished he hurries home to a bath and changes his male clothes for his female ones. He keeps his wardrobes entirely separate, not allowing one role to merge into the other. He used to dress so that, in an emergency, he could quickly resume his male appearance, but later on, as he felt more confident and 'in' the feminine role, he would invite any callers in as he was, and if they were friends tell them about himself. This gave him particular pleasure. As the novelty of each new satisfaction wears off he buys more and more clothes, only to want something else. The life as a man during the day has become unbearable, and he smokes increasingly to relieve his nervous tension. He has been from one medical specialist to another for help, and has followed up any possible methods adopted by others whom he has read about, only to be disappointed. But another friend always seems to turn up and offer new hope.

There seems no hope of adjustment to normality in this case whatever, for the determination to live permanently as a woman is all-powerful. Indeed, his plan to do this is now in the process of being carried out. He has mentally castrated himself, but still has hope of a surgical castration to help him better assume the feminine role. There seems little doubt that he will continue to press his claim for such help, and will equally be restless and unsettled until he gets it. The chances are that even then the limit of his satisfaction will not be reached, and the loss of his sexual function may only cause more frustration, new problems, and more devious behaviour. Unfortunately, the disadvantages of the social and employment aspects, in such a case as this who has so much to lose, apart from the emotional upheaval of finding that a change of role will still demand conformity, are likely to outweigh the advantages of the mental satisfaction. It can only be hoped that he will find happiness, but he will have to realise that life will not alter and that all his efforts will still be necessary to pursue life to the full and to the mutual good. His goal will not be the end of the road; it will be the beginning.

The Anti-Social type

This type rather follows the pattern of the homosexual type, but the degree of perversion is marked and no account is taken of society in the satisfaction of the obsession. It is not the writer's place to condone or condemn these cases, for it is quite possible that they cannot be held responsible for their state, but they do nevertheless represent the least desirable and acceptable group with which we are concerned. We cannot omit them, however, on this basis, but it seems that these cases reflect unjustly and harshly on most of the transsexualists under discussion. The origin of their condition appears to be essentially homosexual, latent or otherwise, and this manifests itself in extreme

243

transvestism regardless of morals, loved ones, or society. The transsexualist part is pseudo, then, and is but a symptom of the homosexuality and transvestism; this is in direct contrast to the homosexual type. By nature they are selfish and cowardly. They want all they can get out of life with the least possible effort, and a lot of their desire to be a woman revolves around the conception that everything must be easier in the feminine world. They feel society will look after them and pamper them, and not expect them to work too hard, etc. On the other hand, the actual masquerade provides ecstatic pleasure in the fooling of the public, as well as giving sexual gratification. They are great exhibitionists; sex is an essential factor in their satisfaction, and their whole attitude to life is rooted in sex, often seeing ahead for themselves an easy life as prostitutes. However much pleasure they get from their masquerade they are rarely settled for long, since their assumed role seems incomplete without a male partner.

The transvestist behaviour is often looked upon callously; they lack moral sense, and if their appearance should offend they do not seem to care. Often they are married with children and even these are not spared the tragedy and humiliation. The fact that these transsexualists are still men anatomically, in possession of male organs under their female clothes, far from giving them a guilt complex because it is repugnant and antisocial gives them sexual satisfaction from the knowledge of such a state of affairs. Indeed, they are so introverted and selfish that they show complete lack of self-consciousness in the achievement of their desires. Generally these types eventually take to living as women all the time, and are not in a hurry to seek medical advice or surgery. Their sexual feelings promote the satisfaction of their role and discourage any wish to have operations; instead they are usually frightened at the thought of them. In spite of living in the role of their desire and getting, as it were, the best of both worlds, these types never remain settled in themselves. Quite often their parasitic nature may even cause them to find themselves in police hands for stealing or other such offences. Often their word cannot be trusted. Once established, this condition is not likely to alter throughout life, and there is no happy ending.

Having covered the significant features of this type we need only briefly give the details of a particular case, as relevant to the subject. Mr E is 56 years old. His transvestist behaviour has always been marked, and although married and with several children he has even dressed as a woman in front of them. He has lived on and off as a woman for a large part of his life, his occupations being various and mostly of a domestic nature. He is now living continuously as a woman, and although his appearance is mostly passable his masculinity is not entirely hidden. There is some uneasiness of action and temperament, and a tendency to a high-pitched giggle. He has made no effort to seek treatment, and his male anatomy does not seem to worry him. Some homosexual inclinations seem to be indicated by his desire to meet up with a man friend. His ability to live and work as a woman has become possible by his own ingenuity in procuring a female National Insurance card. He has also come into contact with the law for stealing. Unfortunately, there is little hope that this individual will gain more of life than he already has, but will only become more frustrated as satisfaction eludes him. Nevertheless, he will almost certainly end up seeking surgery as a further means of expression and in a bid to 'resolve' his troubles, and it is this that warrants his inclusion here as a particular type of transsexualist. Society has no choice but to accept the position and be grateful for their own normality. Unless he treads on their toes, society can do no more than pity or condemn.

The Glandular type

Although transsexualism is regarded as a syndrome which affects normal physically healthy individuals there are some who, as a result of some endocrine imbalance, may appear to have more justification than those who seek to change their sex on purely psychological grounds. Indeed, glandular influences can cause some men to remain effeminate in physique and mannerisms, and the term 'Pretty Boy' given to them is often more apt than is sometimes realised. Likewise, the term 'Baby Face' is often used to refer to someone in their twenties who has not yet had to shave. Similarly we may find abnormal glandular factors causing a woman to to be virilised and to have a heavy muscular physique and a tendency to hirsutism. In both cases, the individuals obviously start out in life at a disadvantage as far as normality is concerned. However, of all those affected only few become established transsexualists, so that these factors alone have little bearing upon the aetiology of the syndrome. Nevertheless, when a change of role is under consideration any natural physical features that may aid the so-called transformation must be a bonus. It is these cases that come under this category as belonging to the Glandular type of transsexualist.

In this type then we find the same picture of transsexual feelings and behaviour, although the boy child is not always aware of any physical deficiencies and, in the early stages, often struggles all the more to adapt to his role of upbringing. His ability to more readily pass in a female part, however, soon finds him engaging in transvestism, encouraged on by his friends and enjoying their overtures and praise. This sometimes progresses to public performances on the stage as a female impersonator whilst still in his late 'teens, and it is then that he is but a short step away from becoming a transsexualist, wishing to adopt the female role permanently as far as medical and surgicial help will allow.

Characteristics of all the other types are often found in this group. One can only generalise but they are inclined to be younger when the climax comes, suggesting some degree of immaturity – immaturity which may well be physical as well as psychological. Often the showy nature of their chosen work attracts many friends so that aspects of the Homosexual type are evident. Consequently, they are the ones also likely to seek a partner after a 'sex change' with marriage in view, often regardless of the legality of such. They are also likely to be great exhibitionists and to revel in any publicity that comes their way.

Seeking female hormones early lessens the development of the male secondary sexual characteristics so that any 'change' is likely to be more successful. Having less past to leave behind them is also a distinct advantage. Nevertheless, it must be remembered that however much justification these individuals might appear to have they are no less biologically of the sex they were born, and can still only be called transsexualists. We are *not* therefore speaking here of someone who is intersexual. Indeed, true intersexuality is not just another type of transsexuality but appertains to a special group of individuals all their own, and will be discussed separately. Nevertheless it is possible that the two categories may appear to merge if the degree of physical ambiguity is marked.

The Basic Female transsexualist

There seems little doubt that female transsexualists can be grouped similarly to the types already discussed. It is not proposed to make more than mention of them here, however, since the possible causative factors giving rise to the various types of male transsexualists can equally exert their influence in the opposite direction, and give rise to a similar pattern of feelings and behaviour in the female. Nevertheless, all cases known to the writer had intimate female partners, suggesting that most were probably homosexually oriented. Generally, as in the male, no undue abnormality of genital organs was professed by these cases, although sometimes the physique appeared masculine and the voice husky, no doubt due to the effects of the injections of male hormones which some had managed to obtain. Their sexual satisfaction was usually obtained in the male role with a lesbian partner, and the desire for masculinisation seemed closely associated with this behaviour. In so far that normal heterosexuality eludes them, they must be considered immature. In so far that their early influences may have caused them to fix their attention on their father, they also come into the Oedipus heading, whilst any extreme aggravation of their obsession may involve them in anti-social activities.

Generally speaking, then, female transsexualists belong mainly to one type, incorporating most of the predominant features of the male types into it. Yet in many ways no 'opposite' to male transsexualism exists, so that the syndrome might more correctly be applied only to the male. There is not the significant loneliness or need for secrecy. Family and public acceptance of any change of role is generally more readily available. The ability to wear clothes of a masculine character in public provides an easier outlet for expression, without excessive build-up of tension or guilt complex. The transsexual woman is also often more practical in her outlook upon life, more logical and factual than the transsexual man, whose feelings are all important and whose world is up in the clouds of fantasy. The practical issues are also of less importance, for a woman can wear trousers irrespective of the shape of her legs. She can be going thin, or be actually bald, and it is no deterrent to her in playing the man's role. She can be fat or ugly, rough and dirty, and still it will make no difference but even possibly enhance her masculine appearance. This is all in complete contrast to the man playing the female role, who craves after shapely legs to show off in nylons, a slim waist, well-developed bust, small feet to go gracefully into dainty high-heeled shoes, a face and body free of 'detestable' hair, head hair that can grow to shoulder length, immaculate hands and features, etc. These differences in the needs of male and female transsexualists seem to represent the main causes of variation in the basic types of cases, and it is upon these that pivot the differences in the whole resultant picture of the behaviour, the conflicts, the complexes, the neuroses, the desires and obsessions, and indeed the entire attitude to sex and life itself.

For our typical example we are going to look into the case of Miss F, who is now 25 and a commercial artist by occupation. She is an only child, and tells the usual story of wishing to be a boy from her earliest conscious moments, inwardly feeling that she was. As a child she showed no interest in dolls, preferring boys' toys and her wishes for guns and trains appear to have been met. She grew up with the constant desire to be regarded as a boy, and to dress and behave as such. Although she dressed as masculinely as possible her feelings went deeper than any mere satisfaction from just playing a role, and her wish persisted *actually* to be a boy so that she could grow up as a man, get married, and father children. Indeed, on leaving school she had such a loathing for her feminine Christian name that she adopted, by common usage, another closely resembling a masculine name, to have the satisfaction of hearing herself called by it. She rebelled at being given gifts of jewellery, and her parents were often resentful at her attitude and could not understand her. Later, she showed no interest in make-up and cosmetics, but rather wished she could grow facial hair so that she would be more masculine.

It was not until the age of 18 or 19 that she first sought advice from a doctor about her feelings, and was told then, in no uncertain terms, that she was a girl and that nothing could change her and that the best thing she could do was to forget all about her desire. She was greatly distressed by this, but did reconsider her position and try to accept what she had been told, so that for the next few years life continued as before with her feelings suppressed. At last, however, she found her conflict even more real and demanding, and her attention was drawn to every case reported in the newspaper to have 'changed' in one direction or the other. Once again she tried to get medical help, her travels taking her to several continental countries as well as England, but each time she met with discouragement and difficulties. Not least of her problems is her great regard for the moral code and her belief in God, not wishing to do anything that is other than right in the eyes of society or of her Maker. Yet if only she could change, she feels, she would be able to give of herself better in service to humanity, which she looks upon idealistically.

As typical of these cases, Miss F has had a female companion for many years and, although there has been no actual sexual relationship, she looks upon herself as a man and plays the 'positive' role, indulging in petting and fondling. She has never been attracted to men, and has repelled any approaches made by them. She in no way regards herself as a homosexual, however, in spite of her attachment to her female friend, saying that since she feels like a man she does not view the association as being between two women. If she could change in every respect so that she could honestly know that she *is* a man, her great delight would be to marry her friend. On the other hand, she feels that unless a 'change' can be 'complete' it would be wrong of her just to live as a man and involve her friend with her problem. Although her mother now knows of her wish to find someone to 'turn her into a man', the practical problems of assuming the male role (to convince her medical advisers that she can live in no other way and that she will be passable in the role) are immense, as far as her official documents and her work are concerned. Above all, she feels it is morally wrong to adopt the role without first getting help, and that only when she has had treatment and operations and is officially recognised as a man will she have a right to the role.

Unfortunately, Miss F knows little of the facts of the problem or just what is meant by a 'change'. She has built up her obsession on the belief that she can actually be made into a man, virtually in every respect, and finds it difficult to understand that this is an impossibility. She feels unable to accept any limitation to what she wants, believing that some magical 'treatment' will change her whole appearance and anatomy. She pictures herself as someone entirely different after she has had 'treatment', wondering how long 'it will take' and believing that those who eventually agree to help her will give her this operation and that operation, so that they will have the satisfaction of ensuring success as far as possible. Further, she feels it is part of their duty to help her with the legal aspect of her 'change', giving the necessary certificates to enable her to be officially recognised as a man and to state, if necessary, that she has always been male as an aid to getting all her documents put in order.

Underlying all her desires are doubts, for she is unable to accept any half-measures and wants to know the likely result before she starts. She feels it may be best not to start at all if she may only land herself more in the middle of the sexes, and hates to think of having her documents show that she was formerly a woman. The thought that her past has been as a girl and a woman revolts her, so much does she want to feel able to be a man and only to think of herself as such all her life, and for this reason she dislikes seeing photographs of herself when younger, dressed in a skirt or dress. About five feet eight inches tall, she has adopted a short hair-style and wears slacks continuously, which has no doubt assisted her ability to assume masculine mannerisms without much difficulty when dressed as a man. Her skin is very smooth and there is no facial hair, although she is passable as a male when dressed in a suit, appearing more as a youth than as a young man. Physically, she is well-proportioned for a woman but rather on the robust side, her breasts necessitating loose-fitting clothes of large size to mask them.

Although it seems likely now that she may receive help towards her goal it is difficult to see just how satisfied she will be, when she finally realises that the **maximum** that can be done for her is removal of the breasts, shaping of an artificial soft tissue penis, and the encouragement of male secondary sexual characteristics by hormones. For the most part she still regards all this as leaving her incomplete and in masquerade, and any obsession built on demanding legal correction of her birth certificate may well result in further conflict, disillusionment and regret. As she is she can at least cling to some normality, but if, after surgical help, she is unable to accept her limitations as a man, it would be better that she sought some other solution to her problem. This is particularly so if she does not accept the possibility that a 'change' may only leave her more abnormal than ever. We can only hope that happiness and peace of mind will come to this case, as indeed we do with all those so afflicted, yet embarking on the road to a change may not turn out after all to be the dream come true but, rather, the facing of reality that has never been known before. It is certain that unless the whole picture is known and understood and the limitations faced and accepted the hard realities of life will only be found at the end of the road, instead of the assumed joy, happiness and peace of mind.

The Intersexual group
Within this group are the true physical intersexes and the hermaphrodites. It is the only group in which physical factors of intersexuality are present to lend support for any desire to change the sexual role of rearing, as opposed to the strictly Transsexual types where only psychological factors account for

the sexual disorientation. In true intersexuality, therefore, the sexual ambiguity is caused by a conflict of the biological factors affecting development, and, in contrast to transsexualists who often prove the normality of their sexual function, intersexes are often both physically and sexually immature and may indeed be sterile through a failure of the proper development of the sexual reproductive organs and tract of either sex. As we have seen, intersexes do not necessarily wish to change their sex and may continue through life quite happy in their sex of rearing, regardless of their 'true' sex and in spite of their likely disability. When this is not so, however, the individual may present as an apparent transsexual until investigations later reveal some physical, biological and/or genetic abnormality. Whilst the majority of cases in this group are brought to medical notice at an early age, very rarely a few soldier on after puberty and into later life before the characteristics of one sex dominate enough to establish a definite swing away from the indeterminate state. Should rehabilitation be necessary to the other role it is still a major upheaval in the individual's life, and since we are discussing the whole subject of sex change and not just as it is applied, invariably incorrectly, to transsexualism it is pertinent that this rare special group – the Intersexual group – should be included here.

As intersexes are likely to be immature sexually they often go through childhood unaware of any abnormality or of being at variance with their sex of upbringing. Unlike the physically normal transsexualists who are totally opposed to their sex of rearing and try to adjust accordingly, the physical intersex is more likely to let matters take their course and accept themselves as misfits, using the best of their features of both sexes to assist the easy flow of life. However, inwardly, they have a much deeper sexual identity problem to solve than the transsexualist, whose virile sexual drive is usually well targeted perversely to a 'change'. Indeed, the intersex is more likely to make every possible effort to accept the role of rearing even though the pull in the opposite direction is extremely powerful and biologically motivated, the hormonal influences affecting not only the sexual and body growth but also the mental

252

development and orientation. The very rare and true hermaphrodites possessing gonads, or elements of gonads, of both
sexes are also included in this group, such cases sometimes only
coming to notice after investigative surgery has been necessary
to establish the reasons for mal-development or mal-function
of the sex organs. Although in this group the forces of
upbringing are in one direction and the biological influences
are in the other, the fact that studies show that the biological
forces do not always win shows how very powerful the forces of
upbringing can be. That these are so readily overridden by
transsexualists, however, equally shows just how powerful are
the psychological forces at work in these cases.

Perhaps the greatest advantage with this group is that they
have absorbed during their lifetime all those things which have
inwardly and unconsciously been natural to them, *as well as*
those associated with their supposed sex. The result is that the
individual can play both roles equally without thinking, one
being the taught and the other the natural one. This is not
usually so with any of the transsexual types, whose physical
features and characteristics are not only marked in the direction
of their correct sex of rearing but whose environmental
upbringing has *not* been accepted by them. Thus, transsexual
men are not only unable to cope with their masculine role, but
generally their idea of the female role is artificial and exaggerated. Consequently, because of their philosophical attitude to
life, their acceptance of their surroundings and physical
'weaknesses', intersexes are the ones most likely to find
happiness in any change of role. The following case, typical of
this group, has now been officially recognised as being a female,
and will therefore be referred to in that sex.

Miss G, now aged 37 has lived for much of her life as a male.
She relates, on reflection, that from her earliest years as a 'boy'
a conscious effort was necessary to behave as expected of her,
and although at first at a loss to understand why this should be
she gradually came to realise that her interests and feelings
were those of a girl. Far from easing her conflict, however, this
knowledge made her intensify her efforts to conform, although
she says, "I was so convinced I could be normal if only I were

a little girl that on my way to school I would run between the cracks in the paving stones, and tell myself that if I trod on one my supreme hope of one day becoming a girl would not come true." She tells of growing out of this phase, as her love for her parents demanded that she conformed more and more to her role of upbringing and it was easier to accept her fate than to fight it. This meant accepting that she would just have to keep to herself as someone who did not apparently fit into either sex role. Being immature, she knew little of the differences between the sexes and grew up without knowing how masculine or feminine she really was. She had never seen a boy or girl, or even her parents, in the nude, and being unattracted to either sex her loneliness became acute. In spite of her inner feelings there was never any question of wanting to dress up or resort to transvestism, and it was only when she was eventually obliged to see a sexologist that her physical intersexual state was revealed and her problem brought out into the open. She had not developed masculinity but had remained eunuchoid; facial and body hair were completely absent and the pubic hair was entirely feminine in distribution. Her sexual organs were deficient and dysgenetic. In spite of her justification a change of role was still an immense step, and even her medical advisers felt that it might be too traumatic for her psychologically and were uneasy about the outcome in view of her well established way of life in the male role. Looking back she admits to going through a very difficult few years, but has only praise for all those who so kindly helped her through her change so successfully. There appears to have been no attempt to overplay the part and the adjustment to her new role has been smooth. No doubt the greatest source of satisfaction has been the official acceptance of her true state, and to this more than anything she attributes the success she feels she has now made in re-establishing her place in society. This case has certainly found happiness, and has returned to health in mind and body. She still looks upon life very philosophically and wishes to embrace all the fine and good things she sees in the world. Her past life can never be forgotten, and her memories still offer a challenge at times, for she remembers the good things and not the bad.

Yet it is the future that really matters to her, and although her basic intersexuality can never be wholly lost there seems no doubt that her present role is the correct one. At least she can go forward to meet the challenges of life, at peace and a whole person.

PART II

THE ANALYSIS

CHAPTER SIX

FUNDAMENTAL DIFFERENCES
BETWEEN MALE AND FEMALE

JUST HOW MUCH sex education should be given to a growing
child, and at what age, is still a matter for common argument.
Indeed, a large proportion of us grow to adulthood having to
seek what knowledge we can of sex by our own initiative. This
may be because of the general reluctance of our parents, or
those responsible for our education, to discuss the subject.
Often, it may be because we have been made to believe by our
parents or others that sex is something revolting, and not to be
mentioned, let alone discussed. As a result, it is little wonder
that many of us grow up not only with inhibited sexual feelings
and an immature outlook, but with a very limited knowledge of
even the fundamental differences between the sexes. Generally
we have nothing to go on except our feelings and awareness of
our own body anatomy and state, aided by deductions our
senses are able to make, by perception and supposition.

During the formative years, lack of information may cause us
to identify ourselves more closely with the opposite sex, on the
assumption that the differences between the sexes are small,
internal or external factors suggesting to us that we more
correctly belong to and fit in better with that sex than with the
one in which we are being reared and by convention being
made to conform. Since you are a boy, for instance, you are told
you must do this and must do that, but you mustn't do this and
mustn't do that. You must act your part. It is part of your
upbringing and education into society. Similarly, if you are a
girl, you mustn't get dirty or play with a hard ball, etc. Directly
we rebel at having to toe the line as expected of us we tend to
assume that, because our interests are in the opposite direction,
nature really intended us to be of the other sex and we are really
being brought up incorrectly. What we do not know are the
actual differences that exist in all their complexity between the
sexes, let alone how much more these are to become evident as
we become older. Certainly, we have only to consult a book on

259

any medical subject whatever to find that the sexes are constantly being compared, should it be a book on anatomy in which the sexual variation of each bone is noted, or should it be a book on medicine in which the incidence and course of this or that disease is shown to differ between the sexes.

Since many of the ideas and fantasies of transsexualists are based on these early misguided conceptions, it is essential that the facts relating to these differences should be fully understood, for, although we are all human beings, from the very moment of conception development commences in a certain direction according to the genetic code, and the course of divergence from the opposite sex becomes even wider and more established as growth proceeds. At puberty, the differences between the sexes are increased even more dramatically, with the development of the secondary sexual characteristics and the functioning of the reproductive processes. After this the differences still continue, according to our psychological approach to life and the manner in which the sex hormones produced in our bodies affect us, influencing our emotions, feelings and attitude to sex. Later, too, when reproductive function declines in the male and ceases in the female, lowering of the sex hormone level will cause changes of varying degree and type. To look into these numerous and variable factors, we can do no better than trace the divergent paths of each sex as they develop from the zygote, comparing the differences as we see the individuals grow, from the genetic, anatomical, glandular, psychological and social aspects.

Genetic differences

In Chapter 1 we referred to the existence of two types of sex chromosomes, designated X and Y, and saw that the female, being of XX constitution, can contribute only an X chromosome to her offspring, whilst the male, being of XY constitution, can contribute either an X or a Y. Thus, the female parent plays no part in the determination of the sex of the individual conceived. Indeed, medical science has not overlooked this or the possibility of producing a child of desired sex, should artificial means enable the separation of the X chromosomal spermatozoa from the Y in the male parent. A recent technique of separating male-determining sperm from female-determining sperm has, in fact, been developed, by passing an electric current through the spermatic fluid. That the chromosomal constitution of a normal male is XY and of a normal female is XX is something, therefore, that is established at the moment of conception, so when the future infant is but one cell in size we find a difference already present. It is because of this that males are exposed to certain hereditary defects, which are sex-linked with their only X chromosome, which from the start would appear to give the female an advantage over the male.

Examination of the cells of the body, subjected to a special staining process, has within recent years revealed that in normal females the nucleus exhibits the presence of certain chromatin nodules, which in normal males are absent. When this test is carried out the presence of the nodules is signified as a positive result, and the absence of them as negative. Much as we would expect a positive result in the case of a female and a negative result in the case of a male, and this is nearly always so, anomalies do occur. Nevertheless, irrespective of the anatomical or gonadal state of the individual, sex in the one aspect of 'Nuclear Sex' can thus be determined. However, this means ascertaining the actual chromosomal constitution and not just testing for the presence of chromatin in a cell. At the moment our knowledge of chromosome abnormalities is limited, but the reason why some males exhibit chromatin in their cells making them apparent females has been found to be due to them having a chromosomal constitution of XXY, a condition known as Klinefelter's syndrome. Often these men are sterile and find their way into the infertility clinics of hospitals.

Although examination of cells to try to establish chromosomal constitution may be made at any age, the significant fact remains that the cell being tested has developed by division from the original zygote so that the result will always indicate the fundamental nuclear sex of the zygote and thus of the individual. If, indeed, we could examine the zygote cell at conception it should tell us which sex the baby is to be with accuracy, assuming all factors are normal. This is of course not possible, but it is possible to draw off some of the amniotic fluid which surrounds the developing foetus in the womb, and, since this fluid contains cells derived from the unborn baby, examination of them can reveal the nuclear sex of the developing individual. Obtaining such a sample of amniotic fluid is obviously not without some danger, since introduction of infection to the womb or stimulation to contraction may cause loss of the baby, and the practical value may not, therefore, merit such a risk.

From the single-celled zygote a complete human being will result. The colour of its eyes and hair, shape of its nose, and character of its teeth are but a few of the vast hereditary factors that are stored in the genes it contains. Here, too, has the chromosomal constitution been formed, the genetic sex established, and the whole pattern of future development determined already. An XX (female) zygote will form in one direction, and an XY (male) zygote will form in another. The differences are there at once, for they are basic, and they will manifest themselves more and more as development proceeds. If there are any abnormalities, they too will present themselves more as time goes on. As we have seen earlier, all types of sexual variations may occur in rare instances, and the nuclear sex may appear to differ from the anatomical sex, but nothing suggests that these account for the condition of transsexualism. Possibly, however, other constitutional factors may develop, as yet unknown, to account for anatomical anomalies and glandular disturbances, etc. Indeed, a vast number of influences *are* brought to bear on the developing embryo, both from within and from without, and although the nuclear and anatomical sex are in agreement in nearly all cases, that this is not one hundred per cent conclusive and correct in all cases does indicate the complexities involved in assessing sex, and that the true sex of an individual can only be determined by taking all the relevant and known factors into account.

Until we can be sure of these factors we must rely upon the known fundamental differences that exist between the sexes. Perhaps the greatest significance is attached to the reproductive organs, since if these are normal, and can function to bring a

new being into the world, it represents the greatest distinguishing mark between the sexes, completely determining
masculinity or femininity in the ability to be a father or a
mother. Beyond this we must be rather more careful, for
although we can learn a lot from establishing the nuclear sex of
an individual this is only one aspect of sex, and sex determination depends upon an assessment of all the factors that go to
make up sex and the ultimate form of the developed individual
resulting from these factors. It is these factors we are now about
to consider, for then we can see the differences that are to
result, depending upon male or female influences being
exerted on the growing mass of cells that is already the
commencement of a human life.

Anatomical and Glandular differences

Since the glands play a major part in establishing the development of the anatomical form of the body, we cannot discuss the
anatomical differences between the sexes without also considering the different glandular make-up, and the glands and
hormones that first produced this. We have seen how, according to the sex constitution, androgenic or oestrogenic
activators stimulate the sexual direction of growth and cause
either testes or ovaries to develop from the precursory tissue.
Once formed, these gonads secrete their respective hormones,
influencing the sexual development in the male or female
direction. Even in a young boy or young girl the primary sexual
differences are quite evident, although it is certainly easier for
the two to change clothes and pass as each other than for them
to do so after puberty, when the secondary changes have
occurred. Whereas the primary sexual characteristics in the
young girl represent the basic human form it is only at puberty
that enlargement of the breasts occurs to produce any positive
developmental change. In contrast, the growing boy develops
steadily in a positive direction away from the basic female form,
and at puberty this is all the more emphasised by the
development of the very positive male secondary sexual
characteristics. That the female, in the human, is the basic sex is
also confirmed genetically by the dominance of the X sex

263

chromosome, which may likewise be likened to an unfertilised ovum. This does not imply that the male is just a masculinised female, for the development is on separate lines from the start, but it does indicate the female as the 'negative' sex and the male as the 'positive'. Because of this, as will be seen later, it is easier to produce male characteristics in a female at any age, than for established male characteristics to be removed once they have developed in the male.

Having established that the female is the basic sex in the human, and that both sexes start off their existence from the moment of conception on different paths of development, we need not consider further the nine months of prenatal growth. What features do we note at birth, however, in each sex? In the boy baby a penis has already begun to grow forward from between the legs, formed from two earlier openings in the area, and through it urine is excreted from the bladder. In the girl baby, these two openings still remain. The front one, the urethra, leads directly from the bladder and bears the clitoris, whilst the second opening, lying posterior to (behind) the first, is the vagina. The rectal opening, a third opening found behind the other two, is similarly placed in the male, lying behind the penis. Generally, then, a boy and girl at birth appear very similar externally, apart from the presence of the penis, or clitoris and vagina.

As the new-born infant grows the bone structure takes on a very definite arrangement, according to the androgenic or oestrogenic stimulation. This is because of the different functions the sexes have to play in the reproductive role. In the whole of the animal kingdom nature works with the entire process of reproduction primarily in mind, so that all the factors in early life are directed towards the reaching of maturity, to make reproduction of the species possible. This ability will then gradually decline or cease, the animal becoming old and dying. In plant life, too, the same is seen, the plant struggling for nutriment and water in order to grow, produce its flowers and seeds, afterwards to wither and die. In the human, the growth of the male is directed towards the production of spermatozoa, which when stimulated by secretions from the prostate and other glands are active, fast-moving, energetic cells, challenging each other to be first to enter and 'mate' with the ovum. In the same way, these are the typical qualities of the male, and the body develops accordingly. The bone structure is large, there is maximum muscular development, minimum amounts of fatty tissue, and the build is athletic, combining strength with agility. The reproductive organs are confined to one particular area, which although more susceptible in attack are equally more easily guarded in defence. This constant challenge of a man's life causes him to have a higher metabolic rate than a woman. He is less able to stand extremes of heat and cold, and the body and face grow hair to help maintain the body temperature.

Growth of the female, however, is directed towards the production of the ova, which are, in contrast, slow-moving and passive. Also, only one ovum is normally shed from the ovaries every month, in contrast to the many millions of spermatozoa ejected by the male at coitus as often as the ability and need demand. There is thus no challenging action in the female, the ovum taking a steady course. The male's momentary act of stimulation and coitus frees him from further part in the reproductive process, in the same way that the work of the spermatozoon is done once it has entered and fused with the ovum. For the female, however, it is the commencement of a long period of prenatal care, culminating in labour and childbirth, which in turn marks the commencement of all the love and care that motherhood imparts and implies. For this reason, the female reproductive system forms a more major part of the anatomy, and is situated within the body. The bones are not so large, and the whole structure is proportionately smaller than that of the male. The hips are larger in diameter, however, and the pelvic bones broader, being so arranged as to accommodate the developing foetus in the womb. Because of this internal anatomy, the bladder is also larger than that of the male, and is the reason why a woman is able to go for longer periods at a time without urinating. The thorax and waist are smaller, and in place of the muscular development of the man there is a greater area of fat distribution. This is particularly noticeable on the limbs, especially the thighs. In conformity with the general bone structure the fingers are smaller, finer and more delicate. Indeed, because of these bone differences, an individual of any age can be dug up long after death, and the sex almost invariably determined from the skeleton.

Between birth and puberty the differences become progressively more manifest in every aspect of mind and body, from the largest organ down to the smallest cell. During this phase sexual awareness is present, but since the sex organs have not reached 'maturity' the boy remains to some extent like the basic female type, and thus like a girl. In both sexes the voice is high-pitched, and there is no hair on the face or body. But the primary sexual characteristics will show the different bone formation, both in structure and size. The boy will have larger bones and a bigger frame, tend to be thicker-set, muscular and athletic, and quicker off the mark, etc. Sexually he possesses a penis and a developing scrotum containing the two testes. A tube (vas deferens) leads from each testicle, joining up in the substance of the prostate gland beneath the bladder, to open into the urethra. Posteriorly to the prostate gland are the seminal vesicles which store the seminal fluid. The secretions produced by the seminal vesicles, the prostate, and Cowper's glands is called the semen, which is expelled into the urethra following the same path as the urine from the bladder, being emitted from the external opening of the urethra at the tip of the penis.

An entirely different set of glands and organs is present in the young girl. Anatomically, we see that her features are generally more delicate. Her bone structure is finer and her build more slight; her limbs will be rounded, being more fatty and less muscular, and the general skin texture will be finer and smoother. There will also be the suggestion of some stimulation of the breasts. Sexually, the two ovaries will be developing within the abdomen, lying each side of the growing womb. The womb leads down to the vagina, which opens externally behind the urethral opening, the latter presenting the clitoris above it which is erotic in character and has erectile properties. This vast network of complicated sexual 'machinery', so completely different in each sex, shows us that any early ideas we may have that we are hardly any different to the opposite sex, except in

266

dress and upbringing, are a fallacy and completely unfounded.

Yet the secondary sexual characteristics are still to come. With puberty the male departs from the female more positively, for the voice 'breaks' and deepens as the vocal cords become slacker and the pharynx longer, whilst the adult female retains her original high-pitched voice. Also, whilst the female retains her original smooth textured skin, with absence of facial and body hair, the male develops a beard, body hair, and a coarser skin. This hair growth may be early or late in developing, and the amount and type may vary according to the physical characteristics of the individual, but the distribution is typical. The beard will extend from the head hair down the sides of the face, round under the cheeks, over the upper lip, and extend over the whole lower half of the face and on to the chin and neck. The lower neck is usually less affected but, down on the chest, the growth thickens again and can cover the body and limbs, the arms, legs and the backs of the hands being particularly susceptible. In the female such hair growth is absent, although later on the finer feminine type of fluff may show, slowly growing in the particularly susceptible areas of the upper lip and face, and on the facing aspects of the arms and legs.

Whilst the head hair is profuse in the female the growth usually ceases high up and across the neck, while the male head hair is slower-growing and extends pointedly down the whole length of the neck, to merge in extreme cases with the body hair on the back. In the areas of the body where sweating is most likely to occur we find a fair growth of hair in both sexes. Such areas are under the arms, and between the legs or pubic region. The pubic hair deserves special mention, since the distribution is markedly different in the sexes. Both exhibit a triangular area of hair, but in the male the point of the triangle is directed upwards, with the hair continuing up to the navel and often joining up with the body hair of the chest. In the female, however, the point of the triangle is directed downwards, the hairline marking the base ending horizontally across the lower abdomen.

Perhaps the main positive secondary sexual characteristic in the female is the development of the breasts. These are glandular in nature, their express purpose being to produce milk on which to feed a new-born baby during its period of weaning. Often, in some large, robust men, there may be some enlargement of the breasts with fatty or muscular tissue, but this in no way resembles feminine bust development, and the flat chest of the male is normally a typically masculine feature. It is indeed the bust, narrowing down to the small waist, smoothly expanding again to the wide hips and rounding off down the thighs and legs, that give the female her characteristic hour-glass figure, her curves and her 'vital statistics'.

The testes and ovaries, the male and female sex organs respectively, are responsible not only for the production of the sperm and ova but, as part of the endocrine system of ductless glands, secrete hormones directly into the blood. These sex hormones cause their greatest effect at puberty, when the testes and ovaries become functional and send forth their increased secretions, and it is these which then induce the physical changes of the secondary sexual characteristics and at the same time prompt the physical feelings and awareness of sex. During the following years these secretions continue according to their normal life-span of function. This may be some thirty years or more from puberty, although their activity usually declines towards the end of this time. After this, in the male, the decline is gradual into old age, although the ability to father a child is still occasionally a possibility in men of 70 or more. In the female, however, reproductive function ceases more abruptly, the 'periods' becoming erratic before finally stopping at about the age of 50. This is known as the 'change of life', the climacteric, or menopause, and the sudden reduction of the female hormones in the blood causes certain symptoms to be associated with it, notably hot flushes, irritability, morbid states, and depression. As a rule these pass off after a time, as the body adjusts itself to the changed circumstances, but often hormones in some form may have to be prescribed to relieve the symptoms and tide the individual over until the normal adjustment occurs. Castration in an adult male may cause similar symptoms, and is an important point that will be referred to later.

Whatever the sexual factors influencing development,

whether they are the early genetic activators or the hormones secreted from the gonads, despite the mechanism which exists within the body to regulate these within normal limits disturbances can, of course, occur. Naturally, the earlier these take place the more profound will be the effect upon sexual development, although it may not necessarily be the testes or ovaries at fault in these cases, for the pituitary gland governs the activity of these and may itself have its normal function disturbed. In all these instances, however, the abnormality presents such obvious anatomical and physiological symptoms that medical help is almost invariably sought, to assist the *normal* development that is lacking. The important point to remember is that any effects are essentially false. Furthermore, the differences in the sexes are so immense, and start on their divergent paths from such an early age, that only genetic considerations are likely to bring about any major reversal of the anatomical or functional sex. It should be particularly noted that development can only occur from the negative state, and that development which has already occurred cannot be reversed. Atrophy of tissues can, of course, occur, in which the tissue shrivels in size and may lose its function, but this in no way represents reversed development. The glandular system does no more than follow the pattern set for it by the genes, and, once a male glandular system has developed, the particular characteristics of the male sex will follow, in the same way that a female glandular system will cause female characteristics to result. There are bound to occur, in isolated cases, factors which cause various female characteristics to occur in a male, and vice versa, and it is then a question of deciding to what extent these characteristics merit the opinion that an individual may be living in the wrong role.

As we have seen, however, the anatomical and glandular differences are vast, and each sex possesses an entirely different and complex reproductive system, so that no assessment of masculinity or femininity based on a few external features alone can be other than biased. Indeed, whatever the psychological sex of an individual may be, it cannot be ignored that he or she has been developing in a certain direction from conception, and that the adult man and the adult woman are as opposed to each other, in appearance, structure, function and mentality, as two poles of a magnet. That we have the bodies we have is one thing. The way we think of them, use or abuse them is another. Certainly our teachings, the way we are brought up, and the environment of our particular community and society affect our outlook on life and sex immensely, and it is these important aspects we must consider next.

Psychological and Social differences

To just what extent the psychological difference between a male and a female can be attributed to internal factors such as hormones and body development, or to external factors of environment and upbringing, is still not exactly clear, because of the many variable factors involved. We must therefore accept that no rigid line can be drawn, but that the differences are probably caused by both internal and external factors in varying degrees.

Considering the internal factors, we have the androgenic or oestrogenic substances that exert their influence before puberty as well as the increased effect the sex hormones have after puberty. We have the psychological effect of the individual's awareness of the functional state of the body, sexually, as well as the awareness of the physical or anatomical state. The hormonal substances that promote the development of the sexual characteristics circulate in the blood stream of the growing boy or girl, and with the brain receiving nutriment from this blood it is possible to see how sexual feelings may be stimulated within it. We do know that men and women think in different ways and have a different outlook upon life, and there seems little doubt that glandular secretions play an important part in causing this. Muscular development enables a man to be more aggressive, a state that can be artificially produced in a woman by the administration of androgens. Alternatively, a man can be weakened by excessive oestrogens, and psychologically he will assume the more placid nature of the female because of it, becoming more emotional and sensitive. This does not mean that an individual's nature can be changed by hormones,

270

because the conditioning of upbringing is something that remains powerfully within us all. Our moods may change, in the same way that we may become more irritable if we are ill, or more loving and kind if we push our own troubles into the background, but basically our way of thinking remains the same. Because of this, androgens given experimentally to try to induce masculinity and a heterosexual way of thinking into homosexuals have failed to bring about any change in outlook. Whereas hormonal factors do exert some influence then, they only represent a part of the picture. Dr. West, in his book *Homosexuality*, discusses the cases of intersexuals reared contrary to the true sex as reflected in the internal organs, and states that 'When this happens, upbringing is apt to triumph over the sex glands.'

Puberty brings with it many psychological problems, due to the increased awareness of sexual development, sensitiveness, and feelings. Although the way each of us overcomes our difficulties at this time depends a lot upon our upbringing and conditioning to our surroundings, there is no reason to suppose that our psychological approach to sex would take on such significance were it not for the testes and ovaries becoming mature and secreting their respective hormones into the blood stream. These hormones help to give us our sexual feelings, our sexual libido and drive. If the genitals remain undeveloped through some abnormality or insufficiency, the individual will not only lack these feelings and sexual desire but be psychologically affected, becoming shy, nervous and inhibited because of his 'inferiority'. Indeed, the androgens present in both sexes are credited with being responsible for sexual desire, and the increase in the androgen level at puberty being greater in the male than in the female would seem to account for the greater sexual drive in the male at this time. That androgens, and not oestrogens, produce the sexual libido appears to be confirmed by the evidence that although the oestrogen level is raised enormously in the female at puberty there is slower build up to the arousal of sexual sensitivity. Thus we can assume that the hormonal internal factors do affect us psychologically, although after our initial experiences of sexual gratification in a certain way we can condition ourselves to produce the same urge by our own conscious thoughts, observations and fantasies.

For all this, the psychological and physical nature of the individual is inborn, and the attitude to sex at the critical time of puberty must be attributed, to some extent, to these factors. It is almost as though the internal factors present all the time are striving to make themselves felt, but that the external factors can either accept them or override them according to the conditioning of environmental circumstances and upbringing. Throughout the whole of our life we are constantly being influenced by our surroundings, and according to the society in which we live men and women are given different rights, so that what is acceptable for one sex may be unacceptable for the other, and vice versa. Can we say this is the reason why a man's outlook and thoughts differ so much from a woman's?

Since the woman is physically weaker, and her body more susceptible to injury because of her vital internal reproductive organs and tract, as the bearer of life it is recognised that she should be protected. Her role in life is that of a mother, and as such her place is considered to be in the home, not becoming involved in the challenges of a man's world. All her interests are expected to revolve around her 'mother instinct', and it is considered quite logical that she should like soft clothes, pretty things, jewellery and make-up, and be content to do cooking, housework, embroidery and knitting, undertaking the more menial tasks or embarking on such careers as her soft, kind nature fits, such as nursing, etc. On the other hand, the man's body is so built for him to be the protector and 'breadwinner', the challenger and fighter. He is not expected to be dainty, artistic or emotional, but hard, courageous and logical. He must not feel too deeply, for love, affection and warmth are the female's greatest qualitites. At all times men and women are expected to conform to the recognised pattern set out for them by society, and, from the moment it is announced that a boy or a girl has been born, he or she comes under the influence of those who have brought him or her into the world, and the conditioning commences. All those qualities that belong to the other sex have to be inhibited, and only those of the appropriate sex encouraged.

In modern Western civilised countries today it is the man who is vested with the power of authority and leadership, and possesses the greater rights over the woman, although more recently the cry for equality for women has done much to narrow the gap that was quite wide not so many decades ago. Margaret Mead's investigations amongst certain tribes living in New Guinea are well known, and her studies of their ways of life serve as examples to show us that an individual can be conditioned in any direction, according to the particular recognised pattern of the community. In the Arapesh tribe, for instance, she found that both sexes are levelled on the feminine pattern, both men and women being naturally maternal, gentle, responsive and unaggressive. The Mundugumor tribe, she found, were similarly levelled, but on the masculine pattern, both sexes being the fighters and lacking any of the usual feminine qualities of emotion and tenderness. In both these examples, then, the temperamental and psychological dif-ferences between the sexes had been largely removed. In contrast, however, she described the Tchambuli tribe, in which the roles of the sexes are markedly divergent and in reverse to the pattern of recognised Western society. Although patri-archial in organisation, the women of the tribe are the recognised rulers and workers, take the initiative in sex matters, and encourage the men in their more menial and artistic pursuits.

It can be seen, therefore, that an individual of either sex can be conditioned to accept the qualities that any particular society demands. That a man should think, act and behave as he does in our own modern life, in a specific manner and in direct contrast to a woman, shows how much our society is responsible for the psychological and social differences that exist. Because the man learns that his must be the position of strength, power and responsibility, he will weigh up evidence carefully and tend to be factual and logical in his approach and outlook on life. On the other hand, the woman accepts her 'weaker' characteristics, tends to shelter behind the recognition of her inferior status, can give way to her emotions and rely more on her 'intuition' than on logic for answers to her problems, since if she is wrong it will be no more than is expected of her. This intuition, however, is based on the extra powers of perception that she develops to fit her role as the bearer of life, and although shy, reticent, reserved and placid, her nature will become fearless and aggressive when it comes to defending a new life that she has borne into the world.

In practice, an individual is expected to conform to his sexual role as laid down by society and convention, and no aspect of his life escapes the surrounding forces trying to mould him into the recognised pattern. Indeed, this whole pattern is built around the part to be played in life, not only sexually but also socially. The design of clothes is based on practical, functional and physical considerations, so that the male who is expected to be engaged in more strenuous tasks, needing freedom of movement in getting about, finds his clothes hard-wearing and his shoes stout and flat. On the other hand, the female is allowed unpractical, dainty, soft clothes to go with her more gentle and placid role in life, with high-heeled shoes, colourful costume to complement her graceful figure, and perfume, jewellery, and long curled hair to help her meet her needs in attracting a male partner. The need of a woman to be protected because of her sexual vulnerability means that her freedom must be curtailed, and that she should not go here or there alone without being thought 'loose'. A man is given pockets to his clothes to carry his personal belongings and his money, and the dirtying of his hands by constantly reaching into these will be of little consequence. Any pockets in women's clothes, however, are more for show, and a handbag serves instead to carry essentials such as make-up and the money she may require. The whole time that such differences are marked between the roles and dress of the sexes, transsexualists will find it even more necessary to break away from the bounds of their imposed limitations in order to express themselves. Yet, however near society comes to recognising the equal rights of men and women, the sexual differences can never alter and the roles will always remain opposed.

To sum up, men and women are partners together in the

human race. Each is born into the world with the intended capability of playing a sex role to reproduce life, and in this respect must be opposite, though complementary, to each other. The essential differences that are to be found, whether they are anatomical, functional, psychological or social, are therefore basically sexual in character. *Nothing can detract from this fact*. The sexes are different in structure because they have different functions to perform, and according to these functions society has, through the ages, formulated a pattern of recognised behaviour, manner, code and dress best suited to the performance of these functions within the framework of a conventional community. The way in which an individual is brought up and conditioned to accept these written and unwritten laws depends upon the community, and upon the sex in which the individual is placed according to the recognised sex-determining factors. The psychological approach to sex, and indeed to life itself, is therefore a result of a combination of all the vast complexities we have discussed, each interrelated with the other. Only when we understand this can we hope to accept our differences, recognise and appreciate the way of life of others, whether they be of the opposite sex or of another nationality or creed, and be happy being what we are and with what we possess.

CHAPTER SEVEN

EXAMINATION OF THE SUFFERER'S ATTITUDE

Perhaps the greatest single difficulty in any attempt to assist transsexualists with their problem lies in their inability to accept facts. Even when they can fully understand the facts, and come to know just how impossible certain things are, they still are unconsciously unable to accept them, since it goes against all their feelings and, as they say, their nature. This may be due to their conditioning and general outlook on life, but certainly, once the sufferer has passed a certain stage and becomes determined to achieve the goal of a 'change', the obsessional state that develops is very difficult to break and all logic is thrown to the wind. Because of this, any criticism of the sufferer's point of view or feelings is immediately interpreted as a failure to understand, and as opposition to their desires. Whatever disadvantages may be pointed out to them, they insist that these will not matter. They will know of other cases who did certain things, and had certain things done successfully, because 'they have read about it.' They know little of the inner feelings and struggles of these other cases, or how they are faring long after the glossy picture has been painted. Certainly the cases themselves would not readily admit to having made a mistake, if it should be so, or even that they may have some regrets. In any case, the sufferers will not believe that their desire may be only for novelty, and can only imagine that once they have reached their goal all their troubles will disappear, and they will have happiness ever after. Nothing in life is ever like that. Whatever we strive after, and then get, can only be a passing phase, for we must soon find something else to strive after if we are to take an active interest in life. To have everything you want in life can be dull, and does not necessarily bring happiness. Even as a child we will crave desperately for a certain toy, only to tire of it soon after we get it, and it will end up broken at the back of the toy cupboard, forgotten. As an adult we may crave for a particular recording of our favourite artist, only to find that when we have played it over and over again and know every note by heart, it leaves us unsatisfied.

The danger with the sufferer's obsession is that it tends to cut off all other interests in life, so that all relevant practicalities are dismissed from the mind. Thus it is necessary to inform the individual of all the facts and to discuss the difficulties and misconceptions of a 'change', so that a full analysis must be made of their state, not, as they may believe, to undermine their justification, but to assist them to face up to life in the broadest possible sense and to accept reality. Clinging to their dream world they remain immature, and often shut out all that is going on around them. Their view of life becomes narrowed, their obsession occupying all their thoughts and energies. In an effort to examine the sufferer's attitude here, we must realise that they will always put forward criticisms and counter-arguments in their favour. Their minds work in such a way that they must justify all they say and feel. If no ready answer comes they will search their minds for one to fit in with their plan and mental picture. This is natural enough and to be expected, for every argument has two sides and rarely is either side completely unbiased. To a large extent, then, the male or female wishing to 'change sex' will find all manner of illogicality to convince others of their justification. Equally, those whose advice, help and sympathy are sought must be prepared to accept the sufferer's point of view without prejudice, and aim to put the facts as logically and objectively as knowledge of the subject permits. There is a point where logic ceases and illogicality commences, however, and the sufferer must realise that, to live a 'sane' and happy life, logic cannot for long be suppressed. If we heard that someone was obsessed with wanting to be a canary, and went around chirping and flapping his arms, we should immediately form the opinion that such a craving was illogical, because we should know that such an event as the individual turning or changing into a canary was an impossibility. Society would further suggest 'caring' for this person in a suitable home. Even the transsexualist would agree with this. Yet in the sufferers's minds they see themselves as the other sex, and can see little illogicality in it. It does not matter if a man is six feet tall, takes size twelve in shoes and is covered with facial and body hair; he will accept that it is logical that he could never be a canary, but will refuse to accept any illogicality regarding his ability to be a woman.

The transsexualist can help himself the most by trying, not only to understand all the facts at his disposal but to accept them, realising that they are intended to help and not to decry his feelings. Equally, those who are onlookers must be careful not to pass judgement based on their own outlook on life, because their views are largely a direct result of their own upbringing and the society in which they live. In the same way, none of us could choose our sex, our nationality, or the era in which we were born. We must, of course, criticise as our common sense tells us, according to our knowledge and education, but we must think of ourselves in different circumstances before we condemn. A thriving society must have its rules and its laws, and those who deviate from the accepted path cannot hide behind ignorance, or the idea that they were born that way, as an excuse. The aim must be that peoples should live in harmony with each other. In considering this problem of transsexualism, therefore, we must not be carried away in the belief that it does not matter if it does not affect us. Similarly, the sufferer must understand that he, too, is a member of society, and must study more than his own circumstances before giving way to his feelings.

Aetiology

In medicine, once we know the cause of a condition we are a long way towards a cure, since removal of the cause will usually remove the unwanted stimulation and its effects. Unfortunately, the cause of transsexualism is very deep-rooted, either in the physical make-up or in the unconscious mind. Also, the urge has usually been exerting itself for most of the individual's lifetime, and to change an outlook or attitude built up over this period of time is not only difficult but for the most part impossible. Once the 'computer' of the brain has been fed with ideas and programmed to accept certain things as facts, it is not easy to substitute others for them. Indeed, if the information fed in has become established from the earliest formative years, it may well be impossible to correct it. It is often different and contradictory ideas, which we accept during our education, upbringing and conditioning, that cause the frequent conflicts and emotional upheavals in our daily lives. Usually, our reasoning comes to our aid and enables us to resolve these battles, but sometimes, however hard we try, a subconscious element keeps our battle raging and we are unable to explain why we feel as we do about certain things, or to understand our conflicts, desires and moods. Provided enough of the information we have in our brain conforms to accepted normality for the society in which we live, we are generally able to live at peace in our surroundings and with our fellow beings, and those impulses that may stimulate any abnormality are able to be suppressed.

In the same way, the more we learn of life and the world around us, the more able are we to regulate any of our earlier misguided conceptions. It is not necessarily true that we cannot change our ideas or behaviour, but that to do so we have to add to our knowledge in order to increase our powers of deduction and reasoning. Similarly, anyone who changes his or her environmental sex does not change his or her attitude to life because of the change, but rather, whether they are happy after all with the 'change' or not, tends to accept life more peacefully knowing there is no further choice left to them. It is this inability to accept life as they are that makes the transsexualists' problem such a difficult one. Their whole life is one uphill struggle, fighting themselves, their feelings, their 'nature', their behaviour and their enforced role. They have become more and more apart from their surroundings, wrapping themselves up in their fantasies and dreams, as the only means of satisfaction. They find that less and less are they able to cope with life, and unless they have their heart's desire of a 'change' they feel life is not worth living. Yet this build-up is essentially due to their own attitude to life, and quite often to their behaviour.

Although internal factors play their part, and may bring about anomalies of the sex organs to a great degree as in the case of the hermaphrodite, or anomalies of development physically or psychologically to a lesser degree, it is the external factors of upbringing and environment that play the major role. A girl, for instance, brought up as a boy, will develop masculine traits because she is conditioned to that way of life. This has been demonstrated with true intersexes, who have been reared contrary to the sex suggested by their internal sex organs. It is, however, essential that we are practical, for if a person has developed, and can function sexually, for example as a normal male, we must deal with the individual as he stands to-day. The same applies in the case of a physically normal female, possessing ovaries and capable of conceiving a child. What the writer is trying to impress is that irrespective of all internal factors, whether they are causative or not in a particular case, the influence of environment is far more likely to be the underlying cause of the transsexualist's feelings and state, important as the physical and biological aspects are when considering the justification for help with a 'change'.

We need not consider the different types (see Chapter Five) separately here, but, if the basic underlying influences are all environmental, we might ask 'what makes an apparently normal boy of three feel like a girl and want to be one?' We are told that a boy may like to dress in his mother's clothes because he has moulded himself on his mother, instead of on his father. We are told he may become jealous of his father receiving his mother's love and so develop an emasculation complex because of his guilt feelings and belief that he should be punished. We are told that an individual can remain immature because of his sheltered upbringing, or may engage in self-love and derive pleasure by masturbation, long after this phase should have passed. He may even have homosexual tendencies as a symptom of his feminine feelings. Yet all these things revolve around the first question: what makes an apparently normal boy of three feel like and want to be a girl?

The writer believes the answer lies in the individual's reversal of his conditioning process in his own mind, brought about through one or several causative factors mentioned. There may be some latent biological reason associated with some definite physical abnormality or anomaly, or there may be encouragement from an overdoting parent. Then again, it may be due to the child being made to feel unwanted, because he or she was not in fact born of the sex desired by the parent, whilst some form of perversion may even be openly or suggestively practised by the parent to influence the child's mental state. Since all cases say that they felt of the other sex as long as they can remember, it is evident that these causative factors make themselves felt in our earliest subconscious awareness of our feelings and surroundings. The immediate instinct is for a child to rebel against its sex, instead of conforming and accepting itself normally, and this may be done almost unconsciously to attract more love or conversely because the mother over pampers a delicate son. Obviously, the child is unaware of the reasoning behind the feelings, and, once they have become established within the formative years, any amount of normal conditioning is resisted. The young boy, then, may remember a great dislike of having his long curls cut, or his delight in once being dressed as a girl because of the attraction it caused. Long after the events have taken place they exert their influence on the subconscious mind, and the individual will automatically rebel against anything connected with the recognised sex, tending to absorb all that normally would most attract the opposite sex. Whilst normal boys look in a toy-shop and perhaps admire a cricket bat, the transsexual boy will 'instinctively' find himself looking at dolls. Whilst the normal boy is out playing games the transsexual boy, finding he does not fit in, will perhaps stay at home and reap pleasure from trying his hand at cooking or some other generally accepted feminine task about the house. However much the transsexual boy may be scolded for his unboyish behaviour he will in his own mind infer that, because he is unboyish, his motive and desire in feeling like a girl and wanting to be one has some justification. The scolding therefore has a contrary effect to that intended by the parent, and only helps to provoke the feelings more. Many cases of transsexualism refer to the fact that they were scolded for their unmasculine or unfeminine behaviour.

We have of course only mentioned a few of the many factors

that may interact to bring about this reversal of the child's conditioning. Each case is influenced by a different set of factors, and we must not immediately assume, for instance, that a transsexual girl is a direct result of the parent's wish for a boy, or vice versa, although in some cases this may, of course, be so. The main outcome always remains the same, however, in that the child fails to accept its conditioning. Later in life, as the condition progresses and the need for expression becomes more pressing, we find that the individual has developed mentally as the other sex, saying that he feels as if he has the mind of a woman imprisoned in the body of a man. Having shunned everything masculine, the transsexual boy grows up to find it is easy for him to act and think as a woman. Whilst other men have been busy following masculine interests the trans-sexual man will have conditioned himself to take notice of those things that attract a feminine mind. He will grow up conversant with the latest fashions and shade of lipstick, or drooling over pictures of models in magazines and the woman's page of the daily newspapers, visualising whether the clothes would suit him if only he could be a girl. If he thinks sport is a masculine pastime he will even force himself not to take an interest in it, and instead occupy himself in some domestic chore about the house.

In as much as society divides the sexes, transsexualists tend to exaggerate even more the normal division, and every little aspect of life is divided into what they envisage as being male or female in character. They develop a gross misconception as to what represents masculinity and femininity. Transsexual men generally seem to think that a woman does not or should not drink, smoke or swear, take an interest in sport or enjoy fast cars. Instead they picture a woman sitting passively at home imparting her love to her offspring, tidying up the house, cooking a meal, being treated with courtesy and guarded by some very masculine man. The revolt against their own concepts of masculinity, and their desire to be feminine according to their own concepts, seems the essential factor behind their refusal to accept life as they are, and until they can view life differently there is little hope that their inner struggle will give them enough peace of mind to make the most out of the qualities nature has endowed them with, regardless of the way they dress.

A man can give vent to his artistic feelings in a vast number of ways, such as music, the arts, designing, hairdressing, etc., in the same way that a woman can tackle jobs not so long ago considered the prerogative of men. Yet often transsexualists are lacking in the drive to alter their life, because the energy required for it is used up in fighting their problem. Since the onset is at such an early age, the sooner the individual can be made to understand the facts the better is the chance of their acceptance. If, on the contrary, the individual grows up with these conflicts, the chances are that he will end up embittered towards society, feeling it has done nothing to prevent his suffering. Unfortunately we can do little to help in these cases, since they credit no one with human feelings, and in any case are resentful of the wasted years that can not now be made up. Since we can also do little to remove the causative factors, whether due to biological forces or to the civilisation in which we live, our aim must be to build up our knowledge of the subject as fully as possible, and to assist those so troubled to a better adjustment to life according to their own individual circumstances and merits.

Normality and Abnormality

We are all apt to think of normality and abnormality as terms denoting some definite and set state, but we should for a moment reflect upon these words, for they can really only describe one state in comparison to another. When we speak of a normal individual, we refer of course to the overall picture. We could, however, enumerate millions of factors when considering anatomy, growth, function, behaviour and attitude, etc., and against these in a supposed normal individual we might write 'abnormal' a considerable number of times. The person may have an abnormally large nose, an abnormal heartbeat, or walk abnormally with his toes turned in or out, yet in every other way he may be normal. Because of our way of thinking, we are apt to draw a line between the abnormal things

283

we do not mind and the abnormal things we very much object to. A person with some abnormality or disease of the heart is not looked upon as being abnormal in the strict sense of the word, and yet there is a very great and unjustifiable tendency to consider a transsexualist abnormal because of his feelings, possibly present through no fault of his own, when in every other respect he may be normal. Thus we must recognise that transsexualists are abnormal only in certain respects, although the transsexualists themselves must accept that to be called abnormal is not necessarily a slight on their character. To call a transsexual man immature immediately brings forth a denial on his part; he feels you have wronged him and cannot possibly understand him, and the same happens if he is said to be abnormal. Yet, in blaming nature, society or his upbringing he accepts his abnormality, by saying that had he been reared in his 'correct' sex he would be as normal as everyone else. Whilst we may not agree, we must be prepared that the sufferer will lose our confidence if we say anything that conflicts with his desires. He will say that if he cannot get help with a 'change' he certainly does not want to be readjusted back to normality, but would rather stay as he is. When we speak of normality and abnormality, then, we must qualify in which sense we mean it; we should also remember that both states merge one into the other, and that our concepts of what is normal or not depends entirely upon our own upbringing, education and outlook. The transsexualist in his turn must realise that normality is not meant to imply rigid conformity to extreme masculinity or extreme femininity, but rather a state giving him the ability to accept the facts of life and act upon them with the greatest benefit to himself and his fellow beings.

Sexual attitude

The sex urge is perhaps the most powerful force within us, and no doubt the most important role we have to play in life is in the procreation of the species. Because of this, the whole process of our development and way of life revolves around this ability. However society or religious bodies expect us to perform our duties in lovemaking and marriage, etc., the sexual role itself is something that has to be expressed in all of us, whether we like it or not, in some form or another. It is often a force we have little control over, however hard we try, because of its very basic origin, and we should not feel guilty about its presence or try to suppress it unnaturally. We should, instead, try to realise that sex is there for a specific purpose, not just as a means of giving us excitement and pleasure, and that if we offend against common decency in relieving our sexual emotions we must accept the consequences. Since reproduction is brought about by intercourse between a male and a female the heterosexual attraction of one sex to the other represents normality, and any other attraction must represent an abnormal condition or perversion, although this does depend largely upon our ability accurately to determine sex. The important thing to remember is that sex needs expression, and that any personal consideration of our sexual role, state or function, or rebellion against them, is essentially sexual in character.

The whole desire to 'change' is in fact wrapped up very closely with the individual's sex feelings, and often, because of his own inadequacy in his expected role, he will mentally assume the role of the other partner and 'love himself' as it were (Narcissism – so called by Freud, from the Greek legend of Narcissus, who fell in love with his own reflection). Such narcissistic individuals pay overdue attention to themselves, in their appearance and in their wish for praise and love from everyone, only to become cold once the limelight is turned away from them. Narcissism is often shown in cases of transsexualism, especially in their introverted state and their fussings over trivia in their appearance. The fact that they wish to be made love to, instead of having to exert their own energies in giving it, is often a common feature of the transsexual man, being rationalised by him as part of his feminine feelings. From the inability to cope with the normal heterosexual act, and the revulsion to it, is born the desire to be sexually complete within himself, and the sexual satisfaction of his appearance and his appreciation of the feeling of soft clothes next to his skin are manifestations of this.

A similar association of ideas may give a particular item of clothing a fetish character, and is not far removed from the recognised sex arousal that a 'normal' male may experience on seeing a woman in a 'sexy' dress, or a 'normal' woman on seeing a man in tights. It is part of the normal sex urge that a man should be stimulated by the sight of a woman's body, although often a *nearly* nude woman provides more stimulus by allowing the imagination to provide what the man wants to picture further. Thus, even a normal man may be aroused by a particular item of female underclothing, being able to picture the woman in it, and so develop a sort of fetish in a purely heterosexual way. The transsexual man's state is obviously only a variation of this 'normal' mechanism, based on the fantasy that he is a woman, and can account for his revulsion to his male genitalia and his apparently homosexual attitude.

To all transsexualists 'homosexuality' is a revolting word, and they are indignant if it should be applied to them, although some cases do sincerely look upon sex in a neutral way, attracted to neither one sex nor the other. Cases who openly exhibit latent homosexual tendencies say that if only they could become women they would want to be admired by men and made love to by them, whilst those who are asexual often desire a 'change' to be rid of any involvement in sex, it being the thought of enjoying the role rather than the passive sex act as a woman which appeals. What they do not realise is that, whilst as men their sexual involvements rest with their own actions, so that they can remain 'neuter' if they wish, as women they are subject to the advances of men whether they like it or not, and are never allowed to forget their sex for one moment. On the other hand, those whose desire for a 'change' is more closely associated with a latent homosexual tendency, and is sexually motivated, are probably more concerned with taking the female passive sexual role than whether they are real women. Probably the prime cause of this sexual laziness is selfishness, coupled with the lack of initiative or physical strength necessary to the male in the sexual act.

The wish to be passive, to take the easy course in life and be treated as one of nature's delicate flowers, is a further stimulation to transsexual men, many of whom imagine life to

286

be so much easier as a woman. This often ties up with the inferiority complex that develops from their feelings of inadequacy, since they think a 'change' would raise their status by virtue of having to put less effort into life to gain 'promotion'. Such is, of course, contrary to the generally accepted view that for a man to want to become a member of the 'weaker' sex is degrading and insulting. People can understand a woman wanting to be a man, to become stronger and to raise her status, but generally it is foreign to them that anyone should feel the other way. Investigation shows, however, that nearly all cases imagine they will be automatically admired and desired as 'women', basing this on their own attitude to the female sex and not realising that *normal* men look upon women in an entirely different way. Perhaps the greatest single feature is the emphatic denial by all transsexualists of there being anything sexual in their wish to 'change sex', yet many already have their 'partners' in life, and many profess to want one as soon as they have 'changed'. Even those who have remained unattracted to either male or female will maintain that their only wish in changing is to be rid of sex, as it is abhorrent to them. Yet the fact of hating their own sex organs and wishing to be without them shows the sexual character of the desire, since it is singularly noteworthy that no case seeks out a surgeon to perform the necessary operations and then, satisfied that his 'guilty' sex urges, feelings, and resultant behaviour have been removed, is happy to go on in the original role of upbringing. On the contrary, the desire to be rid of sex is only part of the story, for much as operations will relieve the transsexualist of the parts of the body antagonistic to him, the motive behind the wish for such operations is the essential ability to be able to identify himself or herself with the opposite sex.

The delight of the transsexualist to dress up and picture himself as a member of the opposite sex is, in fact, very closely connected with the sex act itself, and this can be demonstrated by reducing the normal sex urge by the use of the female sex hormone Stilboestrol, loss of sex desire being accompanied by loss of pleasure in the transvestist act, and commonly with loss of transsexualist desire also. In general, it seems safe to say that in by far the majority of cases the condition is a rationalisation of some other sexual anomaly, an anomaly which in other conditions is more readily accepted than among transsexualists, who do not really want to accept that they are abnormal. They therefore take a perfectionist attitude and seek complete sex reversal as far as medically possible, as a means of justifying their state, making them 'normal', and resolving their inner conflicts. Unfortunately, it is only when the obsession has driven the individual to his desperate goal that he can start to take stock of reality and the world around him, realise the misconceptions of his earlier sexual attitude, and have cause to review it.

Discussion of Behaviour

In the same way that the feelings largely give rise to the behaviour, so the behaviour itself is responsible for many of the difficulties, torments and conflicts of the transsexualists. It is strange that these cases force themselves into actions and behaviour which magnify their problem, and that they fail to realise that much of their inability to fit in with society is because of their own determination not to. Because the behaviour is part and parcel of the condition the sufferer may have little choice in the matter, but this is not to say that he should give way to the condition for by controlling this the behaviour can also be controlled. If, indeed, a stage is reached whereby no effort is made at restraint the individual may become like a chronic alcoholic, callously craving more and more for what will satisfy him irrespective of the harm it may be doing and oblivious to his surroundings, only to end up less and less satisfied. The transsexual man will, for instance, more and more look upon himself as a woman until he is living a double life, both psychologically and in his behaviour. Having forced himself away from heterosexual conformity, and into an inbetween state, he will complain he has few friends, is lonely, is not accepted in company, is open to ridicule and embarrassment, is an outcast, and cannot do this or do that, etc. Yet all this is because of his own mental approach to life, regardless of whether it has some physical basis or is just purely psychological. Possibly, the grudge the transsexual man seems to have against society for not understanding and for ridiculing him may be only in his mind, but even if society in fact takes the view complained of it cannot be wondered at, if he goes about with long hair and finger nails, and adopts unnatural mannerisms, as is often the case. The tragedy with these cases then is that so many of their torments and problems are self-inflicted, and are often a direct result of their failure to seek proper medical treatment. Unfortunately, the only treatment they desire is in the nature of having a magic wand waved over them, for although they only profess to want this or that done to help them, they inwardly know a great deal is necessary to enable them to resemble even remotely the picture they see of themselves, in their mind's eye, as the 'perfect' female. Since all women possess masculine qualities, and the female they envisage is one hundred per cent feminine, their idea of the perfect woman is hypothetical, unreal and non-existent.

The transvestist act is a common feature of the behaviour pattern of transsexualists, for, even if it is not practised openly or in private, it exists very much in the sufferer's dream world. Those who do dress up usually commence with one or two items of clothing and go on to build up a complete wardrobe. Although this may be resisted by a few who have strong principles, full scale transvestism is invariably the ultimate practice of all as a prelude to adopting the opposite role permanently. Those extremists who practise transvestism openly from the start, however, condition themselves to see in the mirror what they want to see, and have a fantastic ability to regard their often grotesque appearance as feminine beauty. Every artificial aid is often resorted to, and in having to comment on the final result one can only, with pity, see deep-rooted immaturity, a desire for unknown expression, and a mind living in another world. Such extremists have usually little hope of ever bringing their dream world to life and would almost certainly be dissatisfied with it if it became a reality, and we can only hope to sympathise and to educate them into the real pleasures that life offers beyond the realms of sex and its involvements.

The passive homosexual who dresses up as a woman largely does so to enhance the sexual act. True transsexualists are not homosexual in this sense, although transvestist behaviour generally stimulates sexual function, and often an individual intending to dress fully as a woman may experience orgasm before he has on all the clothes he has laid out and abandon his plans. Quite often the force of the sexual drive and the frequency of the need to express it determines very much the character of the behaviour. On this basis, we should expect to find that the behaviour moderates as the sexual drive diminishes, and in fact this does occur, whether it is a natural process of age or artificially induced by hormones. This is, of course, provided that the transsexualist obsession has not reached its climax and the individual thus become conditioned to his behaviour.

Sado-masochism, also, has another side to it, for apart from the tremendous urge prompting some desperate action to bring about emasculation, the peculiar pleasure derived from being tied up, weak and helpless, associates itself with the wish to be feminine, to be humbled, and to delight in the thought of being a member of the 'weaker' sex. It is this attitude which similarly enables the transsexual man to accept giving up all the advantages he may have gained as a man, in financial earning power, status and respect, and to profess that he would not mind taking the most humble of jobs, for a meagre wage, if only he could 'change' and be happy. It is remarkable how these cases are prepared to give up all to achieve their goal, although this is often rationalised into the view that, since life is not worth living as they are and if they were dead they would have lost everything anyway, it is better to live with nothing if it gives peace and satisfaction. The hole in this argument, however, is that if the 'peace and satisfaction' should be gained, money, a good job, and friends are even more important, and, once sex has gone out of life and the lovely clothes so longingly craved for have been outworn, the money that seemed so unimportant as a man is ever more necessary, and that five-pound-a-week job as a waitress doesn't quite fill the bill any longer.

Even female hormones can increase the transsexual man's

problems, and in his craving to get anything to make him more feminine he will have explored every avenue to procure some of these 'magic' pills. Some fatty enlargement of the breasts will then be construed by him as feminine in character, but, much as inwardly this will thrill him, he will feel over-conscious of them and hate even more having to live as a man and hide his proud possessions. At the same time they will embarrass him, for he will fear they may be noticed and that his workmates will jokingly but innocently pass remarks about them. This situation is again of his own making, and in any case is likely to be greatly exaggerated in his mind. It is not uncommon for many men to have quite pronounced fatty development of the breast tissue, and being normal men they look upon it as on any other part of their body and if any remarks should be passed probably join in the joke with their pals. Others may be proud that it gives them a certain physical prowess. The guilty feelings of the trans-sexualist make him concerned, however, for the role is a forced one, and any suggestion of being shown up for what he really is hits home hard. Usually, he should have little cause to worry, for the breast enlargement is probably small and not, as he would like to believe, two perfectly normal female breasts. Even so, he will probably withdraw from all social activities, and certainly not go swimming or engage in any sport.

Thus the transsexualist's world grows smaller, making him more and more introverted and unable to think of anything but his problem. His mind will go over and over the same things, wondering how it will all end, and he will live to work and sleep, his only interest being to search for his elusive goal of a 'sex change', for the more difficult it becomes the more he wants it. In the end he finds himself obsessed with wanting something he cannot really visualise, except to know that he is not satisfied as he is. And this is so with his behaviour, for however devious it becomes the satisfaction is never quite complete, nor will it be even if he manages to 'change sex', for he will never lose the knowledge of his past behaviour or his present inadequacies. It is certain, however, that no individual can live between the sexes for long without producing great emotional and mental upheaval, and the surest way to ease this suffering is to conform to the expected role, outwardly, as far as possible, so that the cutting off from society is prevented. What behaviour is indulged in, in private, is the affair of the individual alone, and may serve as an outlet to his feelings. There should be no giving in to the problem or it will become overwhelming, but there is no need to be what he is not, and he can be happy in the pastimes and hobbies of his liking because they are not, as he believes, classified into male and female. He must not look upon cooking as the privilege of the busy little housewife, but realise that male chefs are probably the best of all. He must not think that being a typist in his job is not right for a man, for he has only to think of all the able and very masculine newspaper reporters tapping out their news and articles. In this modern world there seems little that cannot be done by both sexes, and for the transsexualist to say that he likes doing this and doesn't like doing that, on the basis that the do's belong to the opposite sex, and the don'ts' belong to his, is being unrealistic, illogical and unworldly.

Before we conclude here we should perhaps consider something of the female transsexualist's behaviour. Generally speaking, they are much more sensible in their approach to the subject and to life, and this is one reason why a change from female to male is often more successful than the other way round. Instead of adopting a negative attitude they take the positive line, are more matter-of-fact, have more drive and energy, and seem better able to face up to their difficulties without the tears and thoughts of suicide. Whilst men are expected to fend for themselves, and can go anywhere alone, it is quite natural for a woman to go about with a girl friend with similar interests. Even so, without a man between them, the two girls are restricted somewhat in their carefree existence, and, if one of the pair should have come through life feeling like a man and wanting to be one, it is easy to see how a 'change' would enhance the relationship. Because of this we find, almost without exception, that transsexual women have their female partners in life, and therefore appear to exhibit strong homosexual tendencies. It is difficult to say just how much sexual satisfaction these partners give to each other, although we are not concerned here with true lesbians, and any apparent lesbianism is defended as being but a symptom of the transsexual feelings.

The transsexual woman therefore seems to have greater scope for expression, and it is usually only her principles and morals which determine whether she is happy living as a man without any form of change other than clothes, or whether she must insist on all the help that medical science can give her and in the meantime resort to slacks and an Eton crop. This mode of dress seems well tolerated by the public, and generally expression in this way prevents any great deviation in sexual behaviour. Some cases may have masculine features, but they are all generally normal women, so that the greatest obstacle to the masquerade is almost certainly their menstrual periods. Hence the first requisite being a source of supply of male hormones. Often the greatest initial delight to transsexualists of both sexes is the masquerade and fooling the public. It is not always being the one or the other that gives the satisfaction, so much as the actual reversal of roles, and a change which only involves environment and clothes can often keep the transsexualist very much between the sexes, swinging from one side to the other and back again. This situation is not likely to last for long, however, opposite sex hormones usually being taken to excess and encouraging the desire to proceed with the 'change'. Nevertheless, much of the novelty of 'changing sex' is the actual change, which is why disillusionment can creep in afterwards. As one case who has made a surgically assisted change of role put it to the writer, "It was much better travelling than arriving."

Sense and Nonsense

Just as there is only a thin dividing line between what may be said to be normal or abnormal, so to speak of sense and nonsense, or logic and illogicality, depends very much upon society's accepted standards and conceptions of different aspects of life. Yet, since nothing can be proved unless we are first prepared to accept certain facts, it is upon the facts that we must judge what is basically sense or nonsense. Indeed, what may be thought nonsense to-day may be thought sense tomorrow, just as not so many decades ago the idea of man being able to fly, let alone get to the moon, was considered fantastic, impossible, and *nonsense*. We, however, are dealing with a problem as it exists to-day, and transsexualists must face up to this fact in trying to deal with their difficulties and not blame the world's 'ignorance' for their suffering. Neither can justification be based on the belief that one day more will be known of the subject. None of us can really be a part of humanity while living in a world of dreams, either of the past or of the future. Certainly, our experience of the past and our awareness of the present enable us to see with vision into the future, but these visions are based on the knowledge we have and it is with such knowledge that we must measure our concepts of sense and nonsense.

This must be clearly understood, for whilst much of what transsexualists feel is, to most of us, nonsense, to them it is so real that they cannot strive hard enough to convince us of the fact. On the other hand, we have to try and convince them that they are out of step, and that they should accept what we consider to be sense. Perhaps the transsexualists' greatest problem is trying to convince others of the genuineness of their feelings. Much of the time, however, they cannot convince themselves, because of the conflict of their own ideas, and they become incapable of accepting anything they do not want to believe; in this respect many, if not most, of their arguments become nonsense. We may all wish to be different in form or character, in some momentary daydream, but our logic soon pulls us back into the reality of everyday life.

In the transsexualist, however, the obsession overrules the logic, so that the fantasy grows and grows and gradually becomes 'real'. Not only does the six-foot, powerfully built man like to see himself as a petite, curvaceous female, but he even comes to regard himself as one, having conditioned himself to believe that it is his body and not his mind which is out of step. We cannot criticise this simply by saying it is all quite nonsense, but we can impress upon him the nonsense of his ambition to do anything about it, try and make him realise that certain things

294

about us cannot be changed, and suggest that he tries to review his approach to the subject and to life in general. All those dealing with this problem will know, however, how these cases refuse to accept facts or their anatomy. They may often show every aspect of good reasoning and appear to understand the impossibility of actually changing sex, but when it comes to accepting the truth and practical sense of the argument their inner forces defeat them, much as they often profess to wish they could control them.

To these cases, sex has become, unconsciously or otherwise, of great importance in their life, either because of their revulsion to it or because of their disassociation from their own sex, and the very fact that it has been inhibited and suppressed tends to make its presence felt more. It is like holding back a spring; in its free position it can be used to effect when wanted, but if it is permanently under tension a force has to be exerted to keep it that way, and the greater the deflection the greater the force required. Similarly, if the force should be suddenly released the effect will be greater than a gradual release of pressure would bring about. This rather describes the sexual state of transsexuals, for having suppressed their feelings they are constantly aware of the tension, and the more they try to conform the greater the conflict. Only when the tension becomes too great does the matter rebound out of control, and when this happens the individual feels compelled to rationalise his feelings and accept them, so that an obsessional state results. One of the main reasons for the tension occurring in the first place is often lack of sex education, or the belief that sex is something about which we should feel guilty. In early life, too much importance may be given to the differences between the sexes; we have drummed into us that only boys can do this and only girls can do that, and that we must not think as the other. Only a little girl should love pretty things and the beauties of nature; a little boy should enjoy a scrap with his chum or go and play with his toy pistol. When we rebel against fitting in like this the boy believes he was meant to be a girl, and the more his free expression is denied him the more he wishes he were.

The argument that nature meant these cases to be of the

other sex is therefore based on their idea of the differences between the sexes, which is further demonstrated by the way in which these beliefs are maintained throughout life. We find their concepts of femininity and masculinity are grossly exaggerated, and consequently their fantasies, of how they see themselves in the other role, are equally out of all proportion to the true picture of things in reality. They build up an erroneous picture of the opposite sex, and fit their feelings into it as parts of a jig-saw, in order to justify their state. In Chapter Three, Mr. X saw himself ecstatically in a woman's world, going into a beauty parlour, into a powder-room, admiring pretty clothes, discussing fashion, having a man give up his seat on a bus, and being whirled around a dance floor in a pretty frock. Yet what would the average woman say to all this? All very well, no doubt, but what about the washing up in the sink, the dirty clothes to be washed, the carpets to be vacuumed, and the meals to be attended to? And where's the time or the money coming from to meet this craving for fashions? A novelty, yes, but the satisfaction wanes as all these things become part of everyday life.

What really troubles the transsexual man is that he does not want to be a man. He may say that he does not necessarily want to be a woman, although we must wonder just what else there is for him to be? What he really objects to is his sexual state as a man and his self-imposed necessity to conform to everything supposedly masculine, and although he can have no idea of what a woman feels, or of her different role, he can only see that he must fit this sex better. Obviously, all his knowledge of how a woman feels and lives is based on his own conceptions, for without her glandular apparatus, her sex function or her upbringing, he is in no position to compare his feelings with those of a woman. Essentially, however, he feels inhibited as a man, inadequate and unable to give of his best, and all his energy is taken up in trying to conform and being repelled by it. Yet he does not realise that the differences he perceives to exist between the sexes are entirely superficial, and that his failure to give an outlet to his emotions is entirely due to his own insistence upon a sharp dividing line between masculinity and femininity. He cannot see that we are all human beings together, and that what matters to his neighbour is not whether he is a man or woman, but what sort of a person he is, in his character, his integrity, and in his personality.

It can cut both ways, of course, for the transsexualist will say that this is one of the reasons why he wishes to change, for when dressed as and feeling a member of the opposite sex he will profess to be a 'nicer' person. We can only believe that this is due to the release of the sufferer's tension, and that in fact, were he able to unburden himself of his conflict by accepting the facts of life, he would equally be able to live as a man and give vent to all the good qualities he feels obliged to otherwise suppress. There seems little doubt that society over-emphasises the differences between the sexes, above and beyond the purpose of sex as a means of reproduction, because there is no reason why a man should not love all the aesthetic things in life as much as a woman, for each and every one of us is capable of feeling and emotion. Society does therefore help to provoke the antagonistic feelings of transsexualists by imposing its restrictions upon them from their earliest years and conditioning them as it feels they should be conditioned. On the other hand, these cases must realise that it is not society that gives them their particular build or organs, and that as far as function and anatomy is concerned these must be the distinguishing marks to determine the role in life and therefore the upbringing.

The widely held belief that the medical profession do not understand, and will only laugh at them or want to make them 'normal', causes a fear of seeking help, for the last thing transsexuals want is to be made normal as far as being pushed back to heterosexuality is concerned. Even if they cannot press on with the 'change of sex' for which they crave, they most certainly do not want to be 'cured' of how they feel, for these feelings have become so much a part of themselves that to be denied them would be to lose their very soul. The fear also of exposing their lifelong secret causes all the other symptoms of the condition; loneliness, introversion, abnormal sexual pleasure, and the withdrawal into a world of fantasy. Much as all this makes sense the need for it is distressing, since so much of it results from ignorance of the facts. If only these cases would try to get at the truth, instead of absorbing things designed to be sensational, they would find their torments eased considerably, for the medical profession are only too ready to assist them to face up to their problem.

The writer has particularly found these cases to have very little knowledge of the subject medically, of facts of sex and life generally, or even of the basic fundamental differences between the sexes. They also have no knowledge of what is entailed by a 'change of sex', and often their ideas of what is possible are quite nonsense. Some, for instance, seem to think that mere removal of the male genital organs will turn them into women. The loss of a source of androgens will, of course, have some effect, and the loss of the organs themselves may have repercussions in either direction on the individual's mental outlook, but the body will remain the same sex, and organically the operation will make the individual no more a woman than would the amputation of a little finger. Indeed, there must be many cases in war time who have suffered the loss of their external genitalia through enemy action, and who remain as much normal men as ever they were, though of necessity accepting their sexual limitations in life. The belief that hormones will work wonders on the body is also often difficult to shake; one case, after taking female hormones for two weeks, complained that he was still having to shave every day!

Yet even after being told that they can never really change whatever is done they will, whilst agreeing that to be a 'normal' woman is impossible, still affirm their desire to be accepted as a woman socially and legally and to be made into a woman to the fullest extent that modern surgery can achieve. Mr. X says he can really live as a woman to-morrow, and yet later on says the only things that trouble him are the persistent growth of hair on the face and body. In fact, Mr X is essentially masculine in physique and appearance, and what he really means is that he can pretend to be a woman to-morrow. He says he would only want this operation and that operation (obviously from what he has read because of the exact nature of his words), and would just want hormones and have it all made legal, etc. And this is, of course, the story of them all, and whatever is done the chances are that they will never quite be satisfied until something else is done, and then they will find that their conflict remains because they are still not normal anyway.

Another popular belief is that they can be taken in hand, as it were, for the 'full treatment'. They seem to think someone will be there to nursemaid them, know just what to do to make them into women, advise them what to wear and what to do, get all their cards changed, and so on. They do not realise that any expression of their 'true self', as they often like to call it, must come from within them, and that if there is any question of having to *learn* how to be a woman the chances are that they are deeply affected psycho-sexual deviants and that a change of environmental sex is for the wrong reasons and likely to end in unhappiness and regrets. The fact is that many really want a 'change' the easy way. Certainly they do not want to pay for it, and most have not the money anyway. 'Why should I be denied what is my "right" for me,' they say, 'when others who can afford it are not?'

Unfortunately, those who search for help are usually impatient and suggest that their life is wasting away, often criticising the most those who are genuinely trying to understand them and assess the true merits of their case. Often, in their hurry, transsexual men say they will accept hormone treatment without operation, if only it will enable them to live as women and help them just that little bit more in the direction they want to go, but it is not long before the individual realises he cannot go for a swim as a woman, or do this or that, and then presses again for more help. If he cannot get help and his plight becomes desperate he may genuinely feel life is not worth living, and, although some may make a half-hearted attempt at suicide to promote sympathy, in others the impulse may be a very real one as the only way out of the torment and conflict. Either way it puts a great deal of responsibility on those dealing with the case, for if their patient has suicidal tendencies, it can be argued, operation may only precipitate this desperate and ultimate action. In any event, such thoughts of suicide are likely to be misconstrued as blackmail, and the transsexualist must realise that any threats can only be detrimental to his own case and to his own well-being. He cannot expect help unless he is prepared to help himself, and whatever he has to face up to must be better than admitting that life has no further interest for him.

What now of the arguments the transsexual man puts forward to justify his feelings and state? Often he will speak of his inability to put over his argument, because of his 'weaker' feminine qualities. There is, of course, a tremendous need for these cases to convince others of their sincerity, and they will examine every aspect of their past life, their present thoughts and ways, and their anatomy, to try and find signs of femininity. They will believe that their genitals are small and shrinking, when in fact no abnormality usually exists. They will believe that they are having to shave less, and that their facial hair is not excessive after all, in spite of the fact that it is often thick and dark. They will be sure that their body form is more feminine than masculine and delight especially in quoting their 'vital statistics', stressing that they have a small waist but disregarding their small hip measurement. They will claim, for instance, a 36-inch 'bust' and a 26-inch waist; they really mean that they have a normal man's 36-inch chest and frame, and are slim and lean in the waist and hips. If they develop some fatty breasts they might then boast a 40-inch 'bust', and be able to wear a certain cup-sized brassière, but the measurement would be due to the size of the frame and not to normal female bust-development, which in contrast is large anteriorly and small round the back. Unless the male transsexualist can boast a *chest* measurement well under his hip measurement, and still show a slim waist between, he can derive no satisfaction from his 'vital statistics', and even then the curves between are a woman's prerogative. If, indeed, he could 'change sex' and put on the feminine distribution of fat on the breasts and body, he would find his final figures were vastly different and not as 'normal' a woman's as he had hoped.

In extreme cases the individual may even mentally 'castrate' himself, firmly believing that he is not in possession of male organs in order to see himself as a woman. To be told that all his feelings are purely psychological is hurtful and unacceptable, for it implies that he has no justification for a change, is not quite all there, and should really pull himself together. He thus refuses the psychological explanation, claiming the fault lies in his genes, and continues to seek justification in his physical state causing him to conjure up such vivid imaginings about the state of his body, devoid of all logic and reasoning. So adept does he become at 'cheating' himself that in the confusion between his world of fantasy and the world of reality truth is a likely casualty. Indeed, in Dr J. B. Randell's study of thirty cases of transsexualism (*British Medical Journal*, 26 December 1959) referred to in Chapter Two, the author states that he found no male in the series to have dysplasia of the genitalia or major anatomical indication of femininity, and that no female showed evidence either of genital dysplasia or male anatomical conformation. The writer's experiences have been similar concerning the hundred or so cases known to her, although a few male cases showed some signs of feminine characteristics in general body form and three female cases showed a tendency to masculine build, perhaps due, however, to opposite-sex hormone administration.

Concerning the monthly build-up, in transsexual men, of sexual urge and increased desire to 'change sex', no evidence suggests any connection with a female cycle, although this monthly manifestation is commonly reported quite independently of other knowledge. This aspect seems worthy of closer study, for although a phasic state is known to occur in such conditions the regular pattern makes one feel it may well have some psychosomatic origin, or more doubtfully be connected with impulses from the pituitary gland.

So the obsession grows, the individual assuming a double life either in behaviour or just in the mind. Little will convince him that living between the sexes is only making things more difficult. Indeed, it can only cause untold suffering and misery, and is a state that should be avoided at all costs. Whereas nail-biting may have been a manifestation of his early conflict, the transsexual man, now mentally in his desired role, will usually swing to the other extreme and let his nails grow to unpractical length, hating to chip or tear one. Similarly the body becomes unduly precious, the slightest cut or graze almost bringing tears. One case professed difficulty in holding his pen to write a letter, due to the length of his nails. Another would wear gloves at every opportunity to prevent soiling the hands, whilst others bathed excessively and enjoyed the lavish use of perfume. When dressing-up, their exaggerated ideas of femininity were expressed in their clothes, and they would choose things much too young for them, trying to re-live the girlhood that was denied them. Tight-fitting jumpers would delight them, although beneath them there was usually only a 'bra' padded out with socks or handkerchiefs. High heels, too, were an essential part of the attire to emphasise femininity, and often were professed to be sheer joy to wear, yet sore and even bleeding toes bore mute testimony to the enforced torture.

For any man to say he enjoys wearing high-heeled shoes more than the flat masculine ones he has known all his life is a sure sign that he has not worn them for any length of time, or that he is so obsessed with femininity that all practical considerations are swept aside. It is natural that a woman should dress to look attractive, and high-heeled shoes are a part of her upbringing, but she is the first to be glad on occasions to get into a pair of casuals to go for a stroll, and these days even into a pair of slacks, because she finds they are more comfortable and practical. For a man to say he is feminine because he loves high heeled shoes and a free and easy skirt is no more than adherence to his own conception of femininity. To state further that he would not wish to wear slacks as a woman, even if they were the height of fashion, is another example of his refusal to compare natural femininity with the set and false picture of femininity he holds in his mind. He will say that feminine clothes are so soft and nice to wear, yet there is nothing soft about a firm girdle, and the average woman looks forward to bedtime when she can remove it and give her body a rest from the energetic exertions of the garment. To say he enjoys cooking and doing housework, etc., is again but the result of the individual's self-conditioning process; indeed, a vast number of men get their own meals and keep their room or flat tidy. On the whole, if he can make the 'change', he will be quite happy to

302

take the easy way out, go on earning his living, and let someone else do the domestic chores. No case known to the writer, having changed his role, has shown more interest afterwards in domestic matters than in earning a living and making money. One lives in a hotel, others go to work from lodgings, having meals provided, and two still live with their wives!

If any man told a psychiatrist that he wanted to live as a woman, he would probably be told that it is much easier to live as a man. Indeed, a man has more freedom of movement and is likely to get a better job with better pay, and can carry his position wherever he goes. A woman, however, is often regarded as someone unreliable, unpractical, and scatter-brained, who may run off at any time to get married and take her job less seriously. Furthermore, her position in life is not such a reflection of her status, and can be raised or lowered by the company she keeps. All this makes the woman's place in life more difficult to uphold. Yet the transsexual man will refuse to accept these logicalities, saying that if anything it is easier to live as a woman. In any event, they say, it is of no consequence, for they feel they are a woman, and such things will have to be accepted as part of the life they crave for, so that weighing everything up there are more advantages if they 'change' than if they stay as they are in a life of torment. If it were not for the transsexual women who put forward the same arguments for a change in the reverse direction we might believe they were right, but, to be fair, what one considers an advantage and pleasure may to another be a disadvantage and displeasure.

This important question must be examined by all trans-sexualists, although it can add little to the logic of wishing to exchange their whole way of life for a dream world, causing great emotional upheaval to themselves and to their families, and the reality of which they have never sampled. Dreams and desires are very different from reality and hard fact; we may picture a man from his voice on the radio, only to be surprised, when we see him on television, that he is not at all as we had imagined or wanted him to look. Similarly, the glamour of the other role, once achieved, can shatter in a rude awakening to reality, once life settles down to its humdrum way again and there is nothing left to dream about.

That the true intersex follows the psychological pattern of his upbringing, rather than that of his physical state, is perhaps the greatest indication that the external influences are the masters over the internal, and that irrespective of physical justification the transsexualist's attitude and condition is essentially psychological. We must remember that all of us are as we are because of the way in which we were brought up; for example, we behave differently to other nationalities, whose ways are not natural for us. It is that we have not been conditioned to those things, and just as we cannot cast judgement on the rites and doctrines of other countries, neither can we fairly condemn transsexualists for their feelings but rather, since they are in our midst and part of the society in which we live, we should try to understand them. They, too, must help themselves, by realising that certain things are sense and other things nonsense, for only in the acceptance of these facts will they find the peace of mind they seek.

CHAPTER EIGHT

THE LOGICAL APPROACH

THERE IS NO SUCH thing as a 'change of sex'. The writer is perfectly confident in making this apparently bold statement, despite whatever has been written before by a medical or non-medical person to contradict it. We are not now speaking of external anatomy or feelings, but of sex as we must rightfully look upon it for its functional purpose in life. No one who has possessed testes and fathered a child has ever had the testes and penis atrophy, ovaries and tubes, etc., develop, and then mothered a child. Those extremely rare cases of true hermaphrodites, who have been born with both organs and may even have been capable of both sexual functions during their lifetime, have still not changed sex, for the organs were there all the time, exerting their opposing influences on the poor individual.

Other cases of supposed sex change are often due to late development masking the true sex, which may only become evident as a child gets older, and this represents a human error of determination resulting in the individual being brought up in the wrong sex. In no way does the individual 'change', except in the environmental role to fit the functional sexual mechanism. Sometimes, in true intersexes, medical and surgical intervention is necessary to push the individual heartily over the sex border, and to assist in a heterosexual adaptation to life according to all the factors which can be used to establish the correct way the person should go. The correction is usually made in the early years and secrecy is maintained, to give the individual the best possible chance of rehabilitation and in order that the past may be forgotten and left behind. Such cases thus very rarely come to light. What we must realise, however, is that they have in no way 'changed sex'.

Of course, the thought of anyone changing sex conjures up all manner of wonders within the majority of us, and provides excellent material for sensationalism, yet although the reported cases seem to be increasing and the words 'sex-change' becoming household ones, it is surprising how very ignorant the public still are of the facts. The popular Press do little to correct any misconceptions for fear of detracting from the sensation value, and still insist on the use of the words 'sex-change' and 'change of sex' irrespective of whether it is a hormonally assisted 'change' by masquerade, a surgically assisted 'change' of external anatomy, or an officially recognised correction of sex. Because of this, 'sex-change' carries with it some mark of abhorrence in the public's eye, some fascination, perhaps, and most certainly sends up the temperature of the transsexualist searching for a solution to his own problem. When we hear of a German boy (in 1951) officially 'changing his sex' twice, we can see even more clearly how illogical such terminology is, and that such a case arose purely through human errors. It is essential, then, that we clarify the position as much as possible here, and get to know the facts more fully.

The transsexualist, having fought to justify his demand for help, is often equally compelled to justify his 'change' publicly. Indeed, in recent years, and in a number of countries, well-known cases who have received surgical help to assist a change of role have endeavoured to justify themselves to the world and show their uniqueness, whilst articles which have appeared about them generally give the impression that they have actually changed sex. Nearly all cases, however, still have male birth certificates, for the authorities, guided by medical opinion, are more inclined to judge that they are only feminised males living in the role more compatible with their essentially feminine feelings and were therefore correctly registered as boys at birth. Only recently an American is reported to have been prevented from marrying because of this. Some years ago, the circumstances of one British case aroused some medical controversy when, following the issuing of an amended birth certificate to show that she was *born* a girl, it was made public that she had previously been married and was the father of children. Today, the Registrar General requires evidence both that an applicant has never been married and could never function normally in the originally entered sex (see page 423). The practical difficulties of non-acceptance and the psychological distress caused cannot be over-estimated, however, and whatever the individual merits of these cases, we can only hope that they have found happiness and peace of mind in their new role and wish them every continued success for the future.

However much an individual may change in his feelings, emotions, external anatomy and way of life, the internal sex does not alter. Of course, sex is very complex in its implications, and we may speak of a sex cell, a sex gland, a sex organ, a sex hormone, psychological sex and environmental sex, etc. When we speak of a 'change of sex', then, it is necessary that we qualify the manner in which we regard sex. We cannot change our genetic sex, make our sex glands secrete a different hormone, or substitute a functioning testis for a functioning ovary. The difficulty of changing our psychological sex is equally well known, for we can make no firm claims to 'cure' homosexuals or transsexualists. Generally, the transsexualist's psychological sex is in the opposite direction anyway, so all we can do is to change the environmental sex, for once sexual organs have developed there is no way in which these can be changed to the opposite denomination and as far as functional sex is concerned a 'change' is impossible.

In some cases, however, glandular disturbances may cause us never to function in our supposed sex; we may remain under-developed and fail to mature, sexually, either in a strictly masculine or feminine direction. For the most part we are likely to be more feminine, for this is the basic sex, and with the deficiency of normal sex hormones and resulting physical inadequacy our psychological approach to life may well be upset also, so that the development of female characteristics may become more accentuated and established both in body and in mind. Such a state of affairs cannot be ignored, for once the individual is so firmly sexually inclined it is obvious that every medical assistance should be given to ensure that complete compatibility of all the sexual factors should exist as far as possible, in order that a normal and uninhibited outlook may result and the person be able to lead a useful and happy life. Whilst this adjustment generally involves a change of role, it can still not imply a 'change of sex', for the sexual characteristics have been there all the time, only manifesting themselves later to show the true direction of swing from the indeterminate state.

When we consider the vast number of births which take place in the world every day, we must accept the possibility of many intersexes occurring. Indeed, there is no reason why sexual abnormalities should not arise, any more than Siamese twins or other physical faults in development. We must not confuse the issue, however, for many 'normal' individuals exist to-day with functional defects of the sexual mechanism, and these unfortunate people who cannot contribute to the multiplying numbers of the human race have to accept their state and divert their interests to the good of humanity in other ways. Although the functional aspect is important and largely determines our concepts of sex, it does not necessarily outweigh all the other factors that give particular sex qualities to an individual. Indeed, should the function be imperfect in one direction and all the remaining sexual factors overwhelmingly in the other, the sex of the individual will be decided by these latter factors. The case will then be no different to those people devoid of sex function, and surgical assistance and readjustment of role may be indicated to help the individual live more at peace with society according to the obvious dominant sexual factors. Such a 'change of sex' may, in rare instances, be correct and well merited.

We must be careful not to read more into this than is implied, for all transsexualists would dearly like to associate themselves with such to justify a 'change of sex'. Although we find the psychological sex of the transsexualist reversed we rarely find any physical characteristic of the opposite sex or abnormal sex function, and because of this a 'change of sex' is out of the question. A transsexual man may change his form to some extent externally, have his beard removed by diathermy, let his hair grow or get a wig, and dress as a woman, but basically he will still be a man and a mutilated man at that. Similarly, a transsexual woman may develop masculine features by the aid of hormones, have her breasts removed and even a soft tissue plastic penis fashioned, but she remains basically a woman beneath her jacket and trousers.

The writer wishes it to be understood that she is here speaking only of transsexualists, individuals psychologically wishing a 'change of sex' without any physical justification for their attitude. There is, of course, a stage between the true intersex and the transsexualist that may be difficult to define, which is why each case must be dealt with on its own particular merit, although probably less than 1 per cent of all trans-sexualists that come to light show any degree of intersexuality in the accepted sense. Although we cannot deny that psycho-logical sex is an important factor and demands the most worthy consideration, the writer's object is to clearly point out to these individuals the myth about being able to 'change sex', which for the majority, if not all of them, means no more than mutilating operations which are arguably illegal and in consequence most difficult to procure except in the most exceptional circum-stances. Certainly, the whole object of the exercise is for these individuals to be able to dress the part and conform sufficiently to be acceptable to society in the desired role. It is said that clothes maketh the man (and no doubt the woman too). What you look like and what you are, however, can be two quite different things. It is not enough for the transsexual man to 'feel like a woman' when dressed as a woman, and the transsexual woman to 'feel like a man' when dressed as a man: logically they must realise that they can get into a pantomime horse's skin and look like a horse, though that in no way makes them a horse.

A transsexual man must take stock of himself, without the dress, the wig, the shave and the make-up, and wonder just how passable he would be as a woman in a nudist colony, or what he would look like after a week in gaol or on a desert island, deprived of shaving facilities and the fineries of his 'wardrobe', or if he were suddenly aroused from sleep. 'But this would not be so', he would say, because if he could get help to 'change' he would have this done, and that done, and be eventually quite passable as a woman in any circumstances. This, then, is an admission that he needs to 'change' in order to be a woman, and that he is not in fact at present a woman. We have said that he cannot change his sex, so just what does he want to satisfy him, and where will the limit to that satisfaction be? Perhaps the greatest danger of helping the transsexualist in any way is knowing that the limit of satisfaction may never be reached. In order to examine this more closely we must follow the road on which a transsexual man may desperately try to make his way, and see where the dangers and the many obstacles lie. He may, of course, only profess to want a little help at first, and here immediately is the first danger, for he feels that, once he can start on his desired path, the subsequent steps will be easier and give him more justification. In fact, as soon as he gets over one hurdle he will discover even more his abnormality, and crave directly for something else to make life easier in this or that respect in the feminine role; to make him more 'normal'.

Unquestionably, his first desire will be for female hormone. He will show enthusiasm to find out the name of it, unaware that there are several or that they can be of natural extraction or synthetic in manufacture. Of the synthetic ones he may come across the names Dynoestrol, Hexoestrol, and Stilboestrol, and discover that the last named is more likely to be prescribed and cheaper than the more potent Ethinyloestradiol. He will conjure with the pronunciation, and when he thinks he is proficient venture sheepishly into a chemist in the hope of obtaining some of these tablets, which he visualises once swallowed will bring about some wonderful and curious metamorphosis in him. To his dismay, however, he will be told that all drugs of this nature can now only be obtained against a doctor's prescription. If there is any hope, then, it means he must go to his doctor and tell him all about himself, and after some weeks or even months of conflict and torture, wondering what to do for the best, he will take his courage in both hands and open his heart to him. Probably he will come away in tears, wishing he was dead, if, having exposed his secret, he is just told to go away and pull himself together. But he will make another effort later on, when he has sufficiently recovered from his depression and shock and again plucked up the courage. This process is wearying and, no doubt, equally so for the doctor or the psychiatrist to whom he may be referred. In the end, however, feeling the patient's desire for sexual neutrality not unreasonable because of his state, the doctor may concede to the patient's wishes by prescribing 5 mg. Stilboestrol tablets, if for no other reason than as a sex sedative measure.

For a moment he is happy, for he has mounted his first hurdle, and anything to make him more feminine must surely give him greater justification for further help. Yet the great excitement dies down when he finds the tablets are having little effect upon him, and, assuming that a greater dose will produce a greater effect, he may take more than he is supposed to, only to find that it makes no difference as his body can absorb only a certain amount and the rest will be excreted. Into the bargain he may find that the tablets have an annoying side-effect, making him feel sick and nauseated. He should soon build up a tolerance for the drug, however, so that even large doses cause no ill-effect, but he will also find that there is a marked drop in his sexual desire and feel that something has gone out of his life. He had forgotten the time when sex meant nothing to him, and now suddenly there is an emptiness of feeling; almost a decrease in his need to be a woman.

Without the urge, sex in either direction seems rather subsidiary to other interests in life, although he has even lost his energy for these now, and finds that he tires easily and is quite happy to spend longer in bed. Somehow, when his thoughts return to his problem, he can see more clearly just how long the road is going to be, and he will often despair and wonder just how right he is in pressing on. How can he leave his work? What will he do afterwards? How will it affect his loved ones? Will he ever really be passable as a woman? The tablets have made him pause, and enabled him to think more clearly; they have made him more placid. But they have also made him more sensitive and emotional; tears flow more easily, and his soul searchings end up in bed at night with his conflict on top of him and his pillow wet with crying. The only saving grace is that something within him makes him feel more rested bodily, and, feeling his breasts every night, he is sure they are slightly enlarging. Certainly they are pricking a little, making him aware of them, to his great delight. What he is not to realise until much later is that however much female hormone he takes, and for however long, the initial enlargement is likely to be the most spectacular, for the breasts will only develop with fatty tissue to a particular size and remain at that, depending upon his own specific glandular make-up. If this were not so we might expect to find many women taking female hormones, to increase their bust and give them a film star's figure.

Another disappointment to the transsexual man is finding that the hormones are making no difference to his shaving. After a very long period of time his beard may grow less quickly, and the hair tend to be finer, but the distribution will remain the same. However long he goes on taking hormones, even in excessive doses, he will find that once his beard has developed little will effect its removal except the long and costly process of electrolysis. (We are not speaking of cases before puberty now, for if the growth of hair on the face has not commenced, hormonal treatment will prevent this male second-ary sexual characteristic from appearing.) Much as the adult male transsexualist may like to believe that his beard is disappearing, and may even profess this to be the case, no evidence substantiates it and if the individual is honest he will eventually admit it. He may feel able, on occasion, to make up his face to his satisfaction, but if he 'changed' and had to be presentable all the time he would find he had to shave as soon as hair showed itself, in order to avoid too much make-up, and thus have to shave even more often than before. Alternatively, if he puts off shaving as long as possible, relying on heavy make-up, he runs the risk of encouraging the hair to grow inwards because of the everyday covering of cream. He might also use a night cream, thinking it will make his skin texture smoother, being unaware that some creams, especially those of animal origin, encourage the growth of hair. Even a vegetable cream, however, cannot work wonders on a skin that is not potentially capable of improvement, and the use of it is more likely to be satisfying only because it is a normal feminine habit. Certainly his complexion is likely to improve with hormones, his cheeks will be rosier, the whites of his eyes whiter, and he will tend to look much younger as a man, though more his age dressed as a woman.

The chances are, then, that the transsexual man will take his hormones and be disappointed with the results. He is also not likely to know that hormones are recognised as having carcinogenic properties, implying that they could cause cancer. Certainly, any form of abnormal stimulation to the body cells may cause a growth that could be malignant in character, and for this reason stimulation by hormones cannot be excluded from causing this condition. Whilst no case is known personally to the writer where hormones have been detrimental in this way, it is a danger that should not be disregarded. Since the transsexualist feels life is not worth living anyway unless he can 'change', he generally dismisses this risk as incidental; they satisfy a craving, and give him at least some mental pleasure in knowing that his body is being 'influenced' by a feminine substance. If the individual maintains his dose of hormones he will tend to put on weight and his muscular development will decrease, giving way to more rounded proportions of the limbs with a deposition of fat upon the body. This is often counteracted by the inhibiting effect of the hormones on the pituitary, however, which normally plays such an important role in governing growth. Sometimes the plumpness may develop first as 'puppy' fat, and disappear as the glandular system compensates for the change in the hormonal balance. In other cases the castration effect may cause a 'middle-aged spread', the individual putting on weight gradually and being unable to reduce it, having to resort to dieting or Turkish baths. The effect depends upon the original glandular make-up of the particular individual, but in most cases the face becomes fuller in association with the general filling out of the body.

Although loss of libido and associated lethargy are symptoms typical of oestrogen administration, it is interesting to note that one particular case known to the writer proved an exception to the rule, female hormones actually increasing the libido and male hormones suppressing it. In addition to the increased sexual desire there was also an accompanying upsurge of energy, and increased immunity to colds and infection. Both physical and sexual immaturity appeared to be marked in this case.

What of our transsexual man, however, struggling to his goal? If his obsession is complete, he will not be satisfied just being able to dress as a woman, even though he still has high hopes that the hormones will make his appearance completely convincing. Although he may be able mentally to assume the absence of his male genitalia, their actual presence makes the difference, in his mind, between being a man or a woman, and he therefore feels he can never be happy unless he can have his offending organs removed. He may be told that some men are actually living as women merely after hormone treatment, and that he should be content to do the same, without any of the medical and legal complications involved in operations. He is told that a castration operation is illegal in this country, and that there is little hope of getting it elsewhere, except in Casablanca. This does not deter him, however, for he probably feels, morally, that he cannot live as a woman unless he first has the operations.

Let us assume that after much effort he has managed to find someone to perform the castration operation (bilateral orchidectomy). If he has not been genuine to himself he will have misgivings, and may become very depressed. At best he will imagine that the loss of this 'androgenic' factory must assist towards his femininity. He may even believe that he will now develop femininity without having to take female hormones, not realising that the adrenal glands are powerful in determining his sex hormonal balance through their own secretions. Any thoughts of having these glands removed, in order to remove all trace of masculine influence upon his body, will be shattered when he is told that these glands are vital to life and that in no circumstances would the danger involved merit any surgical interference with them. He may have come to regard risk and danger as unimportant, and believe he is only being told this as another excuse to restrain him from pressing on to his goal, but, in fact, artificial replacement of the vital secretions lost to the body by removal of the adrenals involves the most delicate treatment for the rest of life, and the condition may even then still prove fatal at any time.

The next step will be removal of the penis. He may think that, because he has no testes, there can be no possible objection to anyone assisting him in this respect, but he will find that there is just as much reluctance because of the likely complications, legally and psychologically. He will, of course, feel that he is still in every sense a man as long as he has a penis, and it is for this reason that its removal is a major step. Even without his testes he will find he is still capable of orgasm, although it may not be accompanied by the normal erection of the penis or by such a profuse ejaculation of fluid, and he will still derive a certain amount of sexual pleasure from the act. Without his penis, however, the full reality of what he has done will come home to him. Certainly, he only wants the penis removed because of his sexual state, and when he no longer has a sexual state through removal of the penis he may find it very difficult to understand what possessed him to have it done. Having used up all his energy, physically and psychologically, he may at last manage to get the operation his heart cries out for, only to find that his peace of mind is short lived as fresh problems become evident.

At least, however, he will now feel entitled to live and dress as a woman, and he will get busy making plans to change his name, his job and his surroundings, shrouding his transformation in secrecy until he can feel presentable as a woman and get into the routine of a woman's life. He will happily shed his male clothes for the last time and never want to see them again, for the moment has arrived when he can go into the town and look into all the shop windows at the fashions, without feelings of guilt or embarrassment. He will hardly be able to wait to give free expression to all those things he has for so long dreamed about. To be able to show himself off as a woman will give him a great thrill, for inwardly he is an exhibitionist, but it will not be long before he realises that people he passes in the street are too busy thinking what they are going to buy for lunch, or whether it is going to rain before they get home, to notice or care whether he is man or woman. Instead, he will be going home to try on his new purchases, or to try and improve on his make-up, or to worry what else he can do to improve his figure or to lessen his facial hair. He almost wants the world to stop, but in fact it goes on just as it did before and in nearly every respect he, too, is the same, for his own world is still very much centred upon himself. All day long he will be thinking of his appearance, how much he enjoyed being called 'Madam', whether his mannerisms fit the picture of his femininity, and whether he is being accepted. All these thoughts will be completely out of proportion to their relative importance, for he will after all feel that he is growing up again, and must also learn all over again. He will be too busy with the novelty of things to let the disadvantages of a woman's life affect him very much, and he will forcibly suppress any undercurrent caused by these limitations, because he must in no circumstances admit to himself that he may have been wrong to give up all that his former life meant to him.

His new world will soon be rudely shattered when he finds his savings gone and that he must now seek new employment. He will await anxiously the result of his application to change his National Insurance card, and if all goes well he will receive a new card marked 'Woman' and study it over and over again, unable to believe that it is really him. 'That must prove I am a woman,' he will say to himself, still not being quite sure and needing everything he can, in comment or in writing, to convince himself that he really is accepted. Work, however, will not prove so exciting as he settles down to the humdrum necessity of earning his living, for his dream of being whirled round a dance floor in a strapless evening gown is still far off. Thoughts of this soon make him realise again that he is not normal, and he begins to wonder how difficult it would be if he did meet up with a nice man who wanted to take him out, for as a woman he has now begun to see life from the other side and to realise that a good time is not likely to be far divorced from sex. Yet he will realise that, as soon as a 'nice man' knows about his state, he is not likely to have much further interest if the relationship cannot have any sexual significance.

Whether or not sex is now important to the transsexual man having friends most certainly is, and so, if for no other reason than wishing to be as normal as possible should the need arise, he will again become dissatisfied with his anatomy. Thus he will want something else – an artificial vagina. However much help he has already had he will still feel short of his goal, and even be ungrateful to his surgeon if he does not now assist him further. Most probably he has no idea of what he asks, just how the operation can be performed, what is involved post-operatively, how functional the 'vagina' may be, or whether he would ever feel 'right' having to pretend it was real. Indeed, it may only be now that he discovers, to his supreme regret and dismay, that the operations he went to such lengths to obtain so long ago, and which seemed at the time to be the obvious first step towards his goal, have deprived him of the very skin which could have been used to such advantage to form an artificial vagina. Even if he now has skin grafts from the buttock or leg to enable some semblance of one to be made, however, and accepts all the limitations and drawbacks, he will still have something at the back of his mind to deny him the peace for which he has so long searched, for however passable and happy he may be in his new role he will have the knowledge that his birth certificate has the word 'boy' on it.

However far he goes towards his goal it will elude him, for the crowning glory would be for him to bear a child and this can never be. After all his long tormented struggle he will never reach his goal of being a normal woman; he will never be quite satisfied or settled, and he will end up still searching for that elusive something. At long last then he must face up to coming to terms with life, if he is ever going to find happiness and peace of mind. Perhaps the long road he has travelled has taught him to do just this and if for no other reason his 'change' may have been worth while, but there is the very great danger that he is the way he is because of his approach to life, and that he will go on chasing rainbows for the rest of his days. Certainly, he will never be able completely to shut out his past memories or the conditioning of his upbringing, for to these belong his very personality. The chances of his overcoming all the hurdles, as we have for argument visualised, are, at the present time, exceedingly remote. The greatest danger is that he will reach a state where he can go neither forward or back, because he will meet along the way an unsurmountable hurdle, either real or in his mind. All he will do then is to land himself in a worse state than ever, between the sexes, and this is the worst possible state to be in. Knowing he must accept the terms of life at some point along the road, or remain as immature, unsettled, and unhappy as he has always been, it is almost invariably easier to face up to things at the beginning, accept himself as he is, divert his attention away from himself, and see that the wonderful things in the world are there to be enjoyed by both sexes alike. Then, by contributing to the good of society, he will reap the pleasure and satisfaction of that contribution, and his own difficulties will assume their rightful proportions.

In considering the path a transsexual woman may take we need not repeat the story of the struggles, but certain aspects are very different in a 'change' from female to male, not only surgically but physically and psychologically. The main reason for this is that, as the female is the basic type, it is much easier to induce the positive male characteristics in a woman than it is to reverse the process and remove already developed male characteristics from a man. The writer feels this may be better understood by means of an analogy. Let us imagine a bowl of clear water; if we put in a drop of ink it will colour the water, and the more ink we put in the more dense the colour will become. By likening the water (the original basic fluid) to the female, and the ink to the positive male characteristics, we see that in colouring the water the female can become masculinised to a great extent. If, on the other hand, we start off with inky water, representing developed male characteristics in a man, to feminise a man means trying to remove colour from the water. Clear water, representing the female characteristics, is therefore added, but it will be seen that a great deal of water will have to be added to lessen the colour of the ink, and however much water we may add a trace of colour will always remain.

Thus, if the transsexual woman manages to get the male hormone testosterone as the first step towards her goal, the effects will be rather more striking than the transsexual man achieves from his female hormone. Facial and body hair will

318

develop, as on a man, the voice will deepen, and menopausal symptoms will probably occur. Reduction of ovarian function may cause weight gain, and often acne will result as during an adolescent phase. Both will resolve themselves in time as the hormonal balance becomes settled, muscular development becoming more pronounced and the acne disappearing. The breasts will tend to diminish in size and the clitoris will become enlarged. In character the individual will become more aggressive and matter of fact, and although retaining her qualities of love she will not over-sentimentalise, but rather tend to look upon life in better proportion to reality.

The breast development forms the primary antagonism, being looked upon with the same revulsion as the transsexual man looks upon his male genitalia. For her, the breasts are the mark of her femininity, and cannot happily be hidden or forgotten when wearing male clothes. She may be able to encourage reduction in size by hormonal treatment and the wearing of a specially modified 'flat' bra', but regardless of this the transsexual woman considers the surgical removal of her breasts (mastectomy) as the first essential to 'changing sex', and it is this operation that she goes all out to obtain to set her on the path to her goal. This operation is not in itself a complicated one, having to be performed, unfortunately of necessity, on quite a large number of sexually normal women for reasons such as cancer. The loss of what, to a normal woman, is likely to cause extreme distress, is viewed by the female transsexualist as something that would make her very happy, although the psychological reaction to such an operation should not be under-estimated and is not something that can always be foreseen. Assuming she is able to get this operation done, she will soon feel that she is neither one thing nor the other. Although problems of menstruation can be reduced by male hormones, and her internal female reproductive system in no way adversely affects her masquerade, she is never likely to be happy whilst still in possession of her female organs and removal of these 'at an opportune time' is very much a part of her plans.

Meanwhile, she will have taken to wearing male clothes and

although at first the role is strange to her and changes in her mannerisms, ways, and even the way she thinks and speaks are necessary, she will, as time passes, come to feel the part and be less conscious of herself. She will by now have to consider the problems of getting her name changed, of getting a new National Insurance card, and also what forceful argument she can put forward to try and get her birth certificate altered. The relationship with her girl-friend can in any case now be maintained on a more 'natural' basis, the guilt complex is lessened, and the ability to go anywhere and be fully accepted together as man and woman has its advantages. Much as the female transsexualist may be quite content to assume the male role with the minimum of treatment, resorting only to male hormones and the adoption of a male name, another may feel dissatisfied unless she can have everything done that is medically possible to make her a man in the widest sense, and be recognised legally and officially also.

It is almost certain that the manner in which she has to pass water will be a thorn in her side, constantly reminding her of her abnormality, and the inability to use public urinals, though not paramount, can lead to embarrassment and an unsettled mind. It is not difficult to realise the threat this may be to her rehabilitation, and before long her tension returns and the need for her to have something done builds up again. This time she returns to her plastic surgeon, beseeching him to fashion her an artificial soft-tissue 'penis', so that she can urinate in the normal male standing position. She implores that she should be helped further in just this 'final' way, especially as, she will say, she is now quite definitely a man. Certainly, the operation she wants is not an irrevocable one; nothing has to be removed, and it is possible that her circumstances may enable her to press her request for help successfully. Even so, the procedure is a complicated one and involves two or more operations.

It could almost be said that medical science has made her a man; indeed, to the outside world she may appear to be one in physique, manner, and behaviour. She will try to forget that she was ever a woman, and if the 'change' has been successful she will no doubt want to 'marry' her partner, settling for a common-law marriage if it cannot be otherwise legal. She will have certainly changed in a number of ways, in appearance and in her attitude to life, but there will always remain the facts and evidence of her biological femininity in her cell structure, her bone formation and her internal organs, and in the memory of her past, her childhood, and her upbringing. The normal woman has not really *become* a man, anymore than the normal man has really *become* a woman. Neither have 'changed sex'. Even if any of these cases are intersexes of the highest degree, have every justification for their feelings and later prove that a change of environmental role has been right for them, we must realise that all that medical science has done and can hope to do is attempt to make them useful members of society.

Whichever direction these transsexualists look in the search for their happiness and peace of mind, the greatest danger lies in their typical inability to accept a limit to their satisfaction. Because of this it is essential that every step be considered from the start, and all possible facts put before the sufferers, for it is often better to continue on the seemingly impossible road with which they are familiar than to take a road beset with obstacles in search of a dream world that exists only in their imagination. The trouble is that there is never an end to the road, and that once they start upon it it is difficult to turn back, sometimes because they cannot, sometimes because they refuse to admit failure, and sometimes because their strange driving force pushes them on irrespective of circumstances or logic.

Generally, in the vastness of their plan, there is a narrowing of outlook, their obsession to reach their goal taking complete charge over all other interests and important aspects of life. This becomes more and more complete as the increasing influence of the opposite sex hormones makes the desire to 'change sex' the sole aim in life. All reality beyond it is so forgotten that to suddenly reach their goal pulls them up very sharply. Everything that was of so little importance before takes on new meaning, and the ecstatic joy of 'travelling' ends in anticlimax since the driving force remains without a further goal in view. You cannot climb a mountain for ever, for somewhere there is a top to it. You can stay at the level you have reached and be satisfied, until you think of going on higher or coming down. Yet if you do go on, and even reach the top, there only remains the anticlimax of having to come down again. The transsexualist can be alone on top of the mountain, with his joy and his dreams, but the reality of the world lies below and he cannot for long remain detached and ignore his surroundings and his fellow beings if he really seeks happiness. When he considers his aim in life he should remember these facts. He may not be able to master his feelings or his inner desires, but dreams are different to reality and there are some things that have to be accepted if he is ever to live at peace with himself. The transsexual man may have travelled the road to becoming what he thinks is a woman, and think that this is not a dream but a reality. The reality is, however, that by thinking this he is *still* living in his dream world. When he refuses to accept what he really is and has in fact become his obsession will have won, and in place of happiness based on reality will be a growing cancer, caring nothing for his physical or mental health, his feelings or the concerns of his loved ones around him. If the six-foot, ham-fisted, middle-aged, hairy man, married, with a loving wife and children, still wants to be the young, petite, dainty female, it is time he looked at himself in the mirror when next he gets out of his bath and is honest about what he sees, comes to terms with himself, and seeks the pleasures that are for all the world to enjoy, irrespective of anatomy or dress. Every one of us has our own troubles and problems, for it is part of living and of our ability to express our individuality. What we search for in life is largely of our own making; it is our powers of thought and reasoning that make us human and the control of our sex urge that places us above the animals. Only by using these powers can we contribute that which is individual to us, and it is how we use them that will determine if that contribution is to be to the good or evil of mankind and of ourselves.

CHAPTER NINE

THE MEDICAL POINT OF VIEW

THE CONDITION OF transsexualism is not like a case of malaria, in which there is a definite causative organism giving rise to a set pattern of effects and symptoms in the body, capable of being treated in a known manner to assist a cure and a return to normal health. It is, instead, a complex condition, in which not only are the possible causes numerous but several of them may combine together in varying degrees to produce a variety of states, each manifesting itself in a different way and calling for a different approach to treatment.

That every one of us is governed by our conditioning and upbringing can be demonstrated by the patriotism we are likely to show towards the country of our birth. What we are taught we tend to accept as right, in the same way that we accept the food we eat and wonder how other nations can enjoy their special dishes, which may not appeal to us at all. We all resent some small aspect of our upbringing, which equally shows itself in later life, and in the transsexualist this resentment is towards their enforced sex role. Whatever influences act on the mind to cause this state, and however much justification there may be for a change, anatomically, gonadally or genetically, the *desire* is therefore essentially psychological, just as every one of us is governed by our psychological approach to life.

It is not surprising, therefore, that the condition of transsexualism, as with so many others, lies in the province of the psychiatrist and psychologist, rather than the sexologist who is concerned with assessing abnormal sexual development as found in the various types of hermaphrodites. The immediate reaction of the transsexualist on being referred to a psychiatrist, however, is likely to be that he feels he cannot possibly be understood and that he must be thought 'not quite all there' for expressing such a desire to 'change sex'. This is a great tragedy when so many able men and women are available to offer help and deep understanding on the subject, only wishing to sort out the sufferer's problems in the most practical and commonsense way. Unfortunately, the reluctance of cases to seek advice and treatment has not helped to build up a very comprehensive picture of the condition, as far as the medical profession is concerned, although recent advances in this field have been rather more dramatic. Also, few specialists have the opportunity to study closely sufficient cases over a long enough period of time to be able to formulate any definite trend, personal contact and experience being essential for this.

The lack of published material, then, is often unfortunately due to lack of any definite knowledge, and, because of the variable factors involved, what applies to one case may not apply to another. With the specialists left to unravel the causes and try to establish the best forms of treatment, often with a large amount of contradiction resulting, the general medical practitioner remains very much in the dark on the subject except perhaps from recollections of what he may have read in a medical journal, although even this material is only presented in the most summarised and generalised form and is more likely to be by those enthusing in their work and, consequently, sympathetically inclined. For a fully developed anatomical male to go to his doctor and say that he feels like, and wants to be, a girl, must make the doctor wonder if he is having his leg pulled; surely he has only to say such a change is impossible and that is an end to it? It is often hard for the doctor to believe just how seriously his patient means what he says, and, human nature being what it is, what we don't understand we often don't believe in. Depending upon the doctor's scanty knowledge of the subject, and his ability to understand and believe in his patient's sincerity, he will act accordingly, and whereas from one doctor the sufferer may get sympathy, understanding, and a letter to a specialist, from another doctor he may get ridicule and leave the surgery in tears. We cannot question a doctor's motives for doing and saying as he thinks best, and either approach described above may best fit the circumstances. A sudden jolt to reality may be as good as a slap to a hysterical person, but the situation requires very careful consideration and the facts should be gone into very fully before any approval or condemnation is given; a complex condition should not have spontaneous judgement passed on it by otherwise busy medical practitioners, whose time is more often than not occupied with more immediate diseases and ailments. It should also be realised that such a first visit to the doctor will not have been occasioned by the sudden onset of the condition, like an attack of influenza, but, on the contrary, have only materialised after many months, if not years, of deep agonising about the decision to divulge a lifelong guarded secret.

If the general medical practitioner has had little or no experience with this sort of thing he is, at least, a good friend and counsellor, and is indeed the only person to whom a sufferer should go with his problem initially. At least the patient may learn the facts and the truth of his state, even if he is unable to accept them, for very little of what he may know or have read is likely to be authentic. The general public's attitude is similarly likely to be confused, and stories of 'change of sex' may cause anything from amazement, puzzlement, excitement and sympathy, to complete indifference, revulsion, or abhorrence. Indeed, much of what the public believes depends upon their own conditioning and what they have been taught to be right and 'nice'. If they have deliberately suppressed their views on any matter concerning sex, because they have been told and have accepted that even the word 'sex' is too vile to mention, they will obviously be quite incapable of understanding the problem. Even if they read of the facts their psychological approach to the subject will, in a way, equal that of the transsexualists, knowing but not wanting to accept, just because their conditioning makes them *unable* to accept anything that has not formed part of their upbringing. Conversely, the attitude to the problem may be sympathetic, if the public realises, through their own experience of the world, that 'there, but for the grace of God, go I.' Knowledge is the only thing that can help us remould our opinions and views, enabling our brains to arrive at a conclusion on some controversial issue. Yet the lack of authoritative published material leaves the general public to their own opinions, and for this reason it is not surprising that there are so many different attitudes to this problem. In addition, we must not lose sight of the influence of often conflicting and misleading information, that not only emerges more and more in print with sensationalism as the motive but which is generally allowed to go uncriticised and uncorrected.

Whilst the subject of sex change with specific regard to true physical intersexuals and hermaphrodites lies in and only in the province of medical science, it is arguable that the treatment of transsexualists who have nothing physically wrong with them should more correctly be considered within the framework of the moral conscience and sympathies of society. Nevertheless, the subject of transsexualism is one which the medical profession is coming increasingly to accept and take over as their responsibility, and in the past decade or so efforts have been made to look deeper into the problem with more realistic understanding. The conclusions of those who have made some special study of the subject are by no means consistent, but the more thought that can be given to the problem and the more cases studied the greater is the chance of getting to the truth. Clinical tests are obviously one means of trying to establish some basis for the feelings and, as science progresses, improved methods will no doubt come into being to help find some underlying cause, but we must remember that, whatever justification a transsexualist or even a hermaphrodite may be found to have, it is the age and developed state of the individual *at the start of assessment* that is all-important. Before considering the various chromosomal, hormonal, and developmental anomalies that may occur, what influences they may have on the sex of rearing and psychological outlook, and what tests may be employed to assess justification for any change of sexual role, let us take a look at some of the recent medical opinions advanced about these cases on the evidence of their physical and psychological state.

It seems generally regarded that transvestism shows features of homosexuality, fetishism and exhibitionism, and according to Weiderman (1957) the desire for castration may be a symptom of schizophrenia. East (1949) states that transvestites usually show no sign of sexual interest in their own sex, and in this respect are distinguishable from homosexuals, although Peabody, Rowe, and Wall (1953), in agreeing with this, feel that some tendency to homosexuality is not entirely absent. Warden and Marsh (1955) consider that masculinity or femininity is not the result of simple factors of function or state, etc., but is a complex psycho-biological product, and that cases of transvestism and transsexualism are in conflict with powerful sexual urges, feeling threatened by all sexual activity whether heterosexual, homosexual, or masturbatory. They regard male transsexualists as having grossly distorted concepts of what a female is like socially, sexually, and anatomically, and their castration impulse as a rationalisation of their desire to be rid of sex, which is in turn rationalised into the belief that without their male organs they would be women and thus they wish to be one. (These views agree closely with the writer's findings.) Hamburger, Sturrup, and Dahl-Iverson (1953) believe the condition is constitutionally determined and that some transvestites are intersexes of the highest degree. Whether this may eventually be proved is for the future but, so far, no evidence whatever has been forthcoming to substantiate such a convenient hypothesis. On the other hand, Plicher (1953) considers the desire for castration is not compatible with the psycho-analytical theory that fear of castration may cause the condition. He does not, however, take into account the rationalisation of fear by the individual, by reversing the process as a means of freeing himself from the very thing of which he is afraid.

Although largely referring to transvestism there seems little doubt that the condition of transsexualism is also very much in mind, as a rationalisation of the transvestist act. Even up to a few years ago the condition of transvestism was the only term used to cover all variations of those who cross-dressed, showed any physical characteristics of the opposite sex or expressed any desire to change sex. Yet cases we now know as typical transsexualists were often the subject of discussion. One such case, a 28 year old male, was elaborately and sympathetically described by Dr. C. N. Armstrong (an authority on intersexuality) under the heading of Transvestism at a symposium on nuclear sex given at King's College Hospital, London in

September 1957. All the features of wishing to be a girl from an early age, of dressing as a girl as soon as he came home from school, and showing a strong preference for girls' games and girls' company, follow the typical pattern of feelings and behaviour documented elsewhere in this work, even to the seeking out of female hormones post-pubertally and self-administering these. Genitalia were male but the build and hair distribution tended to be in the female direction. The wish to be castrated and to achieve female identity was almost fanatical. Of interest at the symposium was that, although endocrine tests revealed deficient testicular and adreno-cortical function, oral mucosal smears from both cheeks were chromatin negative, as found typically in normal males. Of particular interest, here, is the attitude to the condition with regards to treatment. This was amply demonstrated by Dr. P. Bishop during the ensuing discussion, who said:

> "I have had one or two cases with gynaecomastia and I have also had cases where physically the individual was a very virile male, with no suggestion of any feminine traits. I would agree that the problem is to know what to do with these people. From the experience I have had, and I have had considerably more experience of them than I would have liked to have had, it is extremely difficult to know what to do with them. The plastic surgeons won't touch them and the psychiatrists, very often, are completely uninterested in them. I have found psychiatrists who regard them as perverts, schizophrenics, and so on. The one thing I do feel is that these cases are absolutely genuine in their feelings, and are really very tragic. It is time to seriously try to think what is the right thing to do with them."

By 1959 the condition of transsexualism was beginning to emerge more in its own right and, in a paper by Dr. John Randell (a London consultant psychiatrist) in December of that year, fifty cases of transvestism and transsexualism were considered – 37 were males and 13 females. Physically, he found no case showed dysplasia of genitalia or major anatomical indication of the opposite sex, and nuclear sexing and keto-steriod tests when taken showed no abnormality. In his conclusions, he states:

> 'Almost all transvestites wish to appear in public in their assumed attire, and to be accepted as members of the adoptive sex. This tendency seems more pronounced among the male patients, and has an obvious relationship with exhibitionism. The craving for humiliation in female garb, in menial tasks or in subjection to a woman, indicates a masochistic trend in some male patients, and the demand for castration (or mastectomy in the females) echoes this maso-chism.'

He indicates the emergence of two distinctive groups. One, the homosexual men and nearly all the females, who often rationalised their homosexual inclinations by claiming that they were undergoing physical metamorphosis, to justify their desire and belief that they were 'changing sex'. The other he called the obsessive-compulsive group, who were heterosexual in orientation and in which the transvestist act was mainly a fetish to produce sexual satisfaction, although often accompanied also by normal heterosexual relations. Individuals in this group seem to be compelled to practise their behaviour, living the whole of their lives in the shadow of the impulse and being tortured rather than gratified by it, with a resulting tendency to suicide. Dr. Randell continued:

> 'Thought disorder in the schizophrenic sense did not appear, and the occasional delusion of shrinkage of the unwanted organs and change of stature appeared to be motivated interpretation and fantasy. The condition is to some extent associated with other forms of psychopathic behaviour.'

Another London consultant psychiatrist, eminent in the field of psychosexual disorders and well known for his classic 1940 work on the study of sexual deviation, *Sexual Perversions and Abnormalities*, is Dr. Clifford Allen. In a new, very recent book, in a section dealing with transsexualism, writing, he tells us, from his experience of having seen more than a hundred cases over the years, he describes the condition as follows:

> 'The patient, usually a man but occasionally a woman, most often young but not invariably so, complains either that a strange change is taking place and an alteration of sex is occurring or else he or she has always felt as though their physical sexuality was unnatural and there was a sensation as if he or she were occupying a body of the wrong sex. The purpose of the consultation is either that the spontaneous change, which the patient believes is occurring, should be expedited by treatment or else, if nothing is believed to be happening naturally, an operation should be performed to produce the alteration so that the body coincides with the mentality. It is not unusual for the patient, if a male, to insist that menstrual bleeding occurs from the urethra or anus, or sometimes periodically from the nose or elsewhere. Examination shows that the patient has a perfectly normal physique and there are no signs of metamorphosis. It is not unusual to find that the patient is also a transvestite, and, if a male, wears female underclothes often permanently, or, if a woman, dresses in male costume – the usual excuse being that it is more comfortable.'

He goes on to explain why a change of sex is impossible, the accent being on the word *'sex'*, and to state that any surgical 'change' amounts to no more than a 'mutilation' of the individual's sex organs and function and the encouragement of merely superficial features of the opposite sex by the administration of hormones. 'The aim,' he says, 'should be **not** to make the *normal* body fit the *abnormal* psyche but vice versa. The problem, however, is that these patients will listen only to the promise of surgery, and only too often fall into the hands of surgical enthusiasts, who are eager to show their skill. The bizarre views on transvestism and transsexualism expressed by medical men unacquainted with psychosexual diseases sometimes reach beyond astonishment.' He concludes:

'Transsexualism is not satisfactory from any point of view. Psychotherapy is of little value since the patient refuses any help that is not directed towards assisting him 'change sex'. They come carrying a pocketful of newspaper cuttings and try to confute one by insisting that what has been done to others can be done for them. Moreover they are quite ruthless in the attainment of their desire, cheerfully deserting wives and children and disregarding all practical and financial considerations. Socially the man is a failure and brings misery to his family; legally he remains the man he is and can get into all kinds of trouble with the law, and medically he is incurable. The transsexualist presents a pitiable problem, and one which we have not yet solved, but surgery does not provide a solution.'

Little is offered in the way of treatment, the view being that the patient will have just as many problems or more even if he assumes the opposite role aided by hormones and plastic surgery procedures, leaving him always inwardly ill at ease, never being really able to escape from the knowledge of what he is and that he is living out his life 'a lie'. Dr. Allen suggests small doses of oestrogens might be useful to reduce the tension and the sexual urges.

The author's own findings concur with much of what both Dr. Randell and Dr. Allen relate and with their conclusions. What particularly seems to be universally agreed is that the transsexualist's belief in his ability to change sex is held with obsessional strength, and despite repeated explanations of the chromosomal, anatomical and endocrinological basis of sexuality such fixed ideas persist, *though their illogicality is accepted, intellectually*. The italics are the author's, for it is just because these cases are unable to accept what they are told, believing the medical opinions to be biased and unsympathetic, that we must consider the basis for these opinions. In contrast, the various constitutional and physically abnormal conditions of hermaphroditism and intersexuality will be described in order to assess the sort of developmental defects that can occur and why, in some cases, a change or correction of sexual role may sometimes be medically indicated.

Physical examination

There is little need for much amplification here, since a chapter has already been devoted to the differences between the male and the female (see Chapter Six). Examination of the external genitalia is, however, likely to be the first point of note, assessing the normality of their appearance and state of development. In the male, the normal formation and size of the penis and testes will be noted, as will be the clitoris, labia and vagina in the female and the ascertaining of the regularity of the 'periods'. In either sex, general body form or phenotype needs noting, with special attention to individual aspects such as height, weight, length of limbs, bone structure, fat and muscle development, pelvic measurement, hair type and distribution on the head, face and body, pubic and axillary, breast development, character of voice, etc. The finer features, too, are important, such as the face, eyes, hands and feet. On the whole, there are a multitude of factors that must be taken into consideration. Occasionally, a man may remain thin and eunuchoid with his hand span longer than his height, or present with some degree of gynaecomastia, or a woman may be well built, thick-set and somewhat hirsute. Rarely some features of both sexes may be found. It is inevitable that such variations should occur, but this is in no way a true assessment of masculinity and femininity, unless the development and features are dominantly in one direction. For the most part, transsexualists get little comfort from the result of a physical examination to help justify their feelings and are more likely to be upset by the findings.

Tests and Studies

Apart from a physical examination there are a number of tests that may assist in the assessment of how masculine or feminine an individual is, in comparative terms, in various areas of medicine. The virility of a man, for instance, may be determined not only by ascertaining his ability to produce sperm but by undertaking a sperm count. The ability to produce sperm therefore (spermatogenesis), tells us at once quite a lot about our transsexual male patient. Whether the female transsexualist is having regular periods or suffering dysmenorrhoea or amenorrhoea is also of corresponding note, and, should there be irregularities, investigative tests can then be undertaken. When there may be doubt concerning an apparent intersexual individual a biopsy may be undertaken involving the taking of a small section of tissue from a gonad, whether it be from a testis or from an ovary, for microscopical examination, with a view to ascertaining the true nature of the organ. Similarly, it may be necessary to carry out a laparotomy, in which the lower abdomen is opened up surgically and the internal structures examined to ascertain which gonads may be present, their normality and what tubes of the reproductive system have also developed.

A simpler study that may be carried out on male transsexualists is known as a ketosteroid study. Steroids are chemically related organic compounds and are identified by the number of carbon atoms in the molecule. Various steroids are secreted by the cortex or outer part of the adrenal gland and are known as corticosteroids, and one group of these, the androgens, which are similar to those secreted by the testes, are of interest here being secreted in both sexes. Other sex hormones are also steroids, such as the oestrogens and the progesterones. Certain steroids possess a particular chain and are known as keto-steroids. The main ones of interest are the 17-ketosteroids, which are steroids with an oxygen atom at carbon atom number 17, and being resultant products of male hormone secreted in the body and excreted in the urine, levels of these can be measured to ascertain the relative amount of male hormones circulating in the system. Oestrogens are also excreted in the urine so that examination of the relative levels of both androgen and oestrogen in an individual can be made for the purposes of investigating the endocrine function of the gonads and adrenals when sexual abnormality is suspected. This has enabled studies of excretions, and any fluctuations, to be noted over a 24 hour period in terms of units, at different ages throughout life. At puberty, the androgen level in the male rises to about twenty-five units and in the female to about sixteen. The oestrogenic level remains at forty units in the male, but, in the female, rises from forty units to two or three hundred.

Abnormal levels may exist in certain cases; eunuchoid males may be found to have an excess of oestrogen or a deficiency of androgen, whilst masculinised females, possibly with a tumour of the adrenal cortex, may be found to have an excess of androgen and a deficiency of oestrogen. Whilst such studies are of interest in looking into abnormal physical states, they probably have little more than academic purpose in the case of transsexualists who are almost invariably normal in physique and body development and show little deviation from the normal expected levels. Where abnormal levels are found there is usually other evidence already of some physical peculiarity or glandular imbalance.

It was, indeed, believed that a homosexual may feel and behave as he does because of an excess of oestrogen, and that, if this was so, the balance could be adjusted and the condition 'cured'. This however did not prove to be the case, although it is quite possible that androgens were not administered in high enough doses for a long enough period to prove this fact unequivocably. No doubt no homosexual would be happy anyway to take part in such an experiment. Thus it must be accepted that sexual orientation, *once established*, is very difficult to change. Nevertheless, the administration of oestrogen or androgen to young animals has been shown to influence their sexual development and sexual behaviour and it also seems to be the case in the human, the behaviour, sexual attitude, and emotions of transsexualists being quite definitely affected by the continuous high doses of opposite-sex hormones they take.

Malfunction of the adrenals or the liver can also be diagnosed from blood samples, and in certain cases provide useful evidence of disease or other problems. When the results of all the tests we have mentioned are put together a clearer picture emerges of whether we are dealing with a condition with a physical cause or one that may only have a psychological basis. Occasionally there may be a little overlapping but the trans-sexualist is unlikely to find much to support his feelings and desires, or the justification he so desperately seeks.

Nuclear/Chromosomal sex

When we speak of nuclear sex we are speaking of certain features of the nucleus of a cell which have been found to vary between the normal male and female. The first intimation that a sex difference was to be 'found' in the nucleii of mammalian tissue came accidentally during an investigation into fatigue by Barr and Bartram, as reported by them in 1949. Their investigations led them to study the effect of stimulating a particular nerve in the cat, and to note the cell changes. Using cresyl violet as a stain, they noted that a mass of chromatin was present in some cats and not in others, and that the presence or absence depended upon the sex of the cat. It is from this early work that the present-day test has emerged, in which a 'Buccal smear' is taken from inside the mouth and the nucleii of cells from the scraping examined for the presence of chromatin, or 'Barr bodies' as they have come to be called. These were found to show up in cells from females but not from males. Thus, depending upon whether chromatin was present or not, the test was said to be positive or negative. In the absence of further knowledge it was extended beyond this, however, to imply that the person's genetic sex was female or male. Consequently when an anomaly occurred and an apparent male was found to have the 'genetic sex of a female', or an apparent female was found to have the 'genetic sex of a male', all manner of speculation was forthcoming as to why this should be so, and terms such as sex reversal came to be used. Many well known authorities offered their views and possible reasons for the anomalies, and for ten years the belief that some men (perhaps even a transsexualist or two) had the genetic sex of a female, and some women the genetic sex of a male, prevailed.

It was only recently, in 1959, that cytological studies advanced another important step with the discovery by Lejeune of the first human chromosomal abnormality. A year later, in 1960, chromosomal analysis of blood became a reality. It is obvious that there is still a long way to go but the whole concept of nuclear sexing has now begun to be seen in its true perspective. The ability to find a chromosomal reason to account for variations, beyond the XX designation for a female and the XY designation for a male, meant that some explanation of the anomalies was now possible. The reason that some men appeared to have the nuclear sex of a female and to exhibit the features of Klinefelter's syndrome was found to be due to their having a chromosomal constitution of XXY. The presence of two X chromosomes was the reason for the presence of chromatin in the cells, and the presence of the Y chromosome appeared to be the reason for their maleness. Although the XXY chromosomal constitution of those with Klinefelter's syndrome suggests that this may be an intersexual condition – a female XX with an added Y, or a male XY with an added X – there is no variation throughout the cell lines, as in the case of the true intersexes with a bisexual mosaic constitution, the male Y chromosome being present in all the cells and probably dominating the others. These individuals, therefore, are anatomical males and are of the male sex, but some feminine features may be present. At puberty some develop gynaecomastia and there may be obesity, although the body type is typically tall, slender and eunuchoid. The penis and testes remain small and due to hyalisation of the spermatic tubules spermatogenesis rarely occurs, leaving the individual infertile. Although many have personality problems transsexualism is not a condition associated with the syndrome, and should it occur is likely to be due to other causes.

The opposite anomaly, in which an apparent female appears to have the nuclear sex of a male, was found to be due to the presence of only one X chromosome in the constitution, designated XO, 45 chromosomes only being present and known as Turner's syndrome. Hence the absence of chromatin from the cells and the absence of maleness. These females have specific body features, such as short stature and webbed neck, are sexually immature and infantile, and are infertile, having only streak ovaries. In spite of this and other handicaps, psychologically they are generally strongly feminine. Oestrogens nevertheless have to be administered to make up for the body's inability to produce them naturally and to bring about the development of the secondary sexual characteristics. It is highly unlikely that any female with Turner's syndrome would express a transsexual desire to be a man.

Apart from these anomalies, it seems that variations can occur in cells from different parts of the body and in cells which are young and old. Sometimes, but rarely, conflicting sexual chromosomal patterns may exist alongside each other and this is known as mosaic. Examples are when the chromosomal constitution may be XX/XY, XO/XX or XO/XY. Often the result is a true hermaphrodite or a true intersex and sexual development may be so borderline and indeterminate that problems of sexual identity can occur. Usually, physical features of intersexuality give obvious reason for the conflict, but sometimes transsexualism may be diagnosed until a full medical examination and tests reveal the constitutional nature of the intersexuality.

Considerations of Adrenal and Pituitary factors

Because of the large part played by the cortex of the adrenal glands in secreting hormones of sexual significance, we must consider the result of any malfunction when looking into any abnormal sexual state or condition. It is well known that hyperfunction or over-activity of the adrenal cortex, such as may occur with a tumour or growth of this part, will result in virilism in the female. This is due to the tumour causing excessive secretion of hormones with androgenic properties and is often why a woman may apparently change sex and, from being perfectly feminine and perhaps the mother of children, assume masculine characteristics. The features, a deepening of the voice, growth of facial and body hair, regression of the breasts, enlargement of the clitoris and cessation of menstruation, etc., are those of the *adrenogenital syndrome,* a condition in which the hyperfunction may be caused by a tumour of the cortex of one adrenal only or be bilateral, possibly through some abnormal pituitary stimulation.

A similar condition can occur in foetal life, in which failure of the adrenal cortex to fully synthesise cortisone leads instead to the secretion of a substance with androgenic properties, resulting in pseudo-hermaphroditism. Consequently, the girl develops more as a boy, so that at birth, according to the degree of masculinisation, the external genitalia may be anything from an enlarged clitoris to a fully formed penis. Sometimes a scrotal sac has developed but this is empty, the ovaries and internal female reproductive system having formed internally, although these too may fail to develop properly and result in agenesis. More commonly the penis is improperly formed, the skin failing to wrap round the urethra completely resulting in a condition of hypospadias, in which the urethra is open like a gutter for part of its length. If fully open the more normal appearance of a female urinal opening will result, but when nearly closed at birth the baby may appear to have a penis with undescended testes and be regarded as a boy. If the error is discovered, cortisone is usually given to stop the androgenic secretions affecting the body, when the development will continue in the feminine direction. If treated in time, no harm is done, but once the voice has been deepened this problem will remain. Babies with the adrenogenital syndrome may be brought up as boys or girls according to the degree of masculinisation, and at puberty doubts over their true sex may cause some to desire assistance to better establish their role of rearing or, alternatively, assistance to help the development of opposite sexual characteristics to enable a change of sexual role. Cushing's syndrome, in which other marked features result from an adrenocortical tumour, and Addison's disease, in which the tissue of the adrenal cortex is destroyed, are primarily non-sexual in their disturbance of function and do not merit our concern here.

Malfunction or maldevelopment may also be caused by disturbance of pituitary function. The hormones secreted by the pituitary gland are called trophins, and act by stimulating other endocrine glands. The trophins of sexual significance are secreted by the anterior lobe of the gland, and one of these, Gonadotrophin, as its name implies, influences the gonads and, in the male, stimulates the interstitial cells of the testes, whilst in the female it stimulates the ovarian follicles. In the female, however, two gonadotrophin factors seem to be involved, for, apart from the stimulation to ripen the follicles, a second factor is concerned with the monthly release of the ova and the conversion of the burst follicle into the 'yellow body'. The hypothalamus in the brain seems to play a part in this by influencing the pituitary, and it is considered possible that it may also influence sexual behaviour. Another secretion, pro-lactin, stimulates the secretion of the luteal hormone which initiates lactation. There is also adrenocorticotrophin which stimulates the adrenal cortex. Other functions of trophins from the anterior pituitary lobe are the regulation of growth and metabolism, the latter by thyrotrophin which controls secretions of the thyroid gland.

Any stimulation or suppression of the pituitary itself, by tumour, disease, or hormonal influence, can therefore produce a corresponding stimulation or suppression of the sexual and other functions of the body it controls. Indeed, this fact must be remembered when the effect of exogenous androgens and oestrogens on pituitary function later comes under considera-tion. Tumours may act by increasing the trophin secretions, or conversely, may destroy tissue and result in the reduction of secretions. Generally, the abnormal sexual manifestations are only part of the overall picture, however, since other features and symptoms present themselves, and for this reason the need to consider the possibilities of such a condition existing in a physically normal transsexualist can be ruled out.

Male Pseudo-Hermaphroditism

In these cases the chromosomal sex is XY – that of a normal

male – and foetal development and differentiation is as a male with testes forming. Male reproductive tubes also develop as normal by the suppression of the primative (female) Mullerian ducts and the stimulation of the primative (male) Wolffian ducts. The androgens produced by the foetal testes, however, which normally stimulate all the stages of development in the male direction, fail to have any masculinising effect. The reason for this is unclear, but it gives rise to what is termed the *testicular feminisation syndrome.* In the absence of masculinising factors the development is in the feminine direction – this is due not to the presence and influence of oestrogens but to the absence of androgens. As with the adrenogenital syndrome the degree of sexual abnormality varies over a wide range. Sometimes only the tip of the penis may be incompletely fused or, alternatively, the feminisation may be so great that the person appears as a complete female. In such cases the external genitalia are entirely female in formation and there may be a small vagina, but usually the uterus is missing and the testes which have remained in the groins need removing to avoid the possibility of malignancy. Significant is the fact that the body fails to respond to androgens, even to those administered exogenously. Depending upon the degree of disturbance, therefore, the child may be brought up as a boy with a small inadequate penis, or as a girl with a rather large phallus shaped clitoris. Usually the sex of rearing determines the sexual role chosen at puberty. From the foregoing it can be seen how difficult it may sometimes be to determine at once whether the patient is a genetic male with partly feminised genitalia (testicular feminisation syndrome) or a genetic female with partly masculinised genitalia (adrenogenital syndrome).

True Hermaphroditism

This is generally regarded as referring to those who possess gonads of both sexes or elements of each. There may be one ovary and one testis, functional or not, or one of these may be an ovotestis, containing the gonadal tissue of both sexes. There may be varying degrees of intersexuality, some features being masculine and others feminine. These may predominate in one direction and indicate the role of upbringing or it may only be later, at puberty or after, that the direction of sexual development is ascertained. Obviously, surgical and hormonal help is often necessary but the condition is very rare, and generally medical intervention comes early in life. It would seem that the chromosomal sex is more generally female XX although, as mentioned earlier, it may be that true hermaphroditism should really be reserved for those with mosaic chromosomal patterns showing both male and female cells side by side. Once a sex role has been established it would seem that sex of rearing again generally remains the one of choice.

Progestational hormones

As progestational hormones are produced naturally in a woman's body during pregnancy, the normal role these steroids play and the possibility of abnormal sexual development being caused by them deserves some mention. These hormones, produced in the early part of pregnancy by the corpus luteum and in the later part by the placenta, serve to inhibit ovulation during the period of pregnancy, thus avoiding the possibility of another ovum becoming fertilised whilst a developing foetus is already occupying the womb.

Progesterone and many of its allied steroids are, however, known to possess androgenic properties, and, because of this, a developing female foetus may in rare instances be subjected to androgenic stimulation and thus, to some extent, become masculinised, perhaps through some incorrect metabolism of the progestational agents by the mother. When this occurs in early pregnancy female pseudo-hermaphroditism may result similar to that occurring in the Adrenogenital syndrome, with enlargement of the clitoris and varying degrees of fusion of the labia causing the girl baby to appear more as a boy at birth. An internal female reproductive system will be present, however, indicating the intended and true sex of the child, but the degree of abnormality naturally depends upon the period and severity of the influencing factors exerting themselves during vital development.

Progesterone and certain progestational steroids (such as

ethisterone) have for some years been used in the treatment of hormonal deficiency and various gynaecological disorders, but it has now come to be realised that, because of its androgenic properties, administration to an expectant mother during early pregnancy is not without some risk of causing virilisation of a female foetus.

It is interesting to note that the action of progestational hormones in inhibiting ovulation has led to their development for use as effective oral contraceptives. Indeed, Norethynodrel, a steroid with such properties, has come to be produced within recent years, and to-day forms the basis of one of the modern 'birth pills'. It does not possess the undesirable androgenic properties of progesterone and other progestational steroids but is, on the contrary, intrinsically oestrogenic in its action. In both sexes, Norethynodrel inhibits gonadotrophic activity by its suppressing action on the pituitary, an action that is further enhanced by ethinyloestradiol which is generally combined with the steroid for therapeutic use. Effects produced in the male, such as atrophy of the testes and retardation of body growth, are due to the oestrogenic properties of the drug, but as the oestrogenic potency is comparatively low there is nothing to favour its use in the male, over the essential oestrogens, for feminising purposes.

Discussion

The foregoing medical knowledge has been placed before the reader in order that he or she may better understand the approach a doctor may make in assessing any sexual abnormality, and the manner in which he may account for it. Trans-sexualists will certainly put forward all manner of argument in justification for their feelings and their desire to be of the opposite sex, but they must be prepared to accept that, after all the factors have been taken into consideration, the chances are that there is no physical abnormality, no nuclear or chromosomal sex contradiction, and no hormonal malfunction or tumour, but only a psychological explanation for their state. Unfortunately, this does not make the state any less real, and only adds to the distress and the reluctance to accept the truth.

It should be clear, from what has been said on each of the tests, that cases who find themselves before doctors with physical justification are few, and usually have found their way there because of some very definite maldevelopment or malfunction rather than as a result of their transsexual feelings.

As we have stated, tumours generally show other signs of their existence, and may manifest themselves comparatively rapidly. The androgenic/oestrogenic levels do not appear specifically to cause or alter the direction of sexual desire or attraction, and often go hand in hand with other physical aspects of the body. Even the chromosomal sex of an individual is by no means a yardstick of what the true anatomical sex should be, as we have seen in the various intersexual and hermaphroditic conditions discussed, and nuclear sex testing from a buccal smear is even more unreliable in such abnormal cases. Having dismissed all the avenues of exploration, then, we are left with the original physical examination. Whilst it is true that transsexualists are almost invariably physically normal, the greatest danger is to assume that *every* case must of necessity fit the same pattern. The medical profession are not beyond guilt for following this formula at times, and, much as it is possible to rule out the need for certain tests, some transsexualists have been known to be advised and treated without even the thought or trouble of a medical examination. Some intersexuals can pass as either man or woman, according to the clothes they are wearing, and because of this the sex accorded to them by society may well depend solely upon their upbringing. Yet, when feelings of belonging to the opposite sex are related, a snap diagnosis of homosexuality, transvestism or transsexualism is usually made.

It is most important, therefore, that without exception all who profess transsexual feelings should be given the benefit of a full and careful physical examination by a specialist, although the individual concerned must equally be prepared to accept the findings. Only then need other tests be applied, as merited. There must be no room for error by the medical profession if the sufferer is to have faith in those endeavouring to help him and not believe that they only want to stand in his way, for to give happiness is as much a part of medicine as humanity itself.

Treatment

Assuming that the medical adviser has come to learn of the sufferer's point of view and feelings, and that the sufferer has equally come to realise some of the hard facts about a 'sex change', we reach the stage where both meet face to face across a desk to discuss treatment and in what form help may best be given. We all know what the patient wants – to 'change sex' irrespective of all other considerations – and we might assume that the medical adviser has only to assist this 'change' by all the means at his disposal and that this would be the end to the problem. It is not, of course, as easy as that, for whilst the transsexualist is busy picturing himself as a future female, scurrying about happily in skirts and painting the world exaggeratedly as a new and wonderful place to live in, the medical adviser still sees the hard reality of life that will remain, the wearing off of the novelty, the possible regrets, the emotional upheaval, the effect of loss of sex function, a possible breaking of family ties, and the difficulties of starting afresh contrary to all the conditioning of upbringing. Particularly, he may see before him a person little changed other than in the manner of his dress, blind to the possibly grotesque figure that he is, and about to emerge into a coldly unreceptive world. This knowledge, and the fact that the individual's anatomy can only be deceptively changed superficially, means that he must reject the sufferer's plea and the 'battle' between adviser and advised is on.

Just what courses are open to the doctor in any event? His point of view has been reached by sound reasoning, and he can see that the answer is to try to help the individual back along the road to normality, according to the biological sex and sex in which he was reared. Failing this, he can try to put the facts before the sufferer, in the hope that he may be able to live with his problem and, by taking a broader view of life, adjust himself to his abnormality. He may even hope that, if there can be no adjustment, the individual will somehow manage to keep going as he is, feeling that time will assist in his maturity and that the tension and conflict may, of its own accord, ease off. Only as a completely last resort can he see that help with an environmental change may have to be considered, with or without surgery. Because of all the factors involved the line of treatment is always back to heterosexuality initially, and the other possible avenues are only embarked upon in stages according to circumstances, should all other efforts fail.

There can be no doubt as to the extreme wisdom of this procedure. We are dealing with people who have no knowledge whatever of what it is like to be of the opposite sex even if they have assumed the role for quite some time; their only conceptions are based on supposition and imagination. They know nothing of early upbringing in the other sex and their whole conditioning has been against it, yet the feeling still exists, a feeling derived from the social differences between the sexes. These desires to behave and be accepted amongst society as a member of the opposite sex, and to wear the 'right' clothes which give such pleasure and peace of mind, originate from the necessity to conform to a sexual pattern to which they are opposed. How can a transsexual man say that he feels like and wants to be a girl, when he cannot possibly know what it feels like to be one? Can a doctor believe such a person knows what he really wants, and that he will not find one disappointment after another once he has changed his environmental role and realises, only then, that things are not as imagined? Playing at being a woman is one thing but a permanent pretence is another. Much of the transsexualist's world is already based on fantasy, misconceptions, and exaggerations of the differences between the sexes, so what happiness is he to obtain once the bubble has burst and there is a rude awakening to the reality of life, with all its attendant difficulties in a role the individual was not educated for? The doctor is well aware that the whole future happiness of his patient is at stake, and there is no doubt that he bears a great and grave responsibility in any decision he makes. Indeed, however much the transsexualist may plead that he knows his own mind, when dawn breaks it will be the doctor or surgeon who is held responsible, not only by the public and medical profession but by the patient himself. Usually the transsexualist just presses on regardless of details or the chances of success, more often than not expecting miracles.

Often, the question of age, extreme masculine appearance, marital status or family ties are enough to convince the doctor at once that the patient must be helped to live with his difficulty. Psycho-analysis may be resorted to, but the difficulty here is the major upset to the individual's life by virtue of the time involved, since treatment may be necessary once or twice a week for a year or two. Certainly the considerable cost of this, privately, is a great disadvantage, and to undergo such analysis in a National Health hospital, assuming the psychiatrist has the time, again involves immense patience by the sufferer and consultant alike. Treatment by psycho-analysis, then, is not without its limitations and disadvantages, apart from the essential fact that the patient must *want* to be cured if the treatment is to be successful. Since no transsexualist ever wishes this sort of 'cure', but at best wants to stay as he is if he cannot 'change', the problem remains how else hard facts can be given and accepted.

Ignorance of the differences between the sexes, anatomically and psychologically, as well as an immature outlook on life resulting from introversion and inhibition of expression, is one aspect we can hope to improve by facts, facts, and more facts. Unfortunately, the medical adviser is not always completely knowledgeable on all sides of the problem, and unless he can substantiate what he says as *unquestionable fact* there is the danger that the transsexualist will feel the doctor lacks sympathy. When this occurs the patient inwardly reacts against his adviser, loses confidence, and thinks in terms of trying to find someone else who will 'help'. This attitude is common amongst transsexualists, who often spend years going from one specialist to another in search of someone who 'understands' and agrees to help with a 'change'. This is not only harrassing to the specialists, but is also unsettling to the patient. For a confirmed male transsexualist to be told to 'pull himself together and go and find a nice girl to sleep with', in order to mature him in the heterosexual role, is likely to be looked upon with revulsion by the patient and as failure to understand. He may be told to get involved in more activities that interest him, to help take his mind off his problem. The idea is admirable, but in practice his awareness of not 'fitting in' to society is usually against such a measure.

Unfortunately, the transsexualist loathes being thought abnormal, which is why he strives so hard to justify his feelings, but the fact remains that he *is* abnormal. Yet it is dangerous to make comparisons, such as saying he is like a cripple who must learn to live with his abnormality, for the comparison is incorrect and the sufferer will see the slightest flaw in any argument against him. A cripple, he will argue, has no choice but to accept his medical deformity, any more than a person who has lost a leg can do anything but learn to do all he can with an artificial one. Determination here means everything, but the transsexualist feels there is no need for him to be determined to live with his trouble, as it can be 'simply' remedied by hormones and operations. Similarly, it is no good telling him that many women do, in fact, swear, drink heavily, and are vulgar, as an argument against his own conception of femininity, for comparisons can only be made between men and women of the same class and no useful purpose can be served by comparing, for instance, a fishwife with a public school boy. He may be told he is really enjoying the best of both worlds as he is, having the advantageous status of a male yet possessing the finer feelings of a female, and being able to satisfy his desires by dressing up in private and giving vent to his sexual expression. This is probably more true than even those who suggest such a form of adjustment may realise, but rarely will the transsexualist believe it.

When all the practical and psychological aspects have been delved into the specialist will still be on his side of the desk and the transsexualist on the other, and the sufferer will wonder to himself just how much further he has got with making life acceptable. Should he think, as he saunters homeward in pensive mood, that perhaps after all he had better try and be content to stay as he is, a young girl in a gay frock may pass him, hurrying busily on her way, and his heart will miss a beat as he once again thinks of all his longings, and how much of

347

what he wants can never really be, and he will hide his face in a shop window to prevent others seeing the tears in his eyes. The more he tries to sort out his problem the more depressed he will become, so that anything connected with his past, or with memories that may have influenced his feelings, should be left behind. Often, circumstances have all helped to build up against him: his work, his home town, unhappy home life, and being tied down to a set pattern and routine. In such cases a change of surroundings and job, meeting new people and taking up interests of a more bisexual character, may be advised. Yet often the very things which cause the problem to come to a head are the ones which seem to have a hold over the individual, for largely they represent his 'world'; in it he has moulded his life, and the energy required to break from it has been usurped by his conflict and effort to conform.

Do hormones have any use as a palliative in the treatment of transsexualists and is the specialist likely to prescribe them for this purpose? The medical view on this is not conclusive especially as the effects may vary with each case. Whereas some authorities rigidly believe that any possibility of making the individual even slightly more feminine should be avoided, other authorities believe that oestrogens can be useful in relieving sexual conflict and in treating hypersexual deviation. Stilboestrol may be prescribed for a trial period of a month or two for transsexual men, in the hope that the reduction of the sex urge or libido will reduce the demanding pressure for a 'change'. (The calming effect of oestrogen on sexual offenders in male prisons has for some years been closely studied.) Since the desire for a 'change' is wrapped up very closely with the sex drive it can be assumed that Stilboestrol will, therefore, help male transsexualists by easing their tension and, by reducing sexual activity, correspondingly help to reduce the desire. If treatment is continued for long periods at relatively high dosages a castration effect will be produced by destruction of the testicular tissue, but sexual 'numbing' does not necessarily mean the loss of sexual interest, mentally, which, in some cases, can remain at a high level.

Since the whole outlook on sex is largely determined by

348

psychological factors and upbringing, there is little likelihood that oestrogens will cause any change in the direction of desire *once established*. Males who have lost their testes as a result of disease or accident, though sterile, are still able to experience some form of sexual pleasure and orgasm, often by stimulation of the prostate and remaining masculine erotic areas, or by virtue of some fetish object long established as a sex symbol. This applies also to castrated transsexual men, and surprisingly it seems to make only a little difference that the first group take androgens to help restore their masculinity and the trans-sexualists continue to take oestrogens to help feminise themselves.

The high cost of oestrogens, whether taken orally or in implant form, needs some mention and consideration, as the transsexual man has only these to give him any hope of being feminised enough eventually to be socially acceptable as a woman. Even high doses taken orally every day for two years is little enough time for these to have much effect and it is likely that he will need to, or want to, go on taking these for the rest of his life. Either he will have to find the money himself to pay for the prescriptions, a not inconsiderable regular sum, or the National Health Service will – if they are prepared to do so. Medically, the more important considerations are the possible undesirable side-effects. In the male, oestrogens are known to produce pigmentation of the mid-scrotal line, the temples and the nipples, and can cause gastritis, sickness, fluid retention, liverishness, dizziness, toxic headaches, migraine and cramp. More seriously, they are known to cause hypertension and increase the risk of thromboembolism. Taken for a period in excess of five years they also greatly increase the risk of breast cancer, liver damage and pituitary tumours. In spite of these dangers it is surprising how many cases have taken oestrogens in very large doses for long periods without any apparent ill-effect. There seems little to support a physician's reluctance to prescribe small therapeutic doses for short periods, therefore, on the grounds that these side effects may occur. However, refusal on the grounds that oestrogen will probably exacerbate the transsexual urge is another matter and is well founded.

We have already considered closely the effects of testosterone on females and, because it produces such rapid and drastic changes, the only purpose in prescribing it for transsexual women can be deliberately to masculinise them in support of a 'change'. Androgens and oestrogens affect different individuals in different ways, however, and treatment with these to assist an adjustment, or to give an intersexual a hearty push over the sex border, must at all times rest with the medical specialists and depend upon the merit of each particular case.

Only as a final resort is surgery considered. There has to be every justification, both for the health of the patient and belief that such a step will really bring the happiness that is hoped for. By the time this stage is reached the individual should certainly have been feminised (or masculinised) enough by appropriate sex hormones to pass satisfactorily in the assumed role, to have been rendered sterile by them, and to have lived in their desired role long enough to ensure their ability to do so to the satisfaction of both themselves and their advisers.

One main consideration for the transsexual man is his 'abhorrent' testes. Not infrequently cases have been known to attempt self removal or injury, often with disastrous results. Removal of both testes, known as bilateral orchidectomy or castration, although permissible in certain cases of injury and disease is, for other purposes, illegal in this country and most European countries. One of the transsexualist's stumbling blocks, therefore, is that no surgeon is likely to want to risk his name and livelihood by such an operation which may, after all, not give the patient what he imagined and may in turn leave the surgeon open to be sued on the grounds that he should have known the patient was in no fit state to accept responsibility for such a decision. It seems certain that the greatest danger in removing the penis is that the very need and desire for the operation is removed by the operation itself, causing the feelings to change and leaving the individual desperately regretful at what has been done and wondering what possessed him to want such a mutilation.

The full implications of such treatment by surgery will come under discussion later. Unfortunately, transsexualists are in conflict, not only with sex but with many aspects of life, and are searching for something the identity of which they do not even know themselves. They have conditioned themselves to deny what, to others, is normal happiness, and, since happiness is individual and not something that can be given to them, but only gained from their own efforts and experience, whatever the medical authorities can offer will only benefit them when they can take a different view on life and its purpose.

PART III

THE ADJUSTMENT

CHAPTER TEN

CONSIDERATIONS FOR A CHANGE

Before a person can really consider the wisdom or correctness of changing his or her sexual role in society, it is imperative that the particular circumstances relative to the case should be studied carefully and nothing left to generalised assumption. In this respect, every aspect of the problem so far discussed is an essential consideration where any change of role is contemplated, and, although the object of this chapter is to elaborate on some of these and to discuss other aspects not already covered, it must be realised that a comprehensive picture of all the important considerations cannot be obtained from it alone. The writer has already spoken of the general immaturity of these cases, and their inability to come to terms with life is often the result of ignorance and inexperience. Indeed, transsexual men often complain that, because they are weak and 'feminine', it is easy for their psychiatrists to 'bully' them and overpower their ability to express themselves. Whether this is a fact or the result of a complex it leaves us realising that it is the individual himself who must make the effort, not only to learn the facts but to accept them, for however immature or illogical any of us may be there are certain practicalities we must meet face to face, and no amount of pretending or twisting matters to fit the pattern will work in reality.

In considering the adjustment, therefore, it may seem strange that so many aspects of a 'change' are gone into, as if this is, in fact, the form the adjustment should take. Such could not be further from the writer's thoughts; on the contrary, she believes that 'changes' are rarely successful psychologically, physically or socially, the abnormal individual still having to live out his life on his own or stay within his own socio-sexual group, the homosexual, transvestist or transsexualist community. There are a few exceptions, of course, some changes being unavoidable for reasons of physical intersexuality, but on the whole, practical considerations of the vast majority of cases are against any form of assistance being merited in this direction. The writer believes, however, that each case can only sum up the position by discussing such a 'change' in all its complexities, as it affects him personally, and not by being told dogmatically that he is a man and talking nonsense. If we are to help the sufferer at all, we must discuss the matter on his own level, letting him know that we do understand and share his burden, and do want to help him find happiness in spite of having to tell him things that oppose his drive to his goal. We must weigh up all the advantages and disadvantages of a 'change' as they affect him, the considerations for and against, the various involvements of the 'change' itself, and the legal and religious aspects. Finally, we must search our hearts for the right answer. Such will form the basis of our approach to the adjustment.

Anatomical considerations

Our own observations will tell us much of the transsexualist's physical state. His clothes and speech may tell us how he has fared in life, and possibly his social standing. He may be shy and reticent to speak of his problem and have to be coaxed into giving information, or he may unleash his whole story in an avalanche of words to unburden what has for so long been bottled up inside him, and never seem to come to an end of his egotistic ramblings. We may see anyone, from a small, thin, sensitive-looking man with body hair and heavy beard to a tall, broad-shouldered man with enormous hands and feet, possibly nearly bald. Both will tell the same tale, however, and say how passable they are when dressed in women's clothes, although they somehow give the impression they do not quite believe it themselves. However great the desire to play the opposite role, we generally need look no further than basic anatomy to ascertain just how practical a 'change' may be and to foresee the final shape and type of person likely to emerge as a result. The feelings may be real enough, and the need for expression may indicate some uncontrollable inborn urge, but however much we sympathise with the individual it may well be clearly seen from the whole build and anatomy that anything in the form of a 'change' will only result in disaster.

Whatever the male transsexualist may be able to hide under his female clothes and heavy make-up, his masculine beard will remain even in spite of the prolonged high doses of female hormones he will have been taking. It is quite different having a close shave and spending hours making up and dressing up to go out as a transvestist for the evening, from having to rush off to work every day with only a short while to prepare. The beard, although not insuperable, is a worrying problem, at least in the early stages of any change, and the writer has seen one case recently who has managed to get surgery, with heavy make-up still having to be applied to mask dark facial hair. With very few electrolysists prepared to see male customers and the likelihood of any treatment taking two years or more even based on two or more visits a week, it can be seen that the transsexualist is not only going to be kept busy for a long time but will need a large wallet. If he looks in the mirror closely he will see the hundreds of pores in his face from which hairs are growing, apart from those that are there without apparent sign. Can he picture each one being dealt with by electrolysis and does he know that, because of the strength of the growth, a greater current has to be used than for finer female hair? What of the result to his skin texture after all this, and the finer hairs that will keep growing through. Like most, then, he will have to struggle on with the nightmare of having to shave every day before putting on make-up, and if 'living as a woman' for a probationary period to prove himself, as now being advised, he will find this procedure a drudge, a constant reminder of what he is and a disaster for his rehabilitation.

What of his height? Quite average, perhaps, for a man, although he may say, 'What if I am nearly six feet? There are many girls who are six feet tall, too.' This may be true, but it is not a happy height for a girl unless, perhaps, she is young and has the right lean shape to be a model. In the transsexualist's case, at this height and aged about 30, he is likely to be big-chested and to have large hands and feet; and what, too, of those high-heeled shoes which he considers the mark of femininity? How conspicuous will he be at six feet three inches, and even more conscious of what he is. What, too, of his voice?

Hormones will not change that and he has to go about aware of every word he says to give the best possible impression that he is a woman. He can learn to speak more demurely and softly but the original harshness will remain, albeit masked, and he will always run the risk of having the true character of his voice exposed should he become excited, have a drink too many, or otherwise forget himself. Yet, he says he wants to leave the pretence behind him and be natural as a woman. In fact, in the role of a woman he may feel even more strained and unnatural, because of the need for his conscious act. Surprisingly, even time may not change this, the past always influencing how he thinks and what he says and does. The telephone, with its small frequency range, will almost certainly bring out any depth to his voice, and although a normal woman with a deep voice may not mind being called 'Mister' on the 'phone, to any established post-operative male transsexualist it will be a constant reminder of what he is and was, and will not serve to assist the peace of mind which was listed as one of the reasons to justify the 'change'.

Obviously, the more feminine the male transsexualist is the greater the chance that he will be satisfied with his 'change'. Help before puberty, or soon afterwards, before the secondary sexual characteristics have developed or become established will, of course, give him a better chance of being made to look like a normal girl, although again much must depend upon his original build and glandular balance. Also, cases in this category stand a better chance of readjustment psychologically to their changed role, since they have less past to leave behind them and have not as a rule embarked upon a steady career. However, since the transsexualists we usually encounter only present themselves quite some time after puberty, when the mounting tension caused by abnormal channelling of the increased sexual activity demands treatment, we almost invariably find the sufferers completely masculine in form and some even ultra-masculine and married with children. The difficulties they are likely to encounter in trying to change their body to fit their mind cannot be over-estimated, and unless they have features of eunuchoidism, undersized or under-developed genitalia,

358

little or no facial or body hair, and a voice that does not need much adaptation as a woman, the initial factors are against them.

The transsexual man is likely to be unhappy about the effects of the oestrogens he is taking, and even after two years will look little different. No doubt ten years of taking continuous female hormones will do much to feminise even a quite masculine man, but whether the end result is a passable woman or someone who still looks like a feminised man is what has to be considered. He also has to consider how many years of his life he is prepared to give up in 'changing', what he is going to do in that twilight period, and what he will look like and feel like during that time. Has he forgotten, too, that farmyard animals are often castrated to fatten them up for market? What then of the sylph-like figure that he so dreams about? Unless his glandular make-up is balanced already in the feminine direction the 'feminisation' resulting from castration will be false, and the resulting fat distribution ugly and unhealthy-looking. He may look young in the face but bodily he may look more like an elderly grand-mother or even a well made-up pantomime dame.

It is not surprising, then, that there is so much reluctance to assist these cases surgically, and that they are advised that before pursuing surgery they should first prove themselves capable of living as women. Sometimes, the abhorrence of the male genitalia makes waiting so impossible that transsexual men threaten to operate on themselves. This is likely to be taken to indicate a severe psychotic state, however, since the danger of such a procedure is grave and should be known if the individual is in his right mind. More likely it will be taken as blackmail, and only do more harm to his chances of obtaining assistance in the same way that any threat of suicide will be interpreted.

Hair is also an important consideration, as any need to partly live as a man whilst he is waiting for his oestrogens to 'work' or for other medical help requires him to keep his hair short if he is not to embarrass or be embarrassed. Fortunately the oestrogens will encourage his own hair to grow, and assuming that he will eventually be able to let his own hair grow and to go to the hairdressers and have it fashioned this is only a short-term problem, and unless the transsexualist is bald or nearly so this is not of major concern in the long term.

Such individuals must also remember that to live permanently as a woman is entirely different to the world of femininity they know, when they have only to change their minds and nothing is lost. They may long to have their genitalia removed to be at last rid of the masquerade and be able to wear female briefs and lift up their skirt if any policeman stops them. One elderly case known to the writer who had surgery abroad and sadly still looked very much like a man dressed up spoke excitedly of the time 'she' was stopped and taken to the police station and was quite delighted to raise her skirt to 'prove' she was not a man. Certainly once surgery has been performed there can be no looking back. The transsexual can never be a normal person again. He may hail it as the attainment of a lifelong desire but there will be a certain emptiness and much, very much now to be learnt. He will have the rest of his life to debate the question in his mind whether he made the right decision, but more urgently he will wonder what else he can do to feminise himself further and to make himself more passable and acceptable.

Sexual orientation

If the sexual state has remained immature or the sexual drive remained low, and there has been no attraction to either sex due to sexual conflict or to complete withdrawal from sex, the chances are that a successful change may gradually condition the individual to adopt a 'heterosexual' outlook on life in the new role and quite possibly cause him to experience sexual attraction compatible with that role. Such cases are rare, however, for usually other conditioning influences have affected the transsexualist during his lifetime. The heterosexually-inclined male transsexualist has generally experienced heterosexual relations with a woman at some time, probably going through a phase of enjoyment which later becomes superseded by a feeling of inadequacy. Sexual laziness then makes him wish to play the passive role, and in fact he would seem to want the sexual pleasure and yet be free from the constant reminders of his masculinity caused by spontaneous erections. On the other hand the homosexually-inclined male transsexualist largely dreams of being cared for by a man, and often thinks in terms of 'changing his sex' so that he can meet a man and be taken here and there by him and looked after. Thoughts of marriage, too, are not far from his mind, even long before any hoped-for treatment is commenced, and he may even have the final picture rosily in his imagination of being the doting housewife tending adopted children and waiting for the return of the husband from work. Whilst his mind is busy planning this Utopia in fantasy, however, he will probably be deriving every satisfaction from his abnormal sex play.

These cases must realise that it is the very presence of their androgens and libido that gives them the impulse to seek their new world, and the energy to pursue their desires. Once they have had a castration and had the penis removed, sex life as they have come to know it will cease; there can be nothing more certain than this. Yet sex, one of the most basic of all living urges, is something that affects the highest and lowest equally in every country in the world. Nations may be ruled by the very sex moods of its leaders. It is nature's endowment to us all and, as such, equals in importance our work in society and our social relationships. To be deprived of sex can deny an individual much of his purpose in living, and, although transsexualists crave to be free of its involvements, they have no idea of the emptiness that awaits them if they succeed in procuring the operations they look upon as 'changing their sex'. Orgasm is generally still possible after such operations, by devious means of stimulation, but it is a very self-centred act, produces only limited satisfaction, and the conditioned demands for it produce equal, if not more exaggerated, guilt complexes than formerly. Also, once the sex state is neutralised they will find that all that mattered before becomes of little consequence, and the world of fantasy, instead of being enhanced by the female role, takes on a different perspective. The task of getting on with living will become more important and, with the return to reality, the actual sexual state will become secondary. It is then they may look back and wonder why they made all the fuss over which sex they were. On the other hand, they will say how pleased they are the nightmare is over and that being able to get on with living is what they have been wanting to do all their lives.

Since sexuality and direction of sexual drive are basically a matter of conditioning and of nervous implication, hormones or operations will play no part in altering these in an adult whose ways and behaviour are **established**. The transsexualist must in no way attach importance to these aspects of a 'change', for whether he is heterosexually or homosexually inclined his sex-conditioning will continue in the same direction and what has previously sexually excited him will continue to do so, for his nervous constitution will remain unaltered. Even fetish objects will maintain their same significance, if the individual is so conditioned. Of course, playing the different role in society would bring about some form of conscious 'fitting in' sexually, but underneath it all the awareness of the artificial nature of his genital anatomy would never be lost.

It can be seen even more how any individual, who is more truly homosexually oriented, is likely to have great regrets if he endeavours to become the permanent passive partner, assuming the female role in life as well as in sexual relationships by resorting to operations. So much of the satisfaction comes from the pretence and the perversion of the act that the sudden cessation of sexual expression by operation, the resulting apathy and changed status, are factors which contra-indicate surgery. Indeed, a homosexual is more than likely to be greatly distressed and grieved by the result of operations, and yet some hanker after them and are encouraged into them by their partners without following up the consequences.

There are, of course, a few cases of true transsexualism who are neither heterosexual nor homosexual but essentially inter-sexual in their orientation. In these cases it seems the sexual state is complete in itself, and the person, instead of feeling definitely a man or a woman from the sexual aspect, has grown up as neither or as a combination of both. The masculine influence and attributes would then have balanced out the feminine ones, the individual being happy to take an interest in all things equally regardless of their supposed social sexual connections. This is in direct contrast to the accepted feelings of transsexualists as a whole, who only want to belong to the opposite sex and want nothing to do with their own sex. This is not to say that the intersexual person will necessarily accept his role of rearing and indeed, if forced into the sexual mould of his upbringing too severely without any room for expressing feelings of the other sex, may well revolt and seek a 'sex change' as a means of breaking from the rut in which he feels claustrophobic and trapped. The low power of his sexual drive generally means that operation has no fear for him, and having adapted himself already by diverting his energies to other interests in life he is more likely to be successful in re-establishing himself in the opposite role and to be able to carry on his probably lonely but contented life without too much upheaval. No matter who it is, however, who has lived one way for twenty, thirty, forty years or more, the past cannot be shut out; the upbringing, conditioning, and teachings of that sex role are there, and rehabilitation in the opposite role demands courage, patience and determination. To be flippant about such a drastic measure will only lead to hardships and regrets. What is built well must be built slowly, and, if any are to succeed, the true intersexual type of transsexualist has probably the greatest chance. Certainly, those with involved sexual inclinations and perverted states should think again, for *their* answer to the problem may well deprive them of what little they find to give them pleasure in their mixed-up worlds. Otherwise they may land themselves permanently in the sordid twilight world of the prostitute, to seek whatever devious means of sexual pleasure they can.

Practical problems

It is not every one of us who is free as a bird, without ties and able to do as we please without affecting someone around us. Often, because of his state, the transsexualist remains unmarried and very closely attached to his family, relying upon them for his love and building his life around them. In such cases the person finds it extremely difficult to tell his loved ones about himself, feeling that it must hurt them and therefore equally hurt him. He has probably lived a sheltered life anyway, and the outside world presents a mystery and a challenge to him. Such an individual must realise that the chances of success in the other role, if it is ever achieved, will lie in his ability to leave home, avoid any connection with his family which may cause embarrassment, and face up to the hard reality of the world in a new life, a new job, new surroundings and with new friends. Indeed, any attempt to change role whilst maintaining the former way of living would appear to have some exhibitionist motive, and in the long run will not lead to a successful recognition of the new role or to peace of mind, since associations and memories will be revived constantly.

Such single individuals may feel, since they have no ties, that this is a factor in their favour for a 'change', but it is more than likely that only after a 'change' will the past support of the family be realised for, just when it is needed the most in the building of a new world, it must be denied them. This type of individual is more usually found in the younger age groups. In the older age groups we often find cases whose parents are dead, and they have for some time plodded on in life alone, dreaming of their transformation. In as much as the freedom from all ties is a great advantage and really a necessity, even then old friends must be left behind, and a new job sought in a new district, if the rather more numerous years in the former role are to be forgotten. Indeed, however the transsexualist may consciously accept a new role, memories and past conditioning are never lost in the subconscious mind, and anything to prompt a revival of earlier times can only endanger the individual's peace of mind. Dreams can in this respect play an important part in disturbing the rehabilitation, helping to bring about mental confusion and a continued unsettled state.

What of those who are married, perhaps with children, and yet with the problem growing daily more intense? It almost seems as if their sincere efforts to inhibit their feelings, and to be 'normal' and heterosexual, have not only proved a failure but have made things very much more difficult for them. However we may sympathise with such individuals we must not lose sight of the extreme hardship and distress caused to the wife and children, and our sympathies must lie with them. There are some things we cannot alter, however much we may like to, and the impracticality of individuals in this category pursuing a 'change' cannot be over-estimated. Transsexualists can be very introverted and selfish in walking over everyone to achieve their desires, but some responsibilities cannot be shed. It equally puts great responsibility on any medical authority assisting the 'change', and there seems little to condone such heartless action by an individual leaving a wife and children to fend for themselves, open to ridicule and embarrassment should the husband's circumstances come to light. Sadly, even the advisers sometimes seem to care more for the speculative happiness of their patients than the down to earth misery of their families. Much as the transsexualist may profess to love his wife and children, he escapes from his responsibility by saying that he cannot help it. Even if there are no children, however, no peace of mind is likely to result unless, before any steps towards a 'change' are taken, all ties are relinquished and a trial period of living alone in a new area is embarked upon. If, in the light of these new circumstances, a change of role still appears desirable and treatment is agreed to, a divorce should first be obtained and any wedding photographs put on the bonfire.

The next practical aspect to consider is the employment the individual is likely to be able to obtain in his new role. Almost invariably, the transsexual woman has few problems in terms of getting work as a man, since the pay is likely to be better, there will be increased status, and there is likely to be a greater variety of jobs to choose from that will fit her interests and temperament. The transsexual man, however, finds the reverse the case. Anyone who has held an executive position and been used to a good salary will not favourably accept a reduction in status and a lower wage, and if the only job they know is a 'male' one the problem of how they are to earn their living if they 'become' a woman is very real. They will say they will be happy just as a waitress, a factory-hand or as a shop assistant, but they are likely to soon become disgruntled once their reduced status and basic wage become a fact of life. Some may, of course, find their own work can be done equally by men or women, such as in the professional classes, but they must still remember certain prejudices by the public to women in such positions and increased effort is required.

Money is indeed a great consideration, since it is generally at a time when medical advice and help have to be paid for that one is out of work and unable to earn, on account of going through the phase of 'changing'. However rapid the process of a change of role may be there is always some need for the individual to re-establish himself in mind, manner, and dress, and some in-between stage is inevitable. Certainly, if the transsexual man has maintained his 'front' to the end, he will not be happy starting his new role in a wig but prefer to remain out of circulation whilst his hair grows. This may also be desirable if there is any delay or difficulty in procuring a new 'female' National Insurance card for employment purposes. In his new tempor-ary 'home' he will be kept busy anyway sorting out his things and making plans for the future. His wardrobe of male clothes, built up over many years, will serve him no more, and he will find building up a female wardrobe from scratch not an easy job and most decidedly an expensive one. Whereas a suit would probably suffice all the year round before, he soon finds a woman needs to change her outfit with every few degrees' change of temperature and according to circumstances, and as soon as the outer garment is changed the shoes, gloves, hat, top coat and handbag, etc., have to be changed to suit. Much as his love of clothes makes him delight in all this it strains his financial resources, and a limit has to be imposed.

With the prospect of heavy expense, then, he is also faced with not knowing where his next penny is coming from, and his savings, which may have seemed such a substantial sum once, soon dwindle away and the future prospects become less rosy. Even if these financial matters do not bother him, there is the greater expense to be considered of whether he can afford to press for surgery on a private basis or perhaps be fortunate enough to receive it under the National Health Service. He may certainly feel he has the advantage if he can offer to pay cash for surgery and it is naturally more rewarding to the surgeon if he

366

can. Similarly, the surgeon, if willing to help, is in a very happy position of demanding what fee he wishes, since he looks upon any help as a favour and, knowing the transsexualist's desperation, knows his patient will muster his last penny to get what he wants.

Generally, the surgeon is likely to take into consideration all the circumstances of the individual, and is really only too happy to do what he can based on the assessment of his own worth and the value of his skill, provided he can be sure it is the right thing for his patient. Unfortunately, operations, anaesthetist's fees, and nursing home fees are likely to be extremely costly and few may find themselves able to afford these. Those who cannot bear the heavy cost may feel bitter that they should be denied what others who are better off can have. They have little reason to be bitter, however, for the National Health Service provides that all such treatment as may be considered necessary for the health of a person, including the psychological health of that person, may be undertaken free of charge. Of course, the treatment must be advised by the specialist, which puts considerable onus on his shoulders, having to account not only to the patient for what he advises or does but to the health authorities also. Certainly cases are known who have been assisted in a change of role under the National Health Service, but the final word and responsibility lies with those agreeing to help. Not only does the responsibility rest more fully with those cases who themselves demand help and pay for it privately, then, but they are often likely to be more grateful and, indeed, successful, feeling they must prove to themselves that all they have been through and spent has been worthwhile. There can be no doubt that private treatment has a lot to merit it, and the plastic surgeon, too, may feel a case can better prove his sincerity if he has much to give up financially and otherwise, rather than if he feels the patient may be 'down and out' and falsely visualises a 'change' as making things so much different and better.

The Religious aspect
This is another important consideration, for each individual

must weigh up just how a 'change' may affect any practical and spiritual connections he may have with the faith to which he belongs. Firstly, he must seek acceptance of his position by those church officials upon whom he can rely and be sure that any change will meet with their blessing, so that it will impose no restriction on his worshipping in the manner to which he is accustomed. Secondly, he must consider his personal ability to condone any action he proposes in the light of his religious beliefs. Certainly, he must feel no hesitation about the correctness of what he seeks, and be able to maintain his beliefs so that the success of a change of role will not at any future time be threatened by his inability to find spiritual peace of mind. Whilst for some the religious aspect may not be of major consequence, to others it may represent an extremely vital link between life in one role and the happiness of life in the other. Even those who view this consideration lightly should remember that, whatever our beliefs, we all at some time or other in life need faith, to overcome the loss of someone dear or when death is near ourselves, and we should consider not only our spiritual convictions of the present but what they may become in the light of future events. Whatever the circumstances, therefore, no one should fail to appreciate the importance of religion in their everyday lives or dismiss such matters from the reality of the future, for, in assessing the happiness they are likely to get out of a new role, transsexualists must understand that success depends in the first instance on the openness and cleanness of their hearts.

Psychological implications

There is, in all these cases, a peculiar ability to bend truth and circumstances to fit the pattern they prefer to believe in, rather than the one cold logic would otherwise have them accept. It is, however, inevitable that if the transsexualist presses on through any misguided influences, conditions himself to accept an overruling power within him, and is other than completely genuine to *himself*, he will have cause to regret his action later. The writer firmly believes that the success of a 'change' depends largely upon the transsexualist's ability to cope with life in the first instance, for if his conditioning has made him antagonistic to certain aspects of life his outlook will remain the same regardless of the clothes he wears or the role he plays. *Only if he can cope with life before the 'change' is he likely to cope afterwards*. This illustrates the greatest irony of the problem, since it is the very ones with the ability and sense to make a success of a 'change' who, given the right incentive, could make a successful return to 'normality'. Conversely, the very ones who, because of their frail approach to life, are unable to cope in their present state, are the ones who, in the event of a 'change', will find the need to withdraw from the hard reality facing them, still unable to cope but better able to write it off against feminine weakness. In the same way the hobbies and interests will remain the same, and although these may be inhibited to enable closer conformity to the new role they will soon emerge again, and the motor cycle enthusiast, for instance, will soon return to his motor bikes, skirts or no skirts. The 'change' is only likely to affect the transsexual man in his own mind, then, and his general character and personality will remain unaltered, apart from the way he is able to express himself freed from social conventions.

However far the individual may get towards his goal he will never be quite certain if he has reached it, for the limitations of his new role will always leave him not quite satisfied. It is inevitable that he will pass through an in-between stage, and quite likely, too, that even when he has changed his role he will remain confused psychologically and feel more in-between than ever. Indeed, when the immediate pleasure has passed and he takes stock of reality, he will begin to see his inadequacies and that he can never be normal as a woman. It is then that his sexual state may begin to waver and become like a pendulum in character, swinging him first to one side of the sexes and then the other. Depending upon the individual's justification for his change of role and his attitude to life, this in-between stage may remain indefinitely, but, even if it is only passing, it is a state of bewilderment and doubts. He will look back upon his past and all he used to do and was able to do. He will think of his loved ones and wonder how much he may have hurt them. During

369

these reflections, however, he will refuse to accept that he may have made a mistake after all, for he knows that even if it were possible for him to go back he would be unable to admit defeat. Happiness and tears will alternate then, as the emotional effects of the 'change' become established. He knows he can only ever live as a woman but his upbringing is tearing at his heart. There is, of course, by now no turning back, for he has long ago left behind the person he once was.

Such a pattern of reaction is difficult for the transsexual man to visualise but it is one he must prepare himself for, because his inherent exhibitionist trait makes him happy to enjoy his dual sexuality. Often, the greatest disappointment of the 'changed' individual is the pressure on him to maintain secrecy, when, in fact, he bursts to tell someone. He may have too many doubts about himself for this, but the torture of not being able to tell anyone is rather like the murderer committing the perfect crime and giving himself away in the end through having to tell someone it was he who executed such a masterpiece. The release of information, however, perhaps to a new friend, gives little of the anticipated pleasure, so that in the end he rebukes himself for giving his secret away and for having lost his friend's confidence and regard for him.

Once he has passed the point of no return, and must make the most of things whether they are as he envisaged or not, what are the chances of happiness? Is this the goal he aimed for? Is it the end of the road? It is not likely to be so for his new life is yet to come. Busily he will make plans for the future, but perhaps he is still weak from his operations and wonders where all his drive has gone. Like climbing a mountain, he is likely to find the end-result satisfying for a short time only, the main pleasure having been in the struggles and efforts to overcome the hurdles and difficulties which represented a challenge. Once the goal is reached, especially after a lifetime's struggle, there is a brief, calmful pleasure, giving way to an anticlimax and a continued search for a non-existent ideal. Indeed, it is life's way that none of us should ever be satisfied, otherwise the whole purpose of life would be lost and life itself become dull and uninteresting. In the transsexualist's case the post-operative realisation of this causes disillusionment, for the reaching of an objective is not the end of the line but only a passing milestone in life, and all the realities of life, with its everyday work and humdrum ways, must now be faced up to for there is no longer a dream world into which to retreat. The hangover is upon him – the same hangover he complained of in coming away from the 'pictures' or an emotional play, when, having momentarily lost himself, he was rudely awakened by the reality of the rain outside.

He is not, therefore, likely to be settled or satisfied for long, either with the abnormal sexual anatomy or with his new life, and all his past soul-searchings will still continue, his dreams possibly taking him back in time to constantly remind him of his former self. Will the few old friends he occasionally meets ever get out of the habit of calling him 'Jack', and do they do it to be cynical or because they are unadaptive to changing circumstances? The general result is that the boasted peace of mind has been gained on one point but lost on many others, and the guilt complexes and the doubts are still there. Above all there is the loneliness; a loneliness that even the transsexualist has not known before, for previously the building of his dream world and his transvestist activities have been their own reward. Now he has got used to the clothes he is wearing and he has no dream world. He also has no new friends yet, and has doubts how they will take to him once they know about him. This need be only a passing phase in his re-establishment but he must realise that he cannot live amongst people and disassociate himself from them, if he is to gain his sought after happiness. Whether the transsexual man lives out his life as a lonely old woman with neighbours only as friends or can share in life's goings-on, perhaps with a partner, will depend very much upon his basic sexual orientation and his ability to meet up with someone with the 'right chemistry' rather than someone attracted to him sexually. Happiness may come to either, but if the extrovert ends up as the lonely old maid and the shy introvert ends up getting distressingly 'involved', it may be a different story.

Love and Marriage

Following surgery the transsexual man may choose a female partner to live and go about with as girl-friends often do, or, if still married or remaining on good terms with his divorced wife, he may prefer to maintain her companionship to save being alone and, in spite of the many difficulties, take on the role of her 'sister-in-law'. Some cases may feel the attraction and need for a male partner, however, as conforming more to their new role. Apart from the casual acquaintance, what sort of male partner is a transsexual male likely to find? What is the sexual orientation of this partner, and what is in the relationship for him, sexually and socially? Surgical techniques are still improving to form a satisfactory vagina, and a few of the early transsexuals probably had to accept very indifferent structures. To-day, surgery still leaves some more fortunate than others and upon this is likely to depend the transsexualist's attitude to a partner and sex. Even assuming that some form of sexual intercourse is possible this can only be to give satisfaction to the partner, and the nature of such a relationship has to be questioned. One would assume that a normal heterosexual male would prefer a normal heterosexual female for a partner, with whom he could share life in all its aspects including the joys of *normal* intercourse and the bringing into the world of a new life – *his* child. The sexual aspect of a partnership, although important, is not necessarily the main or only aspect, but the chances of a post-operative male transsexualist being successfully adjusted are remote enough, without having to include the chances of a particular heterosexual individual coming along whose interests, ways, and outlook dovetail in with his. And what of the homosexual partner? It is quite possible that such a person may not be too antagonistic to forming a relationship with the 'changed' transsexual man, perhaps in the belief that the change was prompted by homosexual tendencies or that such a relationship would be immune from conflict with the law. This may well be the case but others are more likely to rebel at any form of sex entirely, just wanting to be looked upon as women and having the social attentions of men.

Inwardly, the post-operative male transsexualist may feel that

372

his femininity will be enhanced by getting a 'real' man, tending to disregard what he is, what he was, and his true biological state. This will not help his rehabilitation. Indeed, any trans-sexualist has to consider just what sort of partner he is prepared to join up with should he succeed in changing his role. Can he really picture the type of man who may fall in love with him, for instance, and is that the sort of man he wants? Again, what if he should choose a female companion; will she ever after be happy, nursing him into feminine ways, living with his story, and sharing his secret? Just how lasting are these partnerships or friendships likely to be? Of course, in his dream world the transsexual man may see himself married. He may feel the world owes him a living, and, without fear of being put in the 'family way', may even view the prospects of finding a wealthy husband. If, indeed, the chance of marriage should ever come his way it may be that he does not divulge all the facts to his 'lover' for fear of losing him, or even confide his doubts regarding his legal ability to marry. In any event, the partner may only later discover that consummation of the marriage may not be possible or otherwise be shocked to learn the truth, causing the partnership to end up in the divorce courts with attendant publicity.

There is one other possible way of partnering the changed transsexual man, and that is with another (unchanged) trans-sexual man. This idea at first may appeal to him, since he sees the possibility of being able to talk about himself without fear of being misunderstood. They will soon find, however, that they weary of the same old theme, and each will tend to be so introverted that the other's interests will not really be shared. Also, what roles are these individuals to play together? Each will admittedly have much in common with the other, but probably not in common enough to prevent conflict. Also, what of the one partner being able to supply the needs of the other?

As can be seen, then, the possibility of love and marriage is yet another important consideration for a 'change', and although the individual may feel happy to leave things until afterwards, to see how he feels and how he fares, the transsexualist would do well to remember that he should not enter into a 'change' with any set ideas in this respect. Indeed, his demand for a 'change' is based upon his abnormal sexual orientation, and he must thus view the possibility of remaining lonely for the rest of his life, especially if he holds on to his old outlook on life and his old interests. We must all have masculine and feminine interests, if we are to hold the affection and enjoy the companionship of an opposite partner, and at the same time each must be needed by the other. The transsexual man sees this rather differently, however. Consciously he may conform well to his exaggerated idea of femininity by sitting and sewing, or just by being considered weak and helpless, but unconsciously his male upbringing digs at him and he will hate being thought an idiot when it comes to mending mechanical things, having to take a back seat while some 'novice', in his eyes, makes a 'botch' of it. Often the dominant side remains, then, together with the wish to be independent, so again we must wonder how all this will fit into his happiness as the weaker partner in a 'marriage'.

Whilst many transsexual men are introverted and narcissistic and unlikely to have much experience of true love in their life, many others have married and fathered children. Marriage implies the sharing of every thought and interest with the partner, and whatever the circumstances of these cases it is unlikely that either group will have any idea of the real meaning of 'marriage' or the responsibilities involved, let alone in the opposite sexual role. The adoption of children to cement such a 'marriage' and make it appear more normal may be prompted by the noblest motives, but accepting responsibility for children may not be easy or legally possible and their own re-establishment must in any case first pass the test. Certainly those who have already fathered children and possibly deserted them cannot now hope to adopt any. For those who have remained single, their love of children may be perfect in theory but in practice their ability to care for them must be founded on more than good faith. Their home must be a happy one if the children are to be given the best opportunity and the post-operative transsexual man must have left all trace of his past behind, affording no possible reflection of abnormality upon the growing individuals. No one with any feeling of humanity will other than sympathise with a transsexualist going through life, in either role, suffering the heartache of true cold loneliness, for it is a loneliness beyond all normal imagination, but others must not be involved with the transsexualist's problem, least of all little children, without the most serious thought. Certainly, such thoughts should be well out of his mind in any picture he sees of his rosy dream world, and he should not plan his future happiness upon such wishful thinking.

We have, up to now, spoken of the male transsexualist and of 'he', 'him' and 'his', etc. This has largely been for convenience in the use of a personal pronoun rather than to imply that the same pattern does not fit the female transsexualist. We need not go back over all we have said in this chapter to indicate any slight differences, but the question of love and marriage does merit some enlargement for, as we know well, individuals in this group are considered to be homosexually oriented to a greater or lesser degree. As a result, a female partner has generally become well established in the female transsexualist's life.

Not only can transsexual women more successfully change their role psychologically and practically but, when they do, they often have this already formed partnership, so that the thought of marriage is not an uncommon feature in such cases with the adoption of children as a following aspiration. Her partner is generally aware of her hopes and takes on a share of the difficulties and burdens, comforting her, feeling for her, and being equally conscious of the striving and frustration that, for a time, is to be a part of both their lives. For this reason the transsexual woman is often better placed than the transsexual man for the task ahead following any change of role, since the building of a new future is to be a joint effort and gives hope of a sound and practical partnership. The problems of satisfying sexual need are also likely to be less, the companionship and ability to share mutual interests being probably of greater importance to the final happiness of the individuals than the sexual act itself.

Although transsexualists dream of the life they imagine will give them joy and peace of mind they sometimes do not dare to consider love and marriage in their plans. Once they have become established in the role of their desire, however, love and marriage can take on a new meaning. Some, of course, prefer to continue to have nothing to do with sex and to contain their mixed-up world within themselves, under their own control. For others, particularly those homosexually inclined, seeking love and marriage is a natural sequence to their 'change', although such a partnership is not always well-founded, may be sexually motivated or for outward show, and may break up in disharmony. Perhaps the greatest consideration of all is whether any dreams of love and marriage can be a reality. However much the dream may appear to be fulfilled by the two partners it is the recognition of that partnership, socially and legally, that really matters, and in this respect transsexualists must understand and accept from the start that this is likely to be denied them.

Publicity

We must not omit from our considerations whether or not publicity might ensue as a result of a 'change', and whether this is likely to be desirable, just distasteful, or completely detrimental to the individual. We are not concerned here with the benefits to a publisher, or with the reactions of the public as far as it affects them, for we have commented upon these earlier. As far as the transsexualist is concerned, however, let us imagine an individual who has changed his role, has no job, nothing much lined up for the future, and very little money. He may be tempted to accept offers for his story, delighting in the publicity and the exhibitionism, and perhaps hoping it may bring remunerative work to him in some form of public performance, for instance. If he deliberately exposes his story with this intention he will be failing to take into account the feelings of his family or loved ones, and may well cause them to suffer as a result. He must equally have faith in himself, for unless his case is completely watertight the publicity is more likely to have a boomerang effect and public distaste may die hard, making it difficult for him to get employment. He may find he is offered little for his story, although whatever he gets, large or small, is not likely to provide much towards the many years that lie ahead of him. What, too, of his many helpers, medical and otherwise; is he to fail, or even betray, them? Is he to laugh at any authority who has recognised his right to his role, by boasting that he really was born of the sex of his rearing and has 'changed'. Certainly it makes a better story, but this will bring him little happiness in the end. The fabulous sums he has heard about, and the glory of the 'change', will soon take their place amongst the other disappointments of his dream world and he will find the world outside even colder than before.

If the person concerned is already known to the public, publicity in connection with a 'change' may seriously affect his livelihood. The more he has, in fact, established himself in life, the more serious are likely to be the consequences. An artist in the public eye, a professional person in intimate contact with the public, a professional designer, or a company director holding a responsible position, are all likely to find that withdrawal from their former connections and the building of a new life demands particular courage, fortitude, determination, and faith. Faith there must be, by the individual himself, not only that he is justified in his actions but that he is true to himself and to the whole of society. If there are any doubts at all regarding his chances of acceptance and his ability to fit the new role the effects of publicity could well prove disastrous, since the vast majority of the public, upon whose support he depends for his living, look upon the subject with abhorrence. Whatever the individual's station in life, therefore, publicity is only likely to make things more difficult for him to eventually re-establish himself, forget the past, and rebuild his future. If he is wise he will see this, and that his best possible chance of success lies in a new life in new surroundings, with as few people knowing about his past as possible. Yet it is remarkable that some seek and revel in the limelight of publicity, sometimes looking little different to a drag queen, and then complain the public does not *accept* them.

There are, however, two sides to the publicity problem, for although the transsexualist may wish to avoid publicity at all costs if he relies upon the public's goodwill for his work, maintaining the secret for the rest of his life will involve a certain uneasiness in his own mind and he must live under the constant threat of his past catching up with him. Thus, in the case of a person who has given up all to start afresh and has nothing further to lose immediately following a 'change', some account of his circumstances publicly may be warranted, especially if he is able to prove his state medically and legally. Certainly, once the announcement is out it will not make the same headlines again, for the news value will be dead almost before the printer's ink is dry. As a result he will feel that the worst is over, and that any future life or reputation he builds can be built more solidly, without the fear of an unwelcome headline at any time bringing his newly built world collapsing around him. He will probably go forward much more happily knowing that little remains to harm him, but each case is individual and each must be their own judge.

First and foremost he must consider his work, for his ability to deal with other problems as they arise may well depend on his financial position. Nearly always the individual relies upon an employer to engage him in work, and he must decide whether to keep his 'change' from his new employer, and feel the strain of the secret, or, more wisely, to tell his employer his circumstances and take the chance of being refused the position. Added to this are the complications that may result from any wanted or unwanted publicity at some future time, its effect upon his employer (with the public in mind) and the effect upon the individual himself morally and in prestige. If self-employed, the individual will not have cause to worry about the reactions of a particular firm or employer, but will have the same headache when it comes to starting afresh and risking the public's attitude should they get to know about him.

Whatever the effect of publicity upon his future, much will depend upon his own sincerity and genuineness. He can expect little public sympathy, for instance, if he has co-operated in providing a bizarre sexual story of low taste, posed for undignified photographs and looks little different to a well made-up prostitute. Certainly, the human factor is an important one, and the peace of mind that can come from being able to face up to a new world free from the threat of publicity and without having to withdraw into secrecy depends much upon the morality, integrity and circumstances of each individual transsexualist.

Even if he feels fully warranted in taking the first course, and with the best of intentions submits to publicity, he must remember how easy it is for his case to be misrepresented. The less he says the more will be left to the imagination, encouraging further digging into his past and a possible misconstruction of the facts. Without his co-operation his family or friends may be approached, and this is likely to be disturbing both to them and to him. There is always the danger, too, of a headline implying something entirely different to the text from which it was taken, for, from the newspaper's angle, a story must be different if it is to make news or have any sensation value. Certainly, once the story is out, the individual has no control over the presentation of it in a newspaper or magazine whether he has co-operated or not. If he genuinely feels that getting the facts out into the open is the best thing he should remember that the story stands a better chance of dying quickly if the initial information is given to a general press agency, and not as an exclusive right to one concern. Each newspaper is often less interested in printing what they know is likely to be word for word in every other newspaper. Notwithstanding the possible disadvantages of trying to cover the story up once it is known, however, there are obvious disadvantages, too, in co-operating, since more information is divulged, although the facts, as published, may still be inaccurate or misconstrued by the reader.

Even with a given set of circumstances the effects of publicity may vary, so that no hard and fast rules apply, but from what has been said the transsexualist must see that, with or without publicity, dangers and difficulties lie ahead. If there is anything that he prefers to hide, however, there can be little doubt that publicity should be avoided at all costs. It is only natural that the press should wish to get all possible facts of an unusual story, and it is only when these are denied them that they are likely to be guilty of infringing the rights of the individual. There are bound to be isolated cases where such blame is warranted, but, on the whole, the British press have probably the finest reputation in the world, and are generally to be praised for their courtesy in seeking information and for the manner in which they present it. They also have a habit of seeking the truth, so that the transsexualist who changes his role whilst still married, has children to consider, or knows a divorce will be inevitable, faces having his world exposed and his loved ones hurt. Such cases should know that their own selfishness and medical state is no excuse for shrugging off their responsibilities in this connection, or for deliberately seeking out publicity to revel exhibitionistically in what to many is their own sordid perversion, at the expense of others. Above all, they should remember that it is how they are portrayed in the press that will determine how they are judged by society, and that to retreat into a new and private world without the facts coming out is the only dignified way if personal success and mutual love are to be lasting and assured.

Social considerations

Many of the aspects we have already covered have important social significance. In generalising, however, we should perhaps stress once again that the transsexualist is often forced to 'press on regardless' thinking only of some imaginary rosy future, rather than of the world he will find in reality after he has 'changed' and will continue to face as he grows older and older. Although the unchanged male transsexualist may, in his early years, be conscious of his inadequacy, perverse interests and feelings, his physique and male clothes are unlikely to give the general public any reason to doubt his masculinity. As a man he has the freedom of the world, and the way he expresses himself in it sexually or socially is entirely of his own choosing. As a woman, however, he will suddenly realise that he is not as free as he was before. He cannot seek his dance partner, but must wait to be asked. He is denied the pleasure of that cigarette in the street. He must not give that poor fellow on the road a lift. He must not walk down an unlit street at night, or, if he does, will feel conscious of his vulnerability. He cannot pop round the corner to post a letter without looking presentable and, if it is blowing a gale and pouring with rain, what of his new hair-do? Did he hope to get a mortgage on that house? Why should it have to be looked into more closely, perhaps even denied him, just because he is a woman? And did he say he had nothing to wear for that special occasion? Funny, he thinks, how when he had the money as a man it meant nothing to him because of his conflict and distress, yet now he has the 'femininity' he wanted he has not the money for all the necessary things he now could buy. Nice, maybe, to think that others will so readily help him if he lifts the bonnet of his car and starts to peer inside, but annoying to have to pull on to a side road and out of sight before he can give that slow-running adjuster on the carburettor a slight turn.

In either role, then, the individual is faced with continual awareness of his sex, but now it stems not from within himself but from without, for it is really a reflection of the way the world thinks, reacts, and judges his status. A normal woman can accept all these things as part of her upbringing because of her completeness as a person in the reproductive role, but the transsexual man will never be socially complete after a 'change' and will always have to face that barrier representing the limit to his satisfaction. Probably he will never be other than in-between, psychologically, in spite of surgery and hormones, and at the best he can only hope to be better adjusted and able to live a happier life. But even this may not mean much; whether one is better adjusted and happier is relative and depends on too many factors, some very personal, other communal. The transsexualist's problems will not resolve themselves just by a 'change of sex'. Indeed, they will almost certainly get worse, but perhaps because the big question mark that has hung over them all their lives has been removed they may at last begin to think more clearly, and use their new energy to tackle their problems, old and new.

Such considerations as have been discussed here deserve the close study of any who propose to take the long and unknown road over the sex border, if only to enable them to view the possible consequences better in their own case. We cannot expect them to agree when it is against their own conditioning and hopes, but it is certain that if they undertake the 'change' much of the matter embraced in this chapter will strike home with unexpected impact. Those who have not been through a 'change' can know little of its real meaning, what it involves physically, emotionally and socially, or its full implications. Even the psychiatrists, surgeons and other medical specialists who have studied the problem have examined the flame without having felt the fire. Yet, conversely, those who feel the fire within them almost invariably know little of the devastation it can cause, or what it can consume. The complexities of a 'change of sex' are vast indeed, and even in the most warranted cases too much searching cannot be done to ensure the wisdom of such action. No one can be responsible for the happiness of another, and it is therefore up to all transsexualists to glean all the facts they can on this subject before embarking on what is not a fun escapade but, on the contrary, a very serious venture from which there will be no return. Members of the medical profession cover a wide spectrum of society and it would be surprising if amongst its ranks we did not find homosexuals, transvestites and even transsexualists. It would be wrong, however, to regard the profession other than as a most respectable and responsible body and when help is given it is often out of deep compassion and for the most humane reasons, so the tremendous onus that is put upon those who help and advise must at all times be appreciated, respected, and honoured by those seeking it. When help is refused, therefore, it is not that those medically involved wish to deny the transsexualist happiness but because they know the possible outcome of a 'change' and its limitations. Only an analysis of cases some thirty years on after a 'change' can give any clear indication of how right the medical profession has been to help at all. For this reason, then, every avenue of adjustment must continue to be explored before the final road over the sex border can be condoned, for it seems true to say that the devil we know is, indeed, better than the devil we do not.

CHAPTER ELEVEN

THE 'CHANGE'

Sɪɴᴄᴇ ᴛʜᴇʀᴇ ɪs no such thing as a change of sex the patient can only be helped in a limited way to achieve his goal, and we must, therefore, in looking into the details and practicalities involved in a 'change', bear in mind that any help can only be directed towards an adjustment to the problem. Strictly speaking, then, we can only speak of 'change of role', and not of 'change of sex'.

Because of the immense number of aspects to be considered, no surgeon is likely to come to the aid of a transsexualist without first obtaining a satisfactory report from a psychiatrist, to indicate, firstly, that the person concerned is not likely to commit suicide after surgery and, secondly, that, unknown hazards aside, there seems nothing specifically against it. The surgeon, nevertheless, has still to bear the responsibility for his surgery and has not only to consider the result of such help upon his patient, knowing that charges that he has mutilated his patient may be strictly true, but has to face the possible criticism of 'helping such cases of "sexual perversion"', not only from society but also from within his own ranks of the medical profession. It is almost certain that the majority of cases who come to him with their problem are ignorant of the facts concerning a 'change of sex', and, indeed, of sex itself. Remarkably, many still have to be convinced that they will never be able to bear a child, for instance. The ability to function in a normal feminine way, have 'periods' and bear children, often represents the male transsexualist's basic idea of femininity, and to be denied such feminine attributes if he changes role shatters his dream world. The individual usually has no idea what is possible and what is not; he seems to think he has only to go to a surgeon for help and that, if it is agreed upon, everything will be done to 'change' him. Often, when asked what he wants, he will just say, 'Everything to turn into a girl.' Such transsexualists picture endless operations to change their anatomy, internally as well as externally; they imagine a magical rapid transformation from hormones and even view their appearance with misgivings, feeling the surgeon should give them new facial features without even having to be asked. They look upon it almost as their right to receive such help, and the chances are that they will never be satisfied; whatever is done is not enough.

Because of this attitude, as many aspects of a 'change' as possible will be covered in this chapter, to enable not only the transsexualist but the general public to understand what is involved. Certainly, a transsexualist is more likely to get help if he knows the facts, asks for some specific help or operation, and knows the limitations of any change of role. Also, if he is ever to find the peace of mind he seeks, and is to come to terms with life, he must learn the truth of what he asks, show some initiative and proof of his sincerity, and consider the feelings of society and his loved ones as well as his own. He must, above all, realise that however well he passes in his desired role, up to now it has only been a game. The surgery he wants is irreversible and he can only know for sure afterwards whether his decision was right, but then it will be too late. Yet to every transsexualist the key to their professed 'happiness' is the 'change', and that means surgery to have, at least, their offending organs removed. They will say it is action they want, not words, words and more words.

What is to be the nature of this action, then? What is possible for one is not necessarily possible for another, for each case is as different constitutionally, anatomically, physiologically, psychologically, in social conditioning, class and circumstance, as is indeed every individual. Any attempt at a change of role will therefore vary with each case, depending upon all these factors and depending, too, upon the extent to which he is prepared to accept that what he does or succeeds in getting done morally entitles him to the assumption of the role, legally or illegally, socially acceptable or not. These considerations will also determine the time factor involved, whether it will take him one or several years to satisfy the requirements of his own desires, to resettle, and be able to unconsciously identify himself as a member of the sex he has assumed. In discussing action that may be taken by these cases we must therefore remember the differences in each, as to the way they may go about achieving their goal, how far they want to go towards the limit of treatment, and just what they feel in their own mind makes them a woman and entitles them to regard themselves as such.

In considering these variations we shall have to deal with those who merely change role by changing clothes and mannerisms, those who embark on a change of name as well, those who also receive help with hormones, those who may be assisted with one or more operations, up to the limit of those who, by virtue of being hermaphroditic or completely inter-sexual, receive every possible help to conform to their correct sexual role. In any event, the final result depends upon the basic state of the individual at the commencement rather than on the degree of help given, so that a physically normal male transsexualist, even if psychologically female, has no more chance of changing his anatomical role than a completely normal male, and, similarly, an intersexual individual, who may conform anatomically to the female role, is likely to be no more successful in that role if the psychological orientation is masculine. It must, therefore, be remembered that the success of a change, although depending to a large extent on an-atomical considerations, is ultimately dependent on all the factors, anatomical and psychological, which together deter-mine the final picture.

In the first instance, let us consider the man who feels he cannot live any other way than as a woman, and simply masquerades in the role. He may be reluctant to seek help, have sought it unsuccessfully, or just have adopted the role because he likes his perverted way of living and the sexual satisfaction he gets out of it. Perhaps family ties stand in his way, so that even changing his name may be problematical or undesirable. He may suggest that he can earn a better living as a woman, either because of his particular feminine ability or because of his inability to be any good in a male job, but in any event he is likely to be able to justify his action in his own mind. Although the change involves no more than letting the hair grow, putting on an affected voice, using heavy make-up and wearing the appropriate clothes, the individual's intention to live permanently in this way distinguishes him from those who engage in transvestist behaviour in public only occasionally, and, although still a masquerade in every sense of the word, his action does imply to some extent a change of role. Such individuals will manage to get their name altered on the more important documents, such as the medical card, N.H.I. card, driving licence, etc., by applying for new ones or by posing the problem to the authorities and gaining their help. Often, rather than expose themselves and their secret to public bodies, they may assume another name, claim that they have lost their medical card, get another N.H.I. card by pretending to be an immigrant from Ireland, and obtain another driving licence on the basis of applying for the first time and submitting to another driving test. Invariably, such cases will choose a name to their liking and, for common usage, may only alter the Christian names to assist acceptance in their new role, or they may, on the other hand, assume a new surname as well, such as the maiden name of their mother, to mask their true identity. Some may feel that changing their role in this way is a useful first step in proving their feelings to their medical advisers, and perhaps give them better justification for hormonal or surgical help. Others may not think in terms of help, enjoying the masquerade and feeling that they can always revert to their original role if ever they feel like it.

We may be horrified to visualise an individual living in this way, but the average person is little affected by such behaviour and often knows nothing of its occurrence. The greater tragedy is for the individual concerned, for the adoption of the opposite role represents his only outlet in life, and his desperate measures to relieve his conflicts and sufferings are likely to lead him into more difficulties and trouble. Such an individual finds that he has more than ever to put on a front, and, although aware that he is socially unacceptable, conditions himself to believe that he is passable and that there is really nothing wrong in his masquerade. Whilst living in constant fear of disclosure, then, this conditioning makes him wish he could expose his secret in order to gain delight from telling the unsuspecting that they have been fooled. Sometimes the unreality of their world makes it easy for them to have little regard for the moral code and to even turn to crime. Although an emerging trans-sexualist, it is likely he will be looked upon as a homosexually-oriented transvestite, so that normal heterosexual individuals would be repulsed on hearing the truth. There is little chance that the individual will ever have any peace of mind if he continues in this behaviour, but usually it is not too long before hormones are sought, not, at this stage, as a preliminary to surgery but in order to enhance his female role.

We cannot imagine, in any sense of the word, that such a life represents an adjustment to the problem. It must either be a stepping stone to loneliness and disaster, or a forerunner to a more established role built on common sense and decency, with full co-operation from the medical authorities whose help should, and indeed must, be sought. We can in no way condone such behaviour and action, when male genitalia remain and the testes have not been neutralised by hormones, going as it does against all concepts of decency, and any individual who takes matters into his own hands in this way must fully accept the consequences. Should it represent part of a definite plan and treatment, however, with full knowledge of the medical profession, the individual must be given the benefit of the doubt as to his sincerity.

In the next group of cases we find those who are rather more morally-minded about their behaviour and have gone out of their way to seek medical advice. These are the cases who do not appear to have much to merit operations, but whose own initiative often convinces the doctors that the change of role will be pursued with or without their help. Occasionally, cases who are sufficiently desperate to take matters into their own hands may appear before their medical adviser for the first time dressed in the role of their desire, as proof of their passability and earnestness in meaning what they say. Such shock tactics may gain the transsexualist the first round, although much must depend upon the person himself as to whether such a move proves advantageous or detrimental to him. First, his appearance may leave much to be desired and only prove more than ever that help is unjustified, and secondly, the specialist may well feel affronted by such behaviour, deeming it bad for his staff, his practice in general, and his own respect and reputation.

Confronted with this determination, and whilst not necessarily agreeing with it as a solution, the doctor may feel bound to help by prescribing hormones; much seems in favour of this treatment since the sexual capacity of the individual will at least be reduced, thereby sedating his sexual conflict and protecting the public. The medical argument here is also that nothing has been changed anatomically should the patient's desires change, and the possible physical and psychological complications of operations are avoided. It is essential that the slow effects of hormones should be fully explained, however, so that the patient does not imagine they will turn him into a woman in a few months, or at all, and that at best he can hope for some stimulation of the breasts. Nevertheless, when hormones are given with the express purpose of feminising a transsexual man to assist a change of role, treatment must be directed primarily towards producing a chemical castration.

Normally, the glands provide a steady flow of hormones into the blood stream, depending upon the gland's normal phase or constancy of function. If sex hormones are to be artificially administered, therefore, to provide as near a natural effect as possible, the blood must be continually supplied with them otherwise even large doses will only provide a limited effect for a short period, the excess being excreted. For this reason an implant may be given, in which a high concentration of the hormone, in pellet form, is implanted under the skin of the abdomen just below the waist, being slowly absorbed into the blood stream over a period of several months. Although this method of administration has several advantages, one disadvantage is that when adverse reactions occur removal of the implant can be difficult. Alternatively, monthly injections of oestradiol benzoate intramuscularly may be given to effect a slow release of the hormone over a period of time. Whilst more controllable, there is evidence to suggest that levels of the hormone fluctuate from a high point following injection to a

388

low point shortly afterwards. Consequently, the more usual and convenient method of administration is by means of tablets taken orally, daily, which can provide a steady supply of the hormone and enables treatment to be easily suspended at any time for any reason. However, one disadvantage is that absorption of the hormone through the gut can be unpredictable and the liver is involved in its breakdown. Also, for this reason, in order to provide the equivalent effect of an implant or injection the tablets have to contain a much larger total dose of the hormone. Usually 1 to 15 mg. of stilboestrol is considered an effective daily dose for male patients, perhaps in a fat soluble form, *it being important that vitamin D is added* to better enable the hormone to become incorporated in the fatty tissues of the body. If stilboestrol is not tolerated too well ethinyloestradiol may be alternatively prescribed in equivalent doses, on the basis that 0.05 mg. of ethinyloestradiol equals 1.25 mg. of stilboestrol. Female patients may be given up to 15 mg. of the male hormone methyl testosterone daily in tablet form, these being dissolved slowly under the tongue. Alternatively, intramuscular injections of testosterone propionate may be given monthly to provide a slow release of the hormone over this period of time. The dangers and complications arising from the administration of male and female hormones, apart from the limitations of their effects, have already been dealt with, although the need for proper medical supervision cannot be too strongly stressed.

It is interesting to note that the phasing of hormonal administration is considered by some authorities to be important, and that a greater eventual effect is claimed if the therapy is carried out on an intermittent, rather than a continuous, basis. According to one authority, 15 mg. of stilboestrol may be taken three times daily for three and a half months, followed by an interval of three months, or, alternatively, 5 mg. may be taken three times a day for five months, followed equally by an interval of three months. In both cases the process is repeated indefinitely. According to this authority the principle of the method is as follows:

In the case of the 15 mg. dose, some eight days after the commencement of treatment the oestrogen intake begins its suppressing action on the pituitary, and as this progresses the androgen level falls and the oestrogen level rises. After about three months the suppression of the pituitary is complete, the androgenic-oestrogenic balance of the blood stream has altered in favour of the oestrogens, and, with the suppression of the testicular androgens, a castration effect will have been produced. Following upon the complete suppression of the pituitary, however, there is a rapid collapse of the body's response to the oestrogens, possibly due to the absence of the gonadotrophic hormones, the extremely low androgen level, or the excessively high oestrogen level. Since the length of time for the pituitary to recover is three months the treatment may thus be suspended for this period, as during this time no androgens are being produced by the testes and the body will remain under the influence of the predominant oestrogens. In the case of the 5 mg. dosage the initial effect takes longer to produce, and when, three months later, the suppression of the pituitary is complete, the collapse of the body's response will be less rapid. Thus the treatment may in this case be continued effectively for a further six weeks, before the interval is taken.

The method would appear to have much to recommend it, even when female hormone is administered for feminising purposes after surgical castration, for apart from its effectiveness it reduces the risk of pituitary tumour or atrophy of the prostate which might otherwise occur as a result of prolonged therapy with oestrogens. Whether or not the individual will have to take hormones for the rest of his life, however, to maintain his femininity, must depend upon his own glandular make-up and hormonal balance, the potency of the source of his androgens (adrenals, etc.), his own particular body physique and its responsiveness to oestrogens. Whatever the patient or the specialist treating him hopes to achieve, the result will almost certainly be disappointing if too much is expected. It cannot be too strongly emphasised that, unless the individual has definite intersexual characteristics, hormones will only encourage feminine features to develop on an existing male frame and body, and may turn a normal person from being an accepted member of society into a freak, accepted by, and belonging to, neither sex.

Cases in this category may press for surgical help as the next step towards their goal, although their remarkable ability to ignore the presence of their male genitalia often results in there being no immediate craving for it. Indeed, the thought of operation may hold fears for him, as might any operation, or it may be that he fears the loss of sexual pleasure. In any event, however, the patient is likely to want to establish himself more firmly in the new role by a legal change of name, and, enlisting medical support, he may go to a solicitor and delight in changing his John to Joan by Statutory Declaration or Deed Poll. His solicitor may also get the N.H.I. card changed for him, on the strength of the medical reports, and he will go in search of a job. It is, however, difficult to see that such an individual will ever be better off in this state, and whilst it is a necessary preliminary to surgery this can never be promised at the start, so the question must arise how morally acceptable it is for these cases to walk amongst us dressed as women but with their male genitalia under their skirts. To the majority of society it presents a revolting picture, and the possible invasion of a woman's privacy in the few places she has every right to regard as sacred to her sex must leave her horrified and in fear. Whilst we cannot entirely control the actions of those who embark on such perverted behaviour of their own volition, those who have to shoulder the responsibility in helping cases are being asked to accept a heavy burden, and we must ask them, when this behaviour is recommended to transsexualists to prove themselves, whether partial adjustment by chemical castration serves either the individual or the public when surgical castration provides a more satisfactory answer, logically and morally.

We must be careful to appreciate that we are not dealing with any one case or with a set pattern of events, for, although what has been said is factual in some cases, the particular approach to the problem by any one individual depends entirely upon his psychological outlook on life, his circumstances, his sexual orientation, and his moral standards: neither have we intended the foregoing to represent a definite pattern leading up to the establishment of the individual's desired role. What we have dealt with are two types of cases; one, in which the individual changes his role without any outside help, purely because of his abnormal sexual state and because psychologically he can see nothing wrong in it; the other, in which the individual is desperate enough to accept any help, provided it will enable him to live as he desires and, by pressing unceasingly for that help, gains some medical support for hormonal treatment. Both, then, are definite types, and are distinguished by the way they go about achieving their goal and the limit they reach in this aspiration.

The third type we are about to discuss are those who gain favour for being helped surgically. Although the first two types may eventually be successful in obtaining operations, those in this third group are distinctive in that they generally object to any change of role until their external genitalia conform to the role they seek, regardless of their torture and their conflicts. In fact, they usually feel sufficiently strongly about this to deny themselves any licence or transvestist behaviour, being obsessional and perfectionist enough to say that they want all or nothing.

Occasionally, the ability to receive even offered help may be jeopardised by the difficulty of obtaining a nursing-home or hospital bed. In this respect it must be remembered that the surgeon's name must be upheld; the desired secrecy may not be entirely possible, for, although wonderfully trained, kind and sympathetic, the medical and nursing staff may not entirely condone certain implications of such genital operations. In view, too, of the attitude of the general public, any reluctance to risk giving the nursing-home or hospital a bad name can well be understood. The answer must surely lie with the surgeon himself, for if he has enough faith in the justification of what he proposes, and in the patient himself, there should be little to fear except the cries of the ignorant and small-minded.

Whatever help the surgeon feels justified in giving, however, he is unfortunately often too busy to go into all the complex details for his patient, and, although the responsibility rests with him as the wielder of the knife, he has to rely to some extent upon other medical opinions to weigh up all the circumstances and justification. The surgeon can also have but little experience of the *effects* of these operations, performed as they are so rarely, and it is only on the result of cases he has previously helped or heard about that he is likely to sum up the situation and decide whether to help or not. It may be that a previous case has regrets, remains unhappy, or is still discontented with his body, wanting more and more done. He may be constantly worried by this case for help with legal documents, or, ungrateful for the help he has received, the case may revel in publicity at the risk of the surgeon's reputation. Such occurrences happen all too often, leading to a clamping down on the offer of help to others who may be perfectly sincere and merit help. Once a medical specialist is let down on even one case it does a lot to undermine his confidence in those who seek help, and other authorities are likely to be hesitant about accepting his opinion and judgement in the future. The surgeon's position is indeed a difficult one, and he is not always as free to help as he may wish.

Occasionally, operations are asked for and performed and not until afterwards does the patient learn what has been done. The patient, pressing for help, is usually too overjoyed at getting any to ask many questions about it, and has faith therefore in what the surgeon proposes; afterwards he may be dissatisfied, thinking the surgeon was going to do 'this' and not leave him like 'that'. Since the patient is ignorant on these matters and believes in nothing but miracles, the surgeon cannot be too careful in explaining exactly his full intention and the possible consequences of any operation he intends to perform, and in seeing that the patient is equipped with the necessary plans for the future. Rarely, with so many things on his mind, the surgeon may fail to go into the patient's personal commitments or even ask if he is married. It may be true that if operation is justifiable at all it must supersede all other considerations but, since the whole purpose of the surgery is to endeavour to give happiness to an afflicted individual, these other considerations must be viewed in the light of the reality which operations will bring to life. Since the individual's decision to have operations to assist a change of role is a momentous one by any standard, and one that no one can envisage without having experienced it, too much consideration cannot be given to the individual's personal circumstances with regard to his long-term happiness when such an irrevocable step is to be taken.

Since there are as yet no means whereby the internal sex organs or apparatus of a woman can be transplanted into a male, to speak of a 'change of sex' operation is basically misleading; since there is no such thing as a change of sex, neither can there be a sex-change operation. For the most part, however, loss of the penis and testes does much to cause the genital region to look feminine, and, on this basis alone, amputation of these organs is generally looked upon by the male transsexualist as the major part of his goal. Certainly, once these organs have been removed the individual feels better able to accept, morally and socially, that he is within his rights to assume the female role and way of life, and the ability to wear female undergarments more naturally and to have to pass urine in the female sitting position are facts which enable him to look upon himself, at last, as a woman. Such operations cannot be performed, however, without the possibility of shock or of great mental upset, and, if the patient has not been on prolonged oestrogen therapy, sudden hormonal imbalance giving rise to pseudo-menopausal symptoms (depressive morbid fears, hot and cold flushes, etc.). In its widest sense, therefore, surgery can only come to the aid of these individuals by changing the external appearance of the genitalia from one sex to another, and, in the male, castration and amputation of the penis is usually sufficient to bring about this change, although plastic surgery to reshape the perineum on female lines, mould the female labia, and create an artificial vagina is possible, technically, to complete the picture.

In the case of the transsexual woman, surgery is primarily directed at removal of the breasts. Such mastectomy is often faced with mixed feelings, however, since the possibility of resultant scarring, uppermost in the patient's mind, would affect her ability to show a normal male chest when bathing, etc. As with all surgery, different methods can be employed to bring about the desired result, and improved techniques are constantly being developed. The straightforward method to-day of removing the breasts is by two semi-lunar incisions above and below the nipples, removal of the breast tissue between to flatten the chest, and bringing together the edges of the skin by means of fine sutures (stitches). Whilst the operation is neat, and only leaves two small horizontal scars that fade in time, a big disadvantage is that the nipples are lost, detracting from the normal chest appearance. Even so, this method is used to help some cases who are more concerned with dress problems than with the cosmetic result. The main problem involved in retaining the nipples is that surgery is less likely to be uniform, since operation by incisions just below the nipples, through which to remove the breast tissue, is more likely to leave excess skin in the flattening process and cause puckering. The immediate result may well alarm the transsexual woman, and, although the puckering and scarring will lessen in time as nature heals and the skin shrinks back over the frame of the chest, she must remember that her objective cannot be attained overnight and that a scarred chest is something she may have to accept as a consequence of her self-sought goal. In another technique, the nipple is cut round, retained and then allowed to fall back after the surrounding breast tissue has been removed. In all cases, however, patience is essential, for it will be a year or more before any scarring will have faded and the final result can be properly assessed. Following the operation, the patient will find herself strapped round the chest to minimise movement during the initial healing phase. The drainage tubes inserted will also need removing after a few days. The patient is usually allowed home after a week, but for a month or two afterwards exercise of the arms and chest must be limited, and lifting of heavy weights avoided. Further surgery directed towards the fashioning of an artificial soft tissue 'penis' may, at some later date, be agreed to, when skin, including that from the genital labia, will be used to mould a tube as an extension of the urethra. Such is likely to be more for practical purposes than appearance, however, to enable male urinals to be used normally. In any event, such an operation is only likely to be

OVER THE SEX BORDER

performed when the male role has become fully established and as complete a 'change' as possible is essential to the individual's peace of mind and social acceptance.

We have so far only considered the third group of male cases collectively. In actual fact there are several sub-divisions within this group, so that some, for instance, may have only obtained a castration, some may have also been able to achieve removal of the penis, whilst others may be assisted further with plastic surgery to mould the female labia and create an artificial vagina. Beyond this, other plastic operations may have been desirable and obtained on the nose or ears, etc. Just what is done and agreed to depends both upon the individual himself and upon the surgeon. Sometimes it may be considered wise to deal with the operations singly, allowing a lapse of time between each to assess the full result or ponder the wisdom or correctness of further surgery. Occasionally, therefore, a castration operation may be performed only, in the hope that this alone might enable the individual to gain the necessary relief from his sexual conflict. Whilst such an operation is, to the surgeon, a straightforward procedure, the extreme vascular nature of the area means that any effort by the individual himself or an inexperienced second party to carry out the operation is extremely dangerous, and involves the risk of considerable or even fatal haemorrhage.

Some surgeons may only feel justified and willing to help if the case has already managed to obtain a castration, as it frees him from the legal involvements of this operation; amputation of the penis may then be agreed to, to assist the individual to feel socially acceptable in his desired role. In either event, however, any shaping of the perineum is normally left until later, depending upon it being sought after and its need and practical value being justified. Whether or not the creation of an artificial vagina should be further attempted is debatable, since in all cases it is a hazardous operation and not always successful or functional. For this reason, it is generally only considered when all the operations are carried out together, when full use can be made of the scrotal and penal skin. Unfortunately, however, only rarely does a surgeon feel justified and willing to combine all the possible operations, so that surgery is usually directed to one specific end only, in the hope that the minimum amount will meet the patient's desires. Whilst the method of undertaking operations in stages may have much to merit it there is no doubt that, where full help is contemplated with the creation of an artificial vagina also in mind, as complete an operation as possible seems desirable in the first instance, with the final result in view. This is particularly so in order that the important scrotal and penal skin may be used to line the proposed artificial vaginal pocket and not lost or mutilated as sometimes happens when earlier individual operations have been carried out, much to the regret of cases who often only find this out when it is too late.

The normal vagina may be looked upon as a tube, being a continuation of the uterus and emerging externally between the urethral and anal openings. Any surgery to simulate this is therefore directed towards the provision of a skin-lined tube, leading from the external opening to a depth of some inches within the body, and of sufficient elastic properties to enable its diameter to receive an erect penis. The functional capacity of the vagina will, of course, depend upon this factor and, although a small wide-necked recess barely 1 inch deep may be proudly regarded by the post-operative transsexual man as a 'vagina', it can be seen that if any form of intercourse is to be possible the provision of a tube of required length and width is essential. In any event, since the tube is artificial and not connected with any internal organ, it can only end in a blind pocket, and the difficulty of moulding this pocket or tube is that the walls of any opening made will tend to contract and close, since it is nature's way to treat this as an area requiring healing. To prevent the walls sticking together the tube-shaped cavity has to be lined with outer skin, preferably epithelium (outer mucous skin); scrotal and penal skin may be used for this, but, if previously lost, a piece of skin from the thigh or buttock may be grafted to the required site. Contraction will still occur with healing, however, and tend to cause closure of the pocket, so that after the operation a plastic mould about 1 inch in diameter and from 3 to 6 inches long has to be worn within the pocket to prevent or minimise this. This will not be without considerable inconvenience and often much pain, since it is necessary to maintain constant pressure on the mould to keep it in place, maintain its correct direction, and assist enlargement of the cavity. Obviously, it is also a great nuisance every time there is need to pass water. Such a mould has to be worn constantly day and night for some six months, during which time there is always the possibility of rapid closure, undoing all the previous work, should it be left out for a short period for any reason. The mould has still to be worn at night for a further six months after this, and even so there is always doubt just how satisfactory and functional the final pocket will be. The closed pocket will also tend to become foul with sweat and discharge, causing smell and soiled clothes unless strict cleanliness is adhered to.

When the skin comes from the scrotum it contains hair follicles and is hard 'outer' skin, and although a technique whereby a portion of intestine is used provides skin more closely resembling the soft moist inner skin of a normal vagina, the intestine still goes on secreting its juice and the discharge is not only inconvenient but irritant. In any case, the artificial vagina will have no normal sensory nerve supply to promote feminine-type sexual pleasure during any act of intercourse, although the transsexualist may be content giving pleasure to his partner. Dr. De Savitch (*Homosexuality and Change of Sex*, 1958) sums up the position adequately by saying:

> 'But no matter what technique is used, or how skilfully the vagina is made, it is unlikely that the patient himself will ever be tempted to use it unless masochistically inclined; intercourse would only be painful and disagreeable. It is, in fact, only the immense psychological benefit conferred in certain cases by its possession that justifies the risk involved in constructing what might otherwise be regarded as a completely useless luxury.'

Whilst this may be true, sight should not be lost of the erotic nature of the prostate gland, which will lie in close proximity to the created pocket and serve to give some sexual pleasure if pressure is exerted upon it during the act. Although atrophy and softening of the prostate is regarded as a consequence of loss of the male genitalia and prolonged hormonal treatment, this is not always the case and sexual feeling often remains; even a full bladder may still stimulate the erotic areas at times and create an urge that requires satisfaction, whether the desire is there or not and whether the subsequent orgasm may be said to result from an act of masturbation or masochism.

Whether the creation of an artificial vagina may be deemed a luxury, and whether it is a surgical success or failure from the functional point of view, the need for one is not altogether purely psychological. The individual is faced with the prospect of a lonely life, destined to become an 'old maid', and the thought is always present that perhaps someone would love them for what they are, for their personality, their capabilities, their companionship and their love. There is much more to love than the mere sexual act, for it embodies the unity of two people, in their interests, sharing each other's pleasures and disappointments, each giving and receiving. If this partner should ever come along it may be that, whilst the inability to have children will not bother him, the need for his own sexual expression and his inability to have 'normal' intercourse could turn the scales against the partnership coming to anything. Aware of this situation the changed transsexual man may well feel justified in wanting an artificial vagina, should this at any time make the difference between his being thought a mutilated male or a more normal and desirable female. That the ability to get one may be denied him, or that what is done may prove unsatisfactory and useless, does not detract from the sincerity behind the original motive, although the full implications, complications, and possible failure of such an operation should be well borne in mind before he beseeches his surgeon to assist him with such a procedure. Indeed, after going through the operation, suffering much after-pain and inconvenience, it is quite possible that complete failure will result and only a healing scar on the leg remain as a reward for all the effort. With all these factors to bear in mind no individual, however obsessed, should entertain the thought of such an operation without being prepared to accept the worst or, at the best, a very poor pocket of doubtful size and depth.

In considering the possibility of helping his patient in any way involving the amputation of organs, the surgeon is confronted with the many dangers associated with irreversible operations, for he well knows that his patient may have cause for regret afterwards, however strongly his feelings may have prompted the demand for help. Apart from the dangers of this pendulum swing of sexual attitude the surgeon is faced with the legal and moral issues involved. In consequence of this, when one case recently was desperate for help and these issues were of particular concern, the surgeon devised a procedure whereby the male organs, instead of being removed, were merely replaced within the body so that by their apparent absence the outward appearance would seem to be that of a woman. This operation he called an 'insertion operation'. Although this case, recommended for help by the writer, appears to be happy with the result of the surgery, retraction of the testes and reimplantation of the penis can hardly be considered to be an answer to the problem. Certainly, the patient will still be able to experience sexual feelings and have orgasm, and large regular doses of female hormones will help towards preventing 'erections' of the penis within him. Obviously, this can only be looked upon as a part adjustment and as a stepping stone, but it should not be dismissed too lightly. The ability to live as a woman for a trial period *without male genitalia under the skirt*, to the satisfaction of the patient and the morals of society, does have something to offer. This leaves the options open later for the patient to either have the organs removed to enable him to live permanently as a woman or to have them repositioned outside the body as before if the decision to revert back to the original male role is made, without any structural harm having been done. Unfortunately, the writer has not been able to follow up the case in question to discover the outcome or whether further surgery was subsequently undertaken. Such advice, help and treatment for any one case involves a lot more time and patience, so that no surgeon is likely to choose this method just to get round

400

accepting the full medical responsibility for his actions. It does, however, offer an alternative approach to surgery in exceptional circumstances.

Apart from his genital anatomy the patient often looks to other aspects of his body for improvement so that a surgeon is not uncommonly asked to reshape a nose, retract prominent ears, or, more significantly, reduce the thyroid cartilage – the characteristically male prominent 'Adam's apple'. Being more general procedures that any person might go to a plastic surgeon to have done, the surgeon is generally quite happy to do what he can as long as the patient is prepared to pay privately. When these further operations are requested under the National Health Service, however, the surgeon may have to decide where to draw the line. It may be said that if an operation is necessary for the health of the patient a case can be made out for it, but it will certainly be difficult to justify both the need for various genital operations and a number of cosmetic procedures also.

Wherever the line is drawn, however, the individual will find himself in his new world feeling he has not really chosen it, believing he is the way he is because of how he was born, and that nature has taken a hand in determining his destiny. We must be prepared to accept this where the sexual margin may have been narrow and there were definite characteristics of intersexuality, but we must also feel that some cases have been forced into this change, not through some constitutional cause, but through some underlying psychological, sexual, or conditioned deviation. The fact remains that the individual is now faced with viewing everything from a different angle, and it is surprising how little one sex knows of the life of the other. 'Viewing' is the operative word, however, for no transsexualist can ever become of the opposite sex. All his doubts and psychological conflicts will reappear with the emergence of new problems, and his inability to go here and there as before, his lowered social position in life, the severing of his associations with his family, and, after all the fuss has died down, his loneliness, will become more evident to him. Even if he has friends of his own kind the loneliness is still there in his heart, for inwardly he knows he does not really belong to either sex and that for him there can be no real place in society. It is at this stage that the whole success of his change is challenged, for, in spite of all he has been through, he must still come to terms with life and accept what he is, what is real, and how best to live in society without treading on their toes or becoming upset when they do not understand or accept him.

If the individual is to make a success of his new life, then, he must change his whole outlook and get things in their right perspective. He must leave the dominating sexual factor behind, and at last realise that the cause of his trouble has not been so much with sex as his conflict with life itself. Whether he sees this or not does not mean that he can necessarily do anything about it, even in his new role, for to do so he must accept what he has been unable to accept previously. He may at last see the folly of his lost and wasted years, and take steps to look around himself and mature in his surroundings, but it is the writer's experience that, although cases accept life more peaceably once they have changed, they are no better able to cope with life than they were before since there is no underlying change in their interests, sexual desires or attitude to life. Their peace of mind only comes by forcing themselves to justify their actions, and by realising that whatever regrets they have they can now only accept the situation. All their life they have wondered which sex was right for them, whether they should try to conform or press on, etc., and the peace of mind is not so much in the 'change of sex' as in the disappearance of this factor.

The absence of the testicular androgens, furthered by oestrogen administration, may in itself make the individual placid enough to take life more easily and quietly. Those who have embarked on a change because of essential immaturity or true constitutional factors probably stand the best chance of establishing themselves successfully in a new role, since time may help to mould their outlook and assist in their further development towards maturity. In this respect we are con- sidering maturity as something beyond the sexual notation of love, marriage, and reproduction of the species; we are speaking of being capable of standing on one's own feet, making responsible decisions, earning a living, taking a broad view on life, enjoying the normal pleasures, feeling the pangs of sorrow in their rightful place and proportion, and being capable of giving, receiving, loving and understanding. When an individual learns to possess these qualities in life the change of role will lose its significance, the world before him will take on new colour, and the anticlimax will prove to be no more than a passing phase in his rehabilitation. If he now goes forward he will gradually rebuild from scratch all that he has lost in the upheaval of changing his role, and if he has started from nothing will probably accept less from life. Basically his character and personality will be the same and his conditioning will remain dominant, so he is not likely to climb higher than he otherwise would have had he not 'changed'.

The belief that everything will be so different after a 'change' is possibly the greatest misconception of all, for the answer lies not in the person's sex or role but within themselves. Unfortunately, few who make the change ever succeed in coming to terms with life in this way, for they are rarely satisfied and go on searching to capture an unknown dream. For some, the belief that they have really changed their sex becomes the platform on which they continue to fight, and, instead of settling down to a happy secluded life, go on wasting away their lives pitying themselves and arguing, often publicly, about the lack of sympathy the world has for them. Their past, too, never really escapes thought during their quieter moments, and the ability to lead a normal life is always denied them. In our aim to help these individuals to some form of adjustment we cannot under any circumstances suggest that surgery to assist a change of role is the answer, but we also cannot deny that it may be better than nothing. We must also be very careful not to generalise too much or deny any case the merit of a full examination of their circumstances, and finally we must remember to treat such cases with all the medical care and attention that they deserve and not as freaks or monsters of society. The medical profession has a difficult, arduous, and responsible task to carry out, and members of this noble calling are not likely to be found wanting in their duties provided they are given the assistance and backing of those whose only duty is to sit back and criticise.

CHAPTER TWELVE

THE LEGAL ASPECT

Whatever the medical aspect of a proposed change of role may be there remains the problem of the legal position in connection both with the possibility of obtaining help and with the ability to live in the new role, legally recognised within the laws laid down by the individual's native country. The legal aspects are indeed so important that they must be considered hand in hand with the medical aspects, for the whole future happiness and peace of mind of the individual depends upon lawful acceptance of the new role, being a factor which goes on exerting itself long after the medical problems have as far as possible been resolved. There seems little point in receiving medical help if it is not backed up with legal help, or if the individual is denied the right to benefit from such help.

Unfortunately, however, the medical and legal aspects are divorced very much from each other; it is not difficult to see the reasons for this, since the medical and legal professions are specialist professions in their own right, each with their own principles, codes, etiquette and laws. Whereas the medical specialist, therefore, may feel that one of his cases particularly merits help in a change of role, and gives assistance in that direction, it is not to say that the legal authorities will accept the medical evidence unquestionably, any more than the medical specialist would necessarily agree with action taken by a lawyer if the circumstances were reversed. Cases must understand, then, that however many medical hurdles they overcome in the achievement of their desire, nothing follows automatically from the legal side, and that overcoming all the legal difficulties involved in a change of role represents a major hurdle all its own. It is because of the general misconceptions regarding these facts that so many of those who have received medical assistance in a change of role experience further frustration and unhappiness, instead of the expected peace of mind. So often the individual feels that once he has been helped surgically, no longer possesses male genitalia, and lives as a woman, he is bound to be recognised for what he is and legal recognition is but a formality. He must realise that this is not so, and that, even with his doctor's help, any change of name on his civic and social documents does not mean that his status is legally recognised, and that any fight to make it so is likely to be hard and may easily not succeed.

It is not surprising that sex in all its different and devious aspects forms the basis of a vast number of our laws, many of which go back in time as long as man himself. Man should not do this, woman should not do that, man and woman together should behave in this way or that, and so the law in many cases depends upon the recognised sex of the individual. A change of 'sex' or role then immediately suggests that the individual will be able to reverse all the laws that previously applied. Since no individual can take it upon himself to change the laws that apply to him, it can be seen that a change of role presents many legal problems which can only be resolved by legal methods. We are, also, dealing with every variation of a change, from those without any justification to those with some basic constitutional reason such as intersexuality or hermaphroditism. Everywhere along the line, however, the same laws are applied, so that in some cases only finer points may decide if they are, in fact, inside or outside the law.

The first instance in which we see this is when an individual pleads with a surgeon for removal of genitalia. We are told castration is an illegal operation, and that it is more than the surgeon dare do to help. Even if there are no testes and only a small hypospadic penis to be removed, the same argument is used. Yet amputation of the genitalia has to be performed in cases of disease and injury, and the surgeon has in no way to consider any legal aspect, because it is for the good of his patient and may be to save his life. There seems little difference between saving the patient's life in this way and saving it when the disease has other medical origin, such as that associated with transsexualism. Since surgeons are, in fact, able to be the judge in all cases as to whether operation on the genitalia is desirable for medical reasons, and have been known to perform all manner of operations to change or correct the external sexual anatomy to help a patient change his 'sex', we must ask when are operations of this type illegal? If the support of medical opinion makes them legal the surgeon surely cannot hide behind the argument that they are illegal, but must have the courage to refuse those asking for help if such is believed right by him. On the other hand, those who do receive help must face the fact that it is medical help, and that undergoing operations in no way legalises their change of role.

We must sympathise with the surgeon in his difficult task of assessing the factors of each individual case, and understand that he is dealing with a person who generally knows little of the medical or legal facts. Whilst a surgeon well knows the possibilities and limitations of surgery in assisting such cases, he is usually also aware of the legal problems that face his patient should a change of role be embarked upon as a result of his help. Often, the surgeon will go to great lengths to assist his patient further, by going into the legal matters in order to ensure that every success is likely to come from his efforts. This is, however, a responsibility which the surgeon is not obliged to undertake, and is most certainly a task that should in no way be imposed upon him, much as his patient often expects this further help. It seems quite probable that any effort on the surgeon's part to help sort out the legal aspects is likely to unfairly and sorely try his patience, resolving him into feeling that he has neither the time nor the wish to become involved in the complex machinery of assisting future cases that come to him for help. Indeed, this often applies equally to solicitors as well, who have found that the whole basis on which assistance and information can be given is uncertain, with the law nebulous and ill-defined on the subject.

Much as these problems exist for the sympathetic doctor and solicitor, for them they are problems connected with their professional calling and do not otherwise interfere with their own particular routine or lives. In the end it is the patient who again has to suffer from the lack of co-operation, between the doctor who has the medical side to deal with, the solicitor or lawyer dealing with the law as it can be interpreted, and the government of the country who make the laws. Again, each of these bodies have divergent factions and opinions within themselves, which further magnifies the task of sorting out the complex problems that such cases present. Often, the medical specialists will not act without legal authority first, and similarly, the legal position cannot sometimes be clarified until medical action has been advised and taken, so that the patient is falling between two fires all the time. From the patient's point of view, however, particularly if a true intersexual, it is nothing short of sheer madness that, after full medical co-operation and assistance in a change of external anatomy, to assist him in conforming to his correct sexual role, he should be left struggling by his own devices against the civil and social formalities of recognition before he may begin to be allowed to rebuild his life out of the confusion and torture of the past.

Each country has its own particular laws, as far as giving a lead to the surgeon is concerned, and the failure of sufferers to be understood or helped in their own country often causes greater pressure to be brought to bear upon those countries who take a more sympathetic view of the problem. It is for this reason that Denmark and other continental countries have had to close the door to other than their own kinsmen seeking help, for not only would it involve them in a task of considerable magnitude and responsibility to advise and possibly help all-comers, but the legal position of the individuals on returning home would be difficult and might strain the medical and legal relations of those countries concerned. Before we consider what is legal in England and other countries for those who have been fully assisted, medically, in a change or correction of role or status, let us examine the difficulties and legal aspects of those who are engaged in any form of transvestist activity or are at any stage along the road towards a determined and sincere change.

First, what of the male or female transvestite who relieves his or her feelings by dressing in the clothes of the opposite sex? In private, this is the concern only of the individual, but in public, much as there is no law against cross-dressing in itself, any activity which may cause a breach of the peace or suggest conduct prejudicial to good order can be regarded as illegal. Since the female is the passive partner in any sexual relationship a woman can dress as a man in public and not be considered offensive. On the other hand, the sexual capabilities of the male make him easily criticised for any transvestist behaviour, the act being regarded as symbolic of sexual perversion and desire. Because of this the public view the thought of a man dressed as a woman with abhorrence, and the police have a duty to safeguard all members of the community against offence. Even if the individual is wholeheartedly sincere in his motive, revolts at all sex, and only wants an expression to his bursting feelings, it must be remembered that he is not likely to see himself as others do. It is more than probable that his appearance will give him away, however well he convinces himself he looks the part. Even if his figure, his legs, his wig, the shadow of facial hair, his heavy make-up or his voice do not give him away, it is still likely that his manner will. Few can witness such a masquerade without being disturbed by it, so that the masquerade itself may well be considered a breach of the peace and land the individual in trouble. Often the very act may necessitate exhibitionism to enhance the pleasure, so that what started off innocently enough may end up with a charge and an account in a Sunday newspaper. Even a young male transsexualist charged as a transvestite with importuning can claim no exemption for his behaviour on account of his 'feelings', or be saved from being possibly sent to gaol as a homosexual. Whatever the circumstances it is obvious that the law must protect society, and a potential danger must be regarded as seriously as the danger itself.

Whilst we may take a detached and unsympathetic view of such behaviour, it must be remembered that the individual may not be able to help himself. On the other hand, the individual must realise that the law is there for the greater good of the greatest number, and either he must seek help or avoid any action that may get him into trouble. It is, however, singularly interesting to note the case of one particular transvestite, who took to living as a woman and devised his own ways to get the name changed on his necessary papers, telling no one and seeking no medical advice. Having let his hair grow and assumed the female role as much as his ability would allow, he was on one occasion involved in a motor accident and taken unconscious to hospital. No questions were asked there about his mode of life. On another occasion, when coming before the court on a legal charge, not of a sexual nature, the law made no issue of his masquerade except to refer to it in quoting his real name and sex. It can be seen, then, that the authorities have no wish unnecessarily to call these unfortunate sad cases to task over their behaviour, provided no charges of indecency are involved. Such a sympathetic view is worthy and to be commended, but it should not be taken as evidence that such behaviour is condoned. Indeed, those who embark on such perverted activities with healthy male genitalia under their clothes should not rely on the good nature of their fellow beings, but must on the contrary accept the rights of those who guard the interests of society to deal seriously and severely with them.

Let us now consider the case of a man who is also compelled to live as a woman, but who receives certain medical treatment (e.g., hormonal), is given a medical certificate as to his state, and yet still retains his male genitalia, being advised against, refused help for, or awaiting, surgery. Again, the medical and legal sides conflict, for we must ask how legal is it for a man to live as a woman? The only difference from our first example seems to be that, in this case, the individual has medical approval. No doubt the medical specialist will feel justified in helping such a patient if he proves his behaviour has no sexual motive, and can pass reasonably well in his desired role without the likelihood of causing offence or a breach of the peace. We can equally assume that this would also include help in getting the name legally changed and the necessary civil papers put in order for the purposes of employment, etc. Whilst ordinary transvestites normally live as one sex and enjoy the sexual stimulation of changing temporarily to the other, these other cases cannot be compared to them for they have taken steps to conform permanently to one role and would, if possible, have any treatment or operation to further their establishment in it.

Whether or not the individual is being tested in this role, under medical supervision before operation may be considered advisable, depends upon the circumstances, but in any case a temporary if not permanent situation exists whereby the exact legality of the patient's mode of life must be in doubt.

It would appear from the foregoing that the law is prepared to take a more humane view of a particular problem provided there are strong medical grounds supported by authoritative and responsible members of the medical profession, and in this respect there does seem to be some welcome co-operation between the medical and legal professions. This still does not mean that the laws can be bent, where they are definitely laid down with clear and purposeful meaning, but that vague laws which may have originally been made with other objects in mind can be interpreted according to the facts by those considering the case.

This brings us to consider the actual status of an individual who has received full medical help, including operations, to assist a change of role, who has legally changed his name and all his essential documents, but who still retains the original 'Boy' on his birth certificate. We might assume that the individual is legally both sexes, but in fact the legal sex remains male, since the birth certificate takes precedence over any other legal document as it bears witness to the actual circumstances, and this evidence would be used in any legal argument in which the question of identity arose. To understand this we must consider the possible courses open to an individual, in England or Wales, who wishes to live in the opposite denomination and status, get his essential papers changed to show a name appropriate to that status, and enable a living to be earned and to keep within the law.

A name can be changed merely by adoption and common usage: Mr. Bloomer, for instance, may feel he would rather be Mr. Baker, and therefore tells his friends that he will in future be known as Mr. Baker. Since there is nothing to connect the present Mr. Baker with the former Mr. Bloomer, however, should a distant relative leave a sum of money to him in the name of Bloomer Mr. Baker would not be able to claim it, unless he had proof that he is in fact the person entitled to the money. In the same way there would be nothing to tie up Mr. Baker with Mr. Bloomer as far as the birth certificate was concerned, and there would therefore be difficulties if he wished to obtain a passport, or had to produce evidence of his age in order to claim the old age pension. There would be similar confusion over the other legal and civic documents. If such difficulties arose they could be overcome by Mr. Baker making a Statutory Declaration before a magistrate or commissioner of oaths, swearing that he, in fact, is Mr. Bloomer, and stating his change of name to Mr. Baker. Alternatively, a friend or relative, who knows Mr. Baker and Mr. Bloomer are one and the same person, may make the declaration. The procedure is exactly the same if it is one or more Christian names that are to be changed, and the acceptance of the new name is no more than a formality. It is less often, however, that the Christian name is required to be changed from that of one sex to another, that John should now be known as Joan or vice versa, but such a change is still possible, although the magistrate or commissioner for oaths may well require medical approval before agreeing to draw up the declaration. Even so, this does not always appear necessary, for a case is known to the writer whereby such a change was formalised without a request for medical evidence.

A change of name by statutory declaration is the simpler and cheaper method. If the individual wishes really to establish his change of name, however, and have it officially registered, he can do this for the extra but worthwhile cost of getting a solicitor to prepare a deed poll. Almost certainly, however, medical evidence will be required if the change of name is to be from one sex to another, and once the deed has been signed and sealed it must be registered in the Central Office of the Royal Courts of Justice in London. In normal circumstances the individual would advertise the change in a newspaper, so that his new name may be known, but it is unlikely that such a procedure would be adopted by those wishing to embark on a new life as quietly as possible.

Cases who change their name in this way may then produce evidence of the declaration or deed poll to enable all the other

412

important documents to be changed. These may include National Health Insurance (Employment) card, medical card, driving licence, passport, or papers relating to bank account, car ownership, or house ownership. Although such matters can be dealt with by the individual concerned, it is certainly wiser to get the solicitor to deal with them following the change of name. When the documents are altered, however, it does not mean that the old name is dispensed with; Mr. Baker, for instance, would still find that against his new name would be written 'formerly Bloomer', in the same way that a married woman generally has her maiden name included in official records. This is mainly for identification and record purposes. Having changed the Christian name by statutory declaration or deed poll, then, the individual can obtain the requisite documents to enable the desired role to be assumed and work to be obtained. Some cases may also feel happier to carry around a medical certificate with them, but the individual can in any case settle down in the knowledge that he has done all he can, legally and socially, to become once again a useful member of the community. Even so, his life must of necessity be restricted in many ways, in view of his abnormality, and he must carefully avoid becoming involved in any incident or relationship which may suggest indecency.

At the same time that a deed poll is prepared and registered it is possible for a note to be made on the reverse of a *copy* of the birth certificate, according to the sworn declaration. This is for civic and record purposes and does not mean that the entry of birth registered at Somerset House (the Central Registry Office in London) has in any way been amended or corrected. In law, a change of sexual name by statutory declaration or deed poll, although regarded as satisfactory for the purposes of identification and records, *in no way suggests recognition of the actual sex or medical state of the individual*. Should the person have entered into a marriage ceremony before such a change, therefore, the marriage will remain legal. In the same way the person is not relieved of his responsibilities on other civic matters, and the law applies to him as formerly.

Cases are known of married men who, having changed their

Christian names from one sex to another following medical treatment and approval, continue to live with their wives. The relationship is then on a 'sisterly' basis, and no doubt companionship is the main reason the partnership continues, although spiritual love and a sense of moral duty may be others, but the difficulties of the arrangement and the maintenance of the ties of the past are likely to undermine the settled state and peace of mind of the individual. There is also the situation where the wife is revolted and seeks a divorce, only to find that the law ties her to her 'husband', any treatment he has had to assist his abnormality being considered necessary medical treatment and not constituting grounds for divorce. One must wonder what further grounds the wife needs to prove mental cruelty beyond having to watch her husband go through such a 'transformation', and in such cases the law, as it stands to-day, cannot be condoned for demanding a three-year separation before a divorce can be considered. In this respect the law is well out of date, and too much pressure cannot be brought to bear upon those responsible for these matters to look closer into the circumstances, in the light of medical advances and knowledge on this subject.

What of those, however, who are single and wish to afterwards marry? The circumstances are bound to come out by virtue of the birth certificate or their amended documents. It seems rather pointless for those who retain their male genitalia to expect sympathy from the authorities when it comes to wanting to 'marry' a man, in spite of their feelings as a 'woman', their medical state, and their 'legal' change of name. Even with those who have had operations, however, the procedure of changing the name and apparent status does not alter the position, and *marriage cannot be entered into because they are not legal women*. The majority of cases are revolted by sex, however, and only wish to be left alone to live their lives in peace, but, should this not be so, the wish to find a 'suitable' partner for companionship or marriage represents a false and dangerous idea, since legal marriage is impossible and any sexual relationship can only be frustrated by the abnormality of the partnership, unless accepted on a homosexual plane.

The ultimate, of course, is to obtain official correction of the birth certificate at Somerset House, since it amounts to legal recognition of the true sex of the person at birth and automatically legalises the role, enabling all other papers to be duly amended without question; certainly there would be no problem if the individual wished to marry. The birth certificate is, however, a most solemn and sacred document, not to be altered without the fullest possible justification and certainly not merely to satisfy a whim or make life easier. There can be no question of falsifying the records, and only in the most rare and exceptional circumstances can the birth certificate be corrected or amended. The authorities are well aware of the difficulties of transsexualists, however, and, whilst having to refuse to alter the certificate, they are otherwise generally prepared to help medically approved cases in all other matters involving a birth certificate, such as in the issue of a new passport, or when required for superannuation or employment purposes, etc. In these circumstances, covering letters from the authorities suffice to meet the individual's requirements, and generally the matter is dealt with most humanely, confidentially, and with every regard for the person's feelings.

Since, almost without exception, the male cases with whom we are concerned have been born biologically male, in possession of a penis and testes and functionally capable of producing sperm, they can stand no chance whatever of honestly convincing the authorities, irrespective of their present state, that at birth their sex was female. The converse, of course, applies to females wishing to re-register as males. Whilst all factors relating to sex are taken into consideration, cases must realise that in asking to be re-registered in the opposite denomination the facts are usually weighted very heavily against them. It is natural, of course, that they would like to get their birth certificates changed, to legalise their role and assist, to their way of thinking, their normality, and the medical advantages of giving peace of mind and a more settled outlook certainly cannot be rated too highly. Indeed, even intersexuals who have been helped medically and surgically to conform to their more correct sex, and feel they have every justification to have the birth certificate corrected, can be very hurt should they be told that they are merely 'hankering after something that represents nothing more than a few words on a piece of paper'.

Unfortunately, the individuals usually know little of the complex procedure involved, or of the legal and medical entanglements. They have no idea of the time it will take, the effort required, the facts to be considered by the authorities, the vague nature of the law which someone has to interpret, or the full responsibility of the decision that someone has to accept and answer to others for. A danger also is that cases too often refer to other cases 'who got this and got that' without any knowledge of the reasons or circumstances. Understandably, then, the authorities are very careful not to set a precedent which would be a yardstick whereby other cases of less sincerity and integrity could insist on their 'rights'. Naturally, no loophole must be allowed for the unscrupulous, but in any case we have seen in this work how diverse are the types affected by this abnormality and how immensely the circumstances may vary, so that the authorities have every justification to insist, as they do most emphatically, that each case must be considered on its own individual merit and that at no time will any decision represent a precedent. No good can therefore come of quoting other cases, and it might even jeopardise the application.

Generally, the procedure concerns the parents of young children, who find there has been a human error of determination at birth, or it may concern the individuals themselves who may discover, later in life, that the sex has been incorrectly entered, perhaps because a Christian name given by the person registering the birth was not sufficiently clear to indicate the sex. Other instances occur in which sexual development may be retarded, so that it is not until the child is a few years old that the error is discovered. Whatever the circumstances, and whatever the age of the person concerned, the full facts have to be notified to the Registrar of Births of the district concerned, together with evidence from a qualified medical practitioner. The details are then submitted to the Registrar General at Somerset House in London, who, if he is satisfied that the circumstances warrant a correction, will require two statutory declarations to be sent to him, one from a parent and one from a doctor. Upon receipt of these he can then instruct that the entry be corrected. The original entry, however, is not altered but a marginal note is made, to the effect that in column 2, for example, for 'John Derek' read Joan Dinah', and in column 3 for 'Boy' read 'Girl'. Thereafter follows the date of the correction, the name and official title of the one making the correction, and the names of those who supplied the statutory declarations. For normal purposes a shortened birth certificate can then be issued, in which only the briefest details of the certificate are shown and in which the newly recognised name and sex are carried forward without reference to any correction having been made.

Knowing that cases who apply for amendment to their birth entry are most unlikely to know the exact nature of the circumstances in which an application may be favourably considered, the officials at Somerset House are extremely cautious lest an individual should persuade eminent authority to sign declarations on his behalf, obtain the amendment, and then openly or publicly contradict the evidence on which he obtained it. The fact is that there is no provision in law whereby a person, who has been born a boy and whose actual sex at birth has been entered correctly on the birth certificate as 'Boy', can in any way have the entry amended later to read 'Girl'. The entry of birth is concerned with the state of the child at the time of birth, and does not take into account any present condition of an individual, irrespective of whether the boy has turned into a woman or, for that matter, a donkey. This is a fact that cannot be over-emphasised. It will be noted how carefully *correction* of the birth certificate has been referred to, for there can never be a *change*, only a correction or amendment. One case who has had medical help in a 'change' is at the moment near suicide, because of his repeated unsuccessful applications to Somerset House to *change* his birth certificate. His unhappiness cannot be under-estimated, but neither can his attitude be condoned, for he insists that he has 'changed' sex and feels that, if his birth certificate is only *corrected*, it would deny him the ability to tell the world that he was born a boy and 'look at me now!' If

Somerset House should agree to a correction, which is the only provision open to them, and then have the case openly saying that he was definitely born a boy, perhaps been married and even fathered children, it does little to favour the case, a lot to harm the reputation of Somerset House, and most decidedly disfavours others who may follow with the utmost sincerity and justification.

Let us therefore follow a case of true intersexuality who may feel justified, with good reason, in applying to Somerset House for a correction of the birth certificate, for in that way we shall be able to see the arguments that may be put forward by the individual or his/her solicitor in support of the application, the nature of the law, the delay and resulting effect upon the case, the medical facts that have to be gone into, the attitude of officials at Somerset House, and the possibilities of the application succeeding. In this way it will be seen how little a transsexualist has to merit *his* case or application.

Let us visualise the individual having sought a sexologist's advice and had medical and surgical help, living as a woman for the first time, perhaps unable to work, and without her loved ones or friends. Having already waited patiently to see her solicitor in her quest for help she returns home to wait all over again, wondering what her reactions will be should the post bring anything to shatter all her visions of the future. A month or more may pass before the first letter arrives, and she will be dismayed on reading that no headway has been made. She is soon to learn that this procedure will repeat itself over and over again, winter turning into summer whilst the stalemate continues. Every letter from the solicitor tells of difficulties, yet offers hope that all may not be lost, and each time new questions will be asked about her past, fresh correspondence entered into with the medical authorities and with Somerset House. Over and over again she will plead and suggest new lines of approach, but the months still pass and success appears to be no nearer. Surely, she feels, if she does not get help soon it will be too late, for her rehabilitation will have been wrecked, all her enthusiasm for the new life drained away. It is probable that, by now, her funds are running low, and quite possible that she has little means of improving the position until her amended birth certificate comes through. The absence of official recognition may have other, less apparent, drawbacks too: perhaps, for instance, she has been molested by some man, yet dare not make a scene for fear the circumstances may be misunderstood and jeopardise her application. When all else fails she may think in terms of asking her Member of Parliament to use his influence on her behalf, or even of making her case known to the Press in the hope of bringing public opinion on to her side. Even the desperate thought of resorting to Court action will occur to her, but this is likely to be costly, distasteful to all concerned, and can only serve to make her rehabilitation more hazardous in the light of the searching publicity that would ensue.

Such a picture enables us to see something of the effect on the individual's emotions and rehabilitation of setting herself what may be an impossible goal. Inability to accept defeat often means that the time-factor becomes important, since the delay in getting settled threatens all the happiness she has so far won, sapping the energy to push forward into her new world. Often this goes further, the individual beginning to believe, if it should be insisted that the birth certificate is correct and she was in fact born a boy, that it follows she should now be a man. Not only does this not tie up with her past medical history and present medical anatomy, but it forces her into believing that her mode of life as a woman is wrong, and that unless official recognition can be obtained the only right way she should live is back as a man. Nothing could do more harm psychologically, since there is a danger of a stalemate position being reached whereby to go in either sex direction seems impossible. There is only one way that the individual can go at this stage, however, and that is on, and any attempt to go back to the former role, with her changed anatomy, will fail psychologically if not practically. Not least among the many aspects in this connection is the omnipresent awareness of failure, and the fact that the state and role in life is more than ever abnormal and in-between. It is often because of the knowledge of this that the individual will press on for an alteration in the birth certificate, becoming obsessional in accepting nothing less, and ending up as she began with thoughts of suicide. For this reason the facts cannot be made too clear at the beginning, and any attempt to gain official recognition by getting the birth certificate corrected should be realised as a lengthy and frustrating procedure.

What further argument can she put forward to the authorities to merit re-registration? Basically, she feels she could not be as she is now, with the feminine characteristics she has, had she been born a normal boy. If, in fact, she was not born a normal boy, and has developed along female lines, surely she must have been of indeterminate sex at birth? Certainly, she argues, her state now is more female than male, so it is right to suppose that, of her intersexual state at birth, she was more correctly girl than boy. Perhaps she can say she was under-developed in the genital region, never possessed normal male organs, and could never function normally as a male; anyway, she will say, she has no male organs now, having merely had corrective surgery to assist her to conform to her dominant physical sex, operations that in no way were intended to be or could be considered to be 'sex change' operations. Perhaps her surgeon will verify this and her state before operation, for surely those who helped her medically would not have done so unless they felt she was overall more feminine than masculine, or agreed that it was right for her to change her role. Cannot Somerset House, she thinks, give some idea of the facts they want established in order to give serious consideration to the application, rather than keep querying points in the medical evidence *after* it has been submitted? Can it be that all this delay is meant to test her genuineness, and to make sure that she has no doubts?

Over and over again she finds herself up against the fact that her birth certificate states 'boy', and that the facts at the time of birth must have suggested this to be true or it would not have been so entered. Also, she finds it difficult to account for the fact that she did at some time have some form of male organs, albeit ill-defined, the subsequent surgery on which does not detract from their presence originally. Whilst medical evidence argues, in her favour, that the possession of male organs in some form is by no means the essential and only factor to be taken into account in such a hermaphroditic person, and that such possession does not preclude her from having been indeterminate at birth, she finds other medical opinion advising the authorities may not be in agreement with this. To this it may be argued that the law only requires the sworn opinion of one medical authority, and that it should not be necessary to have the whole medical profession in accord with the findings before the register can be amended. Indeed, if this were so no court could give credence to any one doctor's evidence. The applicant can now argue that, if she was correctly registered as a 'boy', she should now be a normal male, and so ask on what grounds the authorities query her present feminine state as given by the medical evidence. In any event, she thinks, how can her anatomical sex at birth be confirmed by any person alive, or be *proved* conclusively anyway, so how can she argue that she was born of indeterminate sex or a 'girl', or the authorities otherwise argue and insist that she was born a 'boy'?

If the individual has told the truth all along and, knowing all the requirements of the regulations, still feels justified in her fight for official recognition, the very fact that she is genuine in her motives and believes in the right of her own particular case is likely to increase her distress, feeling that adoption of the female role without full legal status will tar her with homo-sexuality, transvestism, or masquerade. To the sincere case such a role would be improper, and the opposition of her mind, morally, to such an existence would conflict with the peace of mind and happiness upon which the whole change was based. Such a person thus feels that her very 'right' to dress and live as a woman is based on full acceptance of her sex status by the authorities, with proof of this by amendment to the birth certificate. It is not true to say that such an individual has reached this state purely as a matter of choice, for, on the contrary, she has no more choice in the matter than anyone has in choosing their sex at birth. Faced with the conflicting moral issues of going on unofficially as a woman and without recognition, she has only the other and impossible alternative of resuming the former male role. Yet with the law as it stands there is very little that can be done, and, after every argument has been put and every known method used by the solicitor and then by the individual herself, the outcome is likely to be as inconclusive and uncertain as at the beginning. In this respect we can liken it to a political argument in which neither side is prepared to accept the other's view, and when at times logic and common sense seem to prevail on neither side.

We have, in our argument, allowed the case to use every possible approach, accepting that some true physical inter-sexuality has merited the application and that the individual understands the serious nature of what she asks, unquestion-ably accepting in her own mind that she was not born a boy, developmentally or constitutionally. Having allowed the applic-ant a free hand, however, we must now look to the other side of the argument, and see what sort of view is likely to be taken by those who find themselves in the difficult position of ad-ministering the law, honouring their responsibility to the Crown and society, yet still endeavouring to be sympathetic, under-standing and humane in dealing with these cases. There is no doubt whatever that the authorities wish to be as helpful as possible, and they are indeed to be highly commended for their deep consideration of the individual's personal difficulties, and for their desire to arrive at the right decision.

Naturally, those in the official positions find it necessary to act on medical guidance in these matters, and have to rely very much upon the opinions of their own medical advisers in weighing up the facts and arriving at their decision. Any assessment of an individual's sex is therefore likely to be influenced by the attitude of this medical body, and to depend entirely on the relative significance of the sex determining factors which they are prepared to consider. Certainly, sex must be regarded in more than the one aspect so commonly and generally accepted, for, as we have already seen, the sexual make-up is very complex, and unless all the factors that go to determine sex are given full consideration the accuracy of any assessment may well be in doubt. Unfortunately, those medical specialists who hold more advanced and realistic views only too often find their evidence open to question, and it is to be regretted that the knowledge and experience on which their opinions are based is not more highly valued by those to whom it is offered.

There are, nevertheless, certain facts which cannot be ignored and these form the basis on which an individual's sex is determined at birth or later in life. Normally an individual's sex, as determined at birth, establishes the role throughout life, and the present state of the individual therefore confirms the original sex at birth. This does not, however, apply to the transsexualist who changes role, and any suggestion that an amendment to his birth entry is justified by his present state bears no relationship to the requirements. When the accuracy of an entry is questioned, then, the first consideration is likely to be the person's sex as far as reproduction is concerned, which revolves around the possession of certain sexual organs, their normal development and their functional ability. If at birth, therefore, male organs were present together with a male anatomy, and the individual has at some time developed normal masculine features and been capable of functioning normally as a male, enabling him to be a father if necessary, there can be NO doubt whatever that the original entry on the birth certificate, showing the sex as 'Boy', was correct and cannot be altered. Whatever operations the individual may undergo, or however hormonally feminised his appearance may become, his true sex remains male, and provides no grounds for a change in the birth entry. For this reason the authorities at Somerset House will maintain that, irrespective of the present condition, the register cannot be altered unless there is evidence forthcoming that at no time were male characteristics *established*, and that at no time was the individual capable of functioning sexually as a male. Even fulfilment of these conditions and acceptance of the possibility that the sex at birth was indeterminate does not necessarily qualify acceptance that the sex at birth must therefore have been 'Girl', unless certain definite feminine features of physique and personality can also be shown to have existed.

The applicant may argue that any acceptance of the medical evidence that he is now female, coupled with a refusal to amend the register, represents acknowledgement of a 'change of sex', but the authorities have no power to give or withhold official recognition of the present sex and so this situation does not arise. Strictly speaking they have no such power in relation to the sex at birth either, since the record is made up from the facts supplied to them at the time and only in that sense forms the basis for official recognition. What is important is that medical evidence can be supplied to indicate that, despite appearances, the sex at birth was not anatomically male. Any case, then, who feels that operation alone is enough to give them a passport to apply should think again, whilst those who possess male organs should realise the absurdity and impossibility of their request, however feminine hormones may have made them look. In this we can assume that we are speaking of normal organs, for, although operation in itself does not bar consideration of an application favourably, much must depend upon the degree of abnormality in the genital region and the medical evidence that can be produced to confirm the original genital and anatomical state before operation. Indeed, the surgeon's evidence may be valuable here if physical as well as psychological reasons can be confirmed to have prompted the surgery. The authorities are concerned with the medical evidence and the proof it can give on all these matters, and unless it proves that the individual was not male at the time of birth they will feel the requirements of the regulations have not been met, and will turn down the application.

The law dealing with a correction of an error of fact or substance in a register of Births and Deaths, and the procedure and qualification for such a correction, is that laid down under 1 and 2 Eliz. II. Ch.20, S.29 (1953). This provides that a statutory declaration shall be submitted from one medical authority, and another from a parent if possible or, failing that, the person concerned, to the effect that an error relating to a particular entry of birth occurred in respect of the said individual. Obviously, there is little point in getting these declarations drawn up if the Registrar General is not satisfied with the medical evidence, so that his approval of the facts is necessary first. Should the applicant be successful the Registrar General

little is gained if, for any reason, the rights of the 'married' parties cannot be upheld in law. In England, for instance, the contract of marriage confers a new status on the contracting parties, who at once are given certain legal rights and privileges, at the same time being bound by certain conditions of law. For such an individual as we have mentioned to go through a form of marriage with another party may mean nothing in law, and be as unofficial and unrecognised as the 'change of sex'. Further, he will be in breach of the law if he pretends to official bodies that he is married, such as for beneficial income tax purposes. Recognition of the marriage therefore depends on recognition of the sex of the individuals concerned, the particular law of the country or state in which the marriage takes place, and *recognition of that law* by other countries and states.

Just how this conflict of laws can complicate matters can be shown by the case of a man and a woman who married in England. The wife then went to the United States of America, where she obtained a divorce and married another man. The divorce, however, was not recognised by English law, so that the woman was apparently legally married to two men, and the English husband, in subsequently filing his suit for divorce, gave as his grounds the fact that his wife had remarried. Whilst the wife's divorce is not recognised in England, however, it is possible that the remarriage might be, so that she could face prosecution for bigamy should she return.

One of the main purposes of marriage is, of course, to legitimise children who may be born as a result of the union, but this does not arise in the cases with whom we are concerned. Whilst marriage may be desired to cement a partnership, its real purpose is more likely to be to satisfy the transsexualist who feels this 'right' must make him a normal woman, since the 'marriage' proposed can only be for companionship and 'show'. However, those who go through a form of 'marriage' claiming ignorance or deliberately withholding their true circumstances may not only face prosecution, but the marriage certificate will be worth no more than the paper on which it is written and have no legal standing. It must remain in doubt, therefore, how successful such a 'marriage' is likely to be, or how firmly the partnership is likely to be cemented by possessing this worthless piece of paper. We cannot criticise those who find happiness in the company of another and genuinely wish to look upon themselves as husband and wife, but in the exceptional circumstances of these cases they are, unless they face up to the facts, only likely to find themselves in a fool's paradise. Assuming that an individual wishes to remain in England, then, and is unable to obtain full legal status as a woman (or as a man if the case should be reversed), it can be seen that any form of legal marriage is impossible. Going abroad to get married does not solve anything since the marriage will still not be recognised in England any more than if the ceremony had taken place here.

In the same way that the laws of countries vary in respect of marriage, so the laws differ when it comes to an individual seeking official recognition of any change of role. In Scotland, for instance, the application has to be made to the Sheriff of the County; he, being a Judge, is given the power of decision, and it is before him that the applicant has to put his case, supported by the necessary medical evidence. Naturally, the Sheriff is not likely to be easily convinced, anymore than the Registrar General in England, but if he is sufficiently satisfied to accept that the correct sex should be in the other denomination the civic bodies are then bound to accept his ruling, so that correction of the individual's official papers becomes no more than a formality.

In the United States of America the law appears equally rigid, and it is extremely difficult, if not impossible, to get any amendment made to the original birth certificate. Perhaps remarkably so for that country, a change of sex is still not recognised officially and, regardless of many operations that the individual may have had or however successful a change of role may be, where the original registration of the sex was obviously correct at the time no law permits this to be altered. This does not mean that an individual may necessarily be in conflict with the law by assuming a new role, if the medical evidence supports that changed circumstances later in life

428

warrant such a change of role. Basically, it seems that the individual is not denied the ability to earn a living and be a good citizen, but it does mean that difficulties are bound to occur in legal matters involving production of the birth certificate, such as in marriage, etc. Whilst some States may be unable to accept the legality of a person's new role and status, and so deny the individual the ability to marry if the opportunity comes along, other States seem more prepared to accept the medical evidence and permit such a union subject to certain conditions. Whether or not such a marriage is recognised outside this State, however, depends upon the interrelationship of the laws of the States concerned.

On the continent of Europe, in such countries as France, Germany, Switzerland and Italy, cases occasionally come to light of individuals claiming to have changed sex, and of them bringing pressure to bear on the authorities to recognise officially their new and 'correct' sex. The individual is not likely to find the law any less rigid, and application for official and legal recognition will meet with all the usual difficulties, although noted cases in France and Switzerland have succeeded after considerable pressure and much controversy in becoming officially recognised as women. In each case, although not admitting that there had been any error in the entry of the sex at birth, the authorities allowed that the person's present state was sufficiently female to enable her to bear such a status legally from the date of the Court ruling. Even so, when one of these cases was later involved in divorce proceedings following a short marriage the authorities appeared to regret their earlier judgement, when new medical evidence emerged which sought to prove that the 'wife' was no more than a transsexualist and had been born a physically normal male.

In Italy, official records are similarly very difficult to change, and, even when it is a matter of remedying a clerical error, most complicated Court processes are necessary. Thus, for an amendment to the sex status, a petition has to be made to the Court, supported by affidavits and very strong medical evidence; even then no 'change' can be recognised but only a correction, provided the original records can be shown to be false. One must wonder how cases in Russia meet the difficulties when faced with this problem, if, indeed, there is medical acceptance or awareness of it, and if the problem is so pressing in view of the less marked social differences between the sexes. Certainly, there seems less ability for the female to pamper herself with frills, soft clothes and make-up; her figure seems of less importance and her work may be any one of numerous and arduous tasks recognised in the West to be singularly masculine. It seems quite certain, however, that every nation and race in the world is affected with this problem to some degree, and it remains for us to realise that, in most civilised countries, the medical aspects are now beginning to be recognised to some extent and the legal aspects are just as problematical.

Whilst the medical condition cannot be ignored and speculation increases that it may have some constitutional origin, the medical impossibility of a biological 'change of sex' remains a fact. The whole time the law only allows a record to be amended if the original entry is proved false, cases who change their role will continue to find it extremely difficult, if not impossible, to get legal recognition in the true sense of the word. Indeed, with increasing medical knowledge and awareness that trans-sexualists do not really change their sex it seems that the law, instead of bending to take account of the circumstances of these cases, has become more fixed in its attitude. This is not surprising since the laws must obviously be applied as laid down and used to full effect to protect society, but we must be careful not to let laws get out of date or be used against individuals, with no useful purpose other than to make life difficult for those who find themselves in a conflicting sexual world. Where young cases show some definite intersexual features, have been rendered incapable of reproduction by surgery and received full hormonal help in a change of role, it can only be hoped that those who make and administer the law will face up equally to their responsibilities in this connection, and realise that what to them may be no more than a piece of paper may, to the individual, mean the difference between mental peace and torture. On the other hand, the majority of cases have only a psychological basis for their desire to 'change sex', and of these many seek hormones and surgery purely for devious sexual reasons. Often they are middle aged, have enjoyed sex as a male for a large number of years, have married, and even fathered children, before they think it might be sexually fun to 'change sex'. To think that the law should be up-dated to allow these individuals to say that they were born female and legally be brides is to turn the world upside down, and obviously the morality of any society would be at risk if such individuals were legally as well as medically assisted in satisfying such devious sexual cravings.

To speak in terms of how legal a change of role may be, however, we must consider in what respect the case is likely to become involved in legal matters. There may, for example, be a law in Britain against a motorist exceeding a certain speed over a particular stretch of road, and yet, to the pedestrian, this law may just as well be non-existent as far as becoming involved in a violation of it is concerned. In the same way, a person who has changed role may have no cause to consider certain laws, and living in a new role may present no difficulties whatever. Provided the individual's circumstances are medically known, then, and the name has been changed legally, this may be all that is necessary for normal purposes and hankering after a change of the birth certificate may only be obsessional. It all depends on the laws with which the individual is likely to find himself involved, such as the laws relating to sexual or criminal behaviour which may land him in a man's prison, to marriage, or to divorce, etc. This, for instance, is like two people living as common law husband and wife; they can have all the sexual advantages of that relationship and all the social advantages of appearing to be husband and wife, but have to accept the disadvantage that in law the marriage is not legal or binding.

There is no doubt that, for his own peace of mind, the individual who has changed role would like to feel that his 'change' is legal, but in wanting this he is often unaware of the sense in which he is using the word 'legal'. He rather looks upon it as a magical passport to everything he wants to do in his desired role, without realising that different laws exist on every possible topic and in every country, and that each affects him according to his circumstances and not according to his possession of some supposed general legal authority. Certainly, an amendment to the birth certificate does amount to legal recognition of the sex status of the individual, and as such any potential legal difficulties of a new role are eliminated, but it does not follow that an individual who has not obtained this recognition is any the worse off, or that he will necessarily come into conflict with the law over the manner of his role, for he may well go through life without becoming involved in any legal entanglements. It is, of course, sometimes difficult for the feelings and behaviour of those who like to think they have 'changed sex' to be condoned morally by society, and so it is, perhaps not surprisingly, difficult for the law to 'legalise' such a change. Certainly many transsexualists damage their own cause by demonstrating only too frequently the outlook and attitude of the sex they were born, and by exhibiting themselves as the freaks they have become. It must be realised, however, that each case *is* individual and that intersexuals and sincere trans-sexualists do exist; sometimes they never find their rightful place in society or feel that they belong to either sex, and to these especially goes our sympathy. It is to be hoped, then, that those who administer the law will not close the doors to all, but will remember that it is in their power to sentence the deserving few either to a lifetime of misery or to bless them with the chance of a lifetime's happiness.

CHAPTER THIRTEEN

THE REAL ANSWER?

WE HAVE COME a long way since we first considered this problem of transsexualism. We have seen the whole picture emerge in all its conflicting patterns, watching the individual become engulfed in a state of hopelessness as his feelings cry out for expression. We have seen his attempts at conformity wreak havoc with his mental reasoning, and his behaviour become overpowered by the resulting torture to take on all manner of bizarre, perverted, and what to the normal person are horrid and unmentionable forms. Whatever we may have learned from looking into the medical aspects, the disheartening fact remains that too many complex factors are involved in the individual's upbringing and social awareness to offer much, if any, hope of fighting the problem by trying to eliminate the cause. We can, however, by a more universal realisation of the existence of the problem, hope to get to grips with it as early as possible in order to educate those afflicted, and thus avoid the situation arising, as it does at present, of cases only coming out into the open when breaking point has been reached and the tragedy is final, for once the obsessional state is in command no amount of help is ever likely to adjust the individual to normality. This situation will reach its inevitable climax when it becomes impossible for the patient to accept his present role any longer without extreme unhappiness, depression, and thoughts of suicide, it being equally impossible for him ever to be a normal person in the opposite role.

The story which can be told by these individuals is thus by no means a happy one, but the fact remains that the story is a true one which is, and will continue to be, a part of life and reality itself. Unfortunately, therefore, this last chapter is not one, as might occur in fiction, in which all the ends are tied up and everyone lives happily ever after. To come to some conclusion is by no means an easy task, but it seems right that we should try, and we must therefore consider whether there is any real answer to the problem. To do this we shall have to summarise much that has gone before, in order to help us see more clearly the many aspects of the problem, and consider just what may be done to enable the sufferer to accept his state and adjust himself accordingly to become a useful member of society. We must first remember that these cases themselves believe the answer is to 'change their sex'; if we could wave a magic wand and transform the person into a normal woman in every sense of the word we might be tempted to perform this feat, but the fact is that we cannot, and any goal that may otherwise be reached is likely to leave him more abnormal than ever, dissatisfied with many aspects of his new role and the body that goes with it.

Behind what appears to be a conflict over sex lies the very real issue of the attitude of mind, and what really amounts to a conflict with life itself. Because of this the sex problem is nearly always secondary, and it is the inability to cope and to come to terms with life that invariably is the underlying factor. None of this will alter just by changing role, for it is part of the very constitution and conditioning that has made the individual the way he is. These cases are so wrapped up in their own world of dreams and desires that they have little time for alternative interests, yet often state that the reason for this is that they do not fit in socially as expected of them. Whatever the real reason may be, the individual finds his life composed of wanting this and that, and he may feel the world owes him something so that he feels justified to take all he can. Often there is a great urge to give, but little knowledge how this can be done. In the same way there is a tremendous capacity for feeling for others, for loving deeply, and for showing great depth of emotion, yet the same inability to express it. Thus he is stifled by his own problem, and so lacks the ability to give or to get enough satisfaction from it. Only when he can give instead of taking is life likely to assume new meaning and to have any real purpose, but, unfortunately, the transsexualist becomes so obsessed with his own vanity, his desire for comfort and an easy life, and his struggle after his goal, that the interests that would enable him to become extroverted do not materialise and his much sought

434

after happiness eludes him.

Happiness eludes not only rich and poor alike but those who have 'changed sex' as well as those still striving. We must all strive for something, or life would become dull and monotonous; for most of us happiness comes and goes, and the novelty of getting at last what we dreamt about passes off, as surely as a child tires of his new toy and proceeds to take it apart in search of further satisfaction. The transsexualist will find little at the end of the road of his dreams unless he has previously come to realise the facts and accept them. He must understand that somewhere along his road there is a limit to what he can achieve and to his satisfaction, which he *must* accept. Unfortunately, there is rarely a limit to the desires of these cases, for as soon as they have passed one hurdle they look to the next, regardless of impossibility, and continue to torture themselves in pursuit of it. Deep down there is, nearly always, the feeling of wanting to be what they are not, and this perversion is often enhanced by swinging from one role to the other, or even by witnessing it amongst others. If such a state is powerful it may well exist after an individual has changed role.

There is no doubt that whatever the transsexualist is told he finds it extremely difficult to accept, even though he may basically know it to be correct. We may just as well tell a person suffering from claustrophobia that there is nothing to fear from a confined space, that it is only in his mind and that he should pull himself together. We can tell people not to be afraid and they may understand there is no reason for fear, but it does not mean they are any more able to accept the position and cease to be afraid. In this respect we may well put ourselves in the transsexualist's shoes and understand a little of what he fights. Much of our effort to help these cases must therefore be directed at getting through to them, for at times what we say may not register at all, either because the facts are rejected unconsciously by them or because their knowledge is too scanty to enable them to understand.

Although the best form of adjustment may well be for the transsexualist to recognise his abnormality and look to the greater horizons that life offers, the main obstacle is his belief that to give up the challenge his goal presents represents failure. Such an attitude most often results from early developmental factors, the individual conditioning himself to believe that in order to get his own way or to push events in the direction of his desires a build-up of tension and anxiety is necessary, in order that he may subconsciously overrule any tendency to weakness on his part. The outcome is that although he may accept the illogicalities of much of what he seeks the subconscious impulse remains, ever driving him on to some imaginary or hypothetical goal rather than permitting him to accept what he has otherwise convinced himself would be defeat and renunciation. It is this attitude, too, which will cause him to become more determined to get what he wants the more it is denied him, and will, conversely, cause him to doubt and reflect when help seems possible. It is quite essential, therefore, that no step towards a 'change' should be taken impetuously, but that the final result is envisaged before any treatment is contemplated or commenced. The individual must be able to see himself, not as some model girl but as he will be in reality, perhaps having to hide facial hair or the crêping from intensive and prolonged electrolysis under heavy make-up, living on the money he is likely to earn, how it may affect his relations with his loved ones or friends, and whether he will ever be fully happy in accepting the limitations of his role, sexually and legally.

Peace of mind will only come when he can learn to accept life and reality, yet in striving after a change he refuses to accept anything that does not fit in with his own wishes and desires. He must, first and foremost, know himself, and realise that all his efforts to convince others are really efforts to convince himself. It matters little what he can prove to others; peace of mind can only come when he can prove to himself the right behind his desires. His misconceptions on what represents masculinity and femininity have much to do with his conflict, and he often feels compelled to do what he does not want to do. He strangely believes that, as a man, he should not like to sew or knit, or to cuddle pets and make a fuss of them, and he feels denied the ability to do these things; yet the same misconceptions are still there even if he has changed his role, for he will feel self-conscious about tinkering with his car because he believes it is not a woman's place to know about anything mechanical, and so again he inhibits his interests accordingly. The biggest misconception of all is to believe that he will change in so many ways by changing his role, for the pattern all through our discussion shows that his thoughts, attitude to life, and interests will remain the same both before and afterwards.

What he must *not* do, then, is to try to conform to his own rigid interpretation of masculinity. If he sees a moving film, and feels like shedding a tear, he must understand that there is nothing unmanly about it; if anything, it shows great depth of feeling, which in the right circumstances is a quality not to be ashamed of but generally to be admired. He must in no way try to suppress these feelings, and he certainly need have no guilt complex about the way he expresses them. So often it is the inhibition of all that cries out within him that causes such conflict and torment, with the rationalisation that the only way he can express himself without fear of ridicule is as the supposed gentle and demure female. To overcome this, he must learn to express himself freely as he wishes, and to realise that he can do this equally as a man or as a woman. If he is unhappy in his job, he should change it for one that will give vent to his feelings, one that is perhaps creative, artistic, or personal. He must learn to stand on his own feet, and realise that maturity will only come when he can face up to life and its consequences in the faith of his own convictions, accepting human nature for what it is and keeping an open and quiet mind. He need not be a woman to do all this; there is no doubt that he does feel a nicer person when dressed as one, but this is only because he has rationalised his problem into believing that a new life will enable him to leave behind all that has revolted him in the past. Although some cases may appear more settled after a change, by the enforcement upon them of a role in which they cannot look back, as far as behaviour is concerned any established mode of sexual expression is only likely to be further deviated by the adjustment. As with all things in life, sex has to some extent to be controlled if we are to consider ourselves above the animals, capable of reasoning and acting in a civilised manner.

In asking ourselves if there is any real answer to this problem we must deal very seriously with facts as they exist, and we must leave feelings out whether we wish to be kind or not. The sufferer is often hurt by the truth, but it is best that he should face up to it from the start and not go on in a dream world that will explode in his face with greater violence the longer he goes on pretending. He must face up to the facts at some time if he is not to go through life in continual torment and conflict, and to tell him things that he wants to hear, just to be kind at the time, is no contribution to the permanent happiness he seeks, and we should in no way be helping him to understand himself or live better. We know the impracticality of his desires, and yet we also know the tortured hell he lives in; what then can we say to such an individual? Firstly, we must be very practical, and consider his build, size, and features with care, before offering any hope that a 'change' might be successful in his case, for obviously, if he shows very dominant masculine features with considerable facial and body hair it is best that he ceases banging his head against a wall. He may, in his search for justification, turn with hope to the aspect of nuclear sex, but almost invariably this will be found to conform to his recognised and anatomical sex. This is often used as an argument against these cases, although more advanced techniques are constantly being developed in an effort to establish that the condition may, after all, have some constitutional cause. Even should definite proof eventually emerge, however, to indicate that a particular individual should have developed in the opposite sexual direction, the fact still remains that we are dealing with an individual who has developed as a male, and who will encounter the same practical and anatomical difficulties in 'changing sex' as any other individual who can show no known cause for his feelings and state. Whatever value nuclear sexing may have, it is therefore certain that it serves no useful purpose towards offering a *practical* solution to this problem, and every case must look first to his *present* anatomy and development.

It is most unlikely that he will want to be cured of his condition, so that any aim in this direction will probably be resisted by him. He will only believe what he wants to believe, regard all advice as unsympathetic, and be unable to accept that he can possibly be understood if it is suggested he should be helped in any other way than a 'change'. Thus continual discussion may only frustrate him more and aggravate his already sensitive emotional state, for the more the individual tries to solve his problem in his own mind the more he comes to feel the impossibility of finding any other solution. If we cannot help him by trying to trace the cause, then, we must rely on educating him; we must tell him the medical differences between the sexes, what is possible and what is not, what hormones can do and cannot do. Operations, we must tell him, are seldom justified and certainly not easy to obtain, because of the possible medical and legal complications, and they will have no effect in so far as making him more of a woman *in himself.* Strictly speaking, he can look the same in a skirt whether he has his male genitalia or not, and mere removal of these in no way legalises his status or automatically gives him permission to regard himself as a female. On the other hand, the antagonism to the male genitalia is generally such that operation produces considerable and permanent satisfaction, by removing what is probably the main cause of the original sexual conflict. Whilst the patient presses for this treatment, however, in the belief that operations and hormones only are necessary to enable him to 'change sex', it must be pointed out to him very emphatically that the primary urge behind his desire for a 'change' is a sexual one, and that once he has lost his genitalia he may well lose the desire for a change, finding an emptiness in the loss of his sexual function and regretting dearly what he has had done.

Cases often seek medical advice and help on the assumption that all will be done for them without any effort on their part. Happiness, however, is not something that can be given out in slices like a large cake, so that when a transsexualist leaves a doctor's consulting room, unhappy about what he is told, he must understand that only by knowing the truth will he be able to know how to go about finding happiness, and that by accepting the unhappy things in life he will be saved the future torment of making a wrong decision in search of it. There is no question of wishing the patient any extra hardship to bear, or to deny him the happiness he seeks, but he must know everything about the road he wishes to take from the beginning, whether it shatters his dream world or not, if any permanent happiness is really to result.

Cases should not imagine that, in their abnormality, they are freaks or monsters best eradicated from the world. Babies who are born blind or without limbs are not put to death, but rather are they more fondled and cared for, and, just as such cases require adjustment to their abnormality, so do transsexualists to their problem. Everyone is abnormal in some way or another and there is nothing derogatory in its implication, so the transsexualist has no need to resent the term or reject the need for some form of adjustment. Certainly, he should not try to carry his burden alone or wrap up his conflicts in secrecy, but should get medical advice as early as possible, for in this way much can be done to assist the individual to think more clearly and assess the really important things that count in life, seeing them in their rightful perspective. In this way, too, should it be decided that a change of role is inevitable, it will be possible to assist the individual medically whilst still young, before his way of life has become too set and established, and while he stands the best chance of rehabilitation physically. Equally, the chances of a good psychological adjustment are better, with less past to conflict with the future.

Unfortunately, it is often only when the patient has suffered all manner of torment, and his whole world has collapsed around him, that he may have proved himself enough to warrant some medical assistance in a 'change' as a last resort. Certainly, if there is little or no physical justification the medical advisers must concentrate on the psychological side, and time, which is so important to the patient, must be allowed to elapse in order to study all the circumstances and reactions of the case. Indeed, whether the patient is an hermaphrodite, an intersex, a Klinefelter's, or indeed shows any characteristics of the female sex at all, the essential factor is still the psychological one. We

440

have discussed how a girl may be brought up as a boy and, because of her upbringing and conditioning, be masculine in orientation and sexual inclination. Whatever may have caused the condition of transsexualism, be it constitutional or not, there has been a resistance to the conditioning of rearing, and such a psychological state must be dealt with by psychology or psychiatry. These patients do not want to be altered or be 'normal', however, and for this reason 'adjustment back to normality' is a bad phrase, although in the wisest and widest sense the adjustment is towards maturity and a better understanding of life, its problems and how best to cope with them.

Sex is something we grow up with and, often, something we are made to feel ashamed about. Anything written about sex is generally considered to be filthy, and yet in its natural sense it is no doubt something wonderful and beautiful. Rarely can sex be mentioned, however, without the seamier side being thought of at once, and the public attitude which causes this makes some individuals so conscious of the abhorrence of their bodies that to be seen on the beach in a bathing costume, let alone be examined in the nude by a doctor, can cause acute embarrassment. It is human nature that we should be perverse, and what we are denied we often want all the more. If we are taken into a large house for the first time and told that we can go into every room except one, our curiosity makes us uninterested in the other rooms and we long to learn the secret behind the forbidden door. Sex is equally a challenge to us, not only during our early and formative years but later in life, when the power of sex and love can come to mean so much. Once, we only knew sex existed because there were boys and girls and men and women, and they looked, dressed, and acted differently. Later, we came to learn the facts of life, and to realise that the world was not just made up of husbands and wives and their children; the children we met in the street or at school may have been born illegitimately, or otherwise be victims of broken or unhappy marriages. Very quickly our faith in the wonderful things of the world is shattered, and reality stares us in the face; the world does not seem such a nice place after all. It is, in fact, a cruel world, with war following war, constant lust for power, greed, and disregard for principles and human life. When we know and realise these things, could it be that we have reached maturity?

Fortunately, our hopes and desires give us heart, and we are able to fine down the weight of the world's problems and concentrate on our own. Many go through a very searching time at puberty, reflecting on all these things and with an increasing awareness of their own sexual feelings, but we do not necessarily come to realise how reproduction comes about. We do not always find the right answer to our sexual problems, or see much beyond the physical aspect of sex. It is only when we understand sex in its fullest sense that we learn that it is something more than a physical relationship, that it combines the pleasure of love and companionship long after the act has ceased. Sex is the means, of course, of procreation of the species, and as such it is very sacred, but we must not be misled into believing that without sex we serve no useful purpose to humanity. Admittedly, if everyone left the reproductive act to the next the human race would soon become extinct, but, as it is, the world's population is increasingly alarmingly. With a mortality figure from starvation alone pathetically high, the transsexualist may take heart that any loss of genitalia or inability to have children need not be harmful to society. Whatever a person's sex or role may be, and regardless of any circumstances throughout life, that person remains separate and individual, capable of thought, opinions, and such freedom as his country permits. Although sharing the world and the life of those human beings around him everything about the individual's world is personal to him, as it is, too, when death comes, with only God to hold out a guiding hand. It is then, indeed, that the real tragedy of his life will be borne in on him, without a family or children or grandchildren around him at his bedside to ease his last hours and give him the comfort of knowing that his life continues in them. Although we must not look upon sex out of proportion to its relative importance, transsexualists must therefore view life on a broader plane if they are to get any happiness out of their troubled existence, in the same way that all peoples alike should view the

442

transsexualist's problem with broad thinking, charity, and human understanding.

The individual's sexual state has been built up by a particular set of conditioning circumstances, originating from early childhood. It is normal that a man should be stimulated sexually by a woman, her figure, her clothes and what lies beneath them, many aspects of which may represent a fetish for him. The early desires of the male transvestite and transsexualist to seek gratification by possessing or wearing female clothes is but a deviation of this, and when pleasure is found in this way he repeats the process over and over again until he conditions himself to accept that such behaviour is necessary to satisfy his sexual urge. We have only to consider the dogs of Pavlov, whom he conditioned to expect food every time a bell was rung, to realise how simply the process can be initiated even though it may take time to establish. When we speak, therefore, of trying to break the transsexualist of his complexes, of his fetish behaviour, and of his misconceptions, we are in effect trying to break him of these early conditioning factors which, by any standard, is a most difficult task. Often we can only hope to achieve this by a long and tedious process of re-conditioning, and before we can begin it is essential that we have the full confidence of the individual. He must understand that his conflict with sex is out of all proportion to the main issues involved; he has divided the world up into two parts according to sex, and fails to see that everyone is capable of the same feelings and emotions regardless of the shape of the body or the clothes worn, and that it is the character and personality of an individual that really matters to his fellow beings.

Sex, being one of the primary urges in life, is not something we can dismiss from our minds at will. Whether we like it or not we all essentially possess this animal instinct, being part of nature's way to ensure a continuance of the species. Our conditioning largely teaches us to control our feelings, however, telling us that there is a right time and place for everything, and only then under certain circumstances. But it is very likely that we fight against these social conventions during our upbringing, and that the enforced suppression of our natural urge leads us into conflict, with society who made the 'rules', and with sex itself. Many of us grow up, then, without knowing much about sex, and we are left to fumble in the dark with our own thoughts, searching for information and growing more and more guilty over any behaviour which seems to be unnatural, wrong, or insane. Masturbation in early puberty, although quite normal, may be looked upon with such views, and the sexual significance of our behaviour at this time may cause our minds to become indelibly impressed by it. Since it is far easier to prevent a habit from forming than to break one, the importance of correct upbringing, an understanding of the child's problems, and proper sex education cannot be too highly emphasised. The parents who push their artistic and sensitive sons into strenuous masculine pursuits, to 'make a man of him', may well complete the boy's rejection of his sex and what it stands for, and many are guilty of trying to live their lives over again in the person of their children, irrespective of the different views and temperaments these growing individuals may possess. There is no doubt that a boy should be trained to face the man's world that lies ahead for him and to develop his character and personality, for it serves him well in his future life, but the child should not be denied his individuality to express himself or be forced into activities for no other purpose than to try and encourage something within him that just is not there. Since the answer to the condition lies very largely in the child's upbringing and his sexual education, parents must be prepared to shoulder the responsibility that falls upon them and make it their duty, not only to seek advice and help if they suspect any undue deviation from the normal, but also to learn all they can of the condition to enable them to understand, sympathise, and help in a normal adjustment, rather than stand by horrified, ignorant, and antagonising the condition even more.

Whilst there are a large number whose problem has become a cancer to them, and to whom advice and treatment come too late to really do much to help, there are others who at this moment are at the beginning of their suffering, in silent and secret torture, as indeed there are others as yet unborn who are to go through the same pattern of agony. It is the duty of every one of us to recognise this and to do anything we can for these latter cases, and to do this we need do no more in the first instance than understand that it needs treating with patience, understanding, and kindness, as surely as we would give this to a person stricken with poliomyelitis. For this reason trust in the medical profession must be built up, and the individual must know how to seek help and who to go to. The family doctor must learn that a patient may just as easily come to him with this condition as with an aching back, and when confronted with it must know something of the problem and of the specialists to whom he can refer his patient. Lack of integrity by the doctor, in reporting back the nature of such a confidential matter to parents, can also be tragic, since one of the patient's greatest fears is often that of his parents knowing and of the knowledge hurting them deeply. In certain circumstances it may be essential that the parents know of the trouble in order that they can help, but unfortunately, where the complexes may have arisen through parental dominance, far from helping the sufferer the parents are likely to cause even greater harm, for they are most probably as ignorant of the condition as any member of society and in no position to help. Adjustment on specific medical lines can be difficult enough without the attempts of those who are unknowledgeable on the subject, for more than love and good intentions are necessary.

Perhaps the greatest problem in assisting these cases is the wide divergence of views amongst the medical profession itself. Whilst the condition continues to be swept under the carpet by the majority of the general public there is little wonder that the medical profession are torn between their responsibilities to society and their patient. It is a pity, however, that the members of the medical profession have to be left to their own devices in the matter, and often have to face the possible criticism of their colleagues. It is poor consolation to the sufferer in all his confusion to find the body from whom he seeks help equally confused, and divided on the main issues as to how best he should be helped. It is just such a position which causes the individual to go from one end of Harley Street to the other, or from one end of the world to the other, in search of someone whom he prays will understand and help him, and yet the doctors themselves do not take kindly to this procedure or to having to see cases who have already been elsewhere and laboured out their long and woeful story so often before. Those who may be more sympathetic and understanding on the matter therefore find that they are burdened with more cases than they can cope with, involving more time than they are able to give. Because of the varied medical opinions, however, it does mean that some cases may be fortunate in receiving help whilst others may not, but it does not, unfortunately, always follow that those who receive it are the ones who show the greatest justification.

The need to treat the whole problem mysteriously also gives rise to a great dislike amongst doctors of transsexual cases meeting, on the basis that one may influence the other, that they will compare notes, and that what help one manages to get the other will feel entitled to also. Since the patients are not in a position to assess all the factors in favour or against themselves the doctor's attitude in this can well be understood, but behind it all is the shroud of secrecy which surrounds the condition, for the protection of the public and medical profession but to the detriment of the patient. There can be no doubt, however, that as long as transsexualists read of cases who have 'changed sex', and whilst secrecy on the subject is maintained, they will always feel hopeful that such help can be given to them with equal success regardless of their physical state, and for this reason mystery is a dangerous thing. It may sometimes seem that those who have changed role and are at last safely on the other side of the fence appear to discourage others who wish to follow suit. There is obviously no motive in this, except perhaps to try and give good advice based on knowledge of the subject learnt so dearly through tears and sweat.

What answer can the medical profession offer as a means of helping these cases, however? There is the psychological approach, of course, and the prescribing of sedative drugs, such as may be given in general psychological disorders and obsessive-compulsive states. Beyond this, there is little doubt that the prescribing of oestrogens has much to merit it, by dampening the sex urge, easing the nervous tension, and helping the individual to return from his dream world sufficiently to take stock of his position. Usually, a course of two or three months is enough to give the patient a clearer and calmer view of life, and to help him assess his own reaction to any effect on his sexual behaviour and feelings. The greatest drawback is in the encouragement of the transsexual desires, because of the feminising influence of the hormone. Although this is small in terms of making a man into a woman physically, emotionally the effect is more definite, so that the patient may become more sensitive, cry easily, and need more outlets for his finer feelings. There seems scope here for investigation into finding a drug which will have the same tranquillising and sexual negating effects as oestrogen, but without possessing feminising properties. There is no doubt that this would help a great deal towards neutralising the patient, sexually, whilst the main issue involving the conflict with life was sorted out. Even so, the present value of oestrogen given under proper medical supervision cannot be over-emphasised.

Whilst the need for help with a change of role may be medically indicated in the few cases who show some physical as well as psychological justification, it cannot be denied that the vast majority show no physical justification at all, being biologically normal in every sense. Apart from this, much is against the medical profession helping these cases in the direction of a change; first, the individual is generally psychotic and therefore not too well equipped to deal with life and its problems, let alone in a new role; secondly, there is little chance of an individual changing his attitude to life or his sexual orientation, even by changing role; thirdly, there is the question of whether surgery may lead to the hoped for happiness, or only to disillusionment and regret; fourthly, there is the legal side to be considered, and the surgeon's knowledge that the individual will never be normal whatever is done. In view of these considerations it is often surprising that cases are helped at all, and yet we find that a few have managed to overcome the hurdles, whilst others are in various stages of receiving modified help. The illegality of operations and that they are

447

irrevocable are arguments used against help surgically, so that medical help is sometimes given to assist a change of role with surgery avoided. This would suggest that the medical profession apparently condone the action of an individual playing the role of a woman whilst still in possession of male genitalia, and we might classify with these those who have had them hidden by means of an insertion operation. If the reason for this is merely a technical or legal one it is surely time that such was reviewed, so that both surgeon and patient would benefit from not having to get round the difficulty in this way. The mere hiding of genitalia instead of complete removal can only be likened to sweeping dirt under the carpet, on the pretext that out of sight means out of mind. It may be argued that, by the same token, a woman changing to a male role merits having her ovaries removed, but it cannot be denied that the circumstances are different as indeed is the sexual function also. But for this function the woman is as unaware of her ovaries as she is of her liver, and provided the monthly cycle can be stopped by hormones the practical considerations tend to outweigh the need for such a major operation.

Sex is looked upon as something definite by society; we expect to see males or females pass us in the street, not half-and-half freaks. Any effort to adjust a transsexualist should therefore be away from the in-between state, and either we must accept that the individual should be male or we must accept that the individual should be female. We must therefore wonder why, if any help at all is to be given, it should not be full help; if it is argued that the regrets may afterwards be so great that the individual wants to change back, we are only allowing what should be a tremendously serious decision on his part to be taken lightly. Such waverings across the sex border, because of psychological indecision, endocrine changes, or of deriving sexual gratification purely from the act of changing, are not as uncommon as may be believed. If, indeed, the decision is that the patient is justified to change his role, it must be a firm decision on which there can be no looking back, accepted as irreversible by patient and doctor alike. For this reason alone, irrevocable operations should form an essential part of the treatment, for if the patient is ever to feel settled as long as he lives the penis and testes must be removed and forgotten with the past as if they never existed. This is not to say that these should be given as a first part of the treatment, but that, once a case has shown his ability to earn a living and pass satisfactorily in his new role, provided the psychological state permits, operations should not be denied him, be made so difficult to obtain, or be frowned upon as something horrible and distasteful. Back in history, but a fleeting moment in comparison to the existence of the world, it was considered normal amongst certain sects to remove the genitalia of boys in pursuance of custom of the day. To-day, to deny operations on purely moral grounds cannot be condoned when we come to consider it in terms of human happiness, and we must wonder if the thought that the world is now more civilised can seriously be considered as argument with the threat of war and weapons of mass destruction forming part of it.

It is typical of these cases to say that they have reached the limit of how much they can stand, and that to go on as they are in the role of their upbringing will only mean further frustration and misery; yet they little know that the road along which they wish to travel to a 'change' is far more cruel, shows no mercy, and can inflict untold suffering without caring for their health or feelings. Their first hurdle, then, is the least of their troubles, and they must be strong enough to bear the following hardships alone, having enough conviction to walk over everyone to get what they want. If they do not accept the limitations and go on striving after something that is impossible, life is still likely to remain intolerable and thoughts of suicide be as real as ever. Of course, in asking questions these individuals often expect a definite yes or no which is not easy to give, for, in asking if a thing is possible, they believe that if the answer is yes it means it is possible for them. "Can I get operations, will hormones do this to me, will my change be legal, can I marry, etc.?" The answer that matters is not the generalised one but the one that applies to the particular circumstances of the individual. He should in this respect bear well in mind that it may be possible to win a fortune on the football pools, but that his individual ability to do so is another matter. The chances, then, may be against him, as far as his whole make-up, anatomically, is concerned, his ties, or his ability to prove justification, so that his own circumstances are very relevant to what is possible and what is not.

It is particularly important for him to realise that, whatever his justification for help, any assistance he may get will be entirely out of kindness and not as his *right*, in the same way that an elderly man dying at the roadside has no actual right to assistance, but can only look to humanity to take pity and to help him. If the transsexualist decides to press for help, then, and is successful, he must be prepared to accept anywhere along the line that he may not be able to get any further towards his goal. *If he does not accept this he will not be worthy of the help that may have been given to him.*

Those who 'change' with any success are likely to be those who have taken stock of all the facts, can accept and face up to all the problems, and have proved that they can cope with life and have mastered the art of living, *even in the sex of their upbringing.* Alternatively, those more psychologically opposed to their sex and role are only likely to find some peace of mind in a 'change' if it provides a sufficient change in their circumstances, their work, surroundings and associations. Of the rest, however, we find the majority as ill-equipped to cope with life as before, unable to accept the challenge of a new world, needing to maintain the old ties to overcome loneliness, and even with doubts creeping in as to the wisdom of having taken such a drastic step. It is often for this reason that a change of role may appear to meet with some success, since embarking on a new life usually necessitates a change in these circumstances. It is essential, however, that he carries with him more than the prime interest and enthusiasm he has built up in the expression of himself in his desired sex, for this introverted interest will very soon leave him unsatisfied. Rather, he should carry with him a very close interest in some outside sphere, such as in his work, in a hobby, or in a friendship, and he must develop these interests first and reorganise his life and way of thinking.

One of the greatest dangers to his rehabilitation and success will be loneliness. Whilst he is wrapped up in the novelty of changing, expressing himself in the clothes he has wanted to wear for so long, little else will matter and life will seem very exciting, but as time passes and he finds he cannot do as he used to (call on his family as freely as before, for example, without risk of embarrassing them in front of their friends), he will gradually feel more and more aware of being cast off and on his own in life. Up to this time he was probably happy being alone, perhaps unhappy if he was not alone. Now, for the first time in his life, friends probably mean more to him than ever before, and he may suddenly wonder if the result has justified all his efforts and lost years of happiness. He may have a lot to look back on; a loving family, happy days together, a good steady job, perhaps, certain masculine freedoms, etc. He has given up all of this and has to start again from the beginning; perhaps he has even spent his life's savings to reach his goal. Obviously, no one in their right mind would wish to go through such an upheaval from their established way of life if it were not absolutely essential, but, unfortunately, there are those who take the road just to grasp at anything that may, as they suppose, make life easier.

His sexual inadequacy as a female, the truth about an artificial vagina, and the chances that he will see his life out as a lonely old maid, must all be considered. However far he reaches towards his goal he will always remain abnormal, and will still find limitations even in his new life. There is the danger that he will never be really satisfied, that he will only ever feel in-between, and that, for every problem he may appear to have solved, another will have taken its place. Any fetish he may have had will still remain, the complexes will still be there, any inability to cope with everyday problems will remain unaltered, and the need to face up to humdrum routine will become powerfully real to him. He must be able to live without need of his loved ones, and certainly have their blessing if his conscience on the matter is not to undermine any real happiness and peace of mind he has envisaged. The legal aspects, too, require very careful consideration in view of the difficulties that may arise; he must feel fully justified in his own mind regarding the correctness of any 'change', with particular regard to his own moral views concerning his right to adopt the female role, together with his ability to pass, be socially accepted, and his own ability to accept himself as a woman.

It is only too tragic that those with transsexual feelings often marry in a final effort to break themselves of their abnormality, only to find that the problem remains as life-size as ever and even complicated by the union. Such a step is likely to be successful only in certain exceptional cases, who may have shown some original heterosexual orientation and who feel able to adjust their ways accordingly. In all other cases marriage can be fraught with danger and should in no circumstances be considered, for it is surprising how often cases prove their full masculine capabilities by fathering children and then proceed to make the lives of others intolerable as well as their own. If such cases find it impossible to subdue their obsession for a 'change' it is best that they leave home, in order that their families may not be associated unkindly with their difficulties. Divorce, then, is essential, and the three years 'desertion' necessary for this should afford the individual ample opportunity of testing the correctness of the road he feels inclined to take. If he maintains his conviction to the end of this time divorce should be the first step towards his goal, bearing in mind his justification for help and his ability to receive it.

There seems no doubt whatever that no individual can change his role after puberty without considerable emotional and practical upheaval to his life, but in being compelled to express himself in the opposite sexual role he believes he has no choice and cannot help 'how nature has made him'. Even if there should be physical as well as psychological justification for the feelings, however, it does not follow that a change of role is likely to give the individual the most happiness, for the teachings of the formative years, the upbringing and the conditioning, will never be eradicated, and any new adaptation to life will permanently leave some form of psychological conflict between the past, present, and future.

If a change of role is to be denied these cases, however, on the grounds that it is not right or practical for them, what alternative can be offered to these tormented souls? We can, of course, rely on helping them to accept their problem and to live with it, in the same way that vast numbers of individuals, of all nations, creeds, and stations in life, have no course open to them but to accept their own particular troubles and adjust themselves to them as best they can. Whilst we can sympathise with the transsexualists and realise their desperate plight we cannot condone any form of self-pity on their part, for what is impossible to change must be accepted if there is ever to be any meaning or happiness in life. Learning the truth will prove extremely distressing to the transsexualist at first, and, as the impossibility of what he asks registers in his mind, there is the danger that he will withdraw further into his dream world and resist truth and facts. If this attitude persists the individual may already be beyond help, and we may be able to do no more than we would for a patient whose mental state was otherwise in doubt. The use of electro-convulsive-therapy (E.C.T.) is some-times advocated in cases under this category, but it is the writer's experience that this form of treatment has no place whatever in assisting otherwise mentally normal transsexualists with their problem. On the other hand, hypnosis, which is fast gaining repute in the eyes of the medical profession and which does not, so far, appear to have been used in the treatment of these cases, may well bear investigation in the hope of offering a chance of adjustment to those previously considered beyond help. The fact remains that, in helping transsexualists to an adjustment, we must rely upon their mental capacity for assessing the facts that are given to them, and they must realise that, whatever help or advice they are given, in the end only they can help themselves.

The need of anyone to seek power, to try to climb to the top of the ladder, or to be proud of achievement, is all basically a need for expression. The transsexualist often has need to express himself even more than the normal individual and yet finds every way to do so closed to him, because his whole being appears unconsciously inhibited and his energies are sapped by his conflict. Often, because of this, he turns rather more acutely to the sexual form of expression, since his work, his hobbies, or his ability to love never quite seem to satisfy him, whilst music and the arts, instead of stimulating him, may only leave him with a complete sense of inadequacy. Transvestist behaviour to some degree may therefore be necessary as a safety valve, and we cannot expect such behaviour to be immediately discontinued as part of the adjustment. The individual is, of course, much less likely to be in conflict with sex if he can accept the heterosexual role conforming to his anatomy, but those who try to help these cases must equally be prepared to accept that transvestist behaviour may be impossible to suppress, and may be the only safety barrier against suicide or the development of a mania for a 'change' regardless of all practical considerations. The very nature of the condition is progressive, however, so that giving way to transvestist impulses usually leaves the individual craving for some further and more advanced transvestist action. It is, indeed, when the transvestite has gone as far as he can, and savoured every possible means of expression, that he seriously becomes a transsexualist, feeling that to change role completely and permanently must be the answer to his search for satisfaction.

Whilst transsexualism may well exist with but little or no transvestism it seems true to say that, in the majority of cases, the earnestness behind the transsexual impulse develops from progressive transvestist behaviour. We must be very careful, therefore, before we suggest that the transvestist behaviour should be accepted by the individual as the lesser of other perverted and psychotic states. We have really to decide at what point we may agree that the transvestism should be suppressed by the individual, or otherwise be allowed expression as an essential part of the adjustment. Certainly, we would only be increasing the guilt if we told him it was wrong, for, strictly speaking, he has the right to find happiness in life in any way he can, provided his activities are in no way anti-social but are carried out in the privacy of his own home. There seems little doubt that, if the sufferer could suppress his perverted behaviour, his self-imposed frustration would equally abate; on the other hand, what has been built up over a long period, and become established by conditioning influences, is not something that can be just dismissed from the mind. Until we can alter the direction of this perverted but often essential outlet to his feelings, by re-education and by driving home the facts, we can do little more than permit, to some extent, his abnormal behaviour and hope that, in so doing, he will accept that the adjustment must first and last come from within himself, and that he will be able to reorganise his ways before his transvestism grows cancerously into transsexualism.

This serves to emphasise to these cases that any transvestist behaviour should be restricted to a minimum, and not looked upon as a harmless way of expressing their 'finer feelings'. If a change of role is to be right for an individual the important factors determining its wisdom will also be right, so that any transvestite who rationalises his problem into transsexualism is likely to find little pleasure in a 'change' except in its perverted sense. It is particularly important that the wife of a married case should realise that any good intention on her part to try and put up with transvestist behaviour by her husband is misguided, since such permissiveness only allows the condition to get worse. The husband should equally appreciate his wife's position, and not expect her to tolerate such devious sexual expression in front of her. Indeed, he should realise that such behaviour is almost certain to cause her great mental distress, although she is unlikely to admit it in deference to her husband's feelings, and likewise he is unlikely to notice it owing to his obsessional state.

The true transsexualist need not feel stifled in his search for expression, for, if sex really means nothing to him, his interest in life should be widespread. Everywhere we look the world cries out for good to be done, and we need not look far to offer our services in one direction or another, to feel wanted, and that our living is worth while. Often the feeling of completeness gives just such an individual the very ability to do good, for there is no doubt that true transsexualists, in their hearts, are very sincere, sensitive, and loving people, or that their joy in beautiful things and their desire for peace, both for themselves and for every living creature, are qualities that the world cannot afford to be without. Indeed, we must wonder if we should judge these individuals for expressing themselves as they do, well knowing that the world is in its precarious position due to the way in which others seek expression, in a more normal, but, strangely, accepted way. Life is a treasured gift we all possess, and we can either enjoy it or abuse it. Whilst we must conform to the man-made rules that society imposes on us for the good of all we are still individual in ourselves, and our acceptance of life is essentially based on our psychological interpretation of the world around us. As an individual we can love or hate, be happy or sad, and express or suppress. When we have learnt to feel and do all these things, rationally, at the right time and in their rightful circumstances, when we have learnt the meaning of humility and can come to regard life as something to be treasured, being prepared to sacrifice our own needs for humanity's sake, then we shall, in finding a fuller meaning and purpose in life, find ourselves.

Although we have mainly spoken of the transsexual man's desire to achieve femininity our thoughts have not been far removed from the transsexual woman during our discussions here, and, since the adjustment to the problem of transsexualism is mainly in the realm of enlightenment, what we have said of the transsexual man applies for the most part to the transsexual woman. We should not forget, however, that the transsexual woman has many factors in her favour, not least amongst them being the social advantages that she would gain in a change of status. Whilst the transsexual man has to contend with the disadvantages of reduced position, status, and earning capacity, etc., the transsexual woman, although not influenced necessarily by the added advantages that will come her way in assuming the male role, finds in a 'change' that she is going more with the tide than against it. This may be one reason why even doctors appear to give more sympathetic consideration to cases in this direction. It seems that the public's attitude, too, is more favourable to the idea of a woman 'becoming' a man; this may be attributable to the fact that it is more difficult for them to think in terms of a 'man' in dainty clothes, and wanting to be a woman, than it is for them to picture the reverse. Logically, however, there is no difference and the misconceptions are in the public's mind, for they fail to see the individuals as they often are, on the sex border, but see them rather as everyday men and women with sharp divisions of masculinity and femininity between them.

Whatever we have said that may appear to disfavour or discourage the transsexualist, there has been no intention to inflict more suffering upon them. Instead, we have hoped to give them a clearer picture of their problem, and, equally, to put their point of view and desperate plight before the medical profession and the public generally. With only a relatively few cases available to be studied closely, owing to the time involved and the presence of other psychotic states to complicate matters, examination of the subject is of necessity in its early days. Whilst the majority of factors may appear to be against any form of assistance towards a change of role in nearly all cases, therefore, we must realise that constitutional factors as yet unknown may be found to play some part in the condition, and be careful not to generalise too emphatically on superficial facts alone. Provided we are satisfied with the psychological state of the individual, then, we must not ignore the possibility that a change of role may, in fact, be advisable and correct, even irrespective of the apparent genital sex of the case. Indeed, we must not dismiss from our minds the very complex factors which go to make up sex, and we must accept the existence of intersexuality just as much as we do masculinity and femininity. It is often said that the more complex a piece of machinery happens to be the more there is to go wrong, and the development of a human body is by no means an exception. That some individuals are born of indeterminate sex, or on the sex border, is as certain as the fact that some babies are born with a squint, a cleft palate, or a birthmark.

We must therefore understand that some cases do in fact exist in which the sexual qualities and characteristics are equally divided. When, later in life, these qualities and characteristics indicate that the sexual role should more correctly be opposite to that of the upbringing, all the feelings, the frustration, the conflicts and emotional upheaval will occur as in any other type of transsexualist. In the same way, the chances of successful

457

readjustment are likely to be just as problematical, emotionally, practically, and socially. Although we have often spoken of transsexual men who may be six feet tall, hairy, big-boned, and biologically male in every sense, we must be careful to realise that there are as many shades of transsexualism as there are types of men and women, and we must not come to regard all transsexual men as belonging to a group of individuals who indulge in sexual perversion, are psychotic, or who live in devious and horrible ways. We must accept certain facts just as we are asking transsexualists to accept certain facts, and understand that whilst some cases do exist on one end of the scale who change role by no more than a masquerade, there are others who more rightly assume their correct sexual role. Indeed, intersexuality may be present in some form or other, recognisable or not, from birth, and where medical evidence supports this, taking all the facts into consideration, it is vital that those dealing with the legal side of the problem should be as accommodating as possible, allowing the benefit of the doubt in giving recognition to any new status and not feeling prejudiced because of their inability to help other cases of less merit.

It seems essential that the legal aspects of this problem should be reviewed in the light of medical advances on the subject. It is certain that, whether the difficulties facing the sufferer are medical or legal, there comes a time when help, if withheld too long, *can* be too late. Sometimes, medical 'marking time' to ascertain the wisdom of treatment, although to some extent necessary, may leave the individual between the sexes so long that the torture of that state may permanently remain in spite of what may subsequently be done. Equally, irrespective of successful medical treatment, legal complications which leave the individual still psychologically unable to accept either sex can cause irreparable harm, and may well threaten to leave the sufferer permanently **on** the sex border and therefore in a stalemate position and suicidal. The extreme danger of this should in no way be under-estimated by those who possess power over these matters, for if a person cannot live as a man, and equally cannot live as a woman – he cannot live. Whilst the nature of English law on many aspects of this problem could well be looked into and possibly revised, however, praise must at the same time be given that the problem is treated with the humane understanding that it is, which, at present, is not to be found in many other countries of the world.

The time has come for a whole team of experts working in unison to deal with these cases, a body to whom cases may be referred by general practitioners. No longer should there be the one surgeon or the one psychiatrist, persistently being pestered for help because he is the one who spends considerable time assessing the individual merits, understanding the condition, and helping where he feels justified to do so. Even if there were only one such body or team in the whole country, it would give authority to the advice given, give the general public a greater feeling of security, and the sufferer himself confidence in seeking treatment and greater ability to accept what he is told. Every authority possible on each branch of the subject should be included in the team: a psychiatrist, an endocrinologist, a plastic surgeon, a urologist, a legal expert, a government official, a social worker, an official from the General Registrar's office, a philosopher, a church official, and even a Member of Parliament. The non-medical members of the team need only be called in for advice as required, whilst for the most part the medical members would be able to undertake their work relieved of the individual responsibility and, what is more, with the backing of their colleagues. Whilst some eminent medical authorities and, amongst others, the famous London hospitals of Guy's and Charing Cross are doing tremendously useful work in endeavouring to cope with the very difficult problems set them by these cases, there is obvious need for the formation of a body or bodies, as suggested, to ease the burdens of all concerned. Indeed, the help that such a body could offer youngsters, by placing all the facts before them and educating them to live with their problem, cannot be over-estimated, especially in years to come once the existence of these teams or bodies have become both recognised and established, and their authority is known.

Any offer of help in the direction of a change of role could then be completely dealt with by the specialists in question; medical and surgical help would be given as agreed, the social documents dealt with, the legal aspects clarified, and the rehabilitation of the individual to his new life, psychologically, spiritually, and socially, undertaken with as little disruption as possible, ensuring the greatest chance of success. Those with sufficient justification for help in a 'change' would still be few, but at least the long drawn out stages would be eliminated and the sufferer would not be left wondering what more could be done for him. In this way, the seriousness of the decision would be brought home to the patient, and he would know exactly from the start that he would get so much help and no more, and have to accept it or reject it at the beginning. In other cases, the medical team would serve as a joint authority to impress upon them the impossibility of what they ask, and be able to offer the best solution to adjustment by virtue of its accumulated experience of the condition. In this way we would have a medical condition being treated as such, and recognised as much a branch of medicine as any other. As we have said before, we can pretend the condition does not exist and push it into the background, but if we do not recognise its very real existence we are no better than those we are trying to help, for we will be living in a dream world.

All of us can be very introverted at times; the significance of a thousand people dying a thousand miles away in an earthquake may escape us, if against this the river at the end of our garden has flowed into the kitchen and brought that particular event home to us. Admittedly, if we stopped to worry over everybody's troubles, and how we were going to put all the world's troubles right, we should soon find life unbearable, and so often we have to strike a happy balance. This, however, does not mean to say that we should ignore the suffering of others, whether they are a thousand miles away or close at hand. Whilst many problems may remain insurmountable, others can be solved, relatively speaking, with very little trouble, and this is often the transsexualist's argument, for he feels that he has no need to suffer for the sake of a little help when 'so much can be done for him' without affecting anyone but himself. From what we have just said, and provided wives and children are *not* involved, his argument would appear strong, and if we accept this the only part we have to play is to give the medical profession the benefit of our faith in their judgement.

The outstanding point which emerges from our discussion is the doubt that must always exist regarding the materialisation of the transsexualist's professed happiness once his dream becomes reality, and as long as this doubt remains so must the doubt regarding the real answer to the problem. There is thus no real answer in general terms, for it is personal and individual to each case; even then, the answer is not necessarily what the individual himself believes it to be, for it is the right answer that matters and only time will show the wisdom of any decision he makes. So often in the past he will have lost faith in the future, constantly rebuking himself for his thoughts and behaviour and becoming completely depressed in the knowledge that the pattern will repeat itself however hard he tries. So often the repeated and unanswerable question, 'How will it all end?' will have numbed his thinking. Yet if he is ever to find the real answer to his individual problem, whether he has religious convictions or believes in very little, it is certain that he must at all times have faith in himself. Any adjustment he eventually makes must therefore be on the basis of being completely honest and sincere to himself, for only then is the doubt regarding the real answer likely to be resolved and the answer itself prove to be the right one.

In conclusion, we must ask them all to search their own hearts, to find the answer to what they want out of life, and to ask just how much the purpose of their life will alter whether they are man or woman. Before they rationalise all their finer feelings, their love and unexpressed emotions, into feminine terms, and say that life has denied them so much because their minds are prisoners in an undesirable body, they should for a moment hesitate and reflect upon all the great and wonderful men in history, and consider the good they have perpetually left to the world in the manner of their teachings, their crafts, and their examples to humanity. Whether we believe or not, the Christian ideals of love, compassion, meekness and sacrifice are

461

rarely far away, affecting us in our everyday lives. When next transsexualists hear a moving piece of music let them take stock of the world and their place in it, and be stirred to enjoy the many blessings that are theirs, give up fighting the impossible, and turn their thoughts and efforts away from themselves to reap the happiness of giving. Indeed, every one of us would do well to do the same, and put our own house in order before passing any opinion on these cases, for human failing is present in all of us and much of our criticism of others can be aimed so easily at ourselves. The transsexualists' refusal to accept defeat and failure, and their dislike of embarrassment and of having their pride hurt, are little different from the qualities we all possess. We do not like losing a game; we are rarely prepared to admit our failings to ourselves, let alone to others; we do not like to be thought small or to be told how ignorant we are; we hate the embarrassing moment when everyone is looking at us, and what others think of us worries us a great deal, causing us to do things sometimes we would rather not.

All these things show how very little we trust each other and how greatly our lives, thoughts, and deeds are governed by those around us, through our own inadequacy to stand on our own feet. We must feel wanted, to know that we fit in, and that we are, if anything, better than the next person. Yet we shall only begin to have the power to understand life and people when we can be true to ourselves, and are able to face the world with a clear conscience, knowing in our hearts that there is nothing to hide. There is no truer fact than that we come into the world with nothing and go out with nothing, and whether we are among the greatest or the humblest what matters the most is what we can offer humanity during our lifetime, and above all what good we can leave behind us when we are no more. Can we say that we have lived respected and will die regretted? If we can look back from our dying bed and feel that we have served humanity well, have left our love in others and that some good will survive us in thought, word, or deed, we shall then be able to believe that we have not lived in vain. The real answer to this problem lies in the real answer to the purpose in life itself, which is an answer every one of us seeks.

Certainly, if we could all aim to leave the world a better place than when we came into it, by virtue of our own individual contribution, we should all be a long way towards finding the purpose behind life, and towards gaining the supreme happiness out of living that such an answer would provide. Who can blame these transsexualists for their dreams when we all live in a world of outward show, dreaming of our own Utopia? The fact remains above all else that, whether we are speaking of transsexualists or of anyone else in the world, we are ourselves our own worst enemy, and it is only in the power that comes from knowledge and the ability to accept life for what it is that the answers to our problems will be found.

Georgina Carol Turtle
November 1961

INDEX

PUBLISHER'S BLURB 1963

Doctors are still largely in the dark about Transvestism and Transsexualism, and although we hear more frequently to-day of someone 'changing sex', even fewer lay people understand what is meant by this expression or how the 'change' comes about. It is impossible to form any exact estimate of the number of people involved, but at its lowest Miss Turtle puts it at 3,000 in this country, and at its highest at 15,000 – or even more. *Over the Sex Border* is the first comprehensive study of the subject.

In her introductory chapter, Miss Turtle describes the biological processes of reproduction and defines the various abnormal sexual conditions, considering the influences, both prenatal and during childhood, which may be responsible for them.

So far as transvestites are concerned, the act of dressing up in the clothes of the opposite sex may be satisfying in itself, but it generally has a sexual purpose. Transvestites are often fetishists. Transsexualism, the longing to belong to the opposite sex, is also associated with sexual feelings, and arises partly from inability to conform to accepted patterns. Understandably, transsexualists are reluctant to seek medical help. In general, they cover up any abnormality within themselves, and except in the extreme later stages their appearance in public does not give them away. With the onset of puberty the disturbance grows much greater, every aspect of masculinity revolting the sufferer, who often has the sensation of containing both sexes within himself. He is burdened with a constant feeling of guilt, and with a terror that his secret will be discovered. Everything combines to make him turn in on himself, shunning any form of social life. so that eventually he lives entirely in his own private hell. Sometimes he will marry in a desperate effort to escape from his condition, with disastrous results.

Miss Turtle describes the progressive course which the condition may take, the climax generally coming between the ages of 25 and 30, when the act of dressing up, which in the early stages may be confined to one article of clothing, now has to be complete. The sexual act is usually by now almost completely disconnected, and the extremes of feminine behaviour are copied. The frantic need to 'change his sex' may at last lead the sufferer to seek medical help: he has no desire to be helped to 'normality', but believes that hormones and operations will turn him into a woman and that this will bring him fulfilment and happiness.

Such help and operations are, however, most difficult to obtain, since the partial 'change' which may be effected will almost certainly leave him dissatisfied and more in-between than ever. Despite his capacity for self-delusion he will be distressed by, for instance, the continuing need to shave every morning, his body hair, his deep voice, and all the other evidences of his irreversible masculinity. Furthermore, if the sex urge is removed by operation, his former desire to 'change sex' may now even seem to him quite senseless, and he may wonder what possessed him to take such a drastic, irrevocable step.

Miss Turtle then turns to the doctor's viewpoint – the physical examination, nuclear sex, steroid studies, psychological sex, the treatment he may recommend, and his endeavour to steer the sufferer back to heterosexuality. Should a change of role be unavoidable, however, many practical aspects have to be considered, and in her closing chapters Miss Turtle deals with the 'change' itself, the patient's financial problems, the religious angle, marital status, and goes fully into the legal aspect and the difficulties and frustrations attached to any attempt at getting the birth certificate amended.

Transsexualism occurs in women as well as in men, and Miss Turtle discusses their problems, too. The structure of our society, however, makes it easier for the woman to adjust herself. The sex urge is not so strong; no one remarks if she goes about in slacks and with short hair; and it is perfectly feasible for her to live with another woman, whose companionship eases the dreadful loneliness.

As a highly knowledgeable study of a problem which affects

a considerable number of people and is a closed book not only to laymen but also to most doctors, this is a work of great importance. Miss Turtle knows of what she writes. Born in 1923, she lived the first thirty-four years of her life as a man. A dental surgeon and an ex-Navy Surgeon Lieutenant, she started a new life in 1960 when the sex on her birth certificate was officially corrected from 'Boy' to 'Girl'. In 1962 she married Mr. Christopher Somerset, an engineer.

The foreword to the book is written by Mr. Kenneth Walker, the eminent surgeon, sexologist, and writer on religion and philosophy.

POST-PUBLICATION REVIEWS

Sunday Telegraph, **Dr. Alex Comfort, 14 July 1963.**
'This book does not ask for sympathy – but from the author's discussion of the problem it becomes clear that public sympathy and understanding could do more, therapeutically, than any amount of surgery.'

Medical News, **26 July 1963.**
'a very full and persuasively interesting volume.'

The Lancet, **5 October 1963.**
'Miss Turtle writes with obvious knowledge of the subject.'

Brighton Evening Argus, **11 July 1963.**
'is likely to be regarded as an authoritative work on a little understood subject by the people about whom it is written and the medical world.'

Family Doctor, **Dr. Gerald Swyer, March 1964.**
'She is uniquely qualified to write on the subject. This she does with compassion, with deep appreciation of the mental and practical difficulties which all transsexualists face, and with the object of enlightening that more favoured majority of individuals whose sexual outlook has never been other than normal.'

Nursing Mirror, **22 May 1964.**
'The author is well qualified to write – the book is easily understandable and does much to clarify a subject surrounded by mystery.'

Chevalier Publications, **Los Angeles, 1964.**
'Miss Turtle has done a masterful job of surveying the whole problem.'

APPRECIATIONS 1963

Mr. Kenneth Walker, F.R.C.S. Harley Street, London.
'Your book *Over the Sex Border* is **excellent** and I hope you will allow me to quote extensively from your admirable last chapter. I shall advise my transsexualist patients to read your book.'

Mr. Peter Fletcher, Psychologist, Harley Street, London.
'Your book is very impressive both for its breadth of knowledge and depth of insight. I think you have made a most valuable contribution to this difficult subject.'

Dr. John Randell, Psychiatrist, Harley Street and Charing Cross Hospital, London.
'I had written an MD thesis on this topic. Your interesting book seems to suggest that you have in many ways "scooped me".'

Dr. Peter Bishop, Wimpole Street and Guys Hospital, London.
'Your book looks very interesting and is certainly something that needed to be written.'

Dr. Joseph Adler, Wimpole Street, London.
'Your book is certainly a very well written study of the subject and contains much material which needed saying. I am impressed with your work and its frank conclusions.'

Dr. MacSearraigh, General Practitioner, Ireland.
'I was delighted with your book. Its fluency and comprehensiveness and the obvious wisdom, sympathy and understanding of the author, makes it a notable contribution to a most complex and difficult subject.'

Dr. Raymond Bottoms, Specialist Practitioner, Australia.
'Congratulations on the publication of your book. I was delighted to read it and feel that your writings will certainly be of **great benefit** to those struggling in the mists of doubt with problems such as you describe.'

APPRECIATIONS 1963 and later

Dr. B. Sekar, General Practitioner, Middlesex.

'May I say how much I like your book *Over the Sex Border*. It is a very well balanced analytical survey of the problem, and a very objective presentation.'

Dr. Marshall, Scotland.

'I must say I have thoroughly enjoyed reading your book – what a lot of good could have been done had such a thing been available say even ten years ago.'

The British Medical Association, 1965, in a letter to Mr. X.

'The best source of information for your study is a book entitled *Over the Sex Border* by Georgina Turtle, published in 1963 by Gollancz, price 30/-.'

Mr. Justice Roger Ormrod, Royal Courts of Justice, London, 1970.

'I must congratulate you on the way you dealt with the law on this subject. It is a confused area of law anyway and it is a great achievement for a layman to master it and to write so sympathetically about it as you have done. The rest of the book I have found most interesting.'